Praise for Pipe Dreams

"A biting, incisive look at corporate excesses.... funny, opinionated and not shy in offering harsh moral judgement."

The Dallas Morning News

"[A]delicious disembowling of the company.... Bryce has a rare ability to explain complex financial concepts clearly, combined with a breezy, colloquial style that makes his story a page turner."

Salon.com

"While most [missteps] have been reported in some fashion in the buckets of ink spilled on the story, Bryce still packs a punch by gathering all the damning details in one place ... Bryce is most compelling when he sketches the corrupt cast of characters."

BusinessWeek

"There's nothing familiar about what Robert Bryce has accomplished in this superb book ... Meticulously researched ... Bryce presents [financial] stuff with such admirable clarity that even the most numerically illiterate English major can grasp its gist."

Austin Chronicle

"It's a *Barbarians at the Gate*–type read."

Cindy Adams, *New York Post*

"Robert Bryce has done a brilliant job of explaining what Enron was all about and what made it fall apart. Better still, he provides fascinating insights into the lives of the firm's executives who were calling the shots.... a mesmerizing read."

Tulsa World

"Humorous ... entertaining and easy-to-follow.... Bryce's account sets the bar high for other Enron books to come."

San-Jose Mercury News

"No one succeeds in telling the story like Texas journalist Robert Bryce. His straightforward book ... is a must-read for the business set, and an enjoyable read for the rest of us."

National Post (Canada)

"Bryce, who understands the flamboyance built into Texas business culture, clarifies Enron's muddled and deceptive accounting practices, deconstructs the bone-headed and perpetually hyped ventures ... while lacing his account with the sexual foibles that played a tacit part in creating the company's anything-goes executive culture ... There are sure to be many accounts of Enron's collapse, but Bryce's gossipy version will be hard to beat for sheer readability."

Kirkus Reviews

"Enron's downfall was inevitable, and with Bryce as chronicler, it makes for a terrific story.... [Bryce] has mined his sources well and also observes the important investigative rule of 'follow the money,' revealing a systemic corporate breakdown at Enron that was widespread, stretching from the office of the CEOs to the board of directors to various lower-level executives and beyond."

Library Journal

"Finally, an Enron book that actually explains what happened at Enron ... This isn't just the first book to make sense out of the debacle; it's a vivid cautionary tale about the consequences of the lurid excesses—personal and professional."

Publishers Weekly

"A comprehensive piece of investigative journalism."

Booklist

Pipe Dreams

GREED, EGO, AND THE DEATH OF ENRON

Robert Bryce

PUBLICAFFAIRS NEW YORK

Published in the United States by PublicAffairs™,
a member of the Perseus Books Group.

Printed in the United States of America.

Book design by Mark McGarry, Texas Type & Book Works.
Set in Sabon.

Library of Congress Cataloging-in-Publication Data
Bryce, Robert.
Pipe dreams: greed, ego, jealousy, and the death of Enron/Robert Bryce.
p. cm.
Includes bibliographical references and index.
ISBN 1-58648-201-7 (pbk.)
1. Enron Corp.—Corrupt practices.
2. Energy industries—Corrupt practices—United States.
3. Business failures—United States.
I. Title.
HD9502.U54 E573 2002
333.79'0973—dc21
2002031615

10 9 8 7 6 5 4 3 2 1

This book is dedicated to the thousands of current and former Enron employees—hardworking, honest people—who lost so much through no fault of their own.

Contents

ENRON CAST OF CHARACTERS AND THEIR STOCK SALES*

Name	Position at Enron	Shares Sold	Gross Proceeds
J. Clifford Baxter	Vice-Chairman	619,898	$34,734,854
Robert Belfer	Member of Board of Directors	2,065,137	$111,941,200
Norman Blake	Member of Board of Directors	21,200	$1,705,328
Rick Buy	Chief Risk Officer	140,234	$10,656,595
Rick Causey	Chief Accounting Officer	208,940	$13,386,896
Ronnie Chan	Member of Board of Directors	8,000	$337,200
James Derrick	General Counsel	230,660	$12,563,928
John Duncan	Member of Board of Directors	35,000	$2,009,700
Andy Fastow	Chief Financial Officer	687,445	$33,675,004
Joe Foy	Member of Board of Directors	38,160	$1,639,590
Mark Frevert	Chief Executive Officer, Enron Europe	986,898	$54,831,220
Wendy Gramm	Member of Board of Directors	10,328	$278,892
Kevin Hannon	President, Enron Broadband Services	Unknown	Unknown
Ken Harrison	Member of Board of Directors	1,011,436	$75,416,636
Joe Hirko	CEO, Enron Communications	473,837	$35,168,721
Stan Horton	CEO, Enron Transportation	830,444	$47,371,361
Robert Jaedicke	Member of Board of Directors	13,360	$841,438
Steve Kean	Executive Vice President, Chief of Staff	64,932	$5,166,414
Mark Koenig	Executive Vice President	129,153	$9,110,466
Ken Lay	Chairman, Enron Corp.	4,002,259	$184,494,426
Charles LeMaistre	Member of Board of Directors	17,344	$841,768
Rebecca Mark	Chief Executive Officer, Azurix	1,895,631	$82,536,737
Michael McConnell	Executive Vice President	32,960	$2,506,311
Jeff McMahon	Treasurer	39,630	$2,739,226
Cindy Olson	Executive Vice President	83,183	$6,505,870
Lou Pai	CEO, Enron Energy Services	3,912,205	$270,276,065
Ken Rice	CEO, Enron Broadband Services	1,234,009	$76,825,145
Jeffrey Skilling	Chief Executive Officer, Enron Corp.	1,307,678	$70,687,199
Joe Sutton	Vice-Chairman	688,996	$42,231,283
Greg Whalley	Chief Operating Officer, Enron Corp.	Unknown	Unknown
	TOTALS	20,788,957	$1,190,479,472

*All listed sales occurred between October 19, 1998 and November 27, 2001. The number shown under gross proceeds indicates the number of shares times the price of Enron stock on the day the shares were sold. It does not reflect any costs the Enron officials incurred in exercising the sale of the stock. Therefore, the net proceeds to the listed individuals is likely less than the amount shown.

SOURCES: *Mark Newby, et al. vs. Enron Corp., et al.*, Securities and Exchange Commission filings, Congressional testimony, Enron Corp. press releases.

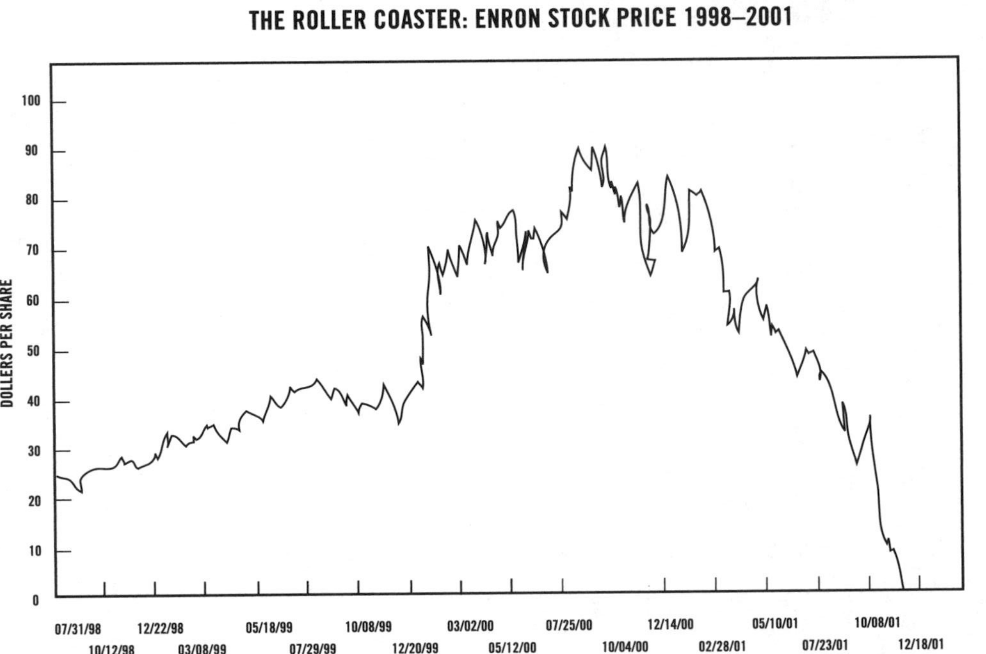

Stock price chart

Author's Note

This book was a joy. Challenging and heart-wrenching, too.

My goal in writing this book was to explain why Enron failed. I did not attempt to tell every facet of the Enron story or to explain all of the legal and accounting issues that came into play. Nor did I attempt to explore the myriad details of how Enron might have profited from California's convoluted electricity markets. Nor did I delve deeply into Enron's efforts to deregulate electricity markets. Instead, I sought to explain why the company got so bollixed up, while avoiding as much business jargon and accounting-related arcana as possible.

My premise throughout this book is that Enron's failure wasn't due to faulty accounting or poor regulation, though both of those factors were—and are—very important. Rather, it failed because key leaders at Enron lost their moral/ethical direction at the same time that the company was making multibillion-dollar bets on fatally flawed projects. From the outset, the key questions were: Why did Enron get corrupted, and why did so many of its bets go bad?

The greatest obstacle in finding good answers to those questions was access. None of the key miscreants—Ken Lay, Jeff Skilling, Rebecca Mark, Andy Fastow, Lou Pai, Ken Rice, or the others—were talking. From their perspective, keeping quiet certainly makes sense. All are being sued. Some will be indicted. Most should be stripped of their ill-gotten gains (fat chance of that) or, at a minimum, flogged in public and sent to bed without dinner. Given those factors and the knowledge that they'll likely be tied up in depositions and court proceedings for the next decade, they kept quiet. The same was true for the Enron board members, the hapless, hoodwinked Greek chorus of fat cats—many of whom had special "consulting" deals with Enron—who stood idly by while Enron was ruined.

Since the miscreants weren't talking to me or anyone else—and I had no interest in dealing with their spin doctors and lawyers—I decided that this would be an "outsider" book. And because I wouldn't have access to the thought processes or conversations of the top executives, I would rely on what *was* available: public records and people in the know. I interviewed as many people as I could who knew what had happened inside Enron. As you'll see, a great majority of those people—many former and some current Enron employees—did not want to be quoted by name. Many of them still work in Houston and feared retribution. All of them want to stay out of court. But they wanted the true story of Enron's failure to be written. So they trusted me. And though I cannot name them, I owe them my sincere appreciation. Thanks.

I had a brigade of longtime friends and former Enron people (many of whom have become friends) who were supportive, candid, and generous with their time. First, thanks to Lou Dubose. He challenged me to do the book, came up with the title, got me an agent, and even proofed my pitch. Thanks, too, to Bob Elder, another terrific reporter, who suffered through many bad ideas and even more bad writing while giving insightful advice. Thanks also to Robb Walsh for his hospitality, educating me about Suite 8-F and introducing me to Houston's amazing food scene.

I also want to thank (in no particular order) Sherri Saunders, Stan Hanks, George Strong, Chris Wasden, Ken Stott, J. Paul Oxer, Lowell Lebermann, Dan Ryser, David and Marty Woytek, Terry Thorn, Rod Gray, Kurt Q. Holmes, Lou Gagliardi, Art Smith, John S. Herold, Inc., Ron and Violet Cauthon, Susan Wadle, Carol Coale, Andrew Wheat,

Texans for Public Justice, Turk Pipkin, María Mondragón-Valdéz, Paul Howes, Dick Heckmann, Mike Muckleroy, Dan Williams, John Allario, David Berg, John Olson, Jim Walzel, Roy Rinard, Richard Reichardt, Ehud Ronn, Ross Patten, Mark Rome, Alvin Thomas, Bob Stein, Ken Wade, Aerodynamics Inc., John Mixon, Bala Dharan, Jeff Dietert, Robert Floyd, Joe Griffin, Robert LaFortune, Randall Dodd, the Derivatives Study Center, Jack Rains, Philip Azar, Sissy Farenthold, Abhay Mehta, Mary Wyatt, Adam Baines, Jim Moore, the 11:30 crew at Guadalupe, and Jim Blackburn. All of these people provided me with a wealth of insights and knowledge that I could not have obtained anywhere else.

I must thank Scott Henson and Amy Smith for their excellent research assistance. Warmest thanks, too, to Mimi Bardagjy for the grace and professionalism she showed during her meticulous job of fact checking the more than 1,250 footnotes contained in the original manuscript.

During my research for this book, I interviewed more than 200 people, some of them multiple times. I did not record my interviews; I typed them on a computer. My written sources were many. In all, I collected over 1,800 electronic documents (spreadsheets, graphics, newspaper stories, lawsuits, and so on), about two dozen books, and dozens of news clips.

This book would not have been possible without the diligent reporting done by journalists at the *New York Times, Wall Street Journal, Houston Chronicle*, *Bloomberg News*, and other outlets. I have tried to credit those reporters and publications where appropriate with footnoted references.

Unless otherwise noted, all of the revenue and cash flow figures cited in this book were taken directly from filings with the Securities and Exchange Commission (SEC). All property valuation and ownership information was obtained through publicly available sources. All the information about property ownership and construction costs for homes owned by Enron officials in Houston was obtained either from the Harris County Appraisal District (available: www.hcad.org) or from the City of Houston.

In reconstructing Enron's finances, I relied heavily on Enron's annual reports, their SEC filings, and the report published on February 1, 2002, by the Powers Committee, which was charged by the Enron board with investigating off-the-balance-sheet entities created by Fastow and his cronies. Of all the documents I used, the Powers Committee report was the most important.

In my effort to be as correct as possible when writing about Enron's financial statements, I relied on a pair of certified public accountants who were familiar with the company's books. The two did not want to be named, but they provided me with a wealth of insight on Enron's practices. Thanks, too, to my brother Wally Bryce, a CPA, who kindly answered 3,761 of my dumbest accounting questions.

Just for the record, I have never owned Enron stock. I have, however, owned a small (and now even smaller) position in the Janus Fund, a mutual fund that owned a huge stake in Enron. So, I, like millions of other Americans, lost money in the Enron meltdown.

Thanks to my agent, Dan Green, who was always professional and warmly encouraging. Also, particular thanks to Lisa Kaufman, my ever-so-patient editor, and Peter Osnos, the publisher at PublicAffairs, for taking a chance on a rookie like me.

Finally, thanks to my first editor and first love, Lorin Bryce, and to my children, Mary, Michael, and Jacob. Without all of you, this book would have been neither possible nor worthwhile. I love you more than chocolate.

ROBERT BRYCE
AUSTIN, TEXAS
AUGUST 2002

Introduction

AUSTIN—I think the single, greatest nonfattening pleasure in life is learning (the other obvious candidate often leads to complications). And that's why this book is such a joy. In Texas, "joy" can be used as a verb—as in, "He joyed in that battle." And one can joy in this book.

So what else is left to be learned about the collapse of Enron? My job is keeping track of the more bizarre forms of Texas weirdness, so naturally I had nothing left to learn when I started *Pipe Dreams*. I'd known about Enron for years, and followed its first teetering steps toward ruin with what I must admit was an annoyingly smug, told-you-so complacency. When the financial equivalent of the World Trade Center collapsed into clouds of toxic dust, my first question was "What took so long?"

So why would Little-Ms.-Know-It-All here need to read a book about Enron? All I can tell you is that I agreed to do it because I know Robert Bryce to be the best Texas investigative reporter of his generation—I have known his work for several years now and it is always impeccable—and so I thought I would do "the boy" a favor. My jaw dropped for the first time before I was ten pages into *Pipe Dreams*, and I laughed out loud for the first time before I was twenty pages into it. And it just kept going like that through the whole book.

Bryce is not only a superb reporter, he's a superb explainer. If you don't know the difference between a denture and a derivative, this is the man you need—done without jargon, condescension, or fuss—clear enough for seventh graders, and then we move right along to the story.

Bryce begins with the singularly useful question: "Why?" Why did this happen? Greed? Stupidity? Deregulation? Corruption? Who knows?

Robert Bryce knows.

"Fish rot at the head," he reports. And proves it.

Over halfway through 2002, it is clear we are looking at something more than a scandal in the financial markets. Implicit, complicit, cooperating, and even totally "whored out," as we say in Texas, is the American political system.

Bryce did not set out to write a book about the corruption of American politics. This is a book about why Enron collapsed. That's what makes it so damning: It's about the corruption of American politics whether it wants to be or not.

Again and again one sees the fatal precipitating step stemming from government action or inaction: the last-minute approval of an exemption from regulation by the federal Commodity Futures Trading Commission granted by Wendy Gramm; Congress consistently underfunding the SEC, leaving it outmanned and outgunned; the massive amounts spent on lobbying and contributions to Congress by the Big Five accounting firms in order to defeat Arthur Levitt's reform proposals; Senator Phil Gramm's Commodity Futures Modernization Act of 2000 containing "the Enron exemption"; the appointment of Ken Lay's selection to the Federal Energy Regulatory Commission; the role of government investment and insurance in Enron's overseas projects—it goes on and on and on.

Any reporter can tell you that much of our work is untangling meaning from jargon. In every field, people develop a specialized vocabulary, often as a way of proving "insidership." Many folks in the "awl bidness" assume they can confuse journalists by using specialized jargon. And they often can—per square inch of pressure in a gas pipeline, the intricacies of writing off drilling costs, what the hell the "allowable" used to be—the bidness is full of initials, acronyms, code, shorthand, none of which, it turns out, is incomprehensible or even difficult once explained. This book will give those unfamiliar with oil that satisfying "Aha!" that comes from the realization, "So that's how it really works."

Although Bryce is kept busy following the money, Enron, like all good stories, is really about people, and that is ultimately the most fascinating part of the book. Supersmart, well-educated people, well-connected people . . . and so stupid, so blind, so greedy. Their folly, their denial, their social climbing, their office affairs, and the corporate culture that pushed them into desperate deal making are all etched clearly in *Pipe Dreams*. The final, shameless plundering of the company by its top executives sets a new record in the annals of greed. We find a few heroes along the way, too—those who ran a tight ship in their time at Enron, or the occasional lonely citizen trying to blow the whistle on those who didn't. "Redeployment" seems to have been their fate.

Although it's a fascinating story, and Bryce tells it with the unquenchable relish of a good investigative reporter on the trail of real scum, this is ultimately a horrifying story. It's horrifying because even after all we have seen, we are still having to listen to people making patently absurd claims that all that has happened only because of "a few rotten apples"; still having to watch exactly the same financial industry lobbyists crawling all over Capitol Hill trying to kill or gut every reform proposal; still standing by as powerful corporations buy the votes of the elected representatives of the people with their huge campaign contributions.

It's time to get mad and get even. And that's where this book leaves us: with a far better understanding of why it is so necessary to make the fixes to our system—or watch it happen again and again and again.

MOLLY IVINS
AUSTIN, TEXAS
AUGUST 2002

Pipe Dreams

1

The Job Fair

We believe in markets. Sometimes there's an aberration.
But over time, markets figure out value.[1]

—KEN LAY, SPRING 1997

DECEMBER 14, 2001
Enron closing price: $0.30

Sherri Saunders was out of place.

She was two decades too old, several shades too gray, and a few pounds too heavy to be at a job fair and she knew it. But she was there anyway, eleven days before Christmas 2001, tiny beads of sweat forming on her forehead as she walked the long, wide curving concourse at Enron Field.

Sherri Saunders wasn't alone. Thousands of other former Enron employees were there, too, all of them hoping to impress one or more of the 200 corporations that had set up tables at the brand-new stadium on the edge of downtown Houston on the unseasonably warm afternoon. All of the companies were hoping to snare a few of Enron's best and brightest for their own.

For Sherri, a woman used to having an orderly daily schedule and an orderly life, the scene at the job fair was discombobulating. And it drove home the fact that she was—for only the second time in her adult life—out of a job. Saunders had been working for Enron for two and a half decades. She had started in 1978 at Northern Natural Gas in Omaha as a Telex operator. Back in those days, before e-mail and high-speed faxes, she was the communications clerk, the one company official who handled all electronic correspondence for the company. In 1980, she moved to Houston and got a different job with Northern Natural, later called InterNorth, the pipeline company that merged with Houston Natural Gas in 1985 and became Enron. Since then, she'd applied her clerical and organizational skills in half a dozen different parts of the company.

She'd been making less than $50,000 per year, a sum that included all of her overtime and bonuses. As a "noncommercial" person at Enron, her bonus was limited to $3,000 per year. But Houston was cheap. She and her husband, Bill, were living in a smallish apartment, saving as much as they could, and dreaming about traveling as soon as Sherri retired. Sherri didn't really expect to get much out of the job fair, but the truth was she and her husband, Bill, a handsome man with a shock of white hair, really didn't have anything else to do.

Bill was seventy-one and already retired. He had a few consulting deals, but they weren't big. And he was curious about the job fair. He wanted to see what was happening and to see the new ballpark. Sherri was there because she needed a job. She also hadn't been able to say good-bye to many of her friends and coworkers. On December 3, she, along with thousands of other Enron employees, had been fired. And when the word came down, her supervisor had told her she had half an hour to get out of the building. The push out the door under watch of security guards and Houston Police Department officers had been disorienting. There'd been no time to seek out her friends, to grieve with them, to exchange e-mail addresses and home phone numbers.

The sting was still fresh. "I worked for that company for twenty-four years. And when the time came, they said, 'You have thirty minutes to get your things and get out of the building.' It was just done so coldly." It was a truly lousy end to what Sherri had hoped would be the last job she'd ever have.

Plus, Enron had good medical benefits, a fact that was particularly important now that she and Bill were getting older. Now all of that was gone. And here she was, two years away from retirement, out of a job, out of prospects, and facing a decidedly unhappy Christmas. The lines of unemployed people waiting to talk to recruiters were only driving home the magnitude of the disaster. Bill had a little money in his pension fund. But he was Canadian, and so was his pension, which meant that those Canadian dollars didn't go far in Houston. Sherri's retirement fund had all been in Enron stock. A year earlier, her 401(k) plan had been worth nearly $1 million. By the time she walked past the concession stand at Enron Field, it was worth less than $100,000.

Sherri wasn't getting much warmth from the recruiters. Sure, they were taking her résumé, but there were no promises. More than 4,000 other former Enron employees were at the job fair, nearly all of them younger than Sherri Saunders. Most were better educated and better dressed, with bigger bank accounts. But Sherri went to as many tables as she could, including the ones for El Paso, the giant gas company that was one of Enron's key rivals. After ninety minutes or so, she had handed out fifteen résumés. The job fair was "for the younger crowd," she said. "There's no way they were going to hire a person like me. I don't care what they say, there's age discrimination. I'm fifty-four, and I'm starting over."

There was plenty of irony in the location of the job fair. Just twenty months earlier, Enron's CEO and chairman, Ken Lay, was on top of the world, and that world revolved around Enron Field.

April 7, 2000, was undoubtedly one of the best days of his entire life. That day, Enron Field opened for business, and the Houston Astros hosted the Philadelphia Phillies in the first game ever played at the new $265-million retractable-roof baseball stadium. Lay threw out the ceremonial first pitch. Then he moved to his private box and watched the game with his friend George W. Bush, governor of Texas, already the odds-on favorite to become the next president of the United States. In addition to having Bush's ear, Lay had one of the biggest plums associated with the Bush orbit: a nickname.

Yes, George W. Bush, the man-who-would-be-president, had slapped Lay with the moniker "Kenny Boy." It wasn't exactly on a par with "Butch" or "Bubba" or any of the myriad other more macho Texas-style nicknames, but the nickname showed that Ken Lay was one of the chosen. W. knew who Kenny Boy was and better still, Kenny Boy knew he could call W. when he needed him. The hundreds of thousands of dollars Lay had invested in the Bush dynasty—including his work as one of the "Pioneers," Big Shots who had pledged to raise $100,000 or more for W.'s presidential campaign—was going to continue paying big dividends. And so he enjoyed the game, a game that he and Bush—and thousands of others who watched the Phillies drum the Astros—would never have seen if not for the clout of Ken Lay.

In 1996, when the Astros were threatening to leave Houston for Virginia, Lay had thrown himself into the campaign to get a stadium built and save the team. He interceded with Houston mayor Bob Lanier and brokered a deal with Astros owner Drayton McLane, raising tens of millions of dollars in corporate subsidies for the team and getting the stadium referendum on the same ballot as Bill Clinton and Bob Dole. Although Houston voters had recently defeated a school bond issue, they approved the funding for the new stadium. And it was all due to Lay's power. Without Lay, the stadium "would never have been built," said Dave Walden, a Houston political consultant who served as chief of staff to Mayor Lanier.

"Never. Ever. Not a chance in hell."

So how was it, then, that Ken Lay—Mr. Houston, friend of the Bushes, revered and feared politico, a man who could, almost single-handedly get baseball stadiums built—had fallen so far? Here was a man who oversaw an empire upon which the sun never set. From pipelines in Houston to power plants in England, Turkey, India, the Philippines, China, and Guam, Enron had a global footprint and global reputation as the company that got things done. And all of that glory reflected back on Lay, the man who fifteen years earlier had taken the reins of a small but well-run gas pipeline company, Houston Natural Gas, and had turned it into an energy colossus.

How, in the span of twenty months, could Ken Lay have gone from world-class CEO to world-class chump?

It was a mind-boggling event. The Enron failure happened so quickly and with such devastating impact that no one could have predicted it. Sure, some analysts and pundits in Houston had said that Enron would fall on hard times or that its stock price would get walloped—but bankruptcy? Not a chance. And yet, mighty Enron had gone Chapter 11. And it had done it Texas-style, in the biggest and gaudiest way possible—with superlatives aplenty.

It was—for the span of seven months—the biggest bankruptcy in American history. (WorldCom's bankruptcy on July 21, 2002, eclipsed Enron.) With $63.4 billion in assets, Enron was nearly two times larger than Texaco when that energy firm went under in 1987. Enron failed thanks to a load of liabilities that exceeded the gross domestic product of Iraq. Suddenly, Kenny Boy was about as welcome in Kennebunkport as the Bush family's old nemesis, Saddam Hussein.

The Enron failure is the biggest political scandal in American history. Teapot Dome—a scandal about payoffs to Secretary of the Interior Albert Fall by a couple of greedy oilmen—was memorable, but involved very few people.[2] The Watergate scandal was bigger and more pernicious than Teapot Dome, but it, too, involved relatively few people: Tricky Dick Nixon, a dozen or two of his henchmen, and a few inept plumbers. Enron was different. By the time of its bankruptcy, Enron owned—or perhaps was just renting—politicians in the White House, Congress, state courts, state legislatures, and bureaucrats at every level.

It's the biggest scandal ever to hit Wall Street. The problems at junk-bond trading house Drexel Burnham Lambert in the 1980s were tiny in comparison to Enron. That scandal involved Michael Milken (who went to jail for securities fraud) and a handful of others. The Enron debacle has ensnared every major investment bank in New York, including Merrill Lynch, Citigroup, J.P. Morgan Chase, UBS, and dozens of others. Those banks not only lent Enron huge sums of money and did investment banking for the company, but their executives invested in Enron's off-the-balance-sheet partnerships. And the same bankers employed a gaggle of analysts who, given enough investment banking work by Enron, were happy to put out "strong buys" on the company's stock.

Enron is the biggest derivatives-trading firm to go bust since the failure of the hedge fund Long-Term Capital Management in 1998. Long-Term, led by a pair of Nobel Prize–winning economists, made huge bets using predictive models based on statistical analysis. The firm lost some $4.6 billion trading derivatives, the complex financial instruments that include futures, forwards options, and swaps. The firm's positions involved so many banks that the New York Federal Reserve organized a multibank, $3.6 billion bailout, lest Long-Term's failure cause a global financial meltdown. And though Long-Term was big, Frank Partnoy, a law professor at the University of San Diego, told Congress in January 2002, that Enron's derivatives business made Long-Term "look like a lemonade stand."[3]

That's a bit of hyperbole, but there's truth in it, too. In 2000, if Enron's derivatives business had been a stand-alone Fortune 500 company, it would have been the 256th-largest company in America. That year, Enron claimed that it made more money from its derivatives business—$7.23 billion—than Tyson Foods made from selling chicken. By the time Enron failed, its derivatives liabilities exceeded $18.7 billion, an exposure that played a key role in pushing the company into bankruptcy.

In addition to the hugely complex derivatives transactions Enron was making with other big energy firms and utilities outside of Enron, it was making mind-numbingly complex derivatives deals inside of Enron with Andy Fastow's off-the-balance-sheet partnerships. Those derivatives deals—all completely unregulated by federal authorities and kept secret from investors—fatally corrupted Enron's books. By the time investors learned the size and scope of Enron's derivatives deals with Fastow, on February 1, 2002, with the release of the report by William Powers, dean of the University of Texas Law School, Enron had already failed.

It's the biggest scandal to ever hit accounting, the world's second-oldest profession. The once-great accounting firm Arthur Andersen wasn't just in bed with Enron, the venerable firm was providing the energy company with auditing and consulting services, while sharing office space—*free shredding!*—all in exchange for $52 million per year in fees. Today, Andersen, which was convicted on June 15, 2002, of obstructing justice in the Enron investigation, has all but disappeared in a cloud of ignominy. The rest of the Big Five, oops, *Big Four*, accounting firms are now struggling to keep investigators at bay and clean up their own practices, lest they be dragged into the Enron mire.

The Enron collapse is the most egregious example of executive piracy in American corporate history. A handful of executives made unbelievable fortunes—tens, even hundreds of millions of dollars—at the same time that Enron was being driven into the ground. Between 1998 and 2001, two dozen Enron executives and board members sold company stock worth more than $1.1 billion—and that's only what's been discovered so far. And that total doesn't include the huge salaries, bonuses, and other cash payments made to Enron executives during their reign of plunder.

The Enron bankruptcy has changed American investors. After losing more than $70 billion in equity value in Enron alone, American stockholders watched companies that have nothing to do with Enron—names like General Electric, Tyco, and others—get hammered because of questions about their accounting.

In addition to all the superlatives, the Enron bankruptcy occurred at a time when the American psyche was badly shaken. Enron went bankrupt eighty-two days after the September 11, 2001, terrorist attacks on Washington, D.C., and New York City. The Al Qaeda terrorist attacks hit America in the heart. Enron's collapse hit America in the wallet.

The attacks on the Pentagon and the World Trade Center shattered America's sense of physical security. The Enron meltdown shook American investors' confidence in the entire financial system. American investors, seduced by the irrational exuberance of the Internet Age and rocked to sleep by the greatest bull market in history, were suddenly hit with the ice-cold water of reality: Even the bluest of blue-chip companies could disappear, or be made nearly worthless, almost overnight.

Enron, the company of the 1990s, the company that epitomized the hyperaggressive New Economy, the company that *Fortune* magazine had named America's Most Innovative Company six years in a row, the first truly transcontinental pipeline company, a company whose history began at Spindletop in the dawn of the Petroleum Age, had gone bust, in a final tragic implosion of the Internet Bubble.

The media knew the story was big. Reporters invaded Houston. By mid-December of 2001, the *New York Times* had eight reporters working on the story full-time. Enron led the national news nearly every night. C-SPAN did a multipart series on Enron. Hundreds of stories were published or broadcast. Everything Enron did was dissected: how it hid its losses, how it bought political access, how it (mis)managed its businesses, how executives lied to Wall Street, how Wall Street analysts whored themselves out in return for big investment banking fees, how Enron executives sold their stock, making big profits while small investors and pension-fund holders lost billions. Congress had hearings on how Arthur Andersen shredded hundreds of pounds of Enron documents. President George W. Bush discussed how his mother-in-law lost money on Enron stock. The *Wall Street Journal* showed how Enron created revenues out of thin air by selling some of its assets over and over to a succession of Enron-controlled entities.

Two reverends, Jesse Jackson and Al Sharpton, brought their flocks to Houston, prompting yet more stories (and more than a few jokes) about the need for more government regulation of businesses like Enron. Meanwhile, the Right blamed the Left. The Left blamed the Right. And the lawyers sued nearly every executive or investment bank ever associated with the "Crooked E."

But amid all the analysis, amid all the hand-wringing and speechifying, something was missing: a discussion of *why Enron failed.*

It's a simple question: Why did it? Why—over a period of four years—did Enron go from thriving and stable to insolvent? Why did a seventy-six-year-old pipeline company with rock-solid cash flow and reliable earnings suddenly flame out in a maelstrom of accounting irregularities, fraud, and skullduggery?

The short answer to why it filed for bankruptcy on December 2, 2001, was that Enron had run out of real money. During the first nine months of 2001, Enron claimed revenues of $138.7 billion. But that number didn't matter. Enron's debts mattered. In the end, Enron had too much debt and too little cash. That fact is proven by a quick glance at the final four years of Enron's cash flow statements. Enron wasn't making enough cash—*real money*—from its operations to pay for its hyperaggressive growth. In the end, a severe cash crunch sank Enron, case closed.

But how did Enron get to be so cash poor? Why did the company get out of control in its growth and expenses? Those questions sent me in search of people with insight, people who could answer those questions.

One of my most instructive discussions was with a former Enron employee. I'll call him Joe.

We'd met through mutual acquaintances and via a series of e-mails had agreed to meet at a dumpy central Houston saloon he selected. He drank beer. I drank Sprite. He had worked on some international energy projects for Enron in the Far East, then worked for a short while at Enron Broadband Services. He'd left the company in mid–2000, apparently because he'd made enough money so he didn't need to work anymore. He then told me how stupid many Enron employees were for not having sold their Enron stock. He had sold most of his stock when it was at $80. Enron really hadn't done much wrong, he insisted. The markets had simply lost faith in the company and that caused it to go downhill. Now, working on some other energy deals as an independent developer (with some other former Enroners), he reminisced about how easy it had been at Enron to get the legal, financial, and technical personnel he'd needed to put his deals together. Enron really had smart people, he said. "You could get the entire project team assembled in one day. They understood what you needed." Now out on his own, in the real world, he was realizing things were just a wee bit harder.

Throughout our conversation, Joe made it clear that he was not going to help me in any way. No, he didn't want to be quoted or named. No, he wouldn't introduce me to his former coworkers. No, he wouldn't give me their names or phone numbers. No, he really didn't want to give me any details about his job at Enron. Joe had the ultimate I-wouldn't-cross-the-street-to-piss-on-you-if-your-brains-were-on-fire attitude.

But Joe said one thing that rang true: "Enron is not an operations company. It is a deal company." A few minutes later, Joe glanced at his $2,400 designer watch and made it clear that he had far more important things to do than talk to dolts like me. So we walked out to his car—a brand new Lexus—he slipped his folding cell phone into his handy belt holster, and off he sped. I would later learn from his coworkers that Joe was considered a very successful Enron employee. In fact, he was the exact type that Enron recruiters loved: young (Joe was thirty-five, tops), smart, and cocky. That didn't mean his coworkers liked him. They thought he was a world-class jerk. But in Enron's view of the universe, he was successful.

A few days later, I realized that I owed Joe a thank-you. His comment about Enron being a deal company was proving to be right on the money. So I rang him up.

He didn't return my phone call.

But that didn't matter. Even though Joe really didn't want to help, he had unwittingly done me a great service. He reminded me that being a Texas-sized sphincter was valued at Enron and that deals—and therefore, deal makers like him—were prized. Enron's headquarters at 1400 Smith Street in downtown Houston had overflowed with young Masters of the Universe just like him. But having a surfeit of sphincters didn't explain it. So I continued collecting theories.

Jack Bowen, the former CEO of pipeline giant Transco Energy (now part of Williams Companies), had his own theory, and having given Ken Lay his first job in the pipeline business in 1974, Bowen was in a position to know. The problem at Enron, according to Bowen, was that it paid its employees too much. "They went way overboard in compensation of their top executives," he said. "They had huge stock options based on the price of stock, and price of stock is based on the earnings they report. So there was tremendous incentive on the part of key people to keep those earnings growing. As earnings went up, their options were worth that much more. You can get too much money."

Bowen was clearly right, too. The top executives were making enormous salaries at Enron, far more than executives at comparable firms in Houston. Plus, Enron was handing out stock options to top executives and lower-level employees all the time. By the end of 2000, over 13 percent of all of Enron's outstanding stock was held in options. Those options were going to make everyone at the company rich, that is, if Enron could just keep impressing Wall Street with big profits.

There were plenty of other theories. A Wall Street analyst said the sexual shenanigans of the top executives could not be discounted. It was well known that Enron president Jeff Skilling had cheated on his wife for years before divorcing her. Other top execs, including Ken Lay, Ken Rice, Lou Pai, and others, had also been involved in adulterous affairs. That raised a red flag among some observers on Wall Street, particularly those who loathed Skilling and his arrogance. "If character has become an issue, then these are important notes to make about a man. This is a guy who felt he could get away with anything," the analyst commented.

One former top executive blamed the company's aggressive accounting. The company's use of mark-to-market accounting had corrupted Enron's books and had allowed the company to be far too optimistic in its assumptions about future profits. That meant, said the executive, who had worked at both Enron and Azurix, Enron's failed water venture, that Enron could show huge revenue growth but have little or no cash—real money—with which to pay its debts. "When earnings go up and cash flow goes down, you can't sustain that. Sooner or later the laws of physics apply," he said.

A former military man who'd spent several years at Enron—numerous West Point graduates worked in Enron's international operations—cut me off at the get-go. "Either you acknowledge that this is all about Ken Lay or we don't have much to talk about," he told me, approximately two and a half minutes after I introduced myself. "This guy was the head of this company for all but six months for the period from 1986 to December 2, 2001. Whether it's willful misconduct or arrogant indifference doesn't matter," he said. "I come from a military background. The command reflects the commander. This is all Ken Lay's fault."

Several other key former Enron people blamed Lay, too.

He "flat couldn't judge people," as one top former executive put it. Another top-level executive said Lay became blinded to other people's faults: "Once Ken became enamored with someone, he couldn't see anything else." Furthermore, they said Lay should have learned his lesson and been more cautious after a group of traders nearly ruined Enron in 1987. "He should have been more wary of traders," said one now-retired executive. Yet Lay was drawn to traders and deal makers, like a moth to a flame.

I began to realize, that all of them—Joe, Jack Bowen, and all the others—were correct. All of the maladies they described were symptomatic of the problem. And better still, the answer to *why Enron failed* could be boiled down to one word—a word that business management gurus love to spout off about. It's a word that consultants and authors charge $1,000 per day to discuss with management. It's an expensive word, a word that has defined civilizations—and companies—for generations. It was the culture, stupid.

Fish rot at the head.

Enron failed because its leadership was morally, ethically, and financially corrupt.

Whether the question was accounting or marital fidelity, the executives who inhabited the fiftieth floor at Enron's headquarters became incapable of telling the truth, to the Securities and Exchange Commission, to their spouses or their employees. That corruption permeated everything they did, and it spread through the company like wildfire. So why didn't Ken Lay see any of this? Sure, he was corrupted by the money just like the rest of the people at Enron, but he was also a smart guy, a Ph.D. economist, a member of the secretive Trilateral Commission,[4] a friend of presidents.

Simply put, how could Ken Lay, this prince of American business, have been so dumb?

2

John Henry Kirby and the Roots of Enron

It must be something in the Texas air.

Every decade or so, the Lone Star State produces an energy baron who willingly pulls his own pants down. And for the next couple of years or so, that former Big Shot becomes the laughingstock of the entire country. In the 1980s, multimillionaire Dallas oilman Nelson Bunker Hunt, who, having far more money than sense, got greedy and tried to corner the world silver market. At one point, Hunt and his partners controlled about one-third of the world's supply of the metal. But the scheme faltered, and Hunt's venture ended up losing hundreds of millions of dollars. After the affair ended, the philosophical—but still rich—Hunt lamented, "A billion dollars isn't what it used to be."

In 1990, Midland oilman Clayton Williams stormed the stage. A jug-eared millionaire Republican, Williams was well on his way to beating Democrat Ann Richards in the race for governor of Texas. But while chatting with some reporters on a cool drizzly day in West Texas, Williams compared the nasty weather to rape and added, "If it's inevitable, just relax and enjoy it." Williams spent more than $20 million in his effort to win the governor's seat, but his rape comment cost him the race. Richards beat him by nearly 90,000 votes.

In 2001, Ken Lay and Enron stumbled onto the scene.

Texas has never had—and never will have—a shortage of colorful, ever-eager Big Shots willing to risk it all. It's a characteristic due, in no small part, to the state's frontier attitude. And no locale exemplifies that attitude better than Houston.

Houston is still on the frontier. Whether the issue is drilling for gas in the Chinese desert or sending rocket ships to the moon (*"Houston, we have a problem"*), the biggest city in the South has long had a swagger, a cockiness, that can't be found in older, Northern cities.

Houston has a fearless "can-do" spirit that stems largely from its energy industry, an industry in which technological innovation and risk taking are the stuff of legend. The new technologies extend from the rotary drill bits invented by Howard Hughes Sr. in the early 1900s to the oil-well fire-fighting technology and personnel from companies like Boots & Coots, who will fly anywhere in the world at a moment's notice to deal with deadly oil-well fires. Whether the technology is pipelines, power plants, or deep-sea oil exploration, Houston has always been at the forefront of the energy business. And the city's reputation and its status as the aorta of the world's energy industry provided the perfect springboard for Enron's success and excess.

Sure, Ponzi schemes and other giant bankruptcies have happened in other cities. But those deals didn't involve energy. Enron didn't trade pork bellies or orange juice. It traded energy. Enron couldn't have happened anywhere but Houston. No other city had the infrastructure, the talent pool, or the history of daring and innovation.

Enron was a perfect reflection of Houston, a place ambitious people go to make money. As soon as they accomplish that goal, they take their money and buy a vacation home somewhere else—anywhere else—where the weather is more agreeable, like Colorado, Hawaii, or Montana. In fact, one of the best views of Houston is the one you get from your rearview mirror. As one prominent Houston journalist told me, "Do you think people live here for the scenery?"

No. They surely don't. That's because there is no scenery. Houston is a table-flat, hot, humid, bug-infested, traffic-choked, soulless city in which every resident is hoping to escape. Most don't. And the crushing poverty evident on the fringes of downtown are a constant counterpoint to the amazing wealth and opulence of the city's West Side, where tanned, toned women dressed in expensive clothes and driving shiny SUVs shop aimlessly for knickknacks at stores like Neiman Marcus and Smith & Hawken. Houston has a sprawling, strip-mall sameness that makes it seem the city and its suburbs never end. The flatness of the landscape and the lack of significant natural landmarks are so disorienting that drivers must pay close attention to traffic signs on the freeway or they might accidentally end up in Sugar Land when they meant to go to Galveston. The sameness is made worse by the lack of zoning laws. Except for a few regulations on fireworks warehouses and sexually oriented business, Houston has no zoning laws. Never has. So you can have a bakery next to a church, next to a high-rise office building, next to an auto salvage yard. The lack of regulation has created a city that has "pockets of civilization surrounded by chaos," as one former city council member described it. "That doesn't make Houston special, it makes Houston a mess."

To be fair, Houston has a tremendous number of attractions. It's one of the most ethnically diverse cities in America. It will soon have no distinct majority. Instead, it'll have one-third Anglos, one-third Hispanics, and one-third everybody else. That everybody else includes a huge Asian population. Its Asian markets on the far western side of town are nothing short of amazing. Every type of live fish, squid, eel, and octopus is available for purchase, along with dozens of exotic teas and herbs from the Far East. The people are invariably friendly. The city's theater district is world class. The Houston Ballet is world class. The de Menil Art Museum, designed by Renzo Piano, is way cool (the collection isn't bad, either). The Rothko Chapel is sublime. Houston has a world-class opera company, along with a clutch of fine art and science museums. Its Texas Medical Center is one of the biggest and most opulent medical facilities in the world. It has one of the world's biggest space installations at the Johnson Space Center.

It also has world-class pollution.

In 1999, the Environmental Protection Agency named Houston the smoggiest city in the land, surpassing even Los Angeles. In 1999, the more than 120 chemical plants, oil refineries, and petrochemical storage terminals located in Harris County released more than 25 million pounds of toxic chemicals into the air, the third-highest total of any county in America.[1] A 1999 study commissioned by the City of Houston found that about 400 people in the region die every year due to high levels of ozone and other air pollutants.[2] In addition, the Houston Ship Channel has, it appears, become a charter member of the "most-polluted waterways" lists published every year or two by various environmental groups. And with all that pollution, Houston's M.D. Anderson Cancer Center—one of the world's most renowned oncology clinics—comes in handy.

Regular floods add to the charm. Every ten years or so, Houston gets hit by a 100-year flood and the city goes through a by-now-familiar routine: The bayous overflow, inundating neighborhoods throughout the city. Thousands of homes are ruined. Soggy discarded carpets line the streets. Landfills get bloated. Politicians get exorcised. Federal aid gets extended. The floods aren't surprising, really. Four river basins lie within seventy-five miles of the city.[3] In 1994, floods killed seventeen people and damaged 22,000 homes. In 2001, when the remnants of Tropical Storm Allison lingered over the city, dumping *three feet* of rain, twenty people died and floodwaters caused an estimated $1 billion in damage to some 20,000 homes and businesses.

The forbidding landscape, pollution, and flooding have never held Houston back. Instead, they somehow add to the city's chest-thumping self-image. The physical environment is just a reflection of the city's always-in-turmoil energy business. Houston is a city filled with schemers and dreamers, men and women who believe that the next deal, the next acquisition, will make them rich. Houston is a city of irrepressible optimists. Despite years of boom and bust, it's a city that still believes that the prices of oil and natural gas will go up and stay up. For more than a century, it's bred fearless deal makers, people who dream Big Dreams and are willing to make Big Bets—people like John Henry Kirby.

The gusher at Spindletop clouded John Henry Kirby's judgment. Kirby, a timberman who'd spent virtually his entire life in the remote, heavily wooded counties of East Texas, had gotten ahead by selling lumber and building railroads. He knew nothing about the energy business. But when Spindletop blew in on January 10, 1901, Kirby—along with thousands of other speculators—was bitten by the oil bug. Spindletop, located in Jefferson County, a few dozen miles east of Houston, was the gusher to end all gushers. The well, drilled by a former captain in the Austrian navy named Anthony F. Lucas, erupted in a volcano of oil, blowing a stream of crude 100 feet into the air.[4] The roar from the well was so intense it could be heard four miles away in downtown Beaumont. The well flowed uncontrolled for nine days, pushing out a river of oil with estimated production of up to 100,000 barrels a day.

Within days of the discovery, Spindletop and nearly all of Houston was in chaos. Throngs of sight-seers, promoters, speculators, and merchants descended on Beaumont to take part in the new gold rush. One Sunday shortly after the well came in, 15,000 sightseers came on excursion trains just to see the well. Land prices shot through the stratosphere. Land that two years earlier had been selling for $10 per acre was suddenly selling for as much as $900,000 per acre. Within months of the discovery, Beaumont's population soared from 10,000 to 50,000—about one-third of the newcomers living in tents. More than 200 wells, owned by over 100 different oil companies, were soon drilled on the same hill as the Lucas 1.

The Texas oil boom had begun, and John Henry Kirby was going to be a part of it.

Kirby was born in 1860 near Peach Tree Village, in Tyler County, Texas, in the heart of what is now known as the Big Thicket. His mother taught him to read and write—his formal schooling consisted of occasional visits to local schools and less than one semester at Southwestern University, in Georgetown, Texas. A natural entrepreneur, Kirby was soon working in the timber business and was able to obtain the backing of a group of Boston businessmen to expand his operations. In 1890, Kirby moved to Houston. Three years later, with financing from his pals in Boston, he began construction of the Gulf, Beaumont, and Kansas City Railway, which stretched from Beaumont into the forests at Roganville. The line was built to service Silsbee, where Kirby's first sawmill was located. In 1900, Kirby sold the rail line to the Atchison, Topeka, and Santa Fe Railway and used the cash to buy more forestland. By the following year, Kirby controlled more than half a million acres of East Texas woodlands. And when Spindletop blew out, Kirby saw his chance to move out of the timber business and into energy. He traveled to the East Coast, where he met Patrick Calhoun, a prominent corporate attorney with all the connections Kirby lacked. Calhoun was the grandson of John C. Calhoun, who served as vice president of the United States under John Quincy Adams.[5]

On April 20, 1901, Kirby and Calhoun struck a deal: They would turn wood into oil. The pair agreed to form two interdependent companies, the Kirby Lumber Company and the Houston Oil Company of Texas. The companies were capitalized at $40 million, which Kirby and Calhoun borrowed from a series of New York and Baltimore banks. The two men used most of the money to acquire 800,000 acres of forestland, which Kirby and Calhoun believed might hold oil. The land would be owned by Houston Oil. Kirby Lumber would harvest and manufacture lumber from Houston Oil's land and pay the oil company for the wood it extracted. Houston Oil would then use those revenues to drill for oil. Sixteen sawmills were involved in the deal, which called on Kirby's company to cut billions of board feet of long-leaf yellow pine from the oil company's vast holdings.[6]

But little more than a year after Kirby and Calhoun agreed on this symbiotic arrangement, the deal started falling apart. Part of the problem was that the two men had scant knowledge of the oil business. In addition, the contract terms were so favorable to Calhoun that Kirby was forced to borrow to meet his contractual obligations. By January 10, 1904, when Kirby was unable to make a $700,000 payment, the Maryland Trust Company asked the federal court in Houston to place Kirby Lumber and Houston Oil into receivership.

For the next four years, Kirby and Calhoun battled in court for control of the timber. In 1908, the sides finally agreed to settle the bankruptcy. And for more than a decade afterward, the bulk of Houston Oil's revenues came from wood, not oil, as Kirby Lumber was allowed to continue cutting the oil company's vast timber holdings. After his split with Calhoun, Kirby stayed in the timber business and began rebuilding his wealth and his social position in Houston.

John Henry Kirby was the Ken Lay of his time.

As a civic-business-political leader, Kirby was interested in, and involved in, nearly every important political and social battle of his day. Like Lay, he was a friend to presidents. He raised huge amounts of money for numerous political campaigns. He was a violin-playing larger-than-life character who dominated Houston society. In 1892, he helped secure the future of the Port of Houston. For months, the City of Houston had been in an uproar over a chain blockade that had been erected across Buffalo Bayou, the muddy stream that served as the city's main port. A citizen who owned land along the waterway insisted that he controlled the waterway, and the city was unable to ship cotton and other goods on Buffalo Bayou while trying to negotiate with the landowner. Kirby went to Washington and was able to convince federal authorities to appropriate money to buy out the landowner and get the blockade lifted.

He was a political animal. He served two terms in the Texas legislature and was a delegate to the 1916 Democratic National Convention. During World War I, at the behest of President Woodrow Wilson, he served as the lead timber representative on the Emergency Fleet Corporation, which was overseeing the construction of ships for the war effort. In 1921, he headed a federal committee on manufacturing at a conference sponsored by President Warren G. Harding. That same year, Kirby got back in the energy business and formed Kirby Petroleum

Company, whose descendant, Kirby Corporation, which operates marine barges on the Gulf Coast and the Mississippi River, is still in business and trades on the New York Stock Exchange.[7] A few years later, President Herbert Hoover appointed Kirby to the chairmanship of the Central Committee on Lumber Standards. In 1920, Kirby quit the Democratic Party, saying it was "honeycombed with socialism." But he couldn't stay away from politics. He fought Prohibition and the Ku Klux Klan. In 1922, he and a prominent Houston oilman, Joseph Cullinan, formed the American Anti-Klan Association in an effort to force the KKK to disband.[8] It was a remarkable stand by Kirby at a time when virtually no whites were interested in protecting the rights of blacks. He favored states' rights and the repeal of the estate tax and ardently opposed Franklin D. Roosevelt, whose policies, he believed, were "made by scavengers from the garbage cans of Europe."

By 1925, Kirby's fortune was estimated at $13 million, and he was one of the most influential men in America. But the Great Depression changed all that. In 1933, he filed for personal bankruptcy with assets of $12.9 million and liabilities of $12.2 million, and he owed the federal government $120,000 in back income taxes. Despite those setbacks, Kirby's name still holds sway in Houston. Kirby Drive, a major thoroughfare in central Houston that runs through the city's nicest neighborhood, River Oaks, is named for him.

By the time of his death in 1940, John Henry Kirby was still a lion of Houston society. And by an accident of geography, the magnificent home he built—and died in—is in Enron's neighborhood.

Ken Lay's old office on the fiftieth floor of Enron's oval glass skyscraper in downtown Houston is less than five minutes by foot from the Kirby Mansion. Six blocks south of Enron, past the YMCA, past the world headquarters for Continental Airlines, and a few steps past the noisy Interstate 45 overpass sits Kirby's home, 2000 Smith Street, one of the oldest and most beautiful houses in Houston. Designed by James Ruskin, the house, which was rebuilt in 1928, was once among the city's most elegant. Today, the building has been converted into office space and is used by a group of lawyers.

The house is the most visible part of Kirby's legacy. But it's also clear that without Kirby's gamble, the Texas energy business would have taken a far different path. As a Kirby biographer wrote, "without his bold enterprise, there might never have been a Houston Natural Gas Corporation."[9]

Although John Henry Kirby was no longer affiliated with Houston Oil Company, the money that he paid the firm following the 1908 settlement agreement allowed it to continue its exploration activities. In the early 1920s, the company discovered vast gas fields in Live Oak and Refugio Counties. And though the discovery was fortuitous, it also forced the company to make some difficult choices. Up to that time, more that 90 percent of Houston Oil's revenues came from oil, not gas. For years, prospectors had viewed natural gas as a problem, not a profit center. Most gas was vented into the air or burned off in flares. Gas was harder to handle and transport than crude oil and had far fewer uses. One of its main uses during the late 1800s and early 1900s was for lighting. It was also gaining favor in industrial applications like steelmaking, but limited infrastructure constrained its consumption.[10] Further, it had a nasty habit of exploding when treated improperly. By comparison, crude oil was not as flammable and could be refined into fuel that could be used for automobiles, heavy equipment, generators, heating, cooking, and lighting.

The first gas pipeline was built in the late 1800s in New York state to carry gas from West Bloomfield to Rochester. It was twenty-five miles long and about one foot in diameter. But it was limited in value because, being made of hollowed-out pine logs,[11] it leaked like a sieve. The first significant high-pressure gas pipeline was built in 1891 by Indiana Gas and Oil company, which installed a 120-mile-long pipeline from a gas field in Indiana to customers in Chicago. But that pipe, too, was riddled with leaks, and by 1907 was shut down; Chicago consumers reverted to using coal gas. For the next few years, urban gas systems were unreliable and expensive.

By 1925, there were only a handful of natural gas pipelines in the entire country, and many of them were plagued by leaks and inefficient operations. But there were positive signs on the horizon. Breakthroughs in metallurgy and industrial equipment were changing the landscape. In the early 1920s, seamless steel pipe began to be manufactured in large quantities. Far stronger than earlier versions of pipe, it allowed gas pipelines to carry gas at higher pressures and thus in greater quantities. Greater quantities meant lower prices, and lower prices meant market share. Breakthroughs in welding technology like oxyacetylene and electric welding allowed pipeline builders to string together long pieces of high-strength steel pipe. Better compression technologies from internal combustion engines allowed gas to be shipped at higher pressures, a development that allowed more gas to be sent through the same pipe. These technologies helped convince the directors of the Houston Oil Company to proceed with a plan to link their new gas fields with a growing urban market. They proposed spending $10.6 million (approximately $104 million in 2000 dollars) to build a 200-mile-long gas pipeline from Live Oak County, just south of San Antonio, all the way to Houston.

At that time, the longest gas pipeline in the country was about 300 miles in length. And it wasn't clear whether the city of Houston would even allow the company to sell its gas to residents, once the pipeline was completed. In fact, the plan was so dodgy that four of the company's thirteen directors promptly quit after the decision to build the pipeline.[12]

On March 16, 1925, the board of Houston Oil Company decided to go ahead with the project and created the Houston Pipe Line Company. Within nine months, the project was completed. And with the completion came the need for Houston Oil to create another company to manage the distribution of the gas. The new entity was christened Houston Natural Gas Company.

Although Houston was an attractive market, the city already had a gas provider, Houston Gas Light Company, which manufactured coal gas for lighting streets and homes. For months, the two companies battled over the right to serve the city. But Houston Natural Gas (HNG) was finally able to win a concession from the city. Within fifteen months of completing the pipeline from Live Oak County to the city's outskirts, the company had laid pipe to hundreds of homes in the city. And it was able to undercut the prices of its major competitor, the coal gas company.

Over the next few decades, Houston Natural Gas expanded rapidly, its growth fueled by the Houston area's astounding growth. The region's population more than doubled every twenty years between 1900 and 1980. In 1920, Harris County had 186,667 residents. By 1980, that figure was 2.4 million.[13] In 1976, Houston Natural Gas sold its retail gas operation, which provided gas to residential customers in Houston, and began focusing on natural gas production and other businesses. And it was doing very well.

By 1975, HNG owned over 300 gas wells and 97 oil wells in Texas, Oklahoma, New Mexico, West Virginia, and Wyoming, containing 356 billion cubic feet of gas and over 2.5 million barrels of oil. It owned coal mines, natural gas gathering systems, natural gas liquids extraction plants, river barges, and thousands of miles of pipelines, both onshore and offshore.[14] By the early 1980s, HNG was one of the most profitable companies in Houston. In 1984, it had over $3.7 billion in assets. Revenues topped $2 billion and profits were $123 million.[15]

That success caught the eye of a hometown Houston millionaire energy speculator and corporate raider named Oscar Wyatt. His greed was to provide Ken Lay with one of the biggest breaks of his career.

3

Buy or Be Bought

Oscar Wyatt was just plain mean. He was the kind of guy who'd sue his own brother-in-law. In fact, he did just that. Three times.[1]

Never mind that his brother-in-law, Robert Sakowitz, had already been forced to take the family's Sakowitz department stores into bankruptcy in 1985 and that the business that his grandparents had founded nearly a century earlier had left him nearly broke. Wyatt and his socialite wife, Lynn, wanted to humiliate Robert Sakowitz, so they sued him over his management of the family's business affairs and got an out-of-court settlement. Wyatt was so much like the caricature of the brash, larger-than-life Texas oilman that when a *Houston Chronicle* story quoted a citizen who likened Wyatt to J. R. Ewing, the duplicitous villain of the television series *Dallas,* Wyatt sued the paper—and got a settlement for that, too.[2]

Not that Wyatt needed the money. By the time he sued his brother-in-law, he was, as they say in Texas, Big Rich. But fighting was in Wyatt's blood. As the founder of Coastal Corporation, he'd grown rich by targeting undervalued oil and gas assets, buying them on the cheap, and selling them for immense profits. He was a devout profiteer and hated losing money, ever. If that meant cutting off gas to businesses and schools in some of the state's biggest cities, as he did during the

1970s—even though he was obligated to deliver the gas—then Wyatt would cut them off and deal with the consequences. As he explained to one reporter in 1985, "As a corporate manager you have to have one objective—to be profitable or popular. I've chosen to be profitable."

By the early 1980s, Wyatt was hungry for acquisitions and HNG was a natural target. Coastal had oil wells, pipelines, and refineries, and HNG's distribution assets were an almost ideal fit with Wyatt's plans to grow his company. At the time, Coastal, with $5.8 billion in annual revenue, was nearly twice as big as HNG. Even better, HNG had little debt, so Wyatt could use HNG's strong credit rating to borrow the money he'd need to do the takeover. So in January of 1984, Coastal launched a $1.3 billion takeover bid for HNG. Although Wyatt had made a hostile takeover bid for another company called Texas Gas Resources just a few months earlier, HNG's leadership was caught completely off-guard. "It was a total surprise," said one longtime HNG executive. "It showed up as an ad in the *Wall Street Journal* one day. Wyatt said, 'I'm offering to buy 51 percent of the stock of HNG.'" The offer sent tremors through HNG's headquarters, and the company's leaders were completely unprepared for a proxy fight. "At that time, Wyatt was generally considered a thug," said the former executive. "And nobody in the company wanted to be in business with him. So we were going to do all we could not to fall into the hands of Oscar Wyatt."

To avoid Wyatt, who already held 5 percent of HNG's stock, HNG made a counteroffer to Coastal shareholders, saying it would buy Coastal for $50 a share, in a deal valued at $1.1 billion. HNG's board also approved an unusual defense, saying it would offer its own shareholders $69 per share for their stock (Wyatt had offered $68 a share) in an effort to acquire 8 million shares of the company. A stock buyback would have allowed HNG to fend off Coastal's offer because it would have prevented Wyatt from gaining a majority of the outstanding shares in the company. The HNG board members also started looking for legal maneuvers that would help them escape from Wyatt. They found one in a 1979 settlement between the state and Coastal that was designed to prohibited Wyatt's company from exerting too much power in the Texas natural gas market. HNG convinced then Texas attorney general Jim Mattox to file a lawsuit against Coastal, and Wyatt's bid to take over HNG was stopped.

But the Coastal takeover attempt was still costly. HNG had to pay Wyatt $42 million in "greenmail" to go away. And HNG was still vulnerable. Other corporate raiders such as Irwin Jacobs were lurking. Wyatt's bid had also convinced the company's board that HNG's CEO, M. D. Matthews, was not a strong enough leader. "There wasn't anything evil about him, but he was a weak CEO," said an executive who was at HNG at the time. "He's not the kind of guy you need when you are fighting a hostile takeover." The members of the board knew they needed someone more dynamic than Matthews, and after a short discussion, they agreed to quietly approach an executive at another pipeline company—Ken Lay.

HNG's board members met Lay while they were searching for a "white knight" who could save them from Wyatt. At the time, Lay was working for Transco Energy, a pipeline company based in Houston that delivered gas to several states in the Northeast. Transco was big enough to merge with HNG, and their pipelines would have been complementary. During their discussions with Transco, the HNG board members met with both Jack Bowen, the company's CEO, and Lay, who was serving as president and chief operating officer. Bowen recalled that Transco was nearly ready to do a merger with HNG when Mattox intervened and sued Coastal. "So HNG didn't need us anymore," said Bowen. "But the board of HNG had become impressed with Ken Lay." Within a few weeks, Lay was named chairman and CEO of HNG.

Finally, Ken Lay had the job he'd been wanting for decades. At HNG, instead of answering to others, he'd be in charge. For a child from miniscule Tyrone, Missouri, the ascent to the executive suite was both improbable and, somehow, almost inevitable.

Kenneth Lee Lay was born on April 15, 1942, to a hard-luck farmer and erstwhile Baptist preacher, Omer Lay, and his wife, Ruth. Omer

Lay was uneducated but hardworking, a man who had held a number of jobs ranging from selling farm implements to working in a department store. Lay's older sister, Bonnie, recalled that Omer always had "two or three jobs to support the family." And charity was always a priority. The family often opened its doors to transients who rode freight trains through town.

From an early age, Ken, who was one of three children, dreamed of being in business. "I spent a lot of time on a tractor and had a lot of time to think," he told one interviewer. "I must confess, I was enamored with business and industry. It was so different from the world in which I was living."

In 1958, when Ken was still in high school, the family moved to Columbia, so he and his younger sister, Sharon, could attend the University of Missouri. That was where Ken Lay met the man who would become his mentor and provide the springboard into public service, economist Pinkney Walker. Lay began taking nearly every economics class that Walker taught. As Walker remembered, Lay was a "straight-A student." He was also a member of the Beta Theta Pi fraternity, a group renowned for its scholars and jocks, and became president as a junior, an unusual accomplishment in the Greek system, where seniority is highly prized. In 1964, Lay graduated from the university as a Phi Beta Kappa in economics. When Lay was preparing to leave school for the workaday world, Walker was able to convince him to continue his studies. Walker found Lay a part-time university job that paid enough to live on while he finished his master's degree. In 1965, with his master's in hand, Lay went to work as an economist for Humble Oil in Houston. Then in 1968, at the height of the Vietnam War, in order to meet his deferred service requirement, Lay entered the U.S. Navy Officer Candidate School. He expected to work at a supply post, but Walker again intervened and got Lay assigned to the Pentagon, where his task was to come up with a better military purchasing system. Although the war was raging and the Pentagon had plenty of other matters to deal with, Lay was able to convince his superior officers that he should be working on his doctorate in economics.

Lay finished his dissertation, "The Measurement of the Timing of the Economic Impact of Defense Procurement Activity: An Analysis of the Vietnam Buildup," in August 1970, while still a commissioned officer in the navy. In the introduction, he thanked his parents "for giving me the desire to complete the doctorate and to my loving and understanding wife, Judie, and son, Mark, for allowing me to satisfy this desire. Without their sacrifices and words of encouragement, this dissertation and the Ph.D. would have been neither possible nor worthwhile."

The dissertation analyzes how the Pentagon's spending on materiel for the war negatively affected the overall American economy. Lay quoted Senator William Proxmire, who said in April 1967 that America was "unprepared for this escalation in military cost and as a result we had these high interest rates, unacceptable inflation, serious problems that we could have avoided with wiser policies, if we had had the information and acted on it."

In his 178-page paper, Lay devised some statistical models that planners and legislators could use to gauge more accurately how war spending would affect the rest of the economy. The models, wrote Lay, "should lead to better forecasts of both the total national output and the composition of this output. Second, the model will permit a more precise measurement of the timing and magnitude of the economic impact of defense procurement activity." Lay's work was lauded and was reportedly adopted by the White House's Council of Economic Advisers.

In 1971, when Lay's naval commission expired, he and Walker crossed paths again. President Richard Nixon had recently appointed Walker to a spot on the Federal Power Commission and Walker convinced Lay to join him as his chief aide. "Ken Lay fit right in," recalled Walker. "He'd go out to lunch with the right people, making the right connections. He always carried his part of the load or more. He always had a smile. He was a delightful person to depend on." Lay helped organize the commission's agenda, writing speeches and letters, planning strategy and making political connections.

After his stint with Walker, Lay went to work at the Interior Department as a deputy undersecretary for energy. He stayed at Interior for about two years. During a hearing regarding offshore lease rights for oil drilling off the coast of Florida, Lay met Jack Bowen, the CEO of Florida Gas. In late 1973, Lay wrote Bowen and asked him for a job. The two later met privately in Washington to discuss Lay's position. Bowen invited Lay to visit Winter Park, where Florida Gas had its headquarters. "He brought his wife, Judie, down and they liked it, and he came down. He went to work right after the first of the year in 1974," says Bowen.

One of Lay's jobs at Florida Gas was managing governmental affairs in Washington, a job he was naturally suited for, given his six years of work there. Lay rose through the ranks at Florida Gas, in Bowen's opinion, because "he was intelligent. He had a good way with people. Everybody liked him. He made a good impression. I could send him off to do something and I didn't have to worry about him making mistakes. He had good judgment." A few years later, Bowen left Florida Gas to take a job at Transco Energy, a much bigger pipeline company based in Houston. Lay stayed behind and rose to president at Florida Gas.

Although Lay's professional life was going very well, his personal life was becoming chaotic. Sometime in the late 1970s, he began having an affair with his then secretary, an assertive (some people close to Lay call her pushy) woman named Linda Phillips. According to executives who knew Lay at the time, his desire to make a clean break with Judie and start a new life with Linda was a major factor behind his next career move. And as he had done before when he was considering a career switch, Lay called Jack Bowen.

Bowen recalled that in late 1980 or early 1981, Lay called him and said he was "having some domestic problems. He and his wife were getting separated." So Bowen hired him again, naming Lay the president and chief operating officer at Transco.[3] Lay would stay at Transco for three years.

But before Lay moved to Houston, he arranged for Linda to get a job in Florida Gas's Houston office, so she could discreetly move out there with him. "The divorce was finalized the day Lay left Florida for

Houston," said an executive who worked closely with Lay. "I remember him getting on the plane for Houston. He went straight there and bought an engagement ring for Linda." They married shortly thereafter.

Many executives have affairs, and many get divorced. But Lay's in-office romance may have been the worst-kept secret in Houston. As one source close to Lay commented, "There wasn't anyone in Houston who wasn't aware that Ken and Judie Lay were divorced while Linda had been his secretary in Florida." The source went on to say that in recent years, Lay's efforts to keep both Linda and Judie happy has bordered on the bizarre. Although he dumped Judie for Linda, he continued to invite—and pay for—his ex-wife and their two children, Mark and Elizabeth, to come on family vacations. Call it a Mormon-style holiday for a Missouri Baptist. According to the source, Ken and Linda would stay with her three children, Robin, David, and Beau in one location. In a nearby house or hotel, he'd install Judie and the other two kids. It was a chance for Ken Lay to show the world that his was just one big happy family.

Whatever the cost, Ken Lay made sure the family vacations were peaceful and that both wives had whatever they needed. Lay's efforts to keep his burgeoning family happy and give them lots of money was to become the template for his management style at Enron. Just as Lay could not—or would not—make a clean break with Judie, he became incapable of firing executives at Enron for bad decisions or poor performance. He avoided confrontations and sought to smooth over any personnel clashes in upper management. "Ken never was able or willing to deal with problem people," said one high-ranking executive who worked with Lay for more than a decade. "He was never willing to give anybody constructive criticism or feedback. He could give praise and stroke them but he couldn't kick their ass or fire them. He blindly trusted people."

Lay's weak management skills might not have been deadly to Enron. But his weakness was exacerbated by his dalliance with Linda. Indeed, his marriage to Linda would help define Enron's culture.

4

The Merger

Ken Lay had only been on the job at Houston Natural Gas for a few months when he got a call from Sam Segnar, the chairman and CEO at the Omaha-based pipeline company InterNorth. Segnar was in a hurry. Irwin Jacobs, a Minneapolis-based corporate raider, had amassed a 5-percent stake in InterNorth. He was looking to make a quick profit, just as Oscar Wyatt had done with Houston Natural Gas a few months earlier. Segnar did not want his company to be taken over by Jacobs. Would Lay be interested in merging the two companies?

It was an intriguing possibility. InterNorth owned one of the best pipelines in America. It connected gas fields in Texas and Oklahoma with cities in the Midwest and extended north to gas fields in Canada. In the months after coming to HNG, Lay had overseen the purchase of two big pipeline systems, the Transwestern pipeline and the Florida Gas pipeline, moves that allowed HNG's pipes to extend from coast to coast. With InterNorth's pipes, the combined company would have 37,000 miles of pipe that would stretch from coast to coast and border to border. Also, InterNorth was a huge company. With $7.5 billion in revenues in 1984, it was more than three times the size of HNG. It had 10,000 employees, more than three times more than HNG, and it had a panoply of other valuable assets, including coal mines, a natural gas exploration business, a petrochemicals business, and other components that could be sold off to pay off any debt incurred to make the transaction.

After several weeks of negotiations, the two sides agreed to terms. And in early May 1985, the companies announced that InterNorth would buy HNG for $2.4 billion. It was a ridiculously good deal for HNG. InterNorth agreed to pay $70 per share in cash for HNG, a big premium over the $47 or so that HNG's stock was selling for at that time. InterNorth's stock cratered when the deal was announced, falling about 10 percent. "It was a classic case of the city slickers taking the country bumpkins," said one former Enron official.

The squabbling between the two newly merged companies started almost immediately. For instance, the company's controller was in Omaha, but the treasurer was in Houston. The leadership plan hatched during the merger was unworkable. The plan called for Segnar to stay on as CEO until 1987, when he would be succeeded by Lay. But, as one HNG executive remarked, "Segnar was weak. Internorth had good line managers and lousy executives." Further, the company had something of an identity crisis. In the months after the merger, it was called HNG/InterNorth. But in early 1986, with the help of a fancy New York consulting firm, Lay proposed changing the name to "Enteron." No one bothered to look in the dictionary. When they did, they saw that the word literally meant "alimentary canal," or "digestive tract." Oops.

The company finally settled on Enron. They also worked out a succession plan. Segnar was going to leave early. Lay would ascend to the CEO job. Somehow, Ken Lay had managed to sell his company and still be in charge. Beyond that, his handpicked executives were going to come out on top. As one HNG executive explained it, "The HNG side ended up with a deal in which they sold the company but still had it. We ended up with control."

A few of the executives from InterNorth were in Lay's inner circle, but for the most part, Lay's team, which included such people as Mike Muckleroy, John Wing, Mick Seidl, and Rich Kinder, had been with him at either HNG or Florida Gas. And Lay had won the battle over location: Enron was going to be based in Houston, damn it, not

Omaha. End of story. Those InterNorth folks could whine all they wanted, but Lay had finally gained control of the board and no self-respecting energy company would be located in Omaha. Houston was the place to be in the energy business. Lay had firm control of Enron, and he could see that Enron's businesses were looking pretty good. The exploration and production business was doing better than it ever had. The pipeline business, while growing slowly, was growing and profitable, and Enron was transporting about 15 percent of all the gas burned in the entire country. The company's forays into independent power generation were gearing up, which meant Enron could potentially make money in electricity and find new markets for its surplus natural gas.

There were still problems, of course. Enron's debt level was way too high. The InterNorth team had agreed to take on debt in order to facilitate the merger with HNG. Lay was slowly working the debt down, but with a total debt of $4.3 billion, the company was in constant danger of default, particularly if interest rates went up again. Furthermore, Lay and Segnar had made a critical error when they did the merger: They didn't entice Jacobs to sell his stock. So just seventeen months after the two companies combined forces, Lay was forced to pay through the nose to make Jacobs go away. The total greenmail payout was $357 million—all of it in cash that Lay sorely needed to pay down Enron's debt.

Nevertheless, things looked pretty good. "I'm having a lot of fun with this," Lay told one reporter at the time. Ken and Linda Lay were having so much fun they decided to move uptown.

5

The Lays Move to River Oaks

If you are Big Rich or Big Important and you live in Houston, you live in River Oaks.

It's one of the rules. It's been that way for decades, and everyone in Houston accepts it in the same way they accept smog, traffic jams, and the sun coming up in the East. And by January 1986, Ken Lay fit the description of Big Important. The uproar over the merger was continuing, but Lay was CEO of the new company, and because the integration of the two companies was going so poorly, the board agreed to make Lay the chairman of the board, too.

So he and Linda needed a house that would reflect his upwardly mobile status. After a bit of looking, they decided that the house for them was 3195 Inwood, a plush home in the heart of River Oaks that had belonged to Robert Herring, the late CEO of HNG. Herring, who headed HNG from 1967 to 1981, and his glamorous former TV-talking-head wife, Joanne, had made international relationships their business. In an effort to gain access to Arab oil and gas reserves, the Herrings had entertained dozens of foreign dignitaries at 3195 Inwood. Their parties included such guests as King Hussein of Jordan, Prince Saud of Saudi Arabia, Saudi oil minister Sheik Ahmed Zaki Yamani, and for good measure, the Herrings would invite the kings of Sweden and Morocco and perhaps a Pakistani diplomat or two.[1]

Ken and Linda Lay were not only going to assume the Herrings' social and business position in Houston, they were going to be sleeping in their bedroom.

Ken Lay was only following tradition. Houston's energy barons have always lived in River Oaks. Ever since the 1920s, when a group of wealthy Houstonians decided they needed a "country place" away from the city, River Oaks and the exclusive River Oaks Country Club around which the subdivision is built have been the redoubt of the richest, most politically connected families in Houston. "It is," said longtime Houston journalist Ray Miller, "our Beverly Hills."[2]

More than just chic, quiet, clean, and safe, River Oaks is blessed with good geography. Whereas lesser executives commute an hour or more each way from suburbs like Kingwood, Katy, and The Woodlands, the Big Shots who live in River Oaks can be through a half dozen stoplights and downtown in less than ten minutes via Allen Parkway—proof of the luxury of location in Houston.

A River Oaks address complete with what one reporter called its "Ralph-Lauren-meets-Scarlett-O'Hara architecture" comes with certain perks and rules. Although it's part of the city of Houston, the two-square-mile area has its own security patrol and its own public areas.[3] The rules include a prohibition on "For Sale" signs. Too gauche. Anyone buying real estate in the area must find it through a realtor or advertisement. The prohibition on signs extends back to 1926, when the area's original developers put deed restrictions on every house in River Oaks. The rules included no hospitals, no duplexes, no apartments, no livestock, and of course, only Caucasian owners.[4] That last rule has, presumably, been rescinded. But the only black or brown faces one is likely to see today in River Oaks belong to the men trimming the grass and tending the well-watered gardens or to the women working as maids or nannies.

At one time, more than one-fifth of the 1,600 homes in River Oaks were occupied by energy industry folks who were not ashamed of making a big show. Billionaire oil tycoon (and bigamist) H. L. Hunt kept one of his three families in a River Oaks home.[5] An oil heiress named Loraine McMurrey became famous for her parties, at which bagpipers invariably greeted her guests, then accompanied them to the foyer, where they were shown tables groaning with mounds of caviar three feet high. A wildcatter named Jim West allegedly kept sacks of silver dollars in the basement of his River Oaks house. When he left, he'd fill the pockets of his jackets with coins that he'd toss to ordinary citizens he'd see on the street.[6] Former Texas governor (treasury secretary under Nixon and one-time presidential candidate) John Connally had lived there.

Lay's former foe, Oscar Wyatt, the head of Coastal, whose bid for Houston Natural Gas had resulted in HNG hiring Ken Lay as its CEO, lived in River Oaks, too. Lay's new home would be just down the street from Wyatt's house. In fact, Wyatt was living in *the* home for the reigning king of Houston's Energy Alley. Wyatt owned the old Cullen Mansion, the house at 1620 River Oaks Boulevard that had been occupied for many years by conservative wildcatter Hugh Roy Cullen, who went on to become one of Houston's most revered philanthropists. The house was built in 1929 and was the most prestigious address in River Oaks.

With his new home in River Oaks, Ken Lay was going to *belong*. He and Linda were the heirs to the type of social and political world that Robert and Joanne Herring had known. As the head of Enron, Ken and Linda would be the talk of Houston. They would be attending the right parties, hobnobbing with diplomats, politicians, and their new Big Rich neighbors. River Oaks was going to be their launching pad.

And with the Lays in River Oaks, other Enron employees would surely follow. Like the Lays, those Enroners would be eager for the money, status, and class that came with a berth in Houston's most prestigious neighborhood. But an obstacle was looming for Ken Lay that would threaten everything he had worked for, an obstacle called Valhalla.

6

The Valhalla Fiasco

Ken Lay was traveling in Europe in early October 1987 when he got an urgent call from Enron's president, John M. (Mick) Seidl. The news was bad. Real bad. And it shouldn't be discussed over the phone. The two arranged to meet hours later in Gander, Newfoundland, the midway refueling point for small jets flying from Houston to Europe. When the two finally met, Seidl's message was simple: "We're broke."

There'd been one part of the InterNorth deal that Ken Lay hadn't paid close attention to. InterNorth maintained a small oil-trading business in Valhalla, New York. The purpose of the business—called Enron Oil—was to speculate in crude oil and refined products. But by ignoring the business, Lay was about to pay a heavy price. A group of unsupervised traders had exceeded their trading limits and were now upside down on contracts that required them to deliver tens of millions of barrels of crude oil—oil that Enron didn't have, couldn't afford, and couldn't deliver.

The Valhalla office had about forty people and was headed by a trader named Louis Borget. Executives in Houston tried to keep tabs on the Valhalla office, but it was far away, and since Borget and his traders claimed that they were making money, Lay and his team left them alone.

The lack of oversight had allowed Borget to get a taste of the good life, and pretty soon he wanted more. Sometime in 1985, Borget, along with Enron Oil's treasurer, Thomas Mastroeni, and several others began manipulating the company's books.[1] The crew set up a series of sham corporations in Panama, which they used to create phony transactions. The phony companies helped Borget show Enron that he was making money and led to substantial bonuses. In 1985, Borget, Mastroeni, and several others split bonuses totaling $3.1 million. In 1986, they shared bonuses of $9.4 million.[2]

To hide their chicanery, Borget and Mastroeni kept two sets of books. According to Mike Muckleroy, who headed Enron's liquid fuels (propane, butane, and so on) business at that time, and an auditor who worked on the Valhalla mess, one set of books—the crooked ones—was fabricated to mislead the auditors from Arthur Andersen and Enron. The other set of books—the real ones—were known only to Borget, Mastroeni, and a few others.

Borget's scam started to unravel in January 1987, when a bank in New York called David Woytek, an Enron internal auditor in Houston, and asked about several large payments from Enron Oil's accounts—totaling $2.1 million—that were being deposited into Mastroeni's personal account. Woytek became suspicious and began looking into the matter. A few weeks later, Borget and Mastroeni met with Lay and a few other Enron officials to talk about the suspicious deals. The two traders assured Lay that nothing illicit was being done. Instead, they claimed they were trying to shift some of their profits. They claimed that they had met their targets for 1986 and were just trying to shift some of that money to another month in case they had a shortfall. Accountants call that type of maneuver "cookie-jar earnings," and it's not only unethical, it's illegal. In addition, Woytek and the other auditors had found that Borget and Mastroeni had falsified bank statements in an effort to hide several unauthorized payments. But Lay and Seidl had ignored those misdeeds and allowed Borget and Mastroeni to go back to work. They dispatched a team of Enron auditors to Valhalla to do some further investigation, but the auditors were stymied by the false set of books that Borget and Mastroeni showed them.

In spring 1987, Muckleroy began getting calls from his acquaintances in the energy business who told him that something was fishy at Enron Oil. His friends said that Enron Oil was short several million barrels of oil. Muckleroy said that, at first, he dismissed the comments as idle gossip. Over the next few months, he began taking them more seriously. But when he tried to get Ken Lay to take action on the traders at Enron Oil, he couldn't convince him that Borget and his traders were out of line.

On April 22, 1987, a team of accountants from Arthur Andersen gave a report to Seidl and the Audit Committee of Enron's Board of Directors. (This august group was chaired by Robert Jaedicke, the Stanford University business whiz who remained chair of Enron's Audit Committee through the end of 2001.) The report said that Borget and Mastroeni had "demonstrated the ability" to do deals "explicitly for the purpose of transferring company funds and deferring company profits." The Andersen auditors said at the time that although they didn't find any "additional unrecorded commitments, we cannot give you assurance that none exist."

Although the tone of Andersen's report was noncommittal, Muckleroy, Woytek, and others inside Enron were convinced that Lay should fire Borget and his entire team immediately, if not sooner. "We knew they couldn't be trusted," said one source who worked closely on the matter. "These guys had falsified bank statements. Any normal officer of a company, when they hear something like that, would fire the guilty parties."

On April 29, 1987, a week after Andersen delivered the report to Seidl and Jaedicke, the Audit Committee met to discuss several matters, including the mess in Valhalla. The minutes of the meeting say that "after a full discussion" of the problems with Borget, "management recommended that the person involved be kept on the payroll." But an executive who was at the meeting recalled that the decision wasn't made by "management"; it was made by Ken Lay. According to the source, Lay said, "I have decided not to terminate these people. I need their earnings."

Lay's decision was undoubtedly motivated by his need for cash. The greenmail payments to Jacobs had been a big hit to cash flow, and the company's long-term debt was still enormous. The problem, Lay thought, could be handled with a few management changes. His solution was to implement new controls on Borget and Mastroeni that, in theory, would prevent them from getting out of hand. Those controls included moving cash control for the Valhalla operation to Houston and removing some of Mastroeni's duties. Everything else would continue pretty much as before.

But it appears that Borget wasn't ready to return to things as they were before. Instead, he may have been under even greater pressure to produce profits for Enron, since the profits from earlier years had been inflated. By mid-1987, he was on the wrong side of the crude oil market, and every time he tried to remedy his predicament, it got worse. In trader parlance, he kept "doubling down," that is, increasing his position, hoping that he could work his way out of the hole. But an unusually volatile market kept working against him. The Iranians and the Iraqis were still shooting at each other. Their long-running war was creating havoc in the oil markets; traders were constantly worried that an oil tanker might be sabotaged and sink in the Strait of Hormuz, cutting off tanker traffic to the Persian Gulf. "Every time he went long, the price went down and every time he went short, the price went up," one Enron official recalled.

By the time Seidl met Lay in Gander, word was leaking out that things were seriously wrong at Enron Oil. Neither Lay nor Seidl knew the extent of the damage because no one in Houston had been able to examine the trading books at the Valhalla office. The best guesses put the damage at about 50 million barrels of oil—meaning that Enron had a liability of $850 million that it would have to meet in less than sixty days. The probability of that was so low it was almost laughable. Enron's credit rating was already wobbly, and once the banks got word of the company's position, they would eliminate Enron's lines of credit altogether. Any efforts to cover the crude oil shortfall would have to be made quickly, and very quietly.

Lay didn't have many choices. He dispatched Mike Muckleroy, who had lots of experience in the trading business, along with an Enron lawyer and an accountant, to Valhalla. Working day and night, they found about six dozen sham contracts. Within a few days, they realized that Borget and Mastroeni had dug a hole so deep that Enron was unlikely to survive. Borget and his traders had promised to deliver millions of barrels of jet fuel in Rotterdam, diesel fuel in Asia, and crude oil in the United States. "We were hung out in every hydrocarbon that had a market except natural gas," recalled Muckleroy.

Enron couldn't deliver on any of it.

In all, Enron was short 87 million barrels of hydrocarbons. That was roughly equivalent to the entire output of the United Kingdom's North Sea oil fields for three months, or, put another way, it was enough fuel to fill about forty supertankers. And the cost was staggering: nearly $1.5 billion.

By fall 1987, Enron's total debt load was about $3.5 billion. But the company's market capitalization (the value of all of its stock) was some $4.7 billion. Adding Borget's trading losses of $1.5 billion to the $3.5 billion in debt meant that Enron Corp. had a negative net worth of $300 million. Or, as Muckleroy put it, "We were screwed."

Worse yet, word was starting to leak out about Enron's short position. If other trading companies knew for certain that Enron was short, they could bid up the price of crude and other refined products, making it more expensive for Enron to buy the product it needed to cover its position. If the price of oil went up dramatically, Enron could have been forced into a "margin call." If that had happened, Enron's trading parties would have asked the company to put up tens or hundreds of millions of dollars in cash—cash that the company didn't have and couldn't borrow—in order to collateralize its outstanding contracts.

Enron was caught in a classic squeeze play. But Muckleroy was able to bluff the market long enough to allow the company to climb out of the hole. In the first few days of the crisis, he bought about 8 million barrels of oil on the spot market. He then began calling the biggest crude oil trading houses, offering to sell each of them 1 million barrels each. Luckily, none of the buyers wanted the oil. And the tactic achieved Muckleroy's goal, which was to give the major oil companies and trading houses the impression that Enron had been able to cover its short position. Over the next two weeks, Muckleroy gradually unwound all of Borget's positions. "Muckleroy and his team saved the company," said Woytek.

Although the public was never told just how bad the Enron Oil situation was, the company was forced to disclose the fiasco. And in October 1987, Enron announced it would take an $85-million charge against earnings in the third quarter. Lay told the *New York Times* the incident was an "expensive embarrassment."[3] He told another paper that it "confirms that oil trading is a very volatile, very risky business. I would not want anyone to think at any time in the future this kind of activity would affect our other businesses. It is the only kind of business we have that is purely speculative."

Within weeks after the announcement of the trading disaster, Lay began damage control. He called an all-company meeting where the Valhalla matter was discussed. At that meeting, Lay told the crowd that he had known nothing about Borget's trading problems and that the incident had blindsided the whole company. According to Muckleroy, Lay said, "If anyone here believes I knew about this, then they should stand up now."

In other words, Ken Lay was covering his ass *and* he was lying about it. Lay had known about the problems in Valhalla. Woytek had warned him. Muckleroy had warned him. Arthur Andersen had warned him. And yet he had heeded none of them because he wanted the profits that Borget had promised. As for Borget, he later pled guilty to several criminal charges, was sentenced to a year and a day in prison, and was ordered to pay about $6 million in restitution. Mastroeni was sentenced to two years' probation.

In the months after the Valhalla embarrassment, assets versus trading became the hot topic of discussion within the company's leadership. Rich Kinder, Enron's chief of staff and a rising star in the company, along with several other executives, became convinced that the trading fiasco was a warning and that Enron had to remain tightly focused on assets and the revenues that the company generated. The problem was that Lay "never understood that the pipelines that are paid for and power and processing plants that are mostly paid for, were the way to make money," Muckleroy stated. "Lay forgot what happened at Valhalla." Another executive from that time period said that Kinder and several others became "adamant that no more than 30 percent of our profits could come from trading. The rest had to come from assets."

Given the magnitude of the near-disaster with Borget, that conservative approach appeared to make the most sense. However, the lead executives couldn't convince one key decisionmaker that their position was the right one. "Ken [Lay] didn't have an opinion either way," he said.

Wow. Lay's lack of opinion on trading as a business in the wake of the Valhalla fiasco is astounding.

He'd nearly lost Enron to a group of traders who were more interested in lining their own pockets than in making money for shareholders; they'd done it right under his nose by convincing Enron people in Houston that they were making money, when they were actually losing money. Lay had been warned months before the disaster not to trust the traders, and he'd been warned to question their financial reporting. The traders had hidden their losses by keeping two sets of books; and finally, after the scam was discovered, Ken Lay stood up to proclaim his innocence and insist that he didn't have any idea that such devious rapscallions could be in his midst.

It was a scenario that would be replayed in almost identical fashion—but with far more devastating consequences—fourteen years later. But first, Lay would have to become enamored with a brilliant trader whose ruthlessness and deceptiveness would make Louis Borget look like a rank amateur.

7

"The Smartest Son of a Bitch I've Ever Met"

J. R. Ewing never talked about pipelines. Jett Rink was interested in drilling for oil, not shipping it through a maze of unseen steel tubes. *Real* men—particularly fictional ones like Ewing and Rink—find oil and gas. Lesser mortals navigate the maze of engineering, metallurgical, and legal wrangles that are needed to get those hydrocarbons delivered to the nearest refinery or storage terminal.

Face it, there's no sex in laying pipe.

For decades, the energy business has been populated by dozens of colorful characters, both real and fictional, who have been immortalized in magazines, books, TV shows, and movies. But virtually all of those characters were *oil*men. They were wildcatters, Texans like H. L. Hunt, W. A. Moncrief, and Sid Richardson, who bet their fortunes on hunches and guesses only to come out either broke or fabulously wealthy. None of the legendary oilmen were transport guys. Getting the oil to the market was a technicality handled by clerks and pencil pushers. Pipelines—and the people that run them—have been relegated to second-tier status in the pantheon of energy gods.

Although they don't get the headlines (or the girls), pipeline builders have played a critical role in the defense and development of the United States. During World War II, the federal government worried about

German submarines and the risk they posed to oil tankers traveling along the coast. So they ordered the construction of the Big Inch and Little Big Inch pipelines from Texas to the East Coast. The Big Inch (twenty-four inches in diameter) transported crude oil. The Little Big Inch (twenty inches) carried refined products. The two lines were constructed in record time and played a pivotal role in the Allied war effort, which depended on oil to fuel its ships, planes, trucks, and tanks. Oil was perhaps the most critical commodity during World War II. The Allies had reliable supplies from Texas, Oklahoma, and elsewhere. The German and Japanese supply routes were longer and therefore more vulnerable to attack. As German general Edwin Rommel wrote after his Afrika Corps was defeated at El Alamein, "Shortage of petrol! It's enough to make one weep."[1] American forces were seldom short of petrol, and that was due in part to the Inch pipelines, which together carried over 350 million barrels of crude oil and refined products to the East before the war ended. The pipes were later sold to Texas Eastern. Today, they are owned by Duke Energy, and instead of carrying oil, they carry natural gas.

Pipelines are the conduit for the American Dream. Every year, pipelines carry some 550 billion gallons of crude and petroleum products to refineries, airports, rail yards, and other locations. Trillions of cubic feet of natural gas are moved through some 2 million miles of interstate, intrastate, and local pipelines.[2] Pipelines are the largely invisible, sometimes dangerous, infrastructure that allows America to consume more energy than any country on earth. Pipelines, like airports, highways, and railroads, have become an essential part of our transportation infrastructure.

By the early 1990s when Jeff Skilling, a former McKinsey consultant, began his rise to power within Enron, the company and its leaders were, says one veteran gas man, "the kings of the American pipeline business." Enron owned the greatest collection of tubular steel infrastructure ever assembled in one company. The company was transporting or selling 17.5 percent of all the gas consumed in the United States.[3]

Those pipelines were profitable, but they were, and still are, heavily regulated by federal authorities.[4] With all of the federal regulations on pricing, the pipeline business is more akin to the utility business than the energy business. Pipelines carry a product from one spot to another, and the owner of the pipe gets paid a fee for the service. It's a straightforward, profitable business. As one former Houston Natural Gas executive said of pipelines, "All they do is make money. It's boring, but it's dependable."

Perhaps that's why Jeff Skilling hated them so much. During his entire tenure at Enron, Skilling never gave any speeches about the wonders of pipelines. Nor did he deign to spend much time with the Enron executives, like Stan Horton, who ran the company's pipelines. Jeff Skilling's brain was too big for pipelines. He was always thinking big thoughts. And big thoughts have no place in the pipeline business. Pipeline companies demand solid managerial skills from people who show up every day and stick to their business. Skilling was not a manager, he was a deal maker. Exotic financing schemes and the deals that came with them excited Skilling. Collecting nickels, dimes, and quarters from what was essentially a new-fangled toll road that no one could even see did not. The only thing that mattered to Skilling about Enron's pipelines was that they kept providing him with cash that he could use elsewhere.

For Skilling, elsewhere meant only one place: the trading business. Skilling may have disliked pipelines, but he was an absolute genius at figuring out how to trade the precious commodity that moved inside them. And he was able to apply his enormous intellect during a time of great tumult in the American natural gas business. That tumult was accompanied by a sharp increase in America's thirst for gas. Both of those factors would help make Jeff Skilling an enormous success.

By 1991, Enron's meetings with Wall Street analysts had become fairly routine: meet with analysts and investors, present Enron's message, discuss a few ongoing projects, then go play golf or tennis or hike in the mountains. Enron had been holding the meetings for years, usually in different locations in Arizona or Colorado. The setting made it all a bit easier. Beaver Creek, which at that time, was still a fairly new resort in the Colorado Rockies, was the location. The conference was to be the forum for Jeff Skilling's first presentation to the analysts as an Enron employee—and he was understandably nervous.

Skilling had only been on the job at Enron for a year or so. He'd had some good success at McKinsey and in his early days at the pipeline company, but he still had to prove to the analysts that he knew his stuff. His job at the conference was to explain how Enron was going to go beyond the pipeline business. He was to lay out the concepts behind Enron's model for commoditizing the natural gas business. Once it was commoditized, Skilling believed that companies like Enron would become traders. Skilling was going to show the analysts why other companies were going to embrace Enron's ideas and how the newly deregulated natural gas market provided Enron with a great opportunity to grow its new business and get into new, sexier areas, areas that had nothing to do with pipelines.

Skilling rose to the occasion. In his distinct baritone voice, he told the analysts that Enron was going to provide hedging tools to major gas consumers that would allow them to manage volatile prices. He showed them how Enron would make money by providing those tools. But the analysts were unimpressed. Several of them who attended the meeting don't even recall Skilling's speech. A decade later, Skilling still had vivid memories of the event. "The crowd yawned. They didn't get it," recalled Skilling in spring 2001. "I was brilliant."[5]

Those three words contain the essence of Jeff Skilling's ego at its acme. They also explain why he was so toxic.

Many things can be said about Skilling, but during his entire stint at Enron, he never doubted that he was the smartest person in every room he ever entered. And there was plenty of reason for him to believe that was so. One former Enroner recalled, "You could give him a 200-page Power Point presentation, give him ten minutes, and he could ask the three critical questions about the project. The uptake speed was phenomenal." Another Enron executive who worked closely with Skilling for five years called him "the smartest son of a bitch I've ever met."

Jeffrey Keith Skilling was born November 25, 1953, in Pittsburgh to Betty and Thomas E. Skilling. He was the second of four children in a middle-class household. His father was a mechanical engineer who sold valves to power plants and other industrial facilities. The family moved twice before Jeff got to high school, first to New Jersey, then to Aurora, Illinois, a town on the outskirts of Chicago. His father traveled quite a bit; his mother stayed home to care for the children. "I've read where my husband was a high-falutin' executive. I don't want to say he was just a salesman, but he was a salesman," says Betty Skilling. "He traveled a lot. We had to be very frugal."

Jeff Skilling's first job was at a small community access station, WXLT-TV, Channel 61, in Aurora. The station shared an old building with a movie theater. "It was small-time, amateurish all the way," recalled Betty Skilling. But it was fun. When Jeff's older brother, Thomas III, was asked to do the weather, he jumped at the chance and began working with Jeff at the station.[6]

In high school, Skilling was a nerd. Smallish, accident-prone, and not overly skilled physically, he shunned athletics but excelled at academics. He was named to the National Honor Society, worked on the school's yearbook, and participated on the school's academic quiz team. But though he made outstanding grades, his mother thought he never had to work very hard at his studies. "He wasn't a great studier," she says, "but he seemed to be able to waltz through." She recalled that Jeff was accepted at Princeton and even got offered a scholarship to the prestigious school. "He was so bright he could have gone to any school. But he wasn't interested in Princeton." Skilling ended up choosing Southern Methodist University after he and his father flew to Dallas. The students there "were clean and neatly dressed—not like at other colleges," said Betty Skilling, who added that the appearance of the students ended up being a big factor in her son's decision to go to SMU, where he accepted an engineering scholarship. At SMU, he joined the Beta Theta Pi fraternity—which was, coincidentally, the same fraternity that Ken Lay had joined at the University of Missouri about a decade earlier.

At SMU, Skilling studied business and earned a B.S. in applied science. He graduated in May 1975 and a few days later married Susan Long, a woman from the Chicago area he'd met at SMU. The newly married couple got an apartment in Dallas, where Skilling got a job at First City National Bank, in asset and liability management. But he was unhappy at the bank, according to his mother. So he applied to Harvard Business School. "He said, 'I'll never make it in but I'm going to try,'" Betty Skilling remembered. "And do you know what? He cried when he got accepted."

At Harvard, Skilling found his element. He was no longer the brightest guy in the class. Instead, he was immersed in a world of smart people. And despite the stiffest academic environment he'd ever faced, Skilling excelled at everything. In 1979, when he left Harvard with his MBA, Skilling was named a George F. Baker Scholar, a designation reserved for the top 5 percent of the students in his class, which contained about 800 students. Being named a Baker Scholar at Harvard opens doors. And the key door that opened for Skilling was the one to McKinsey & Company, the prestigious consulting firm.

Founded in 1925, the firm was started by James O. McKinsey, a University of Chicago accounting professor and prolific author of texts on management and accounting. His books led to a lucrative stream of consulting gigs. And for the next two decades, McKinsey hired industrial managers in their forties to work as consultants. That approach changed in the 1950s, when the firm began recruiting newly minted MBAs at America's best business schools. By the mid-1980s, McKinsey was so heavily entrenched on campus that it was offering summer jobs to 10 percent of the first-year students at Harvard Business School.[7]

During Skilling's time at McKinsey, the firm became known as much for its arrogance as for its enormously high—and nonnegotiable—fees. A 1987 profile of the firm in *Forbes* magazine declared that McKinsey consultants "unabashedly think of themselves as secular versions of the Jesuits, gifted intellectuals uplifting the world of commerce with their vision. Newcomers quickly learn that McKinsey is not engaged in a 'business' but a 'profession.' McKinsey does not work 'for' clients, it works 'with' them. McKinsey consultants do not go out on 'jobs,' they go out on 'engagements.'" One McKinsey leader even bragged to *Forbes*, "We don't learn from clients. Their standards aren't high enough. We learn from other McKinsey partners."

A stint at McKinsey was not only prestigious, it was a way to jump several notches up the corporate ladder. It provided a paying way for the sharpest young MBAs to get noticed by top managers at some of the biggest corporations in America. Dozens of McKinsey alumni are spread among the highest ranks of American corporations. IBM's former chairman Louis Gerstner Jr. was a McKinsey consultant, as was Andrall Pearson, who headed Tricon Global Restaurants, the owner of Pizza Hut, Taco Bell, and Kentucky Fried Chicken.

Skilling, who'd had a strong interest in energy issues at Harvard, jumped at a chance to join McKinsey's Houston office. There, he began working with John Sawhill, who had been deputy secretary of energy under President Jimmy Carter and had served as the administrator of the Federal Energy Administration.[8]

Throughout the 1980s, Sawhill and Skilling worked together, and one of their main clients was InterNorth. "He was very polished and respectful and good. He got noticed because he handled himself very professionally," said one former InterNorth executive. Skilling eventually became the point person on the InterNorth account and became chief of the energy and chemical consulting practice at McKinsey. After the merger with Houston Natural Gas, Skilling advised InterNorth and HNG on the best way to integrate the companies that became Enron. Throughout that time, he impressed everyone at Enron with his intellect and his tenacity. "He loved intellectual arguments," recalled one source who worked with Skilling. "He thrived on it because he won most of them."

More important, Skilling kept coming up with ideas that the leaders at Enron simply couldn't afford to ignore. And it was one such idea that launched his climb to the absolute pinnacle of corporate America. It was simple and elegant, and it arrived just in time for Enron to make a much-needed killing in the gas business. It was called the Gas Bank.

8

Banking on the Gas Bank

By the late 1980s, Enron—along with every other major pipeline company in America—was suffering from the effects of a decades-long regulatory hangover.

A combination of low gas prices and an almost-but-not-quite deregulation of the industry by the Federal Energy Regulatory Commission had forced the pipeline companies into near financial ruin. From the 1930s to the 1980s, pipelines had been heavily regulated by the federal government, which had taken the position that natural gas was a scarce commodity and should therefore be conserved. The regulations were so effective that during several cold winters in the 1970s, a number of cities across the country ran short of gas and had to cut off schools and businesses. The regulations hadn't slowed gas consumption. They had only succeeded in keeping gas prices artificially low, thereby stifling the desire of prospectors to go out and drill for new gas supplies.

Perhaps the easiest way to understand the myriad of federal gas regulations that used to govern pipelines is to imagine a McDonald's franchise that instead of buying gas, purchases federally regulated buns for resale. Under the old federal rules, the franchise was required to buy all of its buns from one seller at a price determined by the federal government, and the buns would then be shipped to the franchise on a federally regulated toll road (pipeline), whose prices were set by the feds.

The regulatory scheme was cumbersome and complex, and it had to be changed if America was to have an effective natural gas supply system. In 1984, under the deregulatory wave being pushed by Ronald Reagan, the Federal Energy Regulatory Commission, the agency that regulates America's pipelines, began repealing some of the restrictions on pipelines. That year, the FERC allowed local gas distribution companies to buy gas from anyone, anywhere. That was fine, but it stuck the gas pipelines with a multitude of "take-or-pay" gas contracts. During the 1970s, when gas shortages were common, many pipelines were locked into long-term gas supply deals that obligated them to buy (take) a certain amount of gas at a stated price that often had provisions that allowed producers to only increase—but not decrease—the prices they were charging. If the pipelines didn't take all the gas they had planned on, they had to pay for it anyway. And it didn't matter if the price they were paying was far higher than the prevailing price of gas. The 1984 ruling, known as FERC Order 380, hit the pipelines hard because they were stuck with dozens of these suddenly very expensive take-or-pay gas contracts. In 1985, the FERC, with Order 436, said that anybody who wanted to use interstate pipelines to transport gas could do so and that the pipeline companies had to provide this service at a federally approved price, and that even though they might be losing money, the pipeliners had to like it. It took two more years for the FERC to create Order 500, which presented a financial methodology through which the pipeline companies could negotiate partial recovery of the costs of their take-or-pay contracts.[1]

Although this upheaval would ultimately prove beneficial to the gas business as a whole, it caused tremendous pain for the pipeliners. Columbia Gas Transmission, a pipeline outfit that served several Eastern states, struggled throughout the late 1980s with overpriced gas it had purchased on take-or-pay deals. It went bankrupt in 1991. Other big pipe owners such as Transco Energy and United Gas Pipe Line spent years fighting with regulators and customers over gas pricing and take-or-pay issues. Enron was able to resolve its take-or-pay problems fairly quickly in the late 1980s, but it still didn't have a viable business plan that would allow it to break out of the pack.

Then, in 1989, Skilling, who was still working at McKinsey as an Enron consultant, realized that there was plenty of gas available—from producers who were being freed from federal price controls—and there was plenty of demand, from new utilities that wanted to burn gas to make electricity. But there was no intermediary that could aggregate—and more important, *balance*—the gas supplies coming from the producers with the demand coming from consumers. Why not create a mechanism that would allow them to hook up? Skilling called his idea the Gas Bank.

In Skilling's model, gas producers were "depositors" in the imaginary bank. Gas consumers were the "borrowers." The producers liked the idea because Enron could give them long-term contracts for their gas, and therefore, predictable cash flow, which allowed them to plan their exploration and drilling budgets over a longer term. Gas users liked it because they would be able to predict fuel costs over multiyear terms. Enron benefited because it could latch onto a ready supply of gas from its subsidiary, Enron Oil and Gas. Flatulent from its new abundance of methane, Enron could guarantee delivery to gas consumers over long periods of time—fifteen years or more.[2] Enron would make its profit on the contracts by pocketing the "spread" between the cost of the gas and the selling price.

Despite the brilliance of the idea, Skilling wasn't sure it would work. For weeks after he hatched the plan, he was racked with doubt, certain he had ruined his career. However, that doubt was accompanied by a parallel belief that he was smarter than anyone else. "I believed this whole world would be different, a huge breakthrough," he told *Texas Monthly*'s Mimi Swartz in 2001.[3]

Skilling needn't have worried. The Gas Bank was a smash.

Shortly after the company launched the concept, Enron Gas Marketing sold some $800 million worth of gas in one week's time.[4] The volume of gas Enron was selling soared. Within months of the launch of Gas Bank, the company was selling 1.1 billion cubic feet of gas per day. To put that amount in perspective, the average American home uses about 88,000 cubic feet of gas per year. By 1990, it was selling 1.5 billion cubic feet of gas per day.[5] Within two years, Enron had signed contracts with thirty-five producers and more than fifty gas customers.

The Gas Bank was "a turning point for Enron for several reasons," said one source who worked closely with Skilling. "First, it put Skilling on the map. He was still at McKinsey. then. It was his concept. It made a major mark." Skilling's strategy really impressed Ken Lay, as well as Rich Kinder, who by 1989 had risen to the rank of vice chairman of Enron. "Second, it demonstrated to the world and to utilities that this was the first big innovation in the gas business and it was being done by Enron, so it solidified Enron's position in the market."

Profits from the Gas Bank were almost immediate. Industrial customers and power generators were willing to pay a premium for a guaranteed gas supply. Within two years of launching the service, Enron was selling fixed-price, ten-year gas contracts with average prices as high as $3.50 per 1,000 cubic feet, even though gas prices were stuck at about $1.30. That meant that on a handful of contracts, Enron was able to make $2.20 per 1,000 cubic feet of gas, a handsome profit by any measure.

In addition to making money, the Gas Bank had several additional, very positive effects for Enron: It made gas-fired power plants much more attractive to lenders. More gas-fired power plants meant more gas consumption, and that meant more business for Enron's pipeline and trading business. And finally, it helped create a futures market in natural gas, a market that Enron would soon dominate.

Today, natural gas–fired power plants are common. But in the late 1980s and early 1990s, almost all of America's electric power came from coal and nuclear sources. Natural gas was hampered by concerns about supply (having enough gas) and price (making sure the gas wasn't too expensive). But with the advent of the Gas Bank, a power company that wanted to build a gas-fired plant could safely estimate its energy costs over a long period of time. That gave lenders the comfort level they needed to provide financing. In December 1990, Enron signed a huge gas deal that achieved that very purpose. The company signed a twenty-three-year-long $1.3 billion contract with the New York Power Authority that called on the company to deliver gas to the authority at a fixed price for ten years. After that, the price would be adjusted monthly based on market conditions. With the fixed-price gas in hand, NYPA was able to go forward with a plan to build a 150-megawatt power plant on Long Island.

The NYPA deal was the first major power plant contract for Enron. It would lead to many more. And though the Gas Bank had quickly proven its worth, Skilling saw another opportunity. Enron was having trouble locking up gas supplies for the Gas Bank because many gas producers couldn't get the financing that they needed. Banks were, for the most part, in terrible shape. The excesses of the 1980s, including wagon loads of bad real estate and oil deals, had decimated banks and savings and loans in the Oil Patch. Lending officers were skittish about everything having to do with energy. Enron needed to lock up more gas production. To do that, Skilling realized the company had to go upstream. That is, Enron had to start locking up gas while it was still in the ground, and to do that, the company would have to start lending money to producers. In short, it would have to step into the role formerly taken by banks: Enron would provide financing to oil and gas producers so they could develop their properties. In return, the producer would promise to sell the hydrocarbons from that oil field to Enron at an agreed-upon price. Enron would then sell the gas through the Gas Bank. The prospectors would get the up-front cash they needed to develop gas fields that otherwise might not be producing at all.

Skilling took the idea to Ken Lay and Rich Kinder, with one proviso: Hire him to run the business. The two quickly agreed. And on August 1, 1990, Skilling walked into the building at 1400 Smith Street as chairman and chief executive officer of the newly created company, Enron Finance Corp.

*

Jim Flores and Billy Rucks had a good idea, they just didn't have enough money. The two landmen had been poring over records on offshore leases and they believed a field that Shell Oil was selling had good prospects. The field was located a few miles offshore from what would be the lips of the mouth of the Mississippi River. Shell assumed the lease was just about depleted and was ready to unload it.

By late 1990 and early 1991, Flores and Rucks—one former Enron official refers to the two as "a couple of broke-assed Louisiana landmen"—were certain that Shell was making a mistake. The two men believed that Shell's field, called Main Pass 69, was likely to contain up to 80 million barrels of oil. Not an "elephant" (the oil industry's term for gigantic fields), but it was certainly worth developing. So the two went to Enron. According to Rucks, "There were no other financing sources at that time. The banks were getting hammered." He also added that he and his partner "weren't broke-assed, but we weren't rolling in dough."

After showing their seismic data to the geology and finance hotshots that Skilling had hired to work at Enron Finance, Flores & Rucks (the eponymous company owned by the two men) had a deal. In early 1992, Enron Finance lent the young company $46 million. A year later, the two parties agreed on another deal, $160 million in financing for a field right near the mouth of the Mississippi called East Bay. With those deals, Flores & Rucks was suddenly on the map, and the old oil fields they'd bought were more prolific than they had ever dreamed. "We were able to increase production in that field to over double of what we bought it for," Rucks remarked. "We did that within two years."[6]

Rucks was quick to give Enron credit for much of his—and his company's—success. "Enron Finance was of paramount importance to Flores & Rucks's becoming a significant E&P [exploration and production] company," said Rucks. "Those financings, initially, were very important." He remembered Enron being full of "bright people who were superexcited about their deal. They wanted to make a great company and they were really focused on it." And he said that Enron forced Flores & Rucks to adopt the discipline it needed to go public, which it did, in 1994. Rucks also credited Skilling. "He had tremendous juice within the company. When we were doing business with them, Jeff was the creator of the concept and the drive behind all of them. He had the power. And at that point, rightly so. He was making it happen over there. He was taking them into areas that were so far out there, that no one had even thought of them."

Prior to the deals Enron Finance did with Flores & Rucks, Skilling had done several other major deals. One deal had provided profits of $11 million. In another deal, Enron provided $38.5 million of the $45 million that Denver-based Forest Oil Corporation needed to purchase some promising properties. Enron got about half of the 48 billion cubic feet of gas Forest was going to produce and was able to sell it for a profit of six to eight cents per 1,000 cubic feet. Spreads of that kind gave Enron profit margins that were higher than any of its competitors.

Although the money Enron made on Forest was good, the profits from the Flores & Rucks deal were the fall-down-laughing kind of money. Rucks estimates Enron profits at $20 to $30 million. Some people within Enron believe the company's profits on the Flores & Rucks deal were closer to $100 million. Whatever the real number, Skilling had learned he could do monster deals—and he loved it.

The Flores & Rucks deal was a perfect complement to Enron's trading business, which, thanks to the Gas Bank, was growing faster than anyone had expected. Although crude oil futures—as well as futures in refined products like gasoline and diesel fuel—had been traded on various exchanges for decades,[7] natural gas futures were not traded for a simple reason: There was no market for them. Federal regulation of the gas business had prevented the creation of a functional gas futures market. The Gas Bank helped change that. There was another major factor that allowed Skilling's trading vision to happen: In 1990, the New York Mercantile Exchange (NYMEX) began trading futures based on delivery of gas to the Henry Hub, a major gas depot in Louisiana where fourteen different intra- and interstate gas pipelines come together.[8] That gave gas traders the catalyst they needed. With the NYMEX's published prices, traders were given a reliable market index that they could then use to establish prices for all kinds of gas contracts. And Enron was leading the charge in almost every part of the business.

As Skilling watched the uptick in trading—the area he believed would be huge—he became convinced that Enron's accounting had to change. He wanted Enron to switch to a bookkeeping method favored by finance companies, not energy companies. That method is called "mark to market."

9

Mark-to-Market Account-a-Rama

For most normal humans, discussions on accounting principles are about as much fun as a prolonged session at the business end of a dentist's drill bit. But Enron's accounting foibles were part and parcel of the company's failure. So take a bit of Novocain and relax. This primer on accounting won't hurt (much).

For panhandlers, housewives, and small businesses, money means one thing and one thing only: cash. For them, money is legal tender or coins that can be redeemed almost anywhere, almost anytime, in exchange for goods and services. But in the Brave New World of Accounting, that's not the case. And the failure of Enron was substantially caused by the company's surfeit of non-cash revenue. Let me say that again, because it's one of the fundamental reasons Enron went bankrupt: Its revenues did not equal cash. And Enron's ability to show sky-high revenues without generating comparable amounts of cash was due to its adoption—at the prodding of Jeff Skilling—of mark-to-market accounting.

Accounting has been called the science of business. It's an appellation that was likely put forth by a lonely pocket-protector-wearing certified public accountant with too much time on his hands. In a real science, like chemistry or physics, there are laws. In physics, certain forces—say, gravity—cannot be denied. They are inexorable truths that simply must be accepted. For chemists, no matter how much they'd wish it to be otherwise, lead cannot be turned into gold. It just can't happen, ever. But in the modern world of accounting, there are no laws. Almost everything depends on "best professional judgment." Better still, Enron and its auditing and consulting firm, Arthur Andersen, knew that there were no cops patrolling their turf (I'll get to the SEC later), so they could act with almost complete impunity. And they did just that.

First, a bit of history. There are more than 500 years of reliable use behind modern accounting methods. They started with a Franciscan friar, Frater Luca Bartolomes Pacioli, who believed that Renaissance businessmen needed a reliable way to assess their financial condition. A pal of Leonardo da Vinci, Pacioli was a polymath. Born in Tuscany in the mid-1400s, he studied religion, business, military science, mathematics, art, music, and law. In his spare time, he helped Leonardo figure out how much bronze he needed for some of his sculptures.

Pacioli's patrons included the traders of Venice and Florence, who needed to be able to analyze their finances on a daily basis. His answer was dual-entry accounting. Every transaction was followed by an entry of both a debit and a credit in a journal. If a trader sold a boat for $100 in cash, he entered a debit for $100 in his asset column and a credit of $100 in his liabilities column. Pacioli decreed that at all times, debits and credits must be equal. If the two sides didn't balance, wrote Pacioli, "that would indicate a mistake in your Ledger, which mistake you will have to look for diligently with the industry and intelligence God gave you." [1] Pacioli's concepts were so brilliant that within a century or so, his treatise on accounting, originally published in 1494, had been translated into five languages and the "Italian method" of bookkeeping became the standard throughout Europe. And although the world has changed radically since the Renaissance, Pacioli's bookkeeping methods have remained largely unchanged.

Under Pacioli's method, known as cost, or accrual accounting, Enron would only have been able to recognize revenues from each deal it made as the money came in. For example, assume Enron was a Venetian company that had signed a contract to sell another company one boat each year for ten years, with each boat costing $100. Under Pacioli's rules, Enron would have only been able to record the $100 debit (and credit) for the sale once each year.

But under mark-to-market accounting, Enron could estimate the total value of the ten-year deal at any price it chose. So although total revenue was projected at $1,000, Enron could slap a net present value on the deal of, let's say $800, and enter that $800 debit in its ledger right away. The deal gets completed by the entry of an $800 liability on Enron's balance sheet.

The problem was, of course, that Enron didn't have $800 in cash. It only had $100 cash from the sale of the first boat and a promise from the buyer that he would buy another boat per year over the next nine years. Further assume that Enron, being an aggressive trader in Venice, saw that the price of boats was increasing and that in three years' time, a boat that it was now selling for $100 might be selling for $150. That meant that under the mark-to-market method, Enron could increase the value of the ten-year contract to $1,050, or even more, and book that revenue right away. The company would arrive at that value by creating a price curve.

Projections of future pricing are mapped on a price curve. Optimistic promoters always use price curves that look like a hockey stick. That is, they assume future prices of the widgets they are selling will soar.

Estimating future prices of anything is difficult. But traders of commodities have to do it to protect themselves from price volatility. For some commodities and time periods, creating price curves is a snap. For instance, the New York Mercantile Exchange has readily available prices for crude oil that will be delivered at the New York Harbor in sixty days. Similar prices are available for commodities like orange juice, coffee, pork bellies, and cotton. But price curves have a limited utility, particularly when the time lines are extra-long. For instance, who can say with any accuracy how much natural gas will cost in twenty years? The Amazing Kreskin might be able to predict that, but no one in the energy business can. For example, futurists and hopeful oilmen have been predicting for years that crude oil would cost $50 per barrel within two decades of whatever day they were making their prediction. Those dire predictions have, so far, been proven wrong, because oil exploration and production companies continue to find ever more oil and natural gas in ever-more-remote locales.

The ability to change price curves to suit the needs of a particular deal can create a tempting option for an accountant. If a company needs extra revenues, an (unscrupulous, or perhaps "creative") accountant can simply "move the curve," that is, adjust the price curve on a particular deal. With a fatter curve, the company can magically generate additional revenue (non-cash revenue) without having to go to the trouble of actually providing any goods or services to a customer. Enron's ability to manipulate price curves on its long-term contracts would become very important as its derivatives business grew ever larger.

Many accountants and traders believe that mark-to-market accounting is the best way to reflect the true value of a business, particularly one that does complex or long-term financial deals with contracts or investments that fluctuate in value. Mutual funds are a good example of mark-to-market accounting. Every trading day, every publicly traded mutual fund prices all of the securities it holds. And at the end of the day, it publishes the net asset value of those securities. Mark to market works particularly well for items that are fungible (stocks, for instance), which is a fancy word for something that is easily bought or sold on the open market. Big Macs and Bic pens are fungible. Nuclear missiles are not.

Mark-to-market accounting is useful, too, when valuing items that are common but not easily exchangeable, like office space. Suppose a real-estate leasing company owns an office building that is leased to five tenants, each of whom uses 2,000 square feet costing $1 per square foot per year. Lease costs are increasing. So the company renegotiates one lease for $1.25 per foot. Under mark-to-market accounting, the company recalculates the value of its other four leases, which, given the new valuation from the new lease, are worth more, even though their rents cannot be increased until the old leases expire. The old leases are only paying $8,000, but under mark-to-market accounting, their true value is $10,000. Add in the value of the new lease, $2,500, and the real estate company now has revenue of $12,500, even though it is only receiving cash of $10,500 ($2,500 from the new lease plus the $8,000 from the old leases).

Within a few months of his arrival at Enron, Jeff Skilling began pushing the company to adopt mark-to-market accounting for his group, which had changed its name to Enron Gas Services Group. Skilling argued that he needed the new method so that his people could properly value the long-term gas-supply contracts they were selling. But there were other motives behind Skilling's push for mark to market. He knew that by recognizing revenues more quickly, his group would be able to show significantly faster growth than any other part of the company. That meant he would get more recognition and move up the corporate ladder faster.

More important for Skilling, the adoption of mark-to-market accounting would put millions of dollars in his own pocket, and it would do it very quickly.

Buried in the 1990 Enron proxy statement (the form distributed to shareholders that lists executive salaries as well as their stock options and stock holdings) are the details of Skilling's employment contract with the company. In addition to a salary of $275,000 and a loan of $950,000, Skilling got Enron to pay him cash bonuses for any increase in the value of the company he was creating. The proxy says Skilling would get "a grant of phantom equity rights entitling him to receive in cash specified percentages of the market value of Enron Finance Corp." Under the deal, if Skilling's company grew to be worth $200 million, Enron would pay Skilling $10 million. If it grew to a valuation of $400 million, Enron would pay him $17 million.

Enron's proxies show that the terms of Skilling's equity-appreciation deal changed slightly in subsequent years. The 1997 proxy says that Skilling was paid about $2.5 million in cash under the terms of the equity deal for the year 1995. That same proxy says Skilling was granted an additional $6 million worth of stock options in Enron Corp. Those payments were in addition to the regular salary and bonuses Skilling received from the company.

The Enron proxies from 1990 through 1996 are silent concerning how much Skilling was paid in those years under the terms of the original contract. Whatever the total, it's clear that Skilling was able to personally enrich himself by many millions of dollars—perhaps tens of millions—because he convinced Enron to adopt the more aggressive accounting method. His arguments, according to sources close to the matter, revolved around the need to have an accounting method that worked well for trading. The big Wall Street firms used mark-to-market accounting for their trading businesses. If Enron was going to be a player in the gas trading business, it couldn't be stuck with accrual accounting. It simply had to change its methods.

"Mark-to-market accounting was Skilling's brainchild," said one executive familiar with the accounting change. "He convinced Ken Lay on it. Then he convinced the Audit Committee and the board."

Skilling began seeing the potential for the new accounting method in late 1990, about the same time that a group of Enron salespeople, led by John Esslinger and Ken Rice, closed one of the biggest long-term gas-supply deals in the history of the energy business. The contract with the New York Power Authority called on Enron to deliver 33 million cubic feet of natural gas per day to power plants built or operated by the authority. The twenty-three-year-long deal gave the authority fixed-price gas for ten years and adjustable prices based on index prices for the remaining thirteen years. The total value of the contract was $1.3 billion. But under accrual accounting rules, Skilling could only take 1/23 of the revenues from that contract every year. If his group could use mark-to-market accounting, he could pull most of that future revenue into the current quarter to make his business unit—and himself—look better.

Enron was particularly aggressive in selling long-term gas contracts like the one with NYPA that extended out ten, fifteen, or even twenty years. At that time, no other energy company was willing to make long-term bets like those because there were no reliable pricing schemes that allowed them to quantify their risks. But Skilling saw that as an advantage. If gas was selling for $2 per thousand cubic feet in 1990, Enron could simply assume (read: make a wild-ass guess) that it would cost $8 in 2010. And through the magic of malleable price curves and mark-to-market accounting, Enron could then assume a juicy hunk of revenue from that contract right away, and enter it on its books.

In short, nobody had ever done the type of transactions that Enron was doing, so no one could evaluate whether the contract was good or bad. The elasticity of the price-curve mechanism allowed Skilling a way to continually adjust the amount of revenues his business was making. It was a methodology that Skilling and his mafia would use repeatedly in the coming years, with disastrous consequences.

The huge—and immediate—revenues he could get from the NYPA deal convinced Skilling that mark to market was the way to go, said another executive who worked closely with Skilling. The former McKinsey man saw the method as "a way to enhance his own pocketbook. He was looking at the value that the New York Power Authority contract would bring to the table. He was never thinking of anything other than how to enhance his paycheck."

But by getting mark to market, Skilling not only enhanced his own paycheck, he started a series of events that took Enron's focus away from cash and cash flow and put it on revenue growth. And therein lies one of the seeds of Enron's destruction: Almost exactly one decade before Enron went bankrupt, the company—and Skilling in particular—began focusing attention not on generating something as old-fashioned as cash but rather on doing deals that allowed the company to foster accounting legerdemain with mark-to-market income.

Revenue growth became more important than cash. It was a mindset that would put Enron in a cash crisis.

Mark-to-market accounting was adopted by Enron's Audit Committee on May 17, 1991, just nine months after Skilling joined Enron. The minutes of the meeting say the committee debated "a new accounting concept to be utilized by Enron Gas Services Group"—the new name for Skilling's group. The new method "will provide a better measure of Enron Gas Services' results in managing its portfolio of contracts than would be reflected by historical cost accounting concepts, and, therefore, is in the best interests of the Company." The motion to approve the concept was made by Robert Jaedicke.

As soon as the method was approved by the Audit Committee, Enron and its auditor, Arthur Andersen, began lobbying the Securities and Exchange Commission for permission to use mark to market. They got that permission in a letter dated January 30, 1992. Walter P. Schuetze, the SEC's chief accountant, said mark to market could be used only within Enron Gas Services for use on its natural gas trading business. The letter also said the SEC "will not object to the proposed change in the method of accounting by Enron Gas Services during the first quarter of its fiscal year ended December 31, 1992."

Thus, with the SEC approval, Enron became the first non-financial company to be given approval to use mark-to-market accounting. Although Enron had the approval it desired, it wasn't quite enough. On February 11, 1992, Enron's chief financial officer, Jack Tompkins, wrote Schuetze back, saying that the company was going to ignore the SEC's approval date and institute mark to market a full year earlier than the SEC expected. "Enron has changed its method of accounting for its energy-related price risk management activities effective January 1, 1991," said Tompkins. "The cumulative effect of initial adoption of mark-to-market accounting, as well as the impact upon 1991 earnings is not material."

In other words, Enron would use mark-to-market accounting as it saw fit, not as the SEC had instructed. And according to auditors who worked at Enron, the company was also lying about the materiality of the use of mark to market. "Without the use of mark to market, Enron would have had a down quarter during the last quarter of 1991 and the market would have killed them for it," said one auditor who worked closely on the matter. "It *was* material to Enron's earnings. And from that point on, Enron started using mark to market in every part of the business, not just Enron Gas Services."

For reasons that aren't clear, the SEC apparently never objected to Enron's retroactive use of mark-to-market accounting in 1991. And the agency's approval of the accounting method gave Skilling all the momentum he needed. On the day the letter arrived from Schuetze, Skilling began celebrating. "He came down to the trading floor with a bottle of champagne that day," said one executive who had worked for Skilling. "He was one happy camper."

And though mark to market helped fuel Skilling's ambition and his drive to remake Enron into a trading company, he had to compete for Ken Lay's attention. Another group at Enron, led by a hyperaggressive Vietnam veteran, was building power plants in Texas and in England that were making money. Lots of money. And that got Ken Lay's attention.

10

Enron Goes International: Teesside

1992 There was no reason to believe it could be done. In fact, most of the people in Houston thought John Wing was wasting his time and the company's money.

Britain's economy had depended on coal for more than a century. The British Isles held vast quantities of the heavy black rock, the fuel that had allowed Britain to become the cradle of the Industrial Revolution. And although they were far weaker than they had been in the years after World War II, Britain's coal miners were still unionized and, despite their dwindling numbers, powerful. How was Wing going to convince the British government and all of its regulators that a dinky outfit like Enron should be permitted to start generating electricity from natural gas when coal was cheap and plentiful? Sure, Britain had access to gas, but the vast majority of it was locked up in the North Sea fields, scores of miles offshore. There were no pipelines to bring it ashore and no companies willing to build them. In addition, there was widespread confusion in the British gas market. In 1986, the government decided to deregulate the gas business and forced the state-owned utility, British Gas, to open its system to other competitors. But few companies were willing to take the chance. Furthermore, British law prohibited the use of natural gas for electricity generation.

Wing saw the obstacles and went ahead anyway. A West Point graduate and former army aviator in Vietnam, Wing was well known at Enron as a brilliant tactician and forceful negotiator. He was also disliked by nearly everyone on Enron's executive team. "Wing is a charming guy—if you don't have to work with him," said one.

Many—if not all of them—viewed Wing as a greedy self-promoter whose only loyalties were to himself, not Enron. Wing was "a genius," said one executive who had worked closely with him. "He was also crazy." Crazy or just crazy like a fox, Wing had a gift for numbers. He had negotiated for Houston Natural Gas during the merger talks with InterNorth, and by all accounts, Wing had taken the crew from InterNorth to the cleaners. InterNorth had paid far more for HNG than it was really worth.

Like Skilling, Wing was a graduate of the Harvard Business School and a Baker Scholar, in the top 5 percent of his class. And again like Skilling, he was damn smart, and he knew it. Wing had some peculiar, but effective tactics. During negotiations, he'd often erupt in screaming fits that were designed to intimidate the other side. They often worked. When they didn't work or when Wing was frustrated with a coworker he was never shy about slamming them with his favorite put-down. "Anybody that didn't measure up, he'd call them a 'pencil dick,'" recalled one former Wing associate.

Ken Lay hired Wing in the mid-1980s. Wing, who'd done a stint at General Electric under GE's revered CEO Jack Welch, was an expert on what was then a new form of gas-fired power plant. The technology, called cogeneration, is more efficient than older methods of producing power. Cogeneration uses the heat from the combustion of natural gas to create electricity and steam. The electricity is sold to big industrial users and utilities. The steam is sold for use in industrial processing or space heating. The steam production made cogeneration a perfect fit for a wide variety of industrial plants, including refineries and chemical producers. Cogeneration caught on quickly and made natural gas into the fuel of choice for electricity production in locations around the world. The technology showed that gas-fired power plants could be built smaller, faster, and cheaper than coal or nuclear facilities. In addition, they emit fewer pollutants than coal plants and were a viable alternative to nuclear plants, which by the late 1980s had ceased to be a viable option.

Ken Lay's relationship with Wing was stormy. Where Lay was quiet and professorial, Wing was loud and profane. Lay preferred calm discussion. Wing liked arguments. Lay was deferential, Wing condescending. Those differences led to a nearly constant running battle between the two. Shortly after Wing negotiated the merger deal with InterNorth, he quit Enron, claiming that Lay had abrogated an employment agreement he had with the company. But about a year later, Wing was back at work for Enron—as a consultant—working on power plant development. The running feud between Lay and Wing would ultimately become very expensive for Enron. Wing always worked under employment contracts that required Enron to pay him several million dollars each time there was a change in control of Enron's electric power business. That meant that any time Enron sold all or a portion of its power-generation assets, it had to pay off Wing. That clause put many millions of dollars into Wing's pockets. By one estimate, Enron was, at one time, paying Wing under the terms of five different employment contracts.

Despite their differences, Lay saw that Wing could get projects done. He also saw that Wing's projects made money. In fact, the first big profits Enron made in the power business came from a cogeneration plant built in Texas City, a small industrial town forty-five miles southeast of downtown Houston that is best known for what may be the worst industrial accident in American history.[1]

The 450-megawatt plant was financed almost entirely with junk bonds provided by Michael Milken's firm, Drexel Burnham Lambert. Wing, through contacts he'd made from his days at Harvard, convinced Drexel to put up about $180 million in junk bonds. Enron put up less than $10 million in cash.

The Texas City deal was just one of many deals Enron made with Drexel. The Wall Street firm had provided Lay with $615 million to help close the HNG/InterNorth merger. Between 1985 and early 1988, Drexel was to provide Enron with more than $2.94 billion in bonds that were spread among eight different transactions.[2]

Finished in 1987, the Texas City power plant began selling electricity to a local utility. It also sold electricity and steam to a nearby Union Carbide plant. With a pittance invested, Enron's profits from the Texas City project were enormous. The company was profiting twice on the same project: from selling the gas to the plant and from selling the electricity the plant generated. From the beginning, according to one Enron finance person, the Texas City facility was making "a ton of money." The success at Texas City convinced Wing that bigger opportunities lay overseas. And in 1989, after convincing Ken Lay and the Enron board of the merits of the project, he left for England. The decision would have profound long-term consequences.

Wing saw a British market ready for competition. Prime Minister Margaret Thatcher, the conservative leader, was pushing deregulation throughout the British economy. She had pushed for the sale of British Gas, and the country was planning to open its electricity markets to competition.

Wing and another Enron official, Bob Kelly, spent most of 1989 and 1990 promoting their plan for a huge cogeneration plant at Teesside, in northeastern England. Like the Texas City plant, the new project would generate power and steam. The steam and a small portion of the power would be sold to a neighboring facility, a nylon and chemical plant owned by ICI Chemicals & Polymers Ltd. Most of the electricity would be sold to four local electric utilities, all of which were expecting to be privatized. By November 1990, Wing had a deal. Enron's project was approved by John Wakeham, Britain's secretary of state for energy, who later became an Enron board member. And the 1,725-megawatt Teesside project became the first independent plant approved in the

United Kingdom. Within weeks, Enron—which owned half of the plant—began construction. By the time Teesside was completed in April 1993, it was the biggest cogeneration plant on earth and was providing about 3 percent of Britain's electricity needs.

It was also hugely profitable. Like the Texas City plant, Wing had found a unique way of financing the project. Enron's 50-percent equity stake in Teesside was granted in return for the company's role in conceiving the plant and acting as general contractor during construction. In other words, Enron laid out almost no cash for the project and still owned half of a plant valued at $1.6 billion. Enron estimated the plant would generate $30 million per year in profits. Enron officials in Houston were astounded. "The fact that it got done was incredible," said one senior Enron executive. Several former Enron people said Enron's profit on the construction contract alone was $100 million.

But Teesside wasn't free. Two elements of the deal—J-Block gas and employee compensation—would have long-term consequences for Enron.

The fuel for the project had to come from the North Sea, and since there were no gas pipelines to Teesside, Enron had to negotiate with a handful of North Sea producers to convince them to build one. Enron agreed to reserve about half of the capacity on the 225-mile-long pipeline. In the course of negotiating with the producers, Enron also agreed to some long-term gas supply contracts that obliged the company to take about 600 million cubic feet of gas per day from three North Sea fields. However, the Teesside plant was only going to use about half of that gas. Enron planned to sell the rest of the fuel, which came from a field known as J-Block, to other customers in the British market. If Enron didn't use all the gas from the J-Block field, it had to pay for it anyway. The arrangement was exactly like the "take-or-pay" contracts that had nearly strangled Enron and other American pipeline companies in the late 1980s. Yet Bob Kelly, who was then chairman and CEO of Enron Europe, thought J-Block was a great deal. In 1992, he told a reporter that the new gas contract would allow Enron to "become a major competitive supplier of gas in the United Kingdom to electric power stations as well as other customers."

There is widespread disagreement among the Enron officials who worked on Teesside as to why the contract was ever signed. The company had already locked up enough gas to fuel Teesside. Some sources blame Ken Lay, saying that he wanted the extra gas so that the company could compete against British Gas and gain a foothold in the European market. Others blame Kelly, saying he simply got outsmarted by the negotiators from the other side. Whatever the reason, it was a colossal blunder. In the late 1980s, Enron had spent tens of millions of dollars to get out of dozens of expensive take-or-pay contracts in the United States, and yet the company was repeating the same mistake in England. In addition, Kelly and the Enron executives who approved the J-Block deal forgot the first lesson about newly deregulated markets: Prices usually fall. That's exactly what happened in the U.K. gas market. The J-Block deal, signed in 1993, locked Enron into a deal when gas prices were high. Within a few months, gas prices crashed, and Enron was suddenly paying more for J-Block gas than gas that was available on the spot market. Enron also got into a dispute with the companies that built the pipeline.

Within two years of Teesside's completion, Enron was locked in nasty litigation against the pipeline owners, a formidable group of foes that included BG Group, BP, Amerada Hess, Phillips Petroleum, TotalFinaElf, and Agip. A year later, the J-Block gas producers sued Enron.

The litigation would cost Enron dearly, and the costs associated with J-Block would lead Jeffrey Skilling and one of his chief minions, an aggressive young MBA named Andy Fastow, into some very creative financing.

Teesside set another precedent, one that would drive Enron's international projects for the next decade. As part of his compensation package, Wing was granted a small ownership interest in the Teesside project. When the project was completed, Enron paid him for his interest in the plant. Although exact figures aren't available, sources close to the matter say Wing got about $11 million for his work on the project. Wing's multimillion-dollar payout "was done over [Enron president and COO] Rich Kinder's objections," said a former senior Enron executive. "It was done because of Ken Lay's infatuation with the international business."

Some people at Enron believe Wing's big paycheck was justified. He had done Texas City and he'd done Teesside, both with minimal exposure to Enron, and both very profitable. Wing may have been worth it. Enron needed him more than he needed Enron, so the company had to pay up. Worth it or not, Wing's paycheck at Teesside became the standard by which future international projects were measured. And every one of Enron's international power plant developers began expecting lucrative bonuses for their deals. "Wing started the excessive-compensation ball rolling," said an executive who worked closely with Lay and Wing. And with so much money at stake, Enron's international team began pushing projects that Wing would likely have never considered.

Teesside also convinced Enron that the international market was ripe for picking. According to one senior Enron executive, the project "made Enron's international reputation. It was a watershed event. It made Enron's name in the international power business. The only problem was it allowed us to get into other bad deals." Indeed, long before the Teesside plant was completed, Enron's money-hungry hordes—led by Wing's protégé and former lover, an executive named Rebecca Mark—began pushing for big power plants everywhere. The most ambitious one was located at a remote port in India that was one of the legendary stopping points for Sinbad the Sailor, a place called Dabhol.

Finally, Teesside convinced Ken Lay that if Enron was going to be a player in the international energy business in places like the United Kingdom and India, it needed to have friends—lots of friends—in Washington.

11

The Big Shot Buying Binge

FEBRUARY 1993

Call it a Big Shot buying binge.

In early 1993, in the span of three or four weeks, Ken Lay hired the just-out-of-office secretary of state and the just-out-of-office secretary of commerce to work as lobbyists. He also snared the just-out-of-office chairman of the Commodity Futures Trading Commission.

But then, Lay was only following tradition. Big Shots in Houston have always had people in government and people-who've-just-quit government on their payrolls. It's been that way for decades. And Lay wasn't going to buck that trend.

Since the turn of the century, Houston businessmen like James A. Baker, one of the founders of the powerful law firm Baker & Botts, have always maintained close ties with Washington. During Reconstruction, Baker—who served a stint as county judge for Harris County—and his firm represented big railroads like the Missouri Pacific and the Southern Pacific. With railroads under constant federal scrutiny, Baker & Botts developed strong Washington ties. Lawyers from the firm served on the War Industries Board during World War I and also on the International Court of Claims.[1] From the 1920s to the

1940s, Houston's main man in Washington was real estate developer, publisher, and banker Jesse H. Jones. In 1932, President Herbert Hoover appointed Jones to the Reconstruction Finance Corporation, the agency that spent billions of dollars bailing out banks, farms, and bankrupt businesses. Jones later became secretary of commerce and was reportedly so enamored of his own abilities that President Franklin Roosevelt sometimes referred to him as "Jesus H. Jones."[2]

Then came Brown & Root.

While Baker and Jones used Washington to further the goals of their clients and their friends, George and Herman Brown, the brothers who owned the construction firm, used their pals in Washington—Lyndon B. Johnson in particular—to build an empire.

Brown & Root, Houston's most famous construction firm (now part of oil field services and construction giant Halliburton) provides the closest thing to an Enron-like case study in Washington influence-buying. In the mid-1930s, the Browns were nearly broke, ruthlessly anti-union businessmen who had won a contract to build a dam on the Colorado River near Austin. But they didn't have much else. They had scant equipment and needed further congressional approval to start the project. The brothers backed the tall young former teacher in his race for Congress. Two weeks after Johnson was sworn in, he made sure the Browns' contract to build the dam was finalized.[3] The Mansfield Dam became the base of their fortune. In his book on Johnson, *Path to Power*, Johnson biographer Robert Caro said the Browns' profit on the dam totaled $1.5 million, "an amount double all the profit they had made in twenty previous years in the construction business."[4]

During World War II, Brown & Root was awarded a massive contract to build several hundred ships for the federal government, even though the firm had never built so much as a dinghy.[5] In 1946, the firm (and two others) was awarded a $21-million contract to build a military base on the island of Guam. Nearly a decade later, construction was still underway and the contract was worth $250 million. In 1947, the Browns were investors in Texas Eastern Transmission Company, which bought the Big Inch and Little Big Inch pipelines from the federal government for $143 million. Two decades later, the pipeline was worth ten times that amount. In his book *The Politician: The Life and Times of Lyndon Johnson*, author Ronnie Dugger wrote that in 1954, a public relations man for Brown & Root boasted that the firm had done "a billion dollars worth of work for the Army and Navy." And many of those contracts were steered, either directly or indirectly, to Brown & Root by Johnson, who, in return for the federal deals, built a pipeline of his own—one that carried a river of campaign cash from the Browns' bank accounts into his own accounts. In 1957, Johnson wrote to his friend, saying, "I invariably find that my chief asset is that I have George Brown as a friend."

In 1960, while Johnson was on the presidential campaign trail with John F. Kennedy, a joke made the rounds. It starts with Kennedy, a Catholic, telling Johnson, "You know, Lyndon, when we get elected, I'm going to dig a tunnel to the Vatican." To which Johnson replies, "That's okay with me as long as Brown & Root gets the contract."[6]

During Johnson's tenure in the White House, the relationship continued and Brown & Root was awarded huge construction projects during the war in Vietnam. The firm built ports, roads, airports, and anything else the Pentagon asked for. In his biography of Johnson, Dugger summed up the relationship: "If Lyndon was Brown & Root's kept politician, Brown & Root was Lyndon's kept corporation."[7]

Brown's political patronage didn't stop with Johnson. He was also a regular in Suite 8-F, the room at the Lamar Hotel where Houston's power elite of the 1950s, 1960s, and 1970s gathered on a regular basis to eat lunch, drink whiskey, play poker, and decide which politicians would get their money and their backing. The "8-F crowd" included the city's richest businessmen, people like insurance magnate Gus Wortham, *Houston Chronicle* publisher Jesse Jones (who owned the Lamar and lived on the top floor), Judge James Elkins, the founder of the law firm Vinson & Elkins, and Oveta Culp Hobby, the publisher of the *Houston Post*. George Brown was the undisputed leader of Suite 8-F, the group that was, in effect, Houston's real government.

By the 1970s, another Houston powerhouse was cultivating friends in high places. Lay's predecessor at Houston Natural Gas, Bob Herring, was a jet-setter and political animal who lunched with former secretary of state Henry Kissinger in Washington and flew to Riyadh for chats with Crown Prince Khaled. When Lay took over at Enron, he not only bought Herring's old house, he also began emulating his style. Like Herring, he became active in local charities and politics, and began supporting Rice University and serving on local boards. And by 1993, with Enron's international business on the rise, Lay needed some friends with big Rolodexes and even bigger résumés.

Ken Lay was going to succeed Herring and Brown with his own version of Suite 8-F. He was going to be Mr. Houston. To do that, he needed to develop a group of powerful friends. So he hired James A. Baker III.

In a February 22, 1993, press release announcing the hiring of Baker—the grandson of the old Harris County judge as well as a former secretary of state and top official serving under three different Republican presidents—and Robert Mosbacher, the former secretary of commerce, Lay gushed that Enron was "delighted to have these two individuals, who have such a wealth of international experience, join us in the development of natural gas projects around the world." And who wouldn't have wanted Baker, the man who used to sign our greenbacks and knew oodles of prime ministers by their first names? Baker, the former secretary of the treasury, as well as chief of staff under Ronald Reagan, was simply passing through the paved-with-gold revolving door between high-level government service and the aristocracy of the lobbyist-fixer. His money grab with Enron—which began almost exactly one month after his boss, George H. W. Bush, moved out of the White House—was the most blatant abuse of the revolving door since Henry Kissinger began pimping his basso profundo and his Rolodex to any company with a big checkbook. (Enron was one of Kissinger's many clients. The company kept him on the payroll for several years in the hope that he'd help open doors in China and elsewhere.)

Baker and Mosbacher had other attributes that made them valuable to Enron. Both were Houstonians. Both were longtime energy guys. And both had strong ties in countries where Enron was pushing power projects, including the still-smoldering ruins of Kuwait, which was just beginning to recover from the damage done by Iraqi troops.

As recounted in a September 6, 1993, article by Seymour Hersh in the *New Yorker*,[8] within six weeks of being hired by Enron, Baker was flying to Kuwait on a Kuwait Airways plane alongside his old boss, former president of the United States, George H. W. Bush. The former president was going to Kuwait in April 1993 to get a medal from the Kuwaitis. Baker was there to lobby them.

The former secretary of state, who just a few months earlier had discussed strategy with the Kuwaitis, was now trying to sell the country's just-back-from-exile royal rulers on the merits of a 400-megawatt power plant that Enron wanted to rebuild at Shuaiba, an industrial zone south of Kuwait City. Also on the plane was former U.S. army lieutenant general Thomas Kelly, who'd joined the Enron board in 1991, shortly after the war against Iraq ended. Kelly had become a CNN regular during the war, thanks to his almost daily appearances before the press corps. By the time of the 1993 trip, according to Enron's proxy statement, Kelly was no longer on the Enron board. However, he was still working as a consultant to Enron, and his compensation was based largely on his ability to get contracts on new power plants. (In addition to Enron, Kelly had another client at the time, the Wing-Merrill Group, an independent power company started by John Wing, who'd parted ways with Enron after Teesside.)[9]

Baker's lobbying for Enron didn't stop in Kuwait. He pushed Enron projects in Turkey, Qatar, and Turkmenistan as well.[10] He also wrote a political risk paper for Enron on the dangers of investing in the Dabhol project in India. Enron never bothered to reveal the amount of money it was paying Baker or Mosbacher. But one published report said that Kelly, who arguably had the least power of the three men, was going to be paid between $400,000 and $1.4 million.[11]

In his report on Enron's new hired-gun lobbyists, Hersh quoted a disgusted former army general, Norman Schwarzkopf, who had commanded American troops during the war. "In the Arab world, your position in government may get you through the door, but it's the personal relationship that gets you the contract. . . . American men and women were willing to die in Kuwait. Why should I profit from their sacrifice?"

Baker and Lay had no such qualms.

"I reject the suggestion there's something inappropriate in this," Baker told ABC shortly after the Hersh story appeared.[12]

Lay was similarly cavalier. "Is there any reason American companies shouldn't profit from the war in Kuwait?" he asked. "What's wrong with hiring former American officials to encourage investments anywhere in the world? Jim Baker has given us some very helpful advice to be more competitive in the world. I ask you, what in the hell is wrong with that?"

There's nothing illegal about hiring former government officials. In fact, Lay began making a habit of it. While the Baker-Mosbacher-Kelly triumvirate was helping overseas, Enron scored a major coup by hiring Wendy Lee Gramm just five weeks after her tenure on the Commodity Futures Trading Commission ended. And if ever there was a case of political payback, Enron's hiring of Wendy Gramm is it.

When Lay announced the hiring of Gramm, a Ph.D. economist, he said her "experience in financial and commodities markets will prove extremely valuable to Enron." What Lay didn't say was that Wendy Gramm had just given Enron a major regulatory bonus. During her very last days as lame-duck chairman of the CFTC (which was short two of its five members), she won hurried passage of a federal rule that exempted energy derivatives contracts—an area that was rapidly becoming one of Enron's most profitable businesses—from federal regulation.

Gramm's regulatory push on behalf of Enron would allow the company to become a giant in the derivatives business. But before continuing this story, let me take a moment to provide a quick explanation of derivatives—the finance world's equivalent of anabolic steroids.

The simplest financial derivative is a stock option.

Let's assume that Wilbur Smith believes Acme Corporation's stock is going to go up. But rather than buy 100 shares of the stock at $50, which would cost him $5,000, he goes to a brokerage house like Merrill Lynch or Charles Schwab and buys an option for, let's say, $100, which gives him the right—*but not the obligation*—to buy 100 shares of Acme Corporation stock at $50 a year from today. In broker parlance, it's a "call option." A call is an option to buy at a fixed price.

If, in a year, Wilbur is proven right and Acme Corporation stock rises to $60 (or higher) his option is valuable. He exercises his option with Schwab, which then sells him 100 shares of Acme Corporation for $50 per share. Wilbur immediately sells that same stock for $60 per share. He then pockets a tidy profit of $900 ($1,000 profit on the stock, minus the $100 cost of his option).

The option allowed Wilbur to use his money more effectively. Instead of investing $5,000 in Acme Corporation stock, he invested $100 in an option and was still able to benefit from the stock's price increase. However, Wilbur might have bet incorrectly. Let's assume that Acme Corporation stock fell to $40 at the end of the option period. In that case, Wilbur simply lets the option expire and does nothing. His only loss is the $100 cost of the option.

"Put options" work the other way. A put is an option to sell at a fixed price.

Wilbur Smith thinks Acme Corporation is overpriced. He goes back to Charles Schwab and buys a put option (again, assume the option costs $100) that gives him the right—but not the obligation—to sell Acme Corporation stock to Schwab in one year, for $50. A year later, if Acme Corporation stock falls to $40 (or lower) Wilbur can exercise his option. Schwab buys the stock from Wilbur for $50 a share. Wilbur again pockets $900 ($1,000 from the sale, minus the $100 cost of the option).

Enron's derivatives business followed a very similar pattern. But instead of selling to individuals like Wilbur Smith, Enron sold them to big industrial customers and energy companies. And rather than purchase stock options, the big companies (small companies, too) were buying and selling put and call options on commodities like natural gas and electricity or interest rates.

For instance, suppose ABC Utility Company owned a gas-fired

power plant and wanted some assurance that its fuel costs for the plant would not exceed a certain limit. ABC could buy a call option from Enron that allowed it to buy 1 million cubic feet of gas per day for a period of one year. The price on the gas could be set at a fixed price or a floating price that fluctuates based on spot market prices set by the New York Mercantile Exchange for certain locations, like the Katy Hub, a terminal twenty miles west of Houston. With the option in hand, the utility could then make more accurate forecasts about its revenues and cash flow. In other words, by purchasing the option, the utility was hedging its price risk. ABC was spending a little money for an option from Enron that protected it in case natural gas prices soared.

That type of contract is a derivative. Simply stated, a derivative is a financial contract between two (or more) parties that is based on an underlying commodity.

In addition to options, Enron sold—and bought—a dizzying array of other derivatives worth tens of billions of dollars. These deals included forward contracts, futures, energy swaps, and one of the most common derivatives, interest rate swaps. Enron could buy and sell these complex contracts alongside big financial institutions like Citibank or J.P. Morgan Chase or Morgan Stanley. But unlike the Wall Street firms, Enron didn't have to get a securities license or register with the Securities and Exchange Commission. It didn't have to comply with the rules of the New York Stock Exchange or report to anyone how much real cash it was using to back all of its derivatives.

Wendy Gramm's exemption allowed Enron to, in essence, run its own derivatives exchange. But unlike exchanges, such as the New York Mercantile Exchange and the Chicago Board of Trade, both of which have collateral requirements that are overseen by the Commodity Futures Trading Commission, Enron could set its own standards, a fact that would allow it to become one of the key players in the burgeoning multitrillion-dollar over-the-counter derivatives market.

Enron's purchase of Mrs. Gramm started on November 16, 1992, just a few days after Americans voted to oust President George H. W. Bush and replace him with Bill Clinton. That day, Enron and several other energy companies began petitioning the CFTC for an exemption from regulatory oversight on energy derivatives contracts. A few weeks later, Gramm complied. She pushed through an exemption that not only prevented federal oversight but also exempted the companies from the CFTC's authority—even, amazingly, if the contracts they were selling were designed to defraud or mislead buyers.[13] Shortly after the exemption passed, Representative Glen English, chairman of the House agriculture subcommittee, which had jurisdiction over the CFTC, said that in his "eighteen years in Congress [Gramm's move] is the most irresponsible decision I have come across."[14] Sheila Bair, the only commissioner to vote against the proposal, argued that deregulation of energy futures contracts "sets a dangerous precedent."[15]

Dangerous or not, Gramm had done what Enron wanted. And on March 1, 1993, Gramm joined the Enron board, a job that would eventually pay her a total of about $1 million in salary, attendance fees, stock option sales, and dividends.[16]

When asked by the *Dallas Morning News* about Wendy Gramm's dash for cash between government and the plush carpets of Enron's fiftieth-floor board room, Lay answered a question with a question: "These people that raise these issues, what do they expect these people to do, leave government and go in a monastery or something?"[17] Wendy Gramm definitely didn't go into a monastery. Instead, she and her husband, Republican U.S. senator Phil Gramm, began feeding at the Enron trough. In the 1993 election cycle, after Wendy Gramm began serving on Enron's board, the company gave more than $25,000 to Phil Gramm's political campaign, and within a few years, Enron had become the arch-conservative's top corporate contributor.[18] Ken Lay would even go on to serve as regional chair of Gramm's failed 1996 bid for the White House.

The Gramms became a wholly owned subsidiary of Enron Corp. And while the Gramms were good, and James A. Baker III would come in handy, Lay was aiming for even bigger Big Shots—a Republican family with roots in all the best places: the energy business, the Central Intelligence Agency, the GOP, and the White House.

12

"Kenny Boy"

No member of the Bush family has ever been on the Enron payroll.[1]

—Ken Lay, June 2000

Surely it's just a coincidence. What else would explain why Enron Oil and Gas, a subsidiary of Enron Corp., would have been in business with George W. Bush way back in 1986?

Bush the Younger was many things, including the eldest son of the vice president of the United States. A successful oilman he was not. Bush's forays into the energy business had been nothing short of disastrous. In 1984, Bush had no choice but to merge his faltering firm, Bush Exploration Company (which had previously been called Arbusto—Spanish for *shrub*) with another firm, Spectrum 7, which had the main virtue of being somewhat profitable. But by mid-1986, Bush had done his magic on the privately owned Spectrum 7. The company wasn't producing much energy of any kind, and Bush was actively trying to sell yet again, this time to an exploration and production company called Harken Energy. Despite Spectrum 7's lousy record, it somehow got into business with Enron Oil and Gas. And on October 16, 1986, Enron Oil and Gas announced that it had completed a well a few miles outside of Midland, Texas, that was producing 24,000 cubic feet of natural gas and 411 barrels of oil per day. Enron owned 52 percent of the well. Ten percent belonged to Spectrum 7.[2]

Now, the oil and gas business is full of speculators, and wells are often drilled with multiple investors with varying backgrounds. But the early Bush-Enron connection, which was first reported by David Corn of the *Nation,* points out just how small the energy business is. Two years later, the energy business—at least as far as George W. Bush and Enron are concerned—was made even smaller. That's when Rodolfo Terragno, Argentina's minister of public works, got a call from—who else? George W. Bush.[3]

Terragno was overseeing the bidding for a major gas pipeline that would connect Argentina's natural gas fields with foreign and domestic customers. He was considering two proposals for the pipeline, which was expected to cost $300 million. One proposal was from an Italian firm, the other was from an Argentine company that was working with Dow Chemical. Then, after nearly a year of deliberation, Enron jumped into the bidding. "I had a lot of reservations about Enron because the company wasn't well established in Argentina," Terragno told Lou Dubose, who broke the story in *Mother Jones* magazine.[4] Terragno said he was lobbied by the U.S. ambassador to Argentina, a fact that didn't surprise him. What did surprise him was the call from George W. Bush, who phoned him a few weeks after Bush's father won the November 1988 election. "He told me he had recently returned from a campaign tour with his father," Terragno told Dubose. And Bush made it clear that he wanted Terragno to give Enron the pipeline deal. Bush told him that the Enron deal "would be very favorable for Argentina and its relations with the United States."[5]

Terragno never got to act on George W.'s recommendation. In 1989, his boss, Argentina's president, Raúl Alfonsín, was voted out of office. In his place came right-wing politico Carlos Menem. And within three years of Menem's election, Enron was able to buy a major stake in Argentina's pipeline system. Perhaps the Spectrum 7 and Argentina deals are coincidental—George W. Bush's handlers deny that he ever called Rodolfo Terragno—but there was nothing accidental about Ken Lay's courtship of the Bush Family.

Lay's ties to George H. W. Bush go back to 1980, when Bush made his first bid for the White House. Bush, who'd recently served as director of the Central Intelligence Agency, needed campaign funds after his surprise win in the Iowa caucuses. So Lay, who had likely met Bush through mutual friends in the energy business in Houston, gave money to Bush's campaign. And though Bush didn't win, Ronald Reagan made him vice president. Bush went on to chair the panel that pushed Reagan's task force on deregulation. One of Reagan's biggest moves in deregulation involved the lifting of federal controls on natural gas markets, a move that Lay had long favored.

In April 1987, Lay reached into his pocket again for Bush, giving him $1,000 (the maximum donation individuals can give to presidential candidates) for his 1988 presidential campaign. In October 1988, when Bush's campaign was in its final days, Lay was one of the candidate's lead fund-raisers and chaired a $1,000-a-plate fund-raiser in Houston for Bush.[6]

When the elder Bush got to the White House, he didn't forget Lay. Bush rewarded Lay during his presidency with one of the most coveted perks of being a presidential pal, a sleep-over at the White House.

By 1990, Lay had become a Big Shot in Houston, and a friend of the Bushes, so he was selected to serve as a co-chairman of the host committee for the Economic Summit of Industrialized Nations in Houston. At that affair, Lay got to rub elbows with the Bushes, as well as Mikhail Gorbachev, Margaret Thatcher, and other world luminaries.

Two years later, when Bush was running for reelection, Lay defended the president against some of his detractors in the energy industry saying, "I'm a strong supporter of the president and his administration. As an industry, we've pretty much gotten what we felt we wanted ten or fifteen years ago." That was certainly true. In addition to the deregulation of the gas business, the Reagan and Bush administrations repealed the windfall-profits tax on oil companies, a levy that was instituted in the late 1970s when Big Oil made huge profits during the run-up of oil prices after Arab nations curtailed shipments of oil to the United States.

Also in 1992, George Bush personally asked Lay to head the Host Committee for the Republican National Convention, which was held in

Houston. And Lay made sure that Enron did its part. Lay's company put up $250,000 to help the GOP defray the costs of confetti, streamers, and stupid hats during the convention. Although the Elder Bush lost the 1992 election to Bill Clinton, Lay didn't disown the Bushes. Instead, he took it as an opportunity to ingratiate himself even further. Lay stepped forward in an (unsuccessful) effort to lure the outgoing president's presidential library to Houston. That library effort, Lay said, allowed him to spend "a little more quality time with George W."

That quality time turned into cash.

When Bush the Younger decided to run for governor of Texas in fall 1993, one of his first stops on the campaign trail was Houston. During his visit, George W. Bush asked Lay to be the finance chairman of his campaign in Harris County, which includes Houston. Lay didn't take the job. He preferred to give George W. Bush a $12,500 check and work behind the scenes. In his stead, Bush's campaign in the county was headed by Lay's second in command at Enron, Rich Kinder. In all, Lay, Kinder, and other Enron executives donated $146,500 to George W. Bush, almost seven times more than the amount they gave to the incumbent candidate, Democrat Ann Richards. The donations by the execs, combined with money from Enron's political action committee, made the Houston firm Bush's biggest campaign contributor. (Amazingly, after the Enron bankruptcy, George W. Bush would contend that Lay was "a supporter of Ann Richards in my run in 1994.")

After George W. Bush defeated Richards, Enron gave $50,000 to Bush's inaugural committee. Lay began lobbying Bush almost immediately. In December 1994, before Bush moved into the Governor's Mansion in downtown Austin, Lay began sending him regular letters on energy policy, tax issues, lawsuit reform, and other matters. That month, Lay asked Bush to appoint Pat Wood, who supported the deregulation of electric utilities, to the state's Public Utility Commission. Bush complied with Lay's request. And later on, Bush would appoint Wood—again at Lay's recommendation—to the Federal Energy Regulatory Commission. On December 21, 1994, Lay wrote Bush, saying tort reform was critically important to Texas and asked the governor-elect to make the matter the "highest priority during the early months of your administration." Bush again complied, declaring tort reform a state emergency, a move that gave the matter priority in the Texas legislature. In 1997, Bush signed a tort reform bill into law that limited jury awards in civil suits and narrowed the definition of liable parties. But in an ironic twist, Enron also lobbied for a provision that would have shielded accounting firms from being held responsible for financial statements issued by the firms they audited. The provision didn't make the final bill.

Some observers have said that Bush and Lay were not that close. Instead, they point out that Lay and Bush were simply on parallel wavelengths. Both men favored less government regulation, and both believed private enterprise and free markets were the way to prosperity. That may be the case, but it is also clear that the Bush-Lay relationship is rife with examples of the two men doing favors for each other.

Shortly after taking office, George W. Bush began considering an overhaul of the Texas tax code. He wanted to reduce property taxes for homeowners and raise the state's sales tax by 8 percent. So he formed a seventeen-member committee to study the issue. One of his appointees was his Enron-based fund-raiser, Kinder. The committee proposed a $3-billion package that would reduce taxes on capital-intensive industries, such as natural gas and petrochemical firms, while shifting much of the burden onto service-oriented entities like doctors, accountants, and attorneys. It also would have meant $9 million in annual tax savings to Enron.

Kinder wasn't the only Enron delegate to get Bush's ear. In August 1995, when Bush was just beginning to formulate his tax scheme, he held a private meeting with Charls E. Walker, a former deputy treasury secretary in the Nixon administration who had also advised Ronald Reagan on tax policy.[7] Walker was chairman of Walker/Potter Associates, a lobbying firm in Washington, D.C. He also chaired the American Council for Capital Formation, a group funded by capital-intensive industries. The group's Board of Directors included executives from Shell Oil, Texaco, Exxon, and of course, Enron. During their meeting,

Walker told Bush that the best way to encourage economic growth was to reduce taxes on expensive plants and equipment because those factors drive productivity and economic expansion. Shortly after their meeting, George W. Bush wrote Walker, saying, "Thank you for your time and ideas. Bush budget director Albert Hawkins will follow up as we develop our models." Bush's final plan was almost identical to the approach Walker was advocating. Although Bush's "Texas business tax" died in the Texas legislature in 1997, his meeting with Walker and his willingness to advocate Walker's position indicates the kind of consideration Bush gave to Enron's point of view.

Why? At the time Bush met with him, Charls E. Walker was an Enron board member and had been serving on the company's board for ten years. And it was no coincidence that Walker was on the Enron board. Charls E. Walker is the brother of Pinkney Walker, Ken Lay's old economics professor. Pinkney Walker told me that Lay had asked him first to be on Enron's board but he had declined and advised Lay to hire his brother instead.[8] In the two years prior to his meeting with Bush, Walker, in addition to his duties as an Enron board member, was working as a paid lobbyist for the company. In 1993, Walker's firm was paid $31,146 for Enron-related lobby work. In 1994, Enron paid the firm $39,750 for its lobby work.

When asked about his meetings with Walker, Bush told the *Dallas Morning News* that he "would like to get him involved more on this down here in Texas. He's very articulate." And though the paper didn't ask about the Enron-Walker connection, Bush offered the comment that he and the Enron lobbyist were "simpatico."[9]

Ah yes, simpatico. If Bush had been any more simpatico with Enron, he could've been charged with a misdemeanor under the state of Texas's buggery laws.

In addition to Bush the Younger, Lay continued to hold sway with Bush the Elder. In summer 1996, Lay was pushing hard on a proposal to build a new baseball stadium for the Houston Astros team, which was threatening to seek bigger, better subsidies somewhere else. Houston voters, though, were wary. Just a few months earlier, they had voted down a $390-million bond package to improve Houston's public schools. And the chances of them approving a stadium deal after the school bond defeat were slim. Lay had raised huge amounts of money for the pro-stadium forces, and the advertisements were helping. But he needed a Big Shot to endorse the project to help put it over the top. According to Dave Walden, former Houston mayor Bob Lanier's chief of staff, Lay tried to convince former first lady Barbara Bush to appear in a TV commercial. She declined, saying it wouldn't be right for her to get involved since her son, George W. Bush, was serving as governor of Texas. But that didn't stop Lay from pressing forward. The Enron boss was somehow able to convince former president George H. W. Bush into making a TV spot endorsing the new stadium. Bush's endorsement commercial, which aired just before the election, "really helped," according to Walden.

In November 1996, Houston voters narrowly approved the stadium deal. A few months later, it was announced that Enron had paid big bucks to name the new stadium Enron Field.

The second coming of the Bush Dynasty coincided with a big surge in Enron's political contributions to candidates at the federal level. In 1992, Enron's political action committees and company officers donated a total of $281,000 to federal candidates. By 1996, that figure had nearly quadrupled, to over $1.1 million, 81 percent of which went to Republicans (by 2000, that figure would more than double again, to $2.4 million, with 72 percent going to the GOP).

The Bushes continued to do favors on behalf of Enron. In October 1997, George W. Bush telephoned one of his Republican pals, Pennsylvania governor Tom Ridge, to assure him that the Quaker State could benefit if it allowed Enron—which desperately wanted to jump into the state's retail energy business—to have access to its markets. Bush's call was, of course, prompted by Lay, who said he told Bush that "it would be very helpful to Enron, which is obviously a large company in the state of Texas, if he could just call the governor and tell him this is a serious company, this is a professional company, a good company." So Bush did as he was asked. His call was one of many bare-knuckle moves Enron made in Pennsylvania. During the fight over deregulation, Enron even hired an airplane to tow a banner around the Philadelphia headquarters of the local utility, Peco Energy, which read, "Enron doubles Peco's rate cuts." Shortly after Bush's call, the Pennsylvania legislature deregulated the state's markets and Enron moved in.

Enron's Texas-based lobbyists always knew that when needed, they could use Lay to carry their message directly to George W. Bush. George Strong, who lobbied for Enron for more than two decades, said that in 1997 while working on an electric deregulation bill, he and other Enron lobbyists were stymied by Bush's staff members, who didn't agree with Enron's position on the bill. "So we'd call Houston and ask Lay to call the governor and explain our position." Strong says other corporate chieftains in Texas had access to Bush, but "from the Houston standpoint, Lay had better access to Bush than just about anybody." That access was important in 1999, when Enron's lobbyists helped push an electricity deregulation bill through the Texas legislature, a bill that George W. Bush promptly signed.

And while Lay maintained close ties to the Bush family throughout George W. Bush's stint as governor of Texas, those connections would be even more valuable to him and to Enron if Bush the Younger could throw the Democrats out of the White House. In December 1999, while Bush was pounding the campaign trail, Lay again wrote his friend, addressing it to "George and Laura" (Bush's wife). "Linda and I are so proud of both of you and look forward to seeing both of you in the White House."

About that same time, Lay sent a letter to some 200 executives at Enron and encouraged them to give money to Bush. He also lined up Enron's political action committee behind his pal.

Enron and Ken Lay were going to bet heavily on George W. Bush's bid for the White House. It was a bet that would pay off handsomely.

13

The Dabhol Debacle

Rebecca Mark wanted to get the Dabhol power plant built so badly she could taste it.

Mark had been at Enron since the mid-1980s, and she needed to make a big score. She needed something that would really impress the people back in Houston. If she could just get the Indian government to finalize the Dabhol deal, she'd make millions of dollars in bonuses, and better yet, she'd finally be out of the shadow of John Wing, the man who had taught her how to make big power deals.

By summer 1993, Mark had been working on the Indian project nonstop for nearly eighteen months. And she was having good success. In July 1992, Enron and the Maharashtra State Electricity Board had signed a memorandum of understanding that laid out the basic terms: Enron would build the power plant at Dabhol, about 150 miles south of Bombay. Mark had the backing of Ken Lay and the somewhat lukewarm backing of Enron's president, Rich Kinder. On the surface, the deal made some sense. India's population was growing, its economy was becoming more stable, its workforce was highly educated, demand for electric power, particularly reliable electric power, was growing, and although the country had plenty of coal reserves, it was going to need new energy sources that were fueled by natural gas.

In addition to those factors, Mark was a damn good salesman. And she was able to use her charm and good looks to her advantage in India in a way that wasn't possible in the United States. The Indian politicians she was dealing with had never worked with anyone like her. "She was able to use her feminine side in a very constructive way and she didn't care to diminish it," said an Enron executive who worked with her in India. "She almost wanted to exaggerate her physical presence but at the same time prove she belonged." That meant that Mark would wear one of her tailored business suits to a meeting in Bombay, and a short time later, don an Indian sari and a pair of sandals for a visit to the project site with local politicians. "She was very good at sensing that a minister or an executive at a powerful company was having difficulty in dealing with her, a woman," the source remembered. "So when that cultural chauvinism came up and there was something we needed, she'd back away and almost become subservient to a male counterpart."

Mark also knew that the risks were enormous. She was working on the biggest single foreign investment project ever proposed in India. In the fifteen years prior to Enron's entry into India, the total of all foreign investment in the country had been less than what Enron was proposing to invest in just one project. But fear and caution weren't Rebecca Mark's style. Action was.

She's a size-six bottle blonde with high cheekbones, extra-straight, extra-big, extra-white teeth, enormous brown eyes, and always perfect makeup. She favors gold jewelry and has more fancy clothes than an upscale shopping mall. Whereas other female executives tend toward navy blue, gray flannel, and conservative pumps, Rebecca Mark likes the very upscale yet slightly trampy look. Her brightly colored outfits are from the likes of Armani and Escada, usually including miniskirts and a pair of come-hither stiletto heels. Mark's clothes-horse act was constant, at work and at play. One former Enron employee said that while skiing in Colorado, Mark would have a morning ski outfit, an afternoon ski outfit, and yet another outfit for cocktails and dinner. Mark certainly isn't shy about displaying the strength of her closets. She bragged to one reporter that her costumes are "a bit of theater." As for the high heels, she said they "make your legs look long when they're not and make them look skinny when they're not."

From India to England and Argentina to Texas, Rebecca Mark was a one-woman blitzkrieg whose only goal was to make gigantic deals backed by even bigger promises. And yet in nearly every case, the deals came with wallet-numbing losses. No one has blamed Mark for the fall of Enron. It appears that she was not behind any of the off-the-balance-sheet deals created by Jeff Skilling and Andy Fastow. But there is also no question that the enormous losses Enron took on Mark's projects accelerated the company's downfall. In addition to losses on the projects, Mark's high-living globe-trotting style was a constant drain on Enron's cash coffers.

Rebecca Mark was Enron's rock star. And just like Britney Spears, everyone has an opinion about her.

Opinions aside, there are a few facts about Mark that cannot be disputed: She could sell ice to Eskimos; she's pretty enough to be a model; she's talented, speaks excellent Spanish, is a Harvard MBA, has a wealth of knowledge about the energy business, and owns a Rolodex filled with the names of important government officials in dozens of foreign countries. And although she wasn't as ruthless as Skilling, she was every bit as cunning and every bit as vain in her quest for power, fame, and mountains of money.

Women are particularly scathing in their assessments of Mark. Maybe it's because women have had a harder time making their way up the corporate ladder than men. To succeed, women have, arguably, had to be smarter, faster, and gutsier than their male counterparts. But the anger of Mark's peers has a unique quality. Perhaps it's envy.

Maybe the women are jealous of Mark's money, success, and good looks. Envious or not, they are clearly angry about what they consider Mark's unflinching use of her sexuality to get where she got. One prominent (female) energy analyst said of Mark, "She got to the top on her back." Women who worked at Enron are scarcely more charitable. They roll their eyes whenever Mark's name is mentioned and almost immediately mention (in appropriately hushed tones, of course) allegations of Mark's affairs with several male executives at the firm. The only affair that Mark had at Enron that has been publicly acknowledged is her fling with John Wing.[1] I'll get to that in a minute.

A prominent former (male) executive at Enron said admiringly of Mark, "She's as good with her sexuality around men as anyone I've ever seen. She knows how to flaunt it. She just knew how to use her intelligence and sexuality to her advantage when sitting across the table from men who didn't know how to handle her." The man wasn't slamming her. He made the comment in a complimentary fashion. And he added, "She's a tremendously smart gal. But she's very scary because she only cared about how much money she could make for Rebecca Mark."

Indeed, much of Mark's marketing campaign for herself depended not on her brains but her butt. "I don't mind being remembered as, 'Oh, that's that beautiful woman I talked to,'" she told *Forbes* magazine in 1998.[2] The fawning profile, which included half a dozen photos of Mark—in half a dozen different outfits—showed her at the height of her power and vanity. "People will make an appointment just to see if you can walk and chew gum at the same time," she said. "I'll take all the advantages I can get."[3]

One advantage that Mark had from the outset was that she was in the right sector to get noticed. Many of her peers were in softer industries: Jill Barad was at toy maker Mattel; Charlotte Beers was at leading ad agency Ogilvy & Mather Worldwide.[4] Mark was in a business dominated by men who have always viewed their industry, and of course, themselves, as macho. "If you want to make a name for yourself and you are a woman, go to the energy business," commented one executive who knows Mark and worked with her. "I'd go to a conference and there'd be ninety-nine guys and one woman. She had advantages by being an oddity."

Although many of her male counterparts respected her intellect, they also questioned her motives. One executive who worked with her in India said Mark was "brilliantly aggressive and tragically reckless. She's brilliant in many respects. But balancing that is, she's reckless."

Rebecca Mark wasn't born into a world of high finance and international power projects, but she managed to grow accustomed to them awfully fast. She was born Rebecca Pulliam in Kirksville, Missouri, in 1954. Her parents were farmers, and she spent much of her youth learning the value of hard work and manual labor. One of four children, she baled hay and worked in the fields. Mark attended Kirksville High School, where she was a member of the National Honor Society and was one of four students selected for Girl's State, an American Legion–sponsored, weeklong event in which the students experience a "mock government situation," the idea being to learn about government and citizenship. Joellen Hayes, the librarian at Kirksville High, remembered Mark. "She had big dark eyes and wore her hair long and straight. She was a beautiful girl. She was not terribly outgoing—more quiet and reserved, and highly respected by teachers. She was just a very pleasant, mature-acting girl."

After high school, she attended William Jewell College, a private Baptist college near Kansas City. From there, she went to Baylor University, in Waco, Texas, where she got an undergraduate degree in psychology and a master's in international management. After graduation, she worked for First City National Bank of Houston, one of many big Texas banks that are now owned by megabanks on the East or West Coast. Along the way, she married Thomas Mark, and together they had twin sons. In 1982, she jumped into the energy business by joining the treasury department at Continental Resources, a natural gas pipeline company. In 1985, Continental was bought by Houston Natural Gas, and Mark's sojourn into the manly world of energy began.

Mark had been at HNG for several years when she began having an affair with her boss, Wing, who was heading Enron's electric power division.[5] The former army captain put Mark through what one person compared to his own private business boot camp. "Wing treated her like a drill sergeant would treat a young private," recalled one executive. "He'd fire her publicly. He'd ridicule her on conference calls, treat her like a secretary, dress her down. He basically had her psychologically from any perspective."

"She had a lay-down sexual harassment suit if she had wanted it. Yet at the same time, they're having an affair," said the executive. "You didn't feel comfortable being around them. But you were more uncomfortable because they were having an affair."

While Wing was berating Mark in the board room and boffing her in the bedroom, he was also showing her how to get deals done in the international electricity market, which was just beginning to open up to foreign investors. He tutored her on the details of the Teesside power plant in England. That schooling provided the groundwork for Mark's ascendance within Enron. In 1988, she and Thomas Mark split. The divorce left her with custody of the couple's twin sons. About that same time, she left Enron to attend Harvard Business School. While attending Harvard—courtesy of Enron, which paid her tuition and reportedly even paid for her child care—she helped monitor the construction of an Enron power plant in Milford, Massachusetts. The Milford plant later became infamous inside Enron because of two rather sticky problems: The plant didn't have access to enough gas or enough water. But Enron wanted the plant built and built by Mark, so she made sure to get the project completed. It was sold a few years after it was built for a slight profit.

After graduating from Harvard, Mark came back to Enron ready to set the world on fire. Within a few months of her return, she convinced Ken Lay that there were many more opportunities on the international front than just the Teesside project in England. So the company created Enron Development Corporation and in 1991, Mark was named CEO. That position led Mark to pursue projects from Qatar to Turkey. Without question, though, the most important project was Dabhol.

Foreign investors had shied away from India for a simple reason: The country's politics were in nearly constant turmoil. And that turmoil scared investors. If they invested in a big project and the Congress

Party, the ruling party in India for nearly half a century, was suddenly thrown out of office, there were no assurances that their money would be returned. Beyond that, India had long despised foreign investment as an insult to the country's self-sufficiency. It was a belief that came from three and a half centuries of experience with outfits like the British East India Company and the Brits who came with it. Foreign companies were colonizers just like the British, and the Indians had already seen plenty of that, thank you very much.

In addition to the political risk, there were huge capital risks. Enron, along with its partners, General Electric and construction giant Bechtel, were proposing a 2,015-megawatt power plant that would cost about $2.9 billion. It would be built in two phases. Phase One of the project would burn naphtha, a fuel similar to kerosene and gasoline. The 740-megawatt power plant would help stabilize the local transmission grid and provide infrastructure for the more expensive second phase. Phase Two meant liquefied natural gas, or LNG, and LNG infrastructure is very expensive. The fuel can only be moved by refrigerated tankers that cost hundreds of millions of dollars each. The infrastructure associated with the LNG terminal at Dabhol was going to be about $1 billion. That overhead and the cost of making LNG (it has to be frozen) and transporting it meant that Dabhol's fuel costs were likely going to be about $500 million per year.[6]

Despite the high costs, Mark and Enron believed LNG would be their foothold in India. After Dabhol got up and running, the company planned to build a pipeline north to Bombay to carry gas from the LNG terminal to other power plants or big industrial customers. Indian officials were also interested in having a new LNG supply to augment their existing energy supplies. The Indian government was excited about Enron's project. Not only would it help stabilize the country's overtaxed power grid, but it would provide a reliable source of power that could attract new foreign investment to the western coast of India, particularly new industries. Sure, the plant was going to benefit Enron, but if it could be built at the right price, it would be very good for India, too.

And though Indian politics, logistics, and other factors were important, the final justification of Dabhol was really very simple. Mark and her fellow Enron employees had to answer two key questions: Did India really need the power? And, more important, could India pay for it?

The answers were probably, and probably not.

India, with about 1 billion people, has nearly four times as many residents as the United States. Most of them are desperately poor. According to the World Bank, the average per capita income in India is just $450. That means that the vast majority of Indians cannot afford electric appliances or the electricity needed to run them. That fact shows up in the country's electricity consumption figures. Although India has four times as many people as the United States, it consumes about one-eighth as much electricity.

And when Indian residents do consume electricity, they often don't pay for it. When they do pay, it is often at prices that are far below the actual cost of producing the power. In his excellent book on the Dabhol project, *Power Play: A Study of the Enron Project*, Indian journalist Abhay Mehta estimated that in the Indian city of Delhi, about 54 percent of the power consumed in the city is simply stolen. Some of the theft in Delhi and elsewhere is by slum dwellers who illegally tap into nearby power lines, but much of it is committed by affluent Indians whose homes do not have electric meters or by industrial companies eager to cut costs. In other cases, the power is not actually stolen, but residents and companies pay a fixed rate for their power that covers only a fraction of the real cost of electricity they consume. In the state of Maharashtra, where Enron was building Dabhol, Mehta reports that the official estimate of the amount of power that was stolen was 15.7 percent. "However, since nearly 40 per cent of the total generation of electricity in Maharashtra is supplied without any metering, it is quite likely that the real losses are much higher than the official figure," wrote Mehta.[7] "A realistic estimate of Maharashtra's T&D [transmission and distribution] losses would probably be around 30 per cent."

Enron officials knew about the power-theft problem when they were negotiating the contract. "The ones who steal the power are the farmers," said an Enron official who worked in India. "They make up half the electric base in every state. So if you anger them, you don't get elected. The state doesn't do anything about the theft because it would be highly unpopular.... The Maharashtra State Electricity Board officials talked about the theft all the time. It's a weekly story in the newspapers there."

The theft of power provides critically important context for the Dabhol project. Who would be crazy enough to build a power plant in a place where 30 percent (or more) of the plant's output was simply going to disappear?

The World Bank thought Dabhol was a bad project and refused to finance it. On April 30, 1993, the huge lending agency sent a letter to Indian authorities that said the Enron project was "too large for base load operation" in Maharashtra.[8] The agency said coal was a better and lower-cost fuel than LNG for producing electricity in the region and that replacing coal-fired electricity with LNG-fired power from Dabhol "would place a heavy financial burden on" the Maharashtra State Electricity Board. The letter went on to say that "local coal and gas are the preferred choices for base load generation."[9] It added that "implementation of the project would place a significant long-term claim on India's foreign exchange resources."[10]

The World Bank report was bad news for Enron. "I think the Bank has a major role to play, so we would like to have their concurrence," Mark told one reporter. But she was quick to add that Enron didn't have to have the World Bank's approval to proceed with the project. And that's exactly what Enron did. A few weeks after the World Bank report came out, Mark's chief lieutenant at Enron, Joe Sutton, a macho, hard-driving former army officer who wasn't used to being told no, wrote a member of the Maharashtra State Electricity Board, saying that Enron was going to hire a public relations firm that would "manage the media from here on.... The project has solid support from all other agencies in Washington. We'll get there!"

Mark and Sutton pushed on with the project. And on August 26, 1993, Mark faxed a letter to Sharad Pawar, the chief minister in the state of Maharashtra, that showed her blind determination to get the Dabhol deal done. She began by saying that Enron officials had been meeting with officials from Maharashtra and the country's main electric power agency, "to answer their questions about the project. The remaining concern," she said, was a state official named Mr. Beg, who "continues to *hold up project approval based upon the question of demand for power in Maharashtra.* No one from the Ministry of Power in Delhi has given direction to Mr. Beg to move forward on this issue" (emphasis added).[11]

Mark went on to say that it was critical that Indian officials sign a power purchase agreement so that Enron could begin financing the project. She concluded, "We are working on financing arrangements prior [to] project approval but the banks in India and externally are losing their enthusiasm based on lack of progress.... We need to make immediate progress."

Mark didn't know it at the time, but her letter would prove to be *the* key document in the story of Dabhol. In it, she is telling Pawar there was no reason for people like Mr. Beg to delay the project based on silly matters like "demand for power in Maharashtra." More important matters like financing needed to be attended to. The message was clear: Forget about questions about who will use the power and how much they might pay. Never mind about demand questions. Never mind if the power from Dabhol is actually needed. Sign the damn papers and get moving. We'll deal with those other questions later.

By early December 1993, Mark had all the signatures she needed. Enron had a deal for Phase One of the project. The Indian government had signed a contract that required it to pay Enron about $1.3 billion per year, or about $26 billion over the life of the twenty-year contract. It was, Mehta said, one of the largest civilian or military contracts ever signed, anywhere on the globe. And it was surely the largest contract ever signed in India. Over the life of the contract, India would pay Enron and its partners nearly nine times what Dabhol had cost. Furthermore, India was required to pay for any cost increases caused by price hikes associated with the plant's fuel, electricity transmission lines, or plant maintenance.[12]

The final insult of the contract was a stipulation that required India to pay Enron in American dollars, even though the Indian rupee was undergoing regular depreciation. Mark had negotiated a can't-lose contract in which fluctuations in international currency and fuel costs would have no impact on Enron and its partners.

The deal really was too good to be true. And to cement it in place, Enron needed help from an obscure but very powerful federal agency.

14

OPIC: Sweet Subsidies

1994 Every newly elected president of the United States gets to reward his friends with cushy jobs in the federal government. To the victor go the spoils. And of all the spoils in the presidential spoils system, a tiny federal agency known as the Overseas Private Investment Corporation may be the sweetest.

Along with the keys to the White House, the president of the United States acquires the privilege of appointing the board, president, and CEO of the smallest but most powerful investment bank and insurance underwriter on earth. The president has quiet but effective control over an entity that decides which American companies will get billions of dollars in loans and insurance on projects all over the developing world, from Angola to Zaire.

When Bill Clinton became president, he used the cushy jobs at OPIC to reward his allies. The most obvious use of the spoils systems was Clinton's appointment of Ruth Harkin—the wife of one of his best buddies, Iowa senator Tom Harkin—to the presidency of OPIC. He also appointed Lottie Shackelford, a pal from his Arkansas days who was the vice chair of the Democratic National Committee, to OPIC's board. And though the jobs at OPIC are good, they also provide a key political platform from which the president and his appointees can affect foreign investment, and therefore foreign policy. The president also gets lots of new friends with deep pockets in corporate America who covet OPIC's backing. Once those corporations have OPIC's backing, they never have to worry about the agency going bankrupt. That's because OPIC is backed by the full faith and credit of the United States of America.

OPIC is a self-sustaining organization, meaning it doesn't draw operating funds from the U.S. Treasury, but it also has another important quality: It helps presidents raise campaign money. More on that in a moment.

OPIC's sway goes far beyond the ability to lend money or provide insurance. OPIC acts as a financial gatekeeper. If OPIC's Board of Directors approves a project, "it sends a signal to the private-sector financial markets," said former OPIC staffer Jon Sohn. "OPIC approval is like the ultimate seal of approval for other international lenders." Indeed, many international banks and insurers require OPIC's involvement in projects before they will sign on.

The argument in favor of agencies like OPIC is that they stimulate economic activity in both the lending country and the receiving company. In addition, OPIC and similar agencies in Japan, Germany, and elsewhere, with their burly backers, are able to finance or insure deals that commercial banks or insurers couldn't. The arguments for OPIC say the agency serves America's interests. When American companies get projects built overseas, those projects benefit American shareholders. They may also provide jobs and investment opportunities for Americans. Further, if American companies are going to compete for international projects, they are going to have to compete with foreign companies that have ready access to insurance and loans from their governments.

American companies can count on OPIC to keep their secrets. Although the agency is backed by American taxpayers, the agency's board operates under a veil of secrecy. The agency insists that the minutes of OPIC's closed-door board meetings—during which the agency decides which projects and companies get federal backing—are not subject to the Freedom of Information Act. That means that decisions about which projects get funding or insurance are made outside of the earshot of taxpayers, even though taxpayers could be on the hook if the project fails. In fact, the agency has aggressively fought reporters (including this one) who have requested documents the agency used to reach some of its decisions.

When Enron was putting together the financing deal on the Dabhol plant in India, it contacted OPIC first. That wasn't the first time Enron called on OPIC for help. The company's relationship with the agency began in 1989, when it got about $56 million in loans and insurance for a chemical plant in Argentina.[1] In 1992, the agency provided Enron with $74 million in insurance on a new power plant in Guatemala. In 1993, the company got $69 million in insurance and $50 million in financing for a power plant in the Philippines.[2] But those deals were miniscule in comparison to what Enron needed to make Dabhol work.

The project was so big that Enron probably couldn't have gone anywhere else to get the funding and insurance it needed. An Enron official who helped create the financing package for the project said OPIC's political risk insurance was particularly critical because "it's either far more expensive in the commercial insurance market or it's just not available." Furthermore, said the official, Enron's president, Rich Kinder, "had a formal policy: We needed political risk insurance for all of our equity investments." But Enron couldn't go to the World Bank for help on Dabhol. The World Bank had already said Dabhol was a bad idea. So Enron had to rely on OPIC, and it didn't leave empty-handed. OPIC agreed to provide $200 million in insurance, as well as $100 million in loans to Enron for the project.

Few companies got more favorable treatment from OPIC during the Clinton administration than Enron. Between 1993 and 2000, Enron gave almost $2 million to Democratic causes. In return, Enron became OPIC's biggest client, getting more than $2.2 billion worth of loans and insurance on more than a dozen power plants, gas pipelines, and other projects ranging from a risky 136-megawatt power plant in the Gaza Strip to a natural gas liquids extraction plant in Venezuela.[3] In addition, Enron officials went on several of the trade missions that the Clinton administration sponsored—at taxpayer expense—to ferret out new investment opportunities around the globe.

Although OPIC had a close relationship with Enron, one senior Enron finance executive who dealt closely with the agency said he saw no evidence that the company brought political pressure on the agency. "I know we were very cozy with the Clinton administration," he said. "We went on all these trade missions and were heavily involved with them to promote our projects. But at the working level, there was no indication that political contributions were being used to gain access to the dollars."

That may be the case, but in at least one instance, the Clinton administration used OPIC to shake down its clients for campaign contributions. In 1995, OPIC, which is required to make sure the projects it sponsors are not overly deleterious to the environment, canceled $100 million in political risk insurance it held on an environmental nightmare, a mine called Grasberg. The mine, in Indonesian-controlled Papua, the western half of the island of New Guinea, contains the world's richest gold deposit as well as enormous quantities of copper and silver. OPIC canceled its coverage on the mine, owned by New Orleans–based Freeport-McMoRan Copper & Gold, after an environmental assessment of the project found it "continues to pose unreasonable or major environmental, health, or safety hazards with respect to the rivers that are being impacted by the tailings, the surrounding terrestrial ecosystem, and the local inhabitants." The move enraged Freeport's thug-in-chief, a colorful ex–University of Texas football player named Jim Bob Moffett, who quickly went on television in New Orleans to say, "There's been no claim by OPIC that we have an environmental problem." Moffett was lying. But in April 1996, he was somehow able to convince OPIC's president, Ruth Harkin, to reinstate the coverage on the mine.

A few months after Harkin agreed to reinstate the insurance, during a Democratic fund-raiser in Iowa in summer 1996, Harkin told a friend, "Guess what? I just got $100,000 for the Democrats from Jim Bob."

Although Harkin denied there was any quid pro quo involved in the reinstatement of Freeport's insurance, Federal Election Commission records show that Freeport executives, or their wives, made big donations to the Democratic National Committee. On August 26, 1996, Freeport-McMoRan gave the DNC $40,000. On September 6, the wives of Freeport's top executives, Chief Financial Officer Richard Adkerson, Vice Chairman Rene Latiolais, and Chief Investment Officer Charles Goodyear, wrote checks to the DNC totaling $35,000. Four days later, Moffett's wife, Louise, wrote a check to the DNC for $2,500. That's $77,500 of the $100,000 that Harkin bragged about.

Perhaps it's a coincidence that Freeport was giving money to the Democrats after Harkin bragged about it. But that's extremely unlikely. OPIC and Vice President Al Gore—who made the final decision to cancel the insurance—had just embarrassed Freeport in the worst way imaginable. Freeport had been claiming that its mine was an environmental showplace. OPIC and Gore had just exposed Freeport to the entire world. And now the very same company was going to decide all was forgiven and give money to the people who'd just finished embarrassing them? Yeah, sure.

Although Freeport was an important customer, it was small when compared to Enron. And the agency was aggressive in pursuing projects that Enron wanted to develop. "Enron basically owned the place," said Jon Sohn. Nearly every deal Enron proposed "sailed right through, despite any environmental, human rights, or financial concerns. There was a culture of what Enron wants, Enron gets."

The record appears to support that contention. In 1997, two months after George Muñoz, a Clinton appointee, took over at OPIC, he invited Ken Lay to speak at an OPIC employee retreat about "the kind of investment support you will need from international agencies like OPIC." In return, Enron made sure that it did favors for OPIC whenever it could.

In fact, Enron would likely never have become involved in the Gaza

Strip power plant project—undoubtedly one of its riskiest projects, both in terms of capital and security—had it not been encouraged to do so by OPIC. According to two Enron people who worked on the Gaza project, OPIC went to Enron in 1998 or 1999 at a time when the Clinton administration was trying to increase investment in Palestine. One of the Enron executives said the Clinton administration hadn't pressured Enron. Instead, the government presented the problem by saying, "Here's a project we think you can do, would you look at it?" Enron did. And top Enron officials dealt directly with lieutenants of Yasser Arafat, chairman of the Palestinian Authority, to seal the terms of the deal. The $140-million oil-fired power plant got built, thanks largely to $22.5 million in insurance provided by OPIC. But the power plant, which was one-third owned by Enron (the other funds came from a public stock offering and Greek investors), has never generated any power. The ongoing bloody battles between the Israelis and the Palestinians have prevented the plant from starting up.

Enron did other favors for OPIC in the mid-1990s, when the agency's funding was threatened by a group of largely Republican fiscal conservatives who contended that the agency was nothing more than a massive subsidy machine for corporate America. The white-shoe Republicans were joined by a number of environmental groups that charged the agency with funding a myriad of mining and other projects that were ruinous to the environment.

Enron immediately rose to OPIC's defense. "Anyone who has paid OPIC's fees knows that this is not corporate welfare," said Lay. The Enron boss also went on a letter-writing binge, trying to rally support for the agency from everyone he could think of. In a March 12, 1997, letter to then Texas governor George W. Bush, Lay wrote that OPIC is "critical to U.S. developers like Enron who are pursuing international projects in developing countries." He asked that Bush "contact each Member of Congress in your delegation" and tell them why OPIC is "important to your state."

Lay wasn't the only Texas energy Big Shot who saw the value of OPIC's loans and insurance. In 1995, former secretary of defense Dick

Cheney became the chairman and CEO of oil field and construction services giant Halliburton. According to the Center for Public Integrity, in the five years prior to Cheney's arrival at the company, Halliburton had garnered only about $100 million in loans and guarantees from OPIC and a similar government-sponsored agency, the Export-Import Bank.[4] In the five years after his arrival, Halliburton received $1.5 billion worth of assistance from those same two entities.

Lay and Cheney both clearly understood the value for their companies of having their projects backed by the U.S. government. That government backing would play a major role in Enron's final days.

15

A Kinder, Gentler Enron

Throughout the early and mid-1990s, Enron grew steadily. And the egos of the key players grew right along with it. Rebecca Mark was gaining stature in the international electricity business. Jeff Skilling was becoming a force in the trading world. But everyone at Enron knew who really ran the company. It wasn't Ken Lay.

Sure, Lay had the titles of chairman and chief executive officer, but the real management of Enron was done by Rich Kinder, the guy who made sure the mundane stuff was taken care of. By early 1996, Kinder was at the height of his power. And he demonstrated that power every Monday morning. The meetings were held in the board room on the fiftieth floor of the Enron building. Every unit leader at Enron, from pipelines to power plants, was expected to show up, ready for grilling. Ken Lay was usually there, but it was Kinder's meeting. As the president and chief operating officer of Enron, Kinder (pronounced KINN-der) was the boss. And he wasn't shy about reminding everyone in attendance of that fact. He demanded that every business unit leader be ready with all the numbers, plans, and strategies for their areas of responsibility.

"Every Monday, I knew exactly how much money my pipeline had made so far that year and had estimates in hand for what it would produce during the rest of the year," said one top executive who worked under Kinder. And although Kinder was a lawyer by training, not an accountant, he was a master moneyman. Everyone who worked with Kinder at Enron marveled at his ability to memorize details of contracts and prices, even though the deals might have been made many years earlier. His recall for facts and figures was legendary. "You could give him a budget number and explain where it came from and he'd say 'that's not what you told me last year.' And then he'd go to his desk and retrieve the year-earlier budget and prove you wrong. It was amazing," said one lawyer who worked under Kinder. Despite all of the reports and information Kinder had to track, he only kept two file-cabinet drawers filled with important data. The rest of the numbers he kept in his head.

When presented with proposals, Kinder would quickly zero in on the deal's weakest point and demand an explanation. "Rich didn't care if you had a great story. He wanted to know several things: How do you plan to make money? How do you secure your risk? And how do you assure your cash flow? It's a simple focus, but it can encompass a lot of things. You could give him a 500-page deal and he would pick out the one number you can't explain," recalled a finance executive who worked at Enron. "He was impossible to bullshit. A lot of people at Enron would lie about their numbers. And at that point, Rich would eat them for lunch."

Kinder had plenty of big snacks during his tenure as president and COO of Enron, which lasted from 1990 to 1996. One former employee called him "Doctor Discipline." That disciplined approach was just what Enron needed. Low natural gas prices and high debt were stifling Enron's growth. But Kinder remained focused on reducing debt and maintaining the company's credit rating. During his first three years as president, he paid off nearly $1 billion of the company's loans.

On any expenditure, Kinder acted "like the money was coming out of his own personal checkbook," said Alberto Gude, a former vice president of information systems who worked with both Kinder and Jeff Skilling.

ENRON CASH FLOW ON QUARTER-BY-QUARTER BASIS, 1Q1997 TO 3Q2001

All figures are from Enron Corp. SEC filings

(All figures are in $ millions)

Every 4Q Enron came up with billions in free operating cash flow to cover up their failing businesses.

	1q97	2q97	3q97	4q97	1q98	2q98	3q98	4q98	1q99	2q99	3q99	4q99
Cash Flow from Operating Activities	–142	–523	–588	501	50	–251	–29	1,640	–660	–38	–43	1,228
Revenues				20,273				31,260				40,112

	1q00	2q00	3q00	4q00	1q01	2q01	3q01
Cash Flow from Operating Activities	–457	–547	127	4,779	–464	–1,337	–753
Revenues				100,789	50,129	100,189	138,718

Kinder's obsessions were cash and cash flow. Bonuses for business unit leaders were often tied to their ability to meet cash flow projections, and each unit was given earnings targets and cash flow targets. In addition to his fiscal conservatism, Kinder was clearly focused on Enron's business model and made sure the company didn't stray too far away from the businesses—pipelines, exploration, and production and gas processing—that it knew and knew to be profitable. With Kinder, "it wasn't enough to just get into a new business, you had to have a strategy that was going to be a natural outgrowth of your existing business. He was a detail person. He wanted to know if there were growth areas, it had to be logical, thought out and have a good reason behind it," said Mike Moran, an attorney who worked at Enron for nearly three decades. Moran and others recalled that Kinder used an oft-repeated line whenever Enron managers would get too cocky or assume that their projects were bound to succeed. "He'd say, 'Let's not start smoking our own dope.'"

In addition to his strength in managing numbers and businesses, Kinder was loyal to people inside Enron. He maintained a collegial atmosphere within the company and went out of his way to show respect for employees. One pilot who spent more than two decades working for Enron said that after his wife died, Kinder "came to my rescue. He flew my family home from Nebraska. He wrote me a personal letter. He took me under his wing. I have a great deal of respect for Rich Kinder."

His personality and management strengths made him the perfect match for Ken Lay. Kinder was "Mr. Inside." Lay was "Mr. Outside." The combination suited both of them just fine. While Lay gave speeches and posed for pictures, Kinder ran the company. He mastered the details of every business, from trading to natural gas liquids, and his knowledge fostered trust inside and outside the company. He handled all the company's negotiations with the rating agencies, the bankers, and Wall Street analysts. "If you get in a room with him, you are really attracted to him," said one Wall Street analyst who has known Kinder for several years. "He knows everybody in Houston and every energy player in the country."

A compact, bullet-shaped man with a mop of thick gray hair who talks in rapid-fire sentences, Kinder has made his mark in the business world by focusing, hawklike, on cash and expenses. One key way Kinder kept a lid on expenses at Enron was by being careful about adding new employees. In 1990, Enron had profits of just over $200 million and almost 7,000 employees. By the end of 1996, Enron's profits had nearly tripled, but the employee count had risen only slightly, to 7,500.[1]

Kinder's successor, Jeff Skilling, wouldn't be nearly so careful.

Ken Lay and Rich Kinder reportedly met while attending the University of Missouri in the early 1960s. After Lay graduated, he went to work in the oil business. Kinder, who got his law degree from Missouri, reportedly began practicing law in that state. In 1980, Kinder got hired at Florida Gas, according to sources, with help from Ken Lay. Kinder worked on a number of issues at Florida Gas. The two separated when Lay went to Transco. But when Lay got to HNG, one of his first acquisitions was the purchase of Florida Gas, a move that brought Kinder and Lay back together.

After the 1985 merger with Internorth, Kinder began making himself increasingly indispensable. Shortly after the merger, he became general counsel and chief of staff. In late 1988, he was named vice chairman of the Board of Directors. Enron's press release announcing the promotion said Kinder's prior jobs included "finance and accounting, law, administration, human resources, management information systems, corporate development and corporate affairs," adding that "he will retain these responsibilities in his new post."

Given all Kinder's duties, it was becoming clear that Enron's president and chief operating officer, Mick Seidl, didn't have much to do. "Seidl was a nice guy but he was never engaged to the degree Kinder was," said one executive who worked under both men. Another commented that Seidl was simply "too nice" to be in a position where he had to make tough business decisions. Furthermore, there was a feeling that someone at Enron had to take the fall for the trading disaster in

Valhalla. Lou Borget's division in Valhalla was Seidl's responsibility. The trading fiasco had happened on Seidl's watch, and that meant he was responsible.

So in early 1989, Seidl left Enron and took a job working for Houston's nastiest corporate raider, Charles Hurwitz, the boss of Maxxam. And in October 1990, Kinder officially took Seidl's old job.

Over the next half decade, Enron grew steadily. Revenues climbed every year, from $5.3 billion in 1990 to $5.7 billion in 1991. By 1996, they reached almost $13.3 billion. Profits rose, too, in near lockstep revenues. In 1990, net income was $202 million. The next year it was $232 million, then $306 million, $333 million, $438 million, $520 million, and finally in 1996, $584 million. Kinder achieved those milestones by holding each business unit to exacting standards. If a pipeline president said he would achieve 17-percent profit growth, Kinder demanded that target be met. And it almost always was. One investment banker recalled a meeting in which an analyst asked whether Enron would meet its profit projects for the quarter. Kinder reportedly replied, "Blood will run in the streets of Houston before we miss our numbers."

Although Kinder was experienced and hard-driving, he also had a good management team. By 1992, the executives running the organization were top-notch. Enron's cash cow, the pipelines, was run by Ron Burns, a longtime pipeliner who had come to Enron in the InterNorth merger. The booming gas services business was run by Skilling. Moderating Skilling's aggressive tendencies was John Esslinger, a longtime energy industry man who excelled at sales and relationship building with customers. The natural gas liquids business was run by Mike Muckleroy. The exploration and production business known as Enron Oil and Gas (which Skilling would later get rid of altogether) was headed by Forrest Hoglund, another longtime energy man whom Ken Lay had lured to Enron from USX a few years earlier. The company's new electric power generation business was led by a group that included Thomas White, a former army brigadier general, who later became secretary of the army under George W. Bush. The company's international operations were being handled by Bob Kelly and John

Wing, who were working on foreign power deals like the Teesside project in England.

By the early 1990s, things could scarcely have worked better for Kinder. All of the executives knew their roles and they worked well, according to executives who worked on that team. While Kinder drove the numbers side, Lay acted as the inspirational leader. He "had the ability to take prima donnas and get them to hover around a central theme," one executive from that group recalled. "Without Ken, they would have exploded into a million different directions." While Lay inspired the troops, Kinder kept the egos—and the budgets—in balance.

Under Kinder, Enron launched a number of successful businesses and projects. The electric power businesses showed phenomenal growth under Kinder. The pipelines showed moderate but steady growth and provided reliable cash. The gas and electric power trading business—headed by Jeff Skilling—enjoyed frenetic expansion and good profitability in their early days. Kinder's slow-but-steady approach was successful, but he had his foibles. In fact, he repeated one of Ken Lay's mistakes: He began sleeping with the hired help.

Sometime in the early or mid-1990s, Kinder began having an affair with Ken Lay's executive assistant, Nancy McNeil. Although several top executives claimed they were surprised when they learned about the Kinder-McNeil affair, the relationship was well known among the company's secretaries. Sources close to the matter say that McNeil was divorced when the affair began. It appears Kinder was not.

McNeil was, according to one executive, "a very ambitious woman." And as Ken Lay's secretary, she had contacts all over Houston. In addition, she was smart and knew how to use her power within Enron.

In summer 1996, one source said, Ken Lay found out about the Kinder-McNeil affair and the romance became a problem. So McNeil, who had been working on the fiftieth floor outside Lay's office (Kinder's office was down the hall), was moved to a different floor, away from Kinder and Lay. "They made up a bunch of excuses" about why McNeil was moved upstairs, one source close to the matter remembered. "But everybody knew it was because she was sleeping with Rich." One secretary recalled that shortly after Kinder divorced his wife, Anne, he told several people in a staff meeting that he and McNeil were "going to try dating." The joke among the women at Enron, she said, was that the two "might as well 'try dating.' They've tried everything else."

Several executives who worked with the two men says the news of the Kinder-McNeil affair immediately caused a rift between Kinder and Lay. Lay became more suspicious of Kinder and began wondering what McNeil had told him about Lay's own dealings, appointments, and decisions. The affair "created a wedge between them," said one source. And although Lay and Kinder were able to maintain cordial relations, there "wasn't much of a relationship between them after that." Another executive said that shortly before the Kinder-McNeil affair was acknowledged, Lay asked Kinder whether he was sleeping with McNeil. Kinder reportedly denied having an affair with McNeil. "After that, Ken lost any trust in Rich, and that meant that Rich wasn't going to be CEO."

The affair with McNeil undoubtedly hastened Kinder's departure from Enron. Staying at Enron while continuing his affair with McNeil didn't appear to be an option. The awkwardness of any social gathering with the other executives would have been too much for any of them to handle. In addition, the board and Lay were in discussions about Lay's future. Sources close to Lay and Kinder say that in 1992, the two men agreed that Kinder would ascend to the CEO job in five years. Under the agreement, Lay would stay on as chairman of the company, but Kinder would be in control of all real decisionmaking at Enron. But by late 1996, Lay and the board reneged on that deal. Lay would stay on as CEO for another five years.

In late 1996, when told about the decision, Kinder accepted it quickly and tendered his resignation. He told another Enron executive that he had no choice. "If you aren't the lead dog, the scenery never changes," said Kinder. While he didn't become the lead dog, Enron threw him some meaty bones, including $109,472 in vacation pay, $1.1

million in severance, $3.8 million in loan forgiveness, and $8,500 worth of club memberships. He also had over $30 million in stock options. He and McNeil, who quit her job at Enron in early 1997, married a short time after he left the company.

Giving Kinder his walking papers would prove to be the single worst decision Ken Lay made in his career. Lay didn't lose one skilled executive. He lost two. By letting Kinder leave, he lost the person who may have been the best operations man in the entire energy business. In addition, he was forced to move Jeff Skilling out of the leadership role he had in Enron's trading group. Skilling loved handling trading and financial maneuvers. Now, with Kinder leaving, Lay had to promote Skilling to Kinder's spot. There wasn't anybody else to do the job. All the other top executives from the Houston Natural Gas and InterNorth team had left, either to take better offers or because they'd gotten sick of Skilling. Also, as one former Enron executive put it, Skilling was "three-for-three. The Gas Bank had worked. The gas trading business had worked. And electricity trading had worked."

Kinder's management and financial prowess had suited Lay perfectly. Lay no longer cared about handling day-to-day issues at Enron. Lay didn't want to walk the floors of the Enron building, talking to run-of-the-mill employees about their concerns, their workloads. Dinner with the Bushes, golf with Bill Clinton, flying to Europe for a meeting or two, that was the kind of management work that suited Ken Lay. He was, said one Enron employee, "the imperial chairman." With Kinder doing all the heavy lifting, Lay indulged himself in politics and privilege. And he assumed that he could continue his imperial act with Jeff Skilling at the helm. Skilling would run the company and Lay would do the vision thing, make speeches, and strut.

It was a fatal miscalculation. "Kinder was aggressive, but in a disciplined way," said Mike Moran. "Once Kinder left, there wasn't any attention given to the day-to-day activities of the businesses. There wasn't the discipline associated with the aggressiveness. It became unbridled aggression."

16
The Reign of Skilling

1997 As soon as Jeff Skilling moved onto the fiftieth floor, he began a hiring binge that didn't stop until the company went bankrupt. But give him credit: He attracted the best and the brightest.

Harvard, West Point, Rice, University of Chicago—every prestigious school in the country began feeding their best MBAs, engineers, and math wonks to Enron. At the same time, Skilling began raiding Wall Street, stealing traders, investment bankers, information technology whiz kids, programmers, and every other skill set that Enron needed. Skilling even changed the titles within the company to make them sound more like the ones at Wall Street firms. Enron didn't have account executives, it had analysts, associates, directors, and best of all, managing directors. A key part of Skilling's overhaul was called the associate and analyst program. Enron recruiters would go to the best schools and offer jobs to the best students. The new hires would enter Enron as midlevel employees and begin rotations in different areas of the company, learning how to structure complicated deals, obtain financing, and most important, absorb the Enron way of doing things. After a series of six-month-long rotations in different areas, the associates and analysts would then be left to find a home within the company. If they couldn't find a spot, they were out.

Most of the analysts and associates did find a home at Enron, and once inside the polished chrome and glass doors, the best and the brightest talked fast, worked insanely long hours, traveled first class, made lots of money, and did all those things among their peers. Every one of them was smart, motivated, and ready to get ahead. Enron provided every amenity to keep them happy—and working. The Enron building had a health club with every imaginable contraption; a concierge, who, for a fee, would handle errands and personal matters; a massage service; a credit union; and, of course, a Starbucks to keep everyone caffeinated.

The health insurance, pension, and other benefits were good, the environment relentlessly competitive. Rotations in good jobs, in areas where real money could be made, like trading and project development, were highly coveted. But there were plenty of other opportunities, particularly working overseas. Want to work in the London office? Go ahead. Be sure to fly in first class.

The competition began in the hiring process. Enron wanted young aggressive people who were ready to take over right away and make deals and decisions. People who needed lots of hand-holding belonged at Exxon or Texaco, or the other old-school energy companies. Enron wanted people who were in a hurry. And that attitude prevailed during what the company called "Super Saturdays," when Enron would interview prospective candidates. Every recruit would sit through eight consecutive fifty-minute-long interviews during which they were scored from 1 to 5 on such factors as intelligence, analytical skill, and aggressiveness. The best and brightest of that group were offered starting salaries of $60,000 to $100,000. Fat bonuses could increase those figures by 30 percent or more.

Enron's caste system was clearly delineated from the beginning. One man, who had a master's in economics from the University of Oklahoma, wanted to get into the analyst and associate program but was instead placed in the risk management group, where he evaluated projects being pushed by peers who were likely to make two to ten times more money than he was making if they could get their projects approved. "I didn't go to the right school," he said. "I was told OU wasn't worthy of the program. The people who'd gone to the Ivy League schools or the big-name schools were paid more and given better jobs." And it was not uncommon for the new hires to remind their coworkers that they'd gone to Harvard or another top-flight school. The OU graduate remembered that shortly after he was hired at Enron, a group of a dozen or so people were introducing themselves to each other. During those introductions, one very proud young woman volunteered, "I went to Thunderbird [the American Graduate School of International Management, in Glendale, Arizona]," she said, "the best international business school in the country."

The fleet of newly hired hotshots were never short of confidence or the belief that they were working at the best, smartest, fastest-moving company in the world. One longtime Enron employee (who held a Ph.D. from the University of Maryland) said, "There's no question that Enron people arrogantly thought they were smarter than everybody else. There's no excuse for that. But they *were* smarter than everybody else."

In addition to being smarter, Skilling's new crowd was far younger than the old Enron culture. Enron "went from being a regulated utility where nearly all the vice presidents were in their forties and fifties to a company that was dominated by a huge number of younger, affluent, well-educated traders and analysts and managers," said George Strong, a lobbyist who worked for Enron for more than two decades. "It was a different ball game."

With the crowd of twenty- and thirty-somethings came a cocksure arrogance that no matter how complex the problem—whether it was how to address price fluctuations in world paper markets or deal with currency risks on a power plant in China—Enron employees could handle it. It was a belief that was fostered by the training they got in business school, where case studies are a major component of the curriculum. Teams of students are often given a set of problems facing a certain company and are told to come back in a few days with a report identifying the solutions. That approach, said one former Enron employee, "trains people to believe everything they need to know can be boiled down into four pages and that all problems can be solved by a few smart people overnight. That's not the real world. In business, there are more wrong answers than right answers."

Right or wrong, the legions of newly hired hotshots believed they held the keys to the kingdom. They were going to get rich and, in the process, teach the rest of the world a few lessons. It was an attitude that perfectly reflected that of Jeff Skilling and his cronies, who wanted Enron to focus on deals and trading. By late 1998, Skilling's inner circle consisted almost entirely of people who loved the trading business: people like Lou Pai and Kevin Hannon, who helped set up the original trading operation in the gas business, and Ken Rice and Andy Fastow, who had been working with Skilling for many years. They had been trained to think, and act, like traders. And anyone who wanted to rise to the top at Enron had to mimic their outlook.

It was an outlook that clashed with the old Enron, where loyalty—and friends—mattered.

Skilling's trader-dominated culture clashed violently with the one established by his predecessor. Under Rich Kinder, Enron fostered a culture that respected, and tried to build, relationships with customers.

"You had the old pipeliners and you had the New York–type financial traders. They were at the opposite ends of the spectrum," remarked one executive who worked with Skilling for much of the 1990s. After Kinder left, all the old pipeline people were viewed as dinosaurs. It didn't matter to the Skilling people that the pipelines always made money—that is, real cash—their business was old, stodgy, and really not worth talking about. The pipelines and the people who worked on them became the ugly stepchildren at Enron.

"Nothing mattered to the New York traders except the deal," said the executive. When Enron was controlled by pipeline guys like Kinder, "it was a relationship business and you did favors for friends. Once Skilling changed Enron into a trading company, relationships counted for zero. Zip. Nada. Nothing. It's 'show me the money.' It's the difference between doing a deal over lunch or over the telephone."

Another longtime Enron executive who left the company in the mid-1990s said, "Skilling never gave a damn about customers' feelings. He said, 'They'll do it if the price is right.'" The source also recalled Skilling saying, "'Relationships don't matter. Trust doesn't matter.' I think he honestly felt that."

Several executives at Enron worried that the trade-first-make-friends-later attitude would hurt the company over the long term. "My idea was, you never screwed somebody on a deal. Why? Because they would always spend the rest of their lives trying to get you back," said one of Skilling's former coworkers. "Under the Skilling culture, a deal was a deal. If I screw you, too bad. Shame on you. The problem is you run out of people to do business with after a while because there are only so many people in the market."

The lingo even changed. Under Kinder, Enron had "customers." Under Skilling, Enron had "counterparties." As the lingo changed, so did old-fashioned ideas like loyalty. Under Kinder, Enron had a more family-based culture in which workers believed their contributions were valued. In return, they were loyal, not just to Kinder and Ken Lay, but to Enron and to each other. As one executive who worked under Kinder said, "When push comes to shove, you can't buy loyalty, you have to instill it in people."

But with Jeff Skilling at the helm, loyalty became a commodity that was bought and sold just like gas, oil, and electricity. He even bragged about it. On one occasion, Skilling told a top Enron executive, Terry Thorn, the company's head of governmental affairs, "I've thought about this a lot, and all that matters is money. You buy loyalty with money. Don't ever forget that."

Given his attitude toward loyalty, it's not surprising that Skilling liked being around traders. "Traders are mercenaries. Their job is to kill. And mercenaries, by definition, don't have any loyalty," said Dan

Ryser, who worked at Enron in the early 1990s before going to work for Enron's hometown rival in the gas business, Dynegy Inc. "With traders, it's rape, pillage, and plunder all the time. They don't care about the shareholders or the business strategy or the long-term interests of the company."

That kind of mindset was pervasive among Enron's traders and deal makers. They didn't want to know about complex issues, they wanted to establish the prices needed to make a deal work. Once those prices were obtained, they wanted to do the deal right away, because if they did the deal—good or bad—their bonus would almost certainly be bigger because of it. That mercenary culture began to pervade everything at Enron. Project developers would refuse to share the details of their projects, lest another developer steal the project—and the bonus that went with it.

The culture at Enron had shifted, and it had shifted in the exact way that Jeff Skilling wanted. And nothing personified the company's testosterone-and-espresso-steeped culture better than the Performance Review Committee.

17

"A Pit of Vipers"

The meeting was over before it had a chance to begin. The executives in the room were all managing directors, which in Enron parlance meant they were above the vice presidents and just below officer level. They were meeting in a crowded conference room in the Enron building to rank all of the executives who worked just below them, a group that included several dozen people.

Before the first name had even been brought up, Enron's chief financial officer, Andrew Fastow, declared, "I'm not going to vote for any employee that I don't know." Even by the cutthroat standards of Enron, Fastow's move was so in-your-face that every managing director in the room was immediately enraged.

"You heard this big 'Oh, man'-kind-of-groan from everybody in the room because we knew that it was basically blackmail," said a source who attended the mid-1999 meeting. Fastow "was saying, 'I'll shut the whole thing down until you go my way.'"

Enron's Performance Review Committee, evil as it was, depended on a modicum of civility and collegiality among the people in the process. Each person doing the ranking had to be willing to barter and trade. If one person knew an employee and thought he or she was a good worker, then the person would vouch for the employee. And if the others didn't know the person, they had to be willing to trust their peer, accept the assessment, rank the employee, and move on. Without that, the PRC simply couldn't work. But someone had apparently irritated Fastow that morning. He was mad. And he was adamant. "I'm not voting for anyone I don't know," he repeated.

"The meeting pretty much ended right then," said the source. "He was saying, 'I don't trust you or believe you, your word is nothing to me.' We couldn't do anything after that. Either Fastow had to cool off, or we had to have a different group do the ranking."

Welcome to the wacky world of the PRC, which was also known by its more colorful name of "rank and yank" or by another moniker, "bag 'em and tag 'em." The system was simple: The company's managers had to rank every person in their business unit on a scale of 1 to 5.

Get a 1 and you're Madonna with an attitude. Get a 5 and you're mopping the floor at McDonald's.

First implemented at Enron during the early 1990s, the PRC had the desired effect when it was used on a small scale. Skilling's business unit, Enron Gas Services, instituted the PRC to help get rid of some of the employees left over from the HNG-InterNorth merger. Many of those employees, once they rose to a certain level, knew that they'd probably never get another meaningful raise, but they'd also probably never get fired, either. The PRC changed that. Hundreds of people who had become part of Enron during the merger were suddenly facing a choice: Perform better or get a new job. "At the time, it was a great tool," a source who worked closely with Skilling recalled. "When we started the ranking process, we were trying to weed out the lower 5 or 6 percent of the company. We had some old dinosaurs, and we had some younger people who needed incentives."

In 1997, when Skilling was promoted to president and chief operating officer, the PRC was gradually instituted companywide. The PRC undoubtedly helped Enron get rid of underperforming employees and create a more aggressive culture. It also spawned a gangrene-like rot that allowed Enron to cannibalize itself.

The PRC created a highly politicized work environment in which, as one employee recalls, "It didn't matter how good you were. It only mattered who you knew." Another employee called it an "institutionalized popularity contest." Another said that with the PRC, every employee "had to find a 'daddy,'" that is, someone to protect them throughout the process. "Everybody who was smart realized that doing a good job was just the beginning. If you went home without working the political system at Enron, you were toast. You had to find a daddy to take care of you. And that person needed to be connected."

The process also created a Sisyphean task for Enron's managers, who had to comb through the mountains of paper generated by the PRC every year. Every employee had to be graded—on paper—by several peers. And each of those peers had to be graded—on paper—by his or her peers. All of those assessments were then handed to the next-higher level of managers, who were themselves being graded—on paper—by their peers. The assessment process required each employee to grade peers on such qualities as leadership, technical ability, and revenue generation. The assessments wasted reams of paper, which all had to be passed among various departments and managers. "I'd get swamped with surveys," said one former executive. "I had probably forty direct reports, so I'm reading 400 different surveys. The PRC would take two months of my time. I couldn't see the cost benefit of the whole process. We had the TV sets in the building blaring out all this propaganda on the four values. [Enron's four values were included in the acronym RICE: Respect, Integrity, Communication, and Excellence.] It was Orwellian. You start to be cynical." The PRC system, he said, "just bred more and more cynicism."

Finally, and perhaps most important, the PRC perverted Enron's internal risk management systems, the processes that were supposed to keep Enron from getting into lousy deals. The corruption of that process would cost Enron millions—perhaps even billions—of dollars.

Despite widespread hatred of the system inside Enron's headquarters, Skilling thought it was great. He told one reporter, "The performance evaluation was the most important thing for forging a new strategy and culture at Enron—it is the glue that holds the company together."[1]

Skilling couldn't have been more wrong. The PRC wasn't glue. It was poison.

The PRC created a culture within Enron that replaced cooperation with competition. "Have you ever seen a team win that wasn't a team?" asks one former Enron employee. "If you have a baseball team or a basketball team with a bunch of superstars on it, they don't win. But if you get a bunch of role players, who understand their jobs, they win championships." The problem with the PRC, said the employee, was that it "didn't reward the grinders." In his opinion, every company needs people who do the thankless jobs, the unglamorous jobs, like sending out invoices, delivering mail, handling payroll. Enron needed those people, too, but instead of letting them do their jobs to the best of their ability, those people were put through the PRC. The result was that many people who were in the service part of Enron simply began creating work to make themselves look better.

Among managers, said one former member of the company's Executive Committee, the PRC became "a great way to stifle dissent and create your own power base. It was used to reward your friends and punish people that weren't."

Although the process was designed to advance the careers of top performers and punish the low performers, it quickly mutated into a numbers game. Every group within Enron had a limited pool of dollars available for salaries and bonuses. The people who were rated 1's and 2's were golden. "It was all based on how much money you were able to make," said one source. With millions of dollars at stake in each annual rating, the fights over individual rankings became intense. "It was a pit of vipers. You can't believe how brutal that process could be. You had people attacking other people's integrity, morality, and values. It wasn't about supporting up, it was about tearing down."

Natural gas or electricity traders who'd booked contracts that were losing tens of millions of dollars might get high rankings because they'd done well in the trading business the year before. Size of trades or deals mattered more than if the deals were good. And though trades and deals were good, trump cards counted. And everyone knew that the best trump card, the one that always worked, was having a champion who was either close to Skilling or close to someone in Skilling's mafia. That card, that personal protector, meant money at PRC time. That money then translated into power and prestige.

The system had few benefits for many of the rank-and-file personnel, including the administrative assistants, clerks, and others who made sure the copy machines worked, the phones were turned on, and everybody had PostIt notes and pens in their drawers. "The highest bonus an assistant could get was $3,000 per year. It didn't matter what you did," said Sherri Saunders, the longtime Enron employee I met at the job fair at Enron Field. "The incident that sticks in my mind was this one guy who was a trader, he was pitching this huge fit because his bonus was only $35,000."

Perhaps most insidious, the PRC gave Enron's Masters of the Universe a baseball bat they could use to intimidate the people who might stop one of their bad deals—and therefore limit their bonuses.

After the disaster of the J-Block contracts that came with the Teesside power plant project, Jeff Skilling created a system known as Risk Assessment and Control, or RAC. The RAC group was staffed with math-savvy people who were experts at risk management and price curve analysis. They would look at issues like currency devaluation, interest rate projections, commodity price projections, and other elements that might factor into a given deal. The group would generate mathematical models in an effort to validate the projections being made on deals proposed by Enron's battalions of young guns. But rather than being viewed as a corporate asset that should be carefully tended and given significant political power in order to prevent lousy deals, the RAC began to be seen as just another hurdle that the traders and deal makers had to surmount. Remember, everyone was in a hurry. The faster a deal maker could get a deal approved, the sooner that deal maker could get a big bonus, buy the BMW, and go skiing in the Alps. Therefore, speed was essential to every dealmaker and the RAC was only capable of gumming up projects, not accelerating them.

"No one ever wanted to stand in front of a deal because you could get killed in the PRC," recalled one source who spent several years in the RAC. People who questioned deals "would get attacked by the business units because they weren't as cooperative on a deal as the developers wanted." In addition, members of the RAC had to fear retribution if they ever wanted to work in other parts of Enron after leaving RAC. "You'd have a hard time finding another rotation if you were too hard on certain deals."

Said another member of RAC, "We did our job. We did it well. But it's like making a meal, and you throw it in the garbage. It was a façade for Skilling to point to when he wanted to impress the rating agencies and the banks and outside investors. In the end, the RAC was destined to fail because the traders' bonus incentives ran counter to what we were trying to do."

The PRC became an ongoing, in-house inquisition, one that perverted the company's morals, its morale, and its ability to kill badly conceived deals. It was, one employee stated, "like everything else at Enron. It started out as a good thing and then it got corrupted." The PRC gave the company's traders and deal makers a method by which they could assure themselves of hefty paydays. They could engineer deals that looked great from a mark-to-market accounting standpoint but produced no cash revenue.

But, of course, those same employees expected their paychecks to be paid in cash. And that disconnect between the need for cash and the mirage of mark-to-market accounting was starting to have an effect. By the end of 1997, Skilling's first year as COO, Enron's cash position was wretched—and it was going to get worse.

18

Cash Flow Problems, Part 1

1997

When it came to strategy and starting businesses, Jeff Skilling was a genius. When it came to understanding the importance of cash, he was dumber than a box of hammers.

Cash is—and always will be—king. Unless a company can generate cash, it cannot survive. As one accounting expert put it, "cash is to a business what blood is to the human body." A company that generates plenty of cash can operate for years without worrying about its ability to pay its debts and its workers or expand its operations. That's why a company like Berkshire Hathaway, the conglomerate created by Warren Buffett, has been so successful: Buffett buys companies that generate lots of cash that he then uses to buy other companies. He once said Berkshire reminded him of "Mickey Mouse as the Sorcerer's Apprentice in *Fantasia*. His problem was floods of water. Ours is cash."

Skilling never had anything like a flood of cash. Instead, his entire tenure was marked by a cash drought.

Rich Kinder understood the value of cash and continually demanded that his managers meet cash flow targets as well as profit projections. He understood that Enron could expand only as fast as its cash flow allowed. And throughout his tenure, he made sure that the amount of cash Enron spent on new projects was about equal to the amount of cash it earned from its operations. That makes perfect sense. If a company invests more in its operations than it earns, it has to borrow money. Companies can borrow money, but whatever they borrow must be repaid *in cash,* and that cash has to come, eventually, from the company's business or it will fail.

Information about a company's cash position is published on a quarterly basis in its cash flow statement. The statement divides cash into three categories. The first category, cash derived from (or used in) operations, is the most important one. It shows whether a company is making or losing money on its core business. The second section is the amount of cash used in investing activities. This includes capital expenditures for new trucks, plants, or other fixed assets. The last section is the amount of cash the company obtained from financing, that is, how much money the company borrowed—or paid back—to finance its ongoing operations.

Kinder was a tightwad. In his seven years as president of Enron, Kinder added very little long-term debt to the company's balance sheet. During that same time period, Enron's profits totaled $2.6 billion. In 1996, Kinder's last year at the company, Enron took in just over $1 billion in cash from its operations, and its long-term debt totaled $3.3 billion.

"Kinder made everybody accountable for every penny," said one senior finance person, but "when Skilling came in, there were no budgets."

In 1997, his first year as COO, Skilling nearly doubled capital expenditures, the expenses companies make to buy more hard assets like factories and trucks, to $1.4 billion. Enron's long-term debt nearly doubled, to $6.25 billion. Along with the increased borrowing came higher interest expenses. In 1997, Enron's interest expenses jumped by 44 percent, from $290 million in 1996 to $420 million. And by 2000, interest expenses would nearly double again, reaching $834 million.

Where was Skilling spending the money? *Everywhere.*

In 1997, Skilling's gas and power trading group, Enron Capital and Trade, spent about $2 million *on flowers,* according to an auditor who worked for the division. "Oh yeah, we had secretaries sending their bosses flowers, bosses sending their secretaries flowers. For a while, we were the biggest customer for about five florists all over Houston," said the auditor. "We found out some secretaries were sending flowers to their friends so the secretaries could get the pretty vases the flowers came in."

Flowers, first-class airfare, first-class hotels, limousines, new computers, new Palm Pilots, new desks—Enron employees began to expect the best of everything, all the time. And there were salaries, lots of salaries. When Kinder left Enron at the end of 1996, the company had 7,500 employees. By the end of 1997, it had over 15,000. The pattern held. By the end of 1999, there were 17,900 employees; by the end of 2000, 20,600. And every one of them had to be paid in cash.

Every time one of the company's traders booked a big power plant deal or gas trade, the company used mark-to-market accounting to book a huge profit for Enron. But all of that "profit" was not cash, and given the incentives for the trader to inflate the value of a given deal, it might not ever become cash. Meanwhile, the trader who'd done the deal got his bonus paid in cash. In addition, the phone, the computer, the desk, the secretaries, the Internet access, and the paper clips—all of the expenses that came with the trader—had to be paid with cash. Yet Skilling told one internal auditor that he did not believe that revenue generators like his beloved traders should ever have to see their expense reports. Predictably, that attitude opened the floodgates. "The excess was obscene. We were just pissing money away." The auditor said that Skilling "absolutely refused to accept the idea of cost accounting. So he had no way to measure the profitability of the trading business. No other Wall Street firm does that. If you don't look at expenses versus revenues, you can't ever figure out what your profits are."

A senior finance executive at Enron who worked closely with Skilling said the former McKinsey consultant knew cash flow was a problem. "But he kept the checkbook open. Skilling thought that you could always find financial ways to come up with cash, and it didn't include managing spending and watching your checkbook."

An executive who worked in Enron's international business vividly recalled Skilling berating Enron's chief accounting officer, Rick Causey, after Causey expressed his worry about the company's cash situation. Skilling responded, "Cash doesn't matter. All that matters is earnings."

One of the easiest ways Skilling could have economized was on construction inside the Enron building. Designed from the ground up by architects and space planners working for Enron, the oval building at 1400 Smith was built for maximum utility. Every floor had conference rooms in the same location so that personnel coming from other floors wouldn't have to search for the meeting room. Each office, except for a few executive offices on the fiftieth floor, was designed to be a standard size, 15 feet by 15 feet, so that office furniture and standard fixtures would fit. The cubicle areas and interior work spaces for kitchens and copy machines were standard. The idea throughout was utility and low cost. If employees needed to move from one space to another, there would be no additional costs incurred in finding special furniture, fixtures, or support materials.

Under Kinder, internal relocations of personnel and departments were kept to a minimum. If one person was added to a new department down the hall, well then, that person could just get off their butt and walk down the hall to talk with coworkers when needed. That attitude kept construction costs and interruptions to a minimum. "Rich understood that moving people and moving walls costs a lot of money," said Mary Wyatt, the vice president of administration at Enron until late 1998. Under Kinder, the cost of construction inside Enron's headquarters was always less than $1 million per year.

When Skilling replaced Kinder, personnel shuffling and construction inside the building went bonkers. Wyatt said Skilling's people demanded that their offices be enlarged, that walls be moved and other expensive modifications made. "Between 1997 and the end of 1998, we had between $5 million and $7 million worth of work underway at any one time," says Wyatt.

And while all of the flowers, salaries, bonuses, perks, and construction contributed to Enron's cash crunch, the biggest problem was that

Jeff Skilling and Ken Lay could not or would not slow down the company's spending spree on big projects both in the United States. and abroad. In 1997 alone, the company bought Portland General Electric Company and bought back the shares of a former subsidiary called Enron Global Power and Pipelines. In all, the company spent more than $3.8 billion in cash and stock acquiring new assets in 1997. In addition, the company's capital expenditures jumped from $878 million in 1996 to more than $1.4 billion in 1997. Those expenditures included investments in power plants in Guam, India, Turkey, Puerto Rico, Italy, Britain, Poland, and Brazil.

All of that spending was showing up in Enron's finances. Around Halloween in 1997, it appears Skilling began realizing he had to do something to shore up the company's cash shortage and he had to do it quickly. If he didn't, his free-spending ways and lack of focus on cash flow would doom Enron.

19

Chewco: The 3-Percent Solution

NOVEMBER 5, 1997 Jeff Skilling's first ten months on the fiftieth floor of the Enron building had been much harder than he ever expected. Enron's stock price was stuck in neutral. The stock, selling for about $19, hadn't budged for months and had actually lost about $2 since Rich Kinder left. Worse yet, Enron had been underperforming its peers in the natural gas sector since 1993. Other gas companies were kicking Enron's butt, and Skilling, who held more than $10,000,000 worth of Enron options, knew it.

There was the ongoing Rebecca Mark problem. Skilling and Mark had been rivals for years. The two were about the same age; they'd both gone to Harvard Business School; they were fully convinced of their abilities and superior intellects; and both wanted to succeed Ken Lay as the next CEO of Enron. Mark was getting a tremendous amount of media coverage, and her international power projects appeared to be doing well. Lay and the Enron Board of Directors liked her. Skilling was going to have to figure out a way to get rid of her.

Despite the annoyances that came with Mark, Skilling was enjoying a few bright spots. In March 1997, Skilling had promoted his closest cronies, including Lou Pai, Ken Rice, and Kevin Hannon to top spots in the company. All of them were now serving on the company's management and operating committees. In addition, the gas and electric power trading businesses were thriving, just as Skilling had expected. Pai, a genius at trading, appeared to be doing well at Enron Energy Services, the company's new retail power business. The pipelines were ticking along. It appeared Enron's purchase of Portland General was going to help Enron solidify its position in the electric power business. Electricity trading volumes were soaring, and new markets were opening. Revenues—thanks largely to the company's use of mark-to-market accounting—were growing like mad. Enron was on pace to exceed $20 billion in revenue for 1997. It would be an increase of more than 50 percent over what Kinder had done in 1996.

But expenses were murderous. Cash flow from operations—the amount of real money the company was making from its businesses—had been negative almost from the day Skilling moved up to the fiftieth floor. In the first quarter, cash flow had been negative to the tune of $142 million. In the second quarter, the losses had nearly quadrupled to $523 million. By the end of the third quarter on September 30, the cash flow situation had grown even worse. Enron's negative cash flow from operations was a whopping $588 million.

Some of the cash problems weren't Skilling's fault. Four and a half months earlier, the J-Block chickens had come home to roost. The J-Block gas deal, struck in 1993 just after Enron completed the Teesside deal, had come back to bite Enron with a vengeance. On June 3, a London court put an end to years of legal wrangling between Enron and a group of North Sea oil companies and ordered Enron to pay the companies a total of $440 million. The ruling forced Enron to take a second quarter restructuring charge write-down of $675 million. That meant Enron's 1997 profits were going to be lousy.

And there was another problem: The California Public Employees' Retirement System, CalPERS, wanted to cash out of a joint venture that it had created with Enron in 1993. The venture, called the Joint Energy Development Investment Limited Partnership or JEDI, was funded with $500 million—CalPERS put in $250 million in cash; Enron put up 12 million shares of its own stock. The partnership invested in natural gas projects. But in fall 1997, CalPERS informed Enron that it wanted to sell its stake in JEDI so it could invest in other deals. That sent Skilling into a tizzy.

With JEDI, Enron had the best of both worlds. As a half owner in the deal, Enron could record any revenues (or losses) on its income statement, but it didn't have to show JEDI's debts on its balance sheet. That was because JEDI's debts really didn't belong to Enron. So Enron could show good revenue growth while maintaining a better-than-average credit rating. And with Enron's trading business taking off, the company's credit rating was critically important to Skilling. That's because when big companies borrow money, the amount of interest they are charged is usually determined by agencies like Moody's or Standard & Poor's, which rate a given company's ability to pay its debts. Enron wanted to keep an investment grade rating so its cost of capital would stay relatively low. Trading businesses need access to large amounts of low-cost capital. If Enron's credit rating fell below "junk" level, its ability to continue trading would have been hampered because its cost of capital would be too high.

Skilling simply had to keep JEDI—and the $600 million in debt that came with it—off Enron's books. So he turned to his financial wizard, Andy Fastow, who quickly came up with the solution: a new entity called Chewco, named for the *Star Wars* character Chewbacca, that would be owned by another Enron official, Michael Kopper. But to make it work, they'd have to get the legal work done in a big hurry and then they'd have to get it approved by the Enron board.

Fastow realized that the easiest way to keep JEDI's debts off Enron's books was to put them on someone else's books. So he'd have Chewco simply buy CalPERS's stake in JEDI. The cost to Chewco: $383 million—an amount that would account for all of CalPERS's original investment and all of its profits from the partnership. Kopper, an upper-level financial manager at Enron, didn't have $383 million, nor was he able to borrow that much money. But Fastow saw a way around the problem. Under the accounting rules, Chewco could qualify as a partnership that was wholly independent of Enron if it satisfied three simple tests:

- At least 3 percent of Chewco's capital came from outside (that is, non-Enron) investors. That meant that Kopper had to raise at least $11 million to make Chewco viable.
- The entity was not controlled by Enron (dubious, since Kopper worked for Enron).
- Enron was not liable for any loans or other liabilities (the key issue for Chewco).

Although $11 million wasn't much for Enron, for Michael Kopper it might as well have been $11 billion. Kopper simply didn't have that much money. He and his domestic partner, William Dodson, were able to come up with $125,000 in cash. But Fastow apparently had another idea. He convinced Barclays Bank to lend Chewco $240 million, a loan that was guaranteed by Enron. Then he arranged for JEDI to lend Chewco $132 million. Then they raised an additional $11.5 million from two other entities that became general and limited partners in Chewco. The two entities, called Big River and Little River, were controlled by Kopper, who later transferred part of his interest to Dodson. Big River and Little River's only real asset was the $125,000 in cash that Kopper and Dodson raised. The rest, about $11.4 million, was borrowed from Barclays. But here's the rub: The loan from Barclays to Big River and Little River was ultimately guaranteed by Enron.[1]

That guarantee meant three things: Enron hadn't made an arm's-length transaction; it was still liable for the debts of Chewco, and that meant Kopper hadn't satisfied the 3-percent ownership requirement. Kopper and Fastow had, wittingly or unwittingly, done a deal that would be a key part of Enron's undoing.

But the deal didn't slow down. Vinson & Elkins, Enron's longtime law firm, helped set up the Chewco deal in what might have been a record time—just forty-eight hours. And although the complex deal was doable, the Enron employees still had another hurdle: The venture had to be approved by the Enron board.

So on November 5, 1997, during a telephone conference call, Fastow and Skilling presented the Chewco deal to the board. But they didn't tell the members several important things. First, they didn't reveal that Kopper was the owner of Chewco. If they had done so, the board might not have approved the Chewco deal because it clearly violated Enron's Code of Conduct. Nor did they reveal how Kopper came up with the $11.5 million in equity for Chewco. According to the minutes of the meeting, Fastow "reviewed the economics of the project, the financing arrangements, and the corporate structure of the acquiring company." He also showed them a diagram of the deal, which looked something like the mess on the following page.

The board, with little discussion, approved the Chewco deal. Skilling and Fastow were hugely relieved.

But the financing wasn't done yet. Shortly after the board approved the deal, Enron gave Barclays enough cash to cut the loans it had made to Big River and Little River in half. That meant that Chewco's 3-percent ownership stake in JEDI was reduced to 1.5 percent. And that meant JEDI—and all of its debts—should have been moved back on to Enron's books.

They weren't. Had the JEDI deal been moved back onto Enron's books, the company's profits for 1997 would have been a paltry $9 million, far below what Wall Street analysts had been estimating. But with the Chewco deal in the bag, Skilling was able to blow the doors off of Wall Street's expectations. When the company reported its fourth quarter 1997 results on January 20, 1998, it showed $105 million in net income. "Some parts of Enron did a lot better than the street expected and that offset the shortfalls," energy analyst John Olson told one reporter.

The Chewco deal also apparently helped Enron's cash flow from operations. The company was able to record the sale of JEDI to Chewco as cash from operating activities. That helped Skilling cover

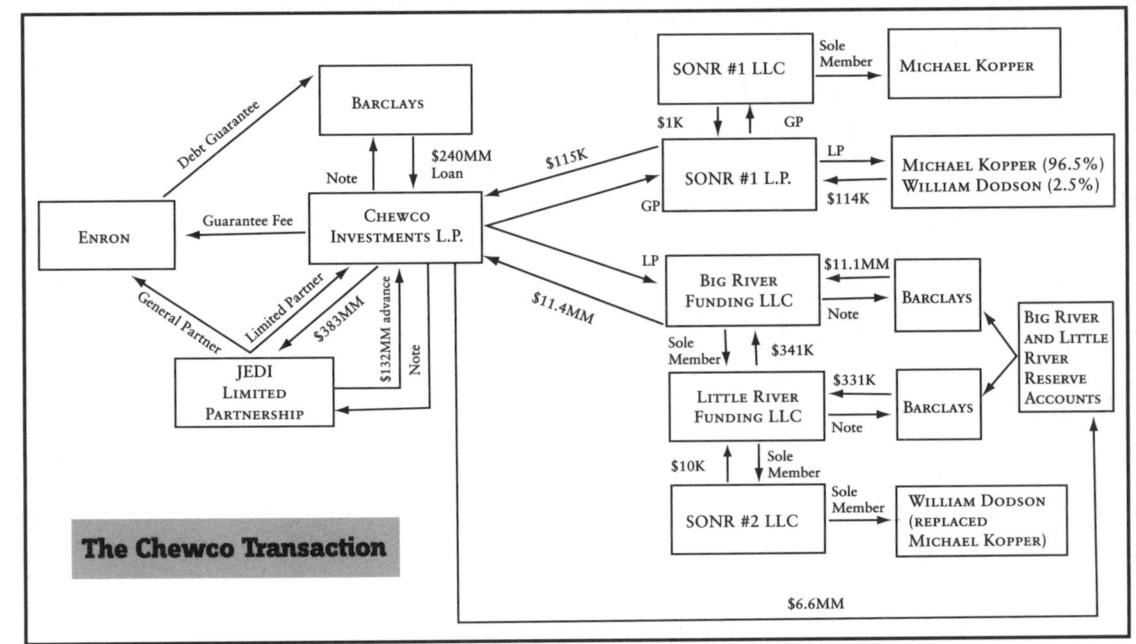

Diagram of Chewco Transaction (graph from p. 51 of the Powers Report)

Source: William C. Powers, Raymond S. Troubh, Herbert S. Winokur, Jr., "Report of Investigation by the Special Investigative Committee of the Board of Directors of Enron Corp.," Enron Corporation, February 1, 2002 (the Powers report).

much of the $588-million cash shortfall and end 1997 with positive cash flow from operations of $211 million.

By mid-February, Enron's stock was beginning a steady upward move, prompting another analyst, Robert Christenson, from Gerard Klauer Mattison to tell *Bloomberg* that Enron was a "growth stock" that was "finally starting to kick up its heels."[2] That was certainly true. And by April—just five months after Skilling, Fastow, and Kopper had talked the board into approving the Chewco deal—Enron's stock had risen by 21 percent.

Jeff Skilling was off to the races and Chewco was forgotten—at least for a while. But the bastard financing that Fastow created in the Chewco deal was only the beginning. A myriad of new off-the-balance-sheet deals were in the offing, deals with names like LJM and Raptor, that would be increasingly convoluted.

Enron had started down a slippery ethical slope. And no one in authority seemed to care.

20

Sexcapades

By late 1998, Jeff Skilling was feeling so comfortable at Enron that he promoted his girlfriend.

Skilling's affair with Rebecca Carter, an accountant who'd been working at Enron since 1990, was one of the worst-kept secrets in the building. Just as everyone at Enron knew that Ken Lay had married his secretary, almost everyone knew that Skilling and Carter had been sleeping together. Carter, a petite, attractive woman with a master's degree in accounting, was regarded as fairly competent by her coworkers in the company's corporate finance department. But as her relationship with Skilling became more widely known, both of them were compromised. "Nobody in the finance unit trusted her because we knew she was sleeping with Skilling," one of Carter's former coworkers remembered. "She became ineffective and they had to find someplace for her to land." That meant moving Carter up the ladder in hurry. So in late 1998 or early 1999, Skilling promoted her to senior vice president. Skilling also named Carter to the company's thirty-one-member Management Committee, making her one of only five women in that group. Within a short time, Carter was working as Enron's corporate secretary. "I knew Enron was corrupt when Jeff made his mistress the corporate secretary and the board never said a word about it," said one top-level Enron executive. "When I saw that, I said, 'There's no hope for this company.' It was like a French court under Louis the Fourteenth."

Carter—whose compensation package from Enron in 2001 included a salary of $261,809, a bonus of $300,000 and a long-term incentive bonus of $75,000 (she also got restricted stock grants valued at $307,301)—wasn't the first woman who got to the top on her back.[1]

"The only women who got ahead at Enron were either very masculine in their nature or were sleeping with somebody," said a (female) auditor who left Wall Street for a job with Enron in the late 1990s.

Sex and extramarital affairs are not, by themselves, a problem for companies. But at Enron, the sexual misconduct happened at such high levels that it became a part of the company's culture. The sex, said one executive, "set the tone for the rest of the company. And you couldn't get away from it. It was like a humidifier. It was in the air." The problem, of course, was that the humidifier was located on the fiftieth floor of Enron's headquarters, and the steam radiated down from there.

The most infamous sexcapade at the company involved one of Skilling's buddies, Ken Rice, whose long-running extramarital affair with another Enron employee, Amanda Martin, became something of a running joke inside the building. "I was shocked when I joined Enron. I had such good morals," said one human resources manager who worked at Enron for many years. "And here were these two, Ken and Amanda, they were wide open about it. They didn't try to hide it at all." Rice and Martin's public displays of affection in the office provided a bit of R-rated entertainment for their coworkers. Sources said that Martin, an attorney and longtime Enron employee, would often go into Rice's office and sit on his lap, or she would sit on his desk in front of him. Or the two would go to Martin's office, which had glass walls, and fondle each other, completely oblivious to the impression they were giving their coworkers.

Rice became so brazen about his infidelities that he bragged about them to his coworkers. One Enron official who'd gotten married a few months earlier told a story about riding on one of the Enron jets with Rice. While coming back from a business trip, Rice turned to his coworker and asked, "So, have you cheated on your wife yet?" The man, surprised, answered that he had not and wasn't planning to. To which Rice reportedly replied, "Well, why not?"

A Wall Street analyst who covered Enron for years said the sexual shenanigans at Enron became an important part of his take on the company and its financial statements. The analyst said when someone like Skilling, who has a wife and three kids and is heading a major company, starts sleeping around, "it addresses the character of the man. This is a guy who felt he could get away with anything. You saw it in his personal life and his business life."

Skilling's affair with Carter (the two married in early 2002) was just a facet of the boys' club at Enron. Several women who worked at Enron said Skilling and the young traders who dominated the company viewed women as a commodity that could be bought and sold just like gas, electricity, or any of the other products Enron was trading. And since Houston's strip clubs are among the best in the country, it was only natural that Enron's boy geniuses visited them with regularity. Joints like Rick's Cabaret, Treasures, and The Men's Club were the most popular venues. Enron executives like Lou Pai reportedly visited them regularly. In fact, Pai's passion for strippers began costing Enron so much money that Ken Lay had to lay down the law. Around 1995, after Pai reportedly submitted an expense report with huge strip club expenditures, Lay sent out a famous companywide memo that said Enron would no longer reimburse expenses from the strip clubs.

But that apparently didn't stop Pai. Numerous sources inside Enron say that late one night in the mid-1990s, Pai brought a pair of women of ill-repute to Enron's headquarters. Pai took them upstairs to one of the conference rooms and allegedly had sex with them on the conference table. (Pai has denied ever taking prostitutes into the building. Lawyers for Pai's wife, Lanna Pai, refused to comment.)

In addition to the affairs occurring among the company's top managers, lower-level employees were also hooking up for romantic adventures. And in many cases, it made perfect sense: Enron was a hothouse environment filled with lots of intelligent, driven young people who worked very long hours and therefore had few opportunities to mingle with members of the opposite sex outside of the workplace. Some of those liaisons ended in marriage, of which there were several among the lower and middle tiers at Enron. And the affairs at those company levels were not conducted maliciously. Nor were those workers supposed to be setting an example for the entire company. Ken Lay, Jeff Skilling, and their highest-ranking lieutenants were.

One headhunter in Houston who worked for a number of energy firms (including Enron) said the sexcapades at Enron even affected how other companies approached hiring. The headhunter remarked that in the late 1990s, he was doing a top-level executive search for Dynegy. After he met with Dynegy's top managers to clarify the skills the company wanted in the new person, the headhunter was pulled aside by Dynegy's CEO, Chuck Watson. "I want to tell you something," Watson confided to the headhunter. "On our executive team, the most important thing is ethics and integrity. All of the executives on this floor are still married to our first wives. Bring us people who fit our ethics and integrity."

Although Ken Lay paid lip service to ethics and integrity, he had been compromised by his own past. As one former top-level Enron executive said, "Leaders cast shadows." And the shadow that Lay cast at Enron was that of a man who couldn't, or wouldn't, do anything to put a stop to the sexual misconduct.

One source close to Lay recalled that several employees complained directly to him about the oversexed atmosphere at Enron. In at least three instances, Enron employees wrote Lay and asked him to put a stop to the Ken Rice–Amanda Martin affair. The source said one letter "came through the office mail threatening legal action if some steps were not taken" to deal with the problem. But Lay was reluctant to do anything about it, according to the source.

So the sexcapades continued. And they became another facet of Enron's corrupt leadership—one that went hand in hand with the company's corrupt bookkeeping practices. "The marital misconduct created an atmosphere where things had to be covered up," said one member of Enron's Executive Committee. "Having secrets, having things not be public, having things be suspected and not known, was part of the deal." Everything at Enron, said the exec, was on a gradation scale. "Are you cheating on your wife? Are you cheating in business? Where do you draw the line?"

There were no lines being drawn at Enron, particularly not by Ken Lay.

21

The Family Lay

MARCH 1999

Will Rogers never met a man he didn't like. Ken Lay never met a relative he didn't put on the Enron teat. And once the Lays latched on, they became sacred sucklings. Evidence of this came in black and white in the company's 1998 proxy statement, sent to shareholders in early 1999.

Under the heading "Certain Transactions," the energy firm reported that during the previous twelve months, it had paid a Houston firm, Travel Agency in the Park, "gross commissions in the amount of $2,504,781 attributable to Enron employee travel." But in 1999, Enron changed the reporting methodology. That year, Travel Agency in the Park got $245,359 in what the proxy calls "net revenue" (most people would call it profit) from Enron. In 2000, the amount paid to the agency would more than double, with "net revenue" jumping to $517,200. In 2001, the payment was $362,096.[1]

Why the change? It appears Ken Lay got spooked in mid-1998 when an internal auditor, who'd been hired away from Wall Street to help Enron reduce its expenses, started raising questions about the huge amounts of money Enron was paying for travel. The auditor believed Enron could get a better deal than the one it was getting with Travel

Agency in the Park. So the auditor made a simple recommendation: Switch travel agencies.

Bad career move. The auditor didn't know that Travel Agency in the Park was half owned by Ken Lay's sister, Sharon Lay. And within a month of making the suggestion, the auditor was canned. "I was allowed to question Jeff Skilling's practices, but I couldn't question Sharon Lay," said the auditor, who went back to work on Wall Street. "It was very clear I couldn't stay in the firm." Another source who was familiar with the firing of the auditor said the reason for the firing was simple: The auditor "violated the taboo of Enron." That is: Don't mess with the Lays.

"We called them Travel Agency in the Dark," remembered one high-ranking executive, adding that he could buy airline tickets for less than half of what was quoted by the agency. Another executive, a math whiz who spent more than a decade at Enron, said, "If I could have booked my own trips, the costs would have been reduced by 80 percent."

"That deal stunk from the word go," said another longtime Enron employee. "We told him it was stupid when that travel company was set up in the late Eighties. Sure enough, they bid on it, they won it, and did all Enron's travel. Plus, I know for a fact that Ken Lay put 'the arm' on different Enron suppliers to get them to use Travel Agency in the Park."[2]

One insider insisted that Sharon Lay's firm won the Enron travel contract fair and square, that the firm bid on the contract in a competitive process and deserved to get it. Furthermore, sources who saw the contract said that Lay's sister's firm provided good service and rebated a good portion of its commissions back to Enron. Sharon Lay defends the deal. She later told the *New York Times*, "There are some who thought it was only because of my relationship to Ken that we got the contract and that's far from the truth.... It's unfortunate that you can be put at a disadvantage because of a relationship."[3]

Mark Lay, Ken's son from his marriage with Judie, didn't experience many disadvantages by being the son of the Enron chairman and CEO.

But Enron did. It appears every deal Enron made with the son of the chairman lost money. Among the most questionable was one involving Bammel Field.

Located about eight miles west of the passenger terminals at Bush Intercontinental Airport in northern Harris County, Bammel Field is one of the wonders of the American natural gas business. The largest gas reservoir in Texas—as well as one of the largest facilities of its kind on earth—the depleted oil and gas field acts like a gigantic storage locker for power companies and other gas users. Bammel allows gas utilities and others to assure delivery to their customers even during times of highest gas demand, like extremely cold or extremely hot weather. It also allows them to hedge against price risk. Gas prices fluctuate constantly and are often tied to changes in temperature. For instance, gas consumption usually rises in the winter, and that generally leads to higher prices for gas. To counter that effect, utilities and other big gas users buy gas during the summer and inject it into storage for use during the winter months. Bammel Field is perfectly situated for that use. The field lies near two major pipelines, one owned by Houston Pipe Line (a division of Enron) and the other by Williams Companies. The location provides access to a broad array of industrial companies that sit near the Houston Ship Channel as well as to the pipelines that feed gas to the residents of Houston and surrounding cities.

The other key attribute that makes Bammel valuable is its size. Bammel Field can store 117 billion cubic feet of natural gas. That's roughly equivalent to 19.5 million barrels (800 million gallons) of crude oil. Bammel alone can hold enough gas to supply America for nearly two days. Since 1952, Bammel Field has been one of Enron's most prized assets. It was the kind of asset that Enron—and Houston Natural Gas before it—would never let anyone else have access to. It was simply too valuable.

That history mattered not a whit when Mark Lay came along. On April Fool's Day in 1994, Enron cut the sweetest of sweetheart deals with Lay the Younger, who, according to Enron's proxy statement, owned one-third of a company called Bruin Interests. Under the terms of the deal, Mark Lay's company was given the right to store and retrieve up to 8 billion cubic feet of gas in Bammel. Bruin paid $800,000 for that service and agreed to make "certain payments" when the company withdrew the gas. For reasons not explained in Enron's proxy statements, Bruin, upon the signing of the contract, almost immediately flipped its right to store the gas to an unnamed third party that was unaffiliated with Enron or Bruin. Although it cannot be proven that Bruin paid less than other companies were paying for gas storage, it can safely be assumed that Bruin couldn't have made a profit on the deal without charging the unnamed "third party" more for the storage than Enron charged Bruin. Nevertheless, Enron's proxy claims the terms of the storage deal with Bruin "are comparable to those available to unaffiliated third parties."

Piffle. "Nobody but Ken Lay's son or brother-in-law could have made a deal like that. That's the only time we ever leased out Bammel," said a former high-ranking Houston Natural Gas official. "It was a bad deal. I couldn't believe it when I heard about it. Bammel was a crown jewel for the company. There's no value that Mark Lay could add by being a customer out there except to cut into Enron's potential margins."

Enron had absolutely no reason to allow Bruin to have access to Bammel. If a company needed gas storage, it could simply buy that capacity from Enron and bypass a third-party interest like Bruin. Furthermore, it was doubtful that a neophyte in the gas business like Mark Lay would have had any contacts in the business whom the gray-heads at Enron didn't already know.

But the deal was done, in part, according to an executive close to the deal, because Jeff Skilling supported it. "Skilling did it to get close to Lay," said the source. "Three of us said, 'We aren't doing that deal.' Ken was naive that it wouldn't come back to haunt him. Most smart people would have known better." The executive said Ken Lay could easily have called on his friends in Houston to hire his son instead of putting him to work at Enron and creating a potential ethics problem. "If it had been me, I'd have called [former Transco chief] Jack Bowen up and said, 'Give him a job.'"

Bammel Field was just the first of a string of deals that Lay did to keep his son in cornflakes. In January 1996, Enron got into another quirky deal with Mark Lay to study "the fixed price purchase and sale of certain paper products." Enron put up $300,000 for the paper study. It appears that Lay the Younger and his partner in the deal, United Media Corporation (a company for whom Lay had done consulting work), put up no serious money. Four months later, that deal was canceled.

But that same year, Enron hired Mark Lay and his friends at Bruin to study an entirely different business: iron carbide, a potential substitute for the scrap metal needed in making steel. Enron agreed to pay Bruin a $2,500-per-month retainer and gave Bruin several incentives, including a $100,000 bonus payment if it made any iron carbide deals. By March 1997, Enron had paid Bruin $33,500 under the terms of the consulting agreement, and two months later, the company decided Mark Lay was so irresistible that the company hired him full-time to work on the development of "a clearinghouse for the purchase and sale of finished paper products."

As part of that deal, Enron agreed to pay off slightly more than $1 million in debts accumulated by Lay the Younger and a group of other people who were former owners of a company called Paper and Print Management Corporation. In addition to the loan forgiveness, Mark Lay got a three-year employment contract with Enron that made him a vice president, gave him a $100,000 signing bonus, a guaranteed minimum annual bonus of $100,000 for 1997, 1998, and 1999, and options to purchase 20,000 shares of Enron common stock.

Once inside Enron, Mark Lay became known—not surprisingly—as one of the untouchables. He not only had the backing of Skilling for all of his pie-in-the-sky deals, but he was the son of the chairman and CEO. "Whenever we were in the PRC [Performance Review Committee] meetings, we always had to rank Mark Lay," said one source. "And it always created this really awkward situation. His name would come up, and no one would say anything. He wasn't the sharpest tool in the shed."

Sharp, dull, or in between, Lay the Younger helped convince Enron to begin investing enormous amounts of money in paper mills. The business plan for Enron's new business, Clickpaper.com, required the company to have ready access to paper products so that it could cover its futures position in what it believed would be a booming business in risk management in paper products. Newspapers were the biggest potential market. Newsprint is important to newspapers because, after payroll, it is their largest cost. By offering hedges, Enron agreed to supply a customer with a set newsprint volume at a set price over a given time period.

On its web site, Clickpaper bragged that between May 1997, the month Mark Lay was hired on, and December 2000, the company had "completed financial transactions totaling over 23 million tons of pulp and paper products having a notional value exceeding $9 billion." But those contracts came with an enormous capital cost to Enron. In early 1999, Enron was part of a group of investors that pumped $193 million into a paper mill in Quebec. In July 2000, Enron bought a newspaper recycling mill in New Jersey, for $72 million. And a year later, it paid $300 million for a paper mill in Quebec City.

Although Mark Lay would later claim that within eighteen months of acquiring Paper and Print Management, Enron's paper business was generating $20 million in operating profit, there is no record in Enron's financial statements or anywhere else that Mark Lay's paper chase ever made a dime. By the time of Enron's bankruptcy, Mark Lay had seen the light. He had quit business altogether and was attending the Southwestern Baptist Theological Seminary in Houston. In explaining his move, Lay the Younger said, "God impressed on me that's where he wanted me."[4]

22

LJM1

By mid-1999 Enron had a sticky finance problem. A year earlier, the company had invested $10 million in a fledgling Internet service provider called Rhythms NetConnections.[1] By early 1999, Rhythms had gone public and the Internet Bubble had sent its stock into the stratosphere. In the first day of trading, the company's stock closed at $69. Suddenly, Enron's share in the company was worth about $300 million. But Enron couldn't sell it. Under the terms of its original investment, Enron had agreed to hold the shares until the end of 1999.

After thinking about the matter for some time, Andy Fastow, Enron's cocky young chief financial officer, came up with a convoluted plan to help Enron preserve the value of its Rhythms NetConnections investment. The plan would be executed by a new limited partnership called LJM Cayman, L.P., which would be controlled by Fastow. The name had Fastow's personal stamp on it, created from the initials of Fastow's wife, Lea, and the couple's two children.

LJM1 would function as a parking lot for Enron, a place where the company could stow and retrieve assets. Those assets would be hidden from Wall Street and small investors because LJM would not be owned by Enron. Therefore, all of LJM1's functions and assets would be separate from Enron's balance sheet.

Enron already had one huge off-the-balance-sheet parking lot called Whitewing, which had a part owner called Osprey. And yes, it's confusing.

Whitewing was among the boldest of Enron's off-the-balance-sheet deals. Formed as an Enron subsidiary in 1997, the company moved Whitewing off its books completely in 1999, when it sold half of the partnership. The company was set up to purchase billions of dollars of Enron's overseas assets. Power plants, pipelines, and other underperforming assets were sold to Whitewing, which was backed by investments from a group of Wall Street investment banks. Whitewing was then to resell Enron's assets on the open market. In return, Enron guaranteed that if the assets were sold at a loss, it would make up the shortfall with shares of its own common stock. That pledge would become very important in late 2001 as Enron hurtled toward bankruptcy.

However, LJM1 would be different. Unlike Whitewing, it would be controlled by an Enron insider, Fastow. On June 18, 1999, Fastow met with Ken Lay and Jeff Skilling. He proposed to create LJM1 with an investment of $1 million of his own money and $15 million from two limited partners. Additional capital for the new entity would come from Enron, which would invest 3.4 million shares of restricted stock in LJM1. Any appreciation in the value of Enron's stock would accrue to the limited partners in LJM1 and not to Fastow. Fastow would be the general partner of LJM1, and through a series of interlocking companies, he would manage all of the investments.

Lay and Skilling apparently thought Fastow's idea was a good one, even though on the surface it appeared that LJM1 failed to meet the test for off-the-balance-sheet deals. As with the Chewco deal that Fastow had engineered with Michael Kopper in 1997, LJM1 was going to be used to move debts and risky investments (like Rhythms) off Enron's balance sheet. But to do that, LJM1, like Chewco, had to satisfy three requirements:

- At least 3 percent of the equity had to come from outside (that is, non-Enron) investors.
- The entity could not be controlled by Enron.
- Enron was not liable for any loans or other liabilities.

LJM1 might have qualified under two of the three. But how was Enron going to be able to prove that the special-purpose entity wasn't controlled by Enron when the company's CFO was managing all of the investments? It appears that neither Lay nor Skilling thought about it. Nor did Lay consider how much money Fastow might make on the assets he was buying from Enron.[2] After a bit more discussion, Lay agreed to bring Fastow's proposal to the Enron Board of Directors at the board meeting on June 28, 1999.

At that board meeting, after a short debate, the company's Board of Directors agreed to waive Enron's ethics policy, which prohibited the company's officers from doing deals directly with the company, and approved the LJM1 deal. The approval opened the floodgates. And LJM1 became the cornerstone of Andy Fastow's financial house of cards.

One of those deals included LJM1's September 1999 investment of $15 million in Osprey. Although it's not clear why LJM1 invested in Osprey, the new entity flipped that investment to Chewco, Michael Kopper's company, just three months later.

During the same month that LJM1 bought part of Osprey, it also purchased a 13-percent stake in Enron's Cuiaba power plant in Brazil, even thought the plant wasn't yet operating. In fact, the power plant was stuck in the midst of an international brouhaha over Enron's plan to push a gas pipeline through a rare dry tropical forest. One of Enron's financial backers, the U.S.-taxpayer-backed Overseas Private Investment Corporation, reluctantly agreed to provide millions of dollars in loans on the project after long negotiations. Cost overruns and environmental problems were causing Enron a world of headaches.

Despite the problems, LJM1 paid Enron $11.3 million for the interest in the plant, a move that allowed Enron to change its accounting treatment on the twenty-year gas supply contract it held on the project. That change allowed Enron to—voilà!—realize $34 million in mark-to-market accounting income in the third quarter of 1999. But Fastow wasn't done yet. In the fourth quarter of 1999, he booked another $31 million of mark-to-market revenue for Enron from the same deal with LJM1. The story didn't end there: Enron would go on to claim another $14 million in 2000 and $5 million in 2001 from the same deal.

Stranger still, Enron bought back LJM1's interest in Cuiaba in August 2001 for $14.4 million, apparently because Enron was having difficulty managing the power plant project after LJM1 purchased part of the plant and needed to have more control over the project. Whatever the reason, LJM1 made a very good profit on the transaction.

And though the Cuiaba deal was odd, it was simplicity itself when compared to the scheme Fastow created in his effort to preserve some of the $300 million Enron made on its original investment in Rhythms NetConnections. The complex deal, closed on June 30, 1999, involved two new Fastow-controlled entities called SwapCo and Swap Sub. Enron agreed to give Swap Sub 1.6 million shares of its own stock. That move, in theory, gave Swap Sub "capital" that it could then use to pay for deals with Enron.

The next move is important, because this is the transaction that marks the beginning of the total corruption of Enron's accounting books. Not only was Enron doing hugely complex, unregulated derivatives transactions with companies *outside* of Enron, it was also now doing derivatives deals with companies (controlled by Andy Fastow) that were actually *inside* Enron.

With the Swab Sub deal, Enron began buying and selling derivatives that were based on the value of *its own stock*. Derivatives are risky. Trading derivatives that are predicated on the equity value of your own company is like playing Russian roulette.

As noted earlier, a put option allows its owner to sell an item at a predetermined price. The nut of the Swap Sub deal was a put option that Enron bought from Swap Sub that gave it the right to sell its Rhythms stock to Swap Sub for $56 per share in June 2004. Thus, even if Rhythms stock fell in value (which it would), Enron would still be able to get its money out of its investment. Simple, right?

Not exactly. The deal was fundamentally flawed. Swap Sub's only asset of consequence was the value of the Enron stock it held. Thus, the entire charade was predicated on the belief that Enron's stock and Rhythms stock would not both decline in price *at the same time*. If Enron's stock price fell and Rhythms stock fell, then Fastow's "hedge" would fail because Swap Sub wouldn't have enough capital to make good on its pledge to buy the Rhythms stock back from Enron.

This graph makes it easier to understand. Or then again, maybe it just demonstrates how convoluted the entire scheme was from the get-go.

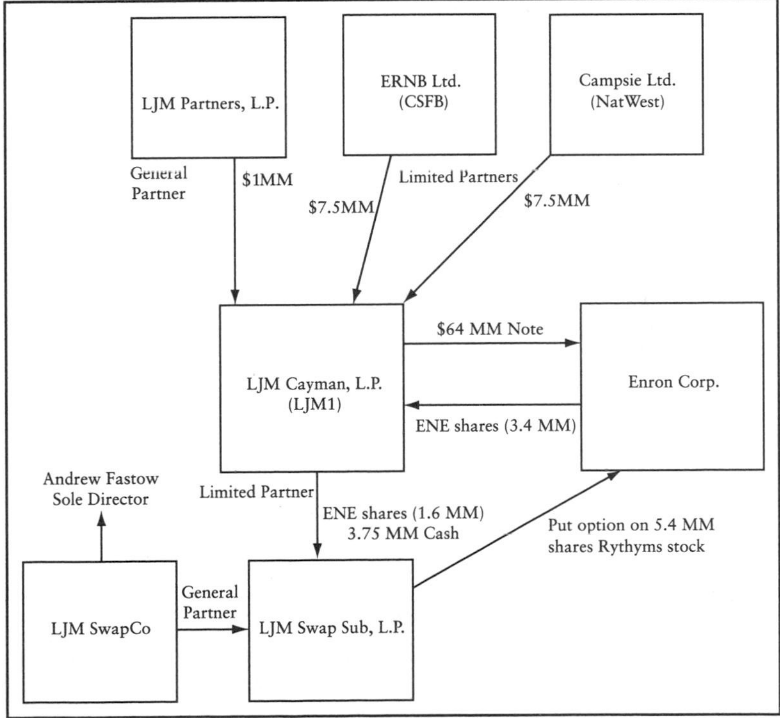

Chart from p. 81 of the Powers Report

Vince Kaminski, Enron's head of research, wasn't convinced. After Enron's chief risk officer, Rick Buy, explained the Rhythms hedge to him, Kaminski concluded the idea was "so stupid that only Andrew Fastow could have come up with it."[3]

Kaminski objected to the deal for three reasons: Fastow had an undeniable conflict of interest; LJM1 was almost certain to make money on the deal (Kaminski told Buy that it was "heads the partnership wins, tails Enron loses"); and the structure of the deal was unstable because most of the capital in the deal was Enron's stock. Again, if Rhythms stock and Enron stock both declined in value, LJM1 wouldn't be able to pay Enron back.

Kaminski's complaints fell on deaf ears. In reporting the Fastow deal to shareholders in its proxy statement, Enron would claim that the "terms of the transactions" with LJM1 were "reasonable and no less favorable than the terms of similar arrangements with unrelated third parties." That point is debatable. The LJM1 deals were—on their face—fairly outlandish. But they would pale in comparison to the deals Fastow would do with yet another entity he would control, LJM2.

23

Buying Off the Board

OCTOBER 11, 1999 The meeting started twenty minutes late. That wasn't really unusual. By October 11, 1999, the Enron Board of Directors had become more like an exclusive men's club than a deliberative body charged with steering a $40-billion global energy business. Whenever the board met, a good part of the time prior to the meeting was spent with members catching up on each other's children, spouses, and, of course, the latest gossip.

Of the fourteen men and two women who gathered in the opulent Whitney Room at the Four Seasons Hotel in downtown Houston for the 7 P.M. meeting, seven had been on the Enron board for fourteen years or more. Another four had served for at least five years. Two of the members, Rebecca Mark and Dr. John Mendelsohn, had just begun serving on the board. All but three of the board members in the room—Ken Lay, Jeff Skilling, and Mark—were independent of Enron. But there was also no mistaking the fact that nearly all of those independent members owed their allegiance, in one way or another, to Ken Lay. And Lay treated them all extremely well. The board members had quickly become accustomed to having the very best of everything. No matter where the meeting was held, the Enron board members could count on having one of Enron's fleet of corporate jets pick them up and deliver them directly to the meeting. It was a great time-saver for the board members, who also avoided the hassle of having to deal with airports and the possibilities of lost baggage or missed flights.

The company's meetings were always held in posh locations. The previous week, the Finance Committee had met at the ultra-plush resort The Breakers, in Palm Beach, Florida. Other times, there would be meetings in London or Colorado, and the board members always stayed in the best hotels. And the pay was great. Each of the independent directors was getting $50,000 a year for sitting on the Enron board. In addition, they got another $1,250 for each meeting they attended. On average, each of the independent directors was getting nearly $87,000 a year in cash and stock options from Enron for about two weeks' work—and there was no heavy lifting.

When the members finally settled down and took their seats, they began dealing with a rather lengthy agenda. The first few matters involved assuring that Enron was ready to deal with any hazards associated with the Y2K problem and selecting members for various committees. An investor relations flack presented figures to the board that showed Enron's stock soaring, up 45 percent for the first nine months of the year, vastly outperforming the S&P 500, which had returned a bit more than 5 percent. The board dealt with a few other things such as compensation and stock sales before turning to a matter involving an entity called LJM2.

Four months earlier, the board had approved the transactions involving LJM1, which was controlled by Fastow. That deal had required the board to waive the company's ethics policy. Now, with LJM2, the board was being asked for another, more far-reaching waiver. Enron's Board of Directors was being asked to approve what was essentially an open-ended transaction machine with which Fastow's newly formed company could do multiple transactions with Enron. And Fastow wouldn't need the board's approval on each deal. As with LJM1, Fastow would be the general partner of LJM2. But whereas LJM1 had only raised a few tens of millions of dollars, LJM2 would raise $200 million or more from a range of limited partners who would agree to invest in Enron's assets. While meeting with the board's Finance Committee, Fastow was calm and reassuring. He presented a list of controls that he felt would assuage their concerns about his obvious conflict of interest in LJM2. First, Fastow said all of the deals between Enron and LJM2 would have to be approved by both Rick Causey, Enron's chief accounting officer, and Rick Buy, the company's chief risk officer. In addition, the board's audit and compliance committee would review the LJM2 transactions once a year to make sure the deals were reasonable. (Management controls added later also required Skilling to review and approve the deals between Enron and all of Fastow's LJM deals.)

The presentation of LJM2 to the full board was made by longtime board member Herbert "Pug" Winokur, a buddy of Lay's. The two had met in the late 1960s when both men were working at the Pentagon. Winokur, a graduate of Harvard, had previously been at the Penn Central Corporation, the entity that survived the massive bankruptcy of the Penn Central Railroad in 1970. Winokur, a board member at Enron since 1985, was the chairman of the board's Finance Committee and had heard Fastow's full defense concerning why LJM2 should be approved by the board. The resolution that Winokur presented to the board said that LJM2 would be a "potential ready purchaser of the Company's businesses and assets or as a potential contract counterparty," and LJM2 "could provide liquidity, risk management and other financial benefits to the Company."

The resolution also declared that Fastow's "participation as the managing partner/manager of the Partnership will not adversely affect the interests of the Company."

The board asked a few questions about the LJM2 deal. In particular, it appears that board member Norman Blake, who was the CEO of the U.S. Olympic Committee, wanted to know whether Enron's auditor, Arthur Andersen, had signed off on the deal. Causey assured Blake that it had. Blake asked again, saying he was still concerned about the appearance of conflict. Causey tried to assure Blake that the matter was under control.

It was an important point. Causey may or may not have known, but Andersen personnel *had* objected to Fastow's plan. Benjamin Neuhausen, a member of Andersen's professional standards group, which specialized in tricky accounting issues, raised questions about LJM1 in May 1999. In an e-mail to Andersen's lead partner on the Enron account, David Duncan, he said, "Setting aside the accounting, idea of a venture entity managed by CFO is terrible from a business point of view.... Conflicts of interest galore. Why would any director in his or her right mind ever approve such a scheme?" On June 1, 1999, Duncan responded, saying, "On your point 1 (i.e., the whole thing is a bad idea) I really couldn't agree more." Duncan told Neuhausen that Andersen would agree to the LJM deal only if the Enron board and Ken Lay approved the transaction. And he added, "Andy is convinced that this is such a win-win that everyone will buy in."

It appears the Enron board wasn't made aware of Andersen's objections to Fastow's conflict of interest. And after presenting all the facts, Winokur made a motion that the resolution be adopted by the entire board. His motion was seconded by his fellow board member John Urquhart. Although Winokur and Urquhart may have been concerned about Fastow's potential conflicts, they had their own conflicts of interest.

Winokur was affiliated with National Tank Company, a privately owned company that provided Enron with oil field equipment and services. Between 1997 and 1999, the company had sold Enron more than $2.1 million worth of goods and services. But even though Winokur's deal was curious, it did not put money directly into his pocket.

By way of explanation, corporate governance experts frown on companies that have outside business dealings with their board members. The potential for serious conflicts of interest are too great. Directors who have consulting or other business deals with the companies they direct may be less willing to object to certain corporate practices for fear that they might lose their sinecures.

Urquhart's deal with Enron was ludicrously lucrative. In addition to the $87,000 or so per year that he was getting for sitting on the board, Enron paid Urquhart to be a "senior adviser to the chairman" on such things as the "implementation of an integrated strategic international business plan and other matters." Urquhart's consulting deal started in 1991, the year after he joined the company's board, and continued through the 1990s. Lay may have believed that Urquhart's experience in the power generation business—Urquhart spent forty years at General Electric—would be valuable to the Enron board. So in 1991, Enron paid Urquhart $257,500 in consulting fees. In 1992, that figure jumped to $580,168. In 1993, Enron paid him $562,500. In 1994, he made $596,354 for consulting and pocketed another $931,000 after exercising options on 56,000 shares of stock. In 1995, he got $592,989 "for services rendered and another $575,000 by exercising Enron stock options." And so on: 1996, $625,126; 1997, $632,156; 1998, $410,106; 1999, $531,710. According to Enron's 1999 proxy, the terms of Enron's deal with Urquhart included a retainer of $33,075 a month for providing up to ninety days of consulting services to the company per year. Any days over that amount were paid at a rate of $4,410 per day. For an eight-hour day, that amounts to $551.25 per hour.

But wait, there's more. In addition to the cash and stock options, Enron paid Urquhart an additional $1.16 million (in cash) in the mid-1990s in exchange for his agreement to surrender the "phantom equity" Urquhart had been granted in Enron's international electric power business. Urquhart kept an office on the fiftieth floor in the Enron building, although sources who worked on that floor said he rarely used the office. In all, it appears Enron paid Urquhart about $7.4 million during the 1990s for his expertise. But several high-level Enron employees said Urquhart wasn't worth it. After Enron finished the Teesside power plant in Britain in 1993, "the company outgrew the need for people like him," said one source who worked in the company's international power business. "After Teesside, we had people inside the company with far more experience than he had."

But Urquhart wasn't the only board member pigging out at the

Enron trough. Take Wendy Gramm. As explained earlier, in 1993 Gramm did Enron a mighty favor by exempting energy derivatives contracts from federal oversight. Immediately after making that move, she joined the Enron board, where she began benefiting in two ways. First, there was the fat paycheck for serving on the board. Second, Enron became a major donor to the Mercatus Center, a free-market think tank at George Mason University, where Gramm is director of the regulatory studies program.

For five years, Gramm sat on Enron's board and ignored the fact that she might have a teeny-weeny conflict of interest, given that her husband sat in the U.S. Senate and could, on any given day, vote on matters that could provide huge benefits to Enron. But in December 1998, Ms. Gramm consulted an attorney who found that—surprise!—she "could have a material conflict of interest." So in 1999, rather than continuing to give her stock options, Enron agreed to contribute $79,763, in cash, to her deferred compensation plan. The company also agreed to give her cash instead of stock options in the future.

Two members of the board, John Mendelsohn and Charles LeMaistre, are highly respected medical doctors with long histories at Houston's M.D. Anderson Cancer Center. But they had scant experience in energy-related matters. Their main connection to Enron appears to be that Enron was a major donor to the cancer center. In 1993, the Enron Foundation pledged to donate $1.5 million toward a clinic at M.D. Anderson.

Robert Belfer gained a seat on Enron's board in the 1980s after he sold his family's oil and gas exploration business to the company. Belfer, who owned 8.4 million shares of Enron stock, had recently been stung by the collapse of the hedge fund Long-Term Capital Management, in which he'd been an early investor.[1] As a member of the Enron board, he was focusing his attention on his newly formed energy business, Belco Oil & Gas. That company traded millions of dollars' worth of commodities with Enron through much of the 1990s. In 1997, Belco did a huge deal with Enron when it bought Coda Energy, a company that was owned by a joint venture whose partners included Enron.

Belco paid $149 million in cash and assumed $175 million in debt to take Coda off Enron's hands.

Joe Foy, a board member who'd been with Enron and its predecessor, Houston Natural Gas, since the beginning of time, also had a conflict. He was a retired partner in the Houston law firm Bracewell & Patterson, which did legal work for Enron.

Then there was Lord John Wakeham, leader of the British House of Lords and chairman of Britain's Press Complaints Commission. In mid-1999, Wakeham rebuked a cheeky London newspaper, the *Sun,* for daring to publish a photo of Prince Edward's fiancée, Sophie Rhys-Jones, who had somehow misplaced her shirt. Although Wakeham was a busy man in London, his position on the Enron board was not a coincidence. It was Wakeham who, while serving as Britain's secretary of state for energy, had granted final approval to Enron's massive Teesside cogeneration power project in 1990. And now Enron was paying him back. Beginning in 1996, Enron, in addition to paying Wakeham his hefty director's check, had the British Big Shot on the regular payroll. Wakeham was paid $6,000 per month for "advice and counsel on matters relating specifically to European business and operations."

Wakeham was supposed to lend more than just advice to the Enron board. He was also a member of the company's Audit Committee and was therefore charged with overseeing the company's financial documents. It was a natural position for Wakeham, a chartered accountant (Britain's equivalent of a certified public accountant) with extensive experience in private practice. Although he was qualified to question some of Enron's accounting practices, it appears Lord Wakeham was too busy cashing his checks to pay much attention. One high-ranking Enron employee who worked in the firm's London office for several years said Wakeham did a few things to help Enron in Europe shortly after he joined the board. "But he never earned his keep after that."

In addition to the deals that Winokur, Urquhart, Gramm, Mendelsohn, LeMaistre, Belfer, Foy, and Wakeham had with Enron, three other members of the board who voted on the LJM2 deal were employees of the company. To a casual observer, it appeared Enron's Board of

Directors was one giant conflict of interest. So adding Andy Fastow's LJM2 deal to the already long list of conflicts must not have seemed like a big deal.

In any case, after a short bit of discussion, the board approved LJM2 without any major objections. The decision would ultimately allow Fastow's LJM partnerships to do more than twenty deals with Enron. It would also allow Fastow to loot Enron's treasury on a scale not seen since, well, since John Urquhart.

One of the board members who apparently voted for the Fastow-led partnerships (the board minutes don't have a tally of the vote) was one of its newest members, Rebecca Mark.

24

The Deal Diva, or How to Lose a Couple of Billion Dollars and Still Be a Rock Star

Water conferences are usually boring affairs. Filled with too many middle-aged men whose fashion sense favors the timeless pocket-protector-and-a-tweed-jacket look, the conferences attract few interesting personalities and even fewer women. But the water wonks who went to New York City in mid-1999 knew to expect something different. Not only would the meeting be held at the World Trade Center, but Rebecca Mark was going to give a speech.

Most of the attendees had never seen Mark. But they had heard of her and they knew enough to expect a show. They weren't disappointed.

According to conference attendees, Mark arrived, as was her custom, via limousine. And although the weather in New York was warm at the time, Mark swept into the meeting room wearing a dark floor-length fur. "It looked like it cost a ton of money. I don't know what kind it was, maybe Russian sable. It was gorgeous," said one attendee. As she walked to the front of the meeting room, she was trailed by an aide, a matronly, decidedly unfashionable woman, who appeared to be in her late fifties or early sixties. Mark bore straight ahead, looking neither right nor left. Her strutting manner made it clear that she was going to show these tweedy know-nothings that Enron was in the water business to stay. Soon, the utility geeks would know that her new company, Azurix, was a force to be reckoned with, a company that would change the water business forever.

As Mark approached the stage, she reached up to unhook the fur, which she had been wearing cape-like, over her shoulders. Just as she reached the stage, with nary a look back, Mark sent the fur flying off her shoulders. The fur hung in the air just long enough to be caught by her faithful Sancha Panza, who folded it in her arms and scurried to the sidelines. Mark then vaulted up the stairs to give her speech. It was a fabulous entrance.

Once at the podium, Mark proceeded to tell all of the attendees how Azurix was going to use Enron's expertise and money to kick their butts in the water business. Never mind that Azurix was a newcomer. Azurix had the secret sauce. After finishing her speech, she was far too busy to hang around and listen to the tweedy set talk about mundane things like reverse osmosis and turbidity. So she hit the door, a fact that left many industry members seething. "We were absolutely determined to bury her because when she'd speak at these conferences, she took the air of the definitive voice in the business," said Dick Heckmann, the founder and CEO of U.S. Filter (now part of Vivendi), who was at the World Trade Center that day in 1999. "She'd say things like 'This is a new day in the water business. Enron is bringing its trading abilities to the water business to bring it out of biblical times.'"

"Then," Heckmann said, "when I got up to talk, she'd leave. She'd come in just in time to give her speech and then leave immediately. It just pissed me off."

Enron would have never allowed Rebecca Mark to attack the world water business had she not brought Dabhol back from the dead.

Mark was successful in pushing through Phase One of the project. But in 1996, Dabhol was stopped before it ever generated a dime's worth of power when India's longtime ruling Congress Party was tossed out of office and the government's agreement with Enron on

Dabhol was tossed out, too. Mark worked tirelessly to revive Dabhol. For months, she shuttled back and forth between Houston and India, negotiating and cajoling a platoon of Indian officials. The Indians finally agreed to reinstate the contract after Enron reduced the cost of the project and offered a slightly better power purchase deal. But Mark's problems continued. Local protesters cut off the water supply to the construction site. Human Rights Watch and Amnesty International both documented serious cases of human rights violations at the Dabhol project site. The abuses carried out by local police including beatings, arbitrary arrests, and threats against local people who were protesting against the project.[1] Human Rights Watch alleged that Enron and the other owners of the project "benefited directly from an official policy of suppressing dissent through misuse of the law, harassment of anti-Enron protest leaders, and prominent environmental activists and police practices ranging from arbitrary to brutal."[2] Opponents filed more than two dozen lawsuits in an effort to stop the project. Enron won them all. But during the lengthy haggling process, the project kept growing in size and cost. Local politicians got new roads, schools, and other projects rolled into Dabhol.

Mark was getting plenty of help from the Clinton administration on the project. Clinton's chief of staff, Thomas F. "Mack" McLarty, pushed hard for Enron's position. So did Clinton's energy secretary, Hazel O'Leary. Enron made sure to compensate the people who helped the project in India. About the same time Mark was pushing to revive the project, Enron hired the just-retired U.S. ambassador to India, Frank Wisner. Enron installed Wisner on the Board of Directors of its subsidiary, Enron Oil and Gas, which had a number of projects in India. Given his expertise, it's no surprise the company appointed Wisner to chair its "International Strategy Committee."

The assistance from the Clinton administration, combined with Mark's doggedness, convinced the Indians to approve the construction of Phase Two of the project, which added another 1,444 megawatts of power and a $1-billion liquefied natural gas (LNG) facility. What had been a billion-dollar project during Phase One would now be a $2.9-billion project.

Mark's ability to push through the second part of Dabhol before the first phase was even completed amazed many Enron employees who were working on Dabhol. They believed the company needed to let the naphtha-fired Phase One get up and running—and more important, show it was profitable—before they built the LNG terminal. But Mark prevailed. She got a bigger project. And a bigger project meant—no surprise—a bigger bonus. Getting the second phase of Dabhol approved right away "meant doubling or tripling her bonus," said one Enron employee who worked on Dabhol. "I'll never again underestimate the power of an incentive compensation program and the desire it can instill in people."

The Dabhol project made Mark one of the most famous women in India. It also did wonders for her ego. Unfortunately, no one was willing—or able—to harness her ambition. "I enjoy being a world-class problem solver," she said in 1996. "I'm constantly asking, 'How far can I go? How much can I do?'"[3] That kind of ambition was obvious to one executive who worked closely with her. Mark "wanted to eclipse [John] Wing. Ultimately, she wanted to eclipse Kinder, Skilling, and even Lay."

By 1997, her division's backlog of international projects totaled some $20 billion. In 1998, *Forbes* reported that Enron International had revenues of $1.1 billion and reportedly contributed about 17 percent of Enron's operating profits.[4] But about that same time, Enron quit breaking out its international revenues, a move that prevented outsiders from seeing whether the company's international ventures ever made any real money.

Profitable or not for Enron, Mark did very well. Company proxies show that between 1996 and 1998, her total compensation was $25.7 million—that's more than any other Enron employee during that time, including Ken Lay ($16.7 million) and Jeff Skilling ($25.4 million). By 1998, she was named vice chairman of the Enron board and held voting power on more stock than anyone else on the board except Robert

Wells like this 1906 gusher at Spindletop helped spawn the creation of dozens of oil and pipeline companies including Houston Natural Gas, which became Enron. (The Granger Collection)

Pipelines like this one being constructed in East Texas during the late 1960s or early 1970s, helped Houston Natural Gas become one of Houston's most profitable companies.

In 1993, Enron CEO Ken Lay was standing tall. (Getty Images)

Rich Kinder, Enron's president and chief operating officer from 1990 to 1996, went on to become one of Houston's truly Big Rich.

Rebecca Mark thinks Big Thoughts while aboard a plush Enron jet. Although her failed water and power projects cost Enron $2 billion, she flew away with $100 million. (© 2002 Michael J.N. Bowles)

Jeff Skilling, the ruthless McKinsey & Co. consultant who became Enron's president, and later, its CEO, never doubted his own genius. After a speech to a group of analysts, Skilling said they "didn't get it. I was brilliant." (Paul Hosefors/*New York Times*)

Andy Fastow, Enron's duplicitous chief financial officer, created a panoply of off-balance sheet entities that totally corrupted the company's books. (Reuters)

Enron temptress Amanda Martin carried on a torrid affair with (married) Enron executive Ken Rice for several years. Her 2001 pay package totaled $10.4 million. She still works at Enron. (*Houston Chronicle*)

Nancy McNeil Kinder (left) and Rich Kinder (right), who began having an affair while both worked at Enron (she was Ken Lay's assistant), chat up the former president and first lady at a charity event in 1998. (*Houston Chronicle*)

Enron CEO Ken Lay awards a silver platter to George H. W. Bush as sons George W. and Jeb look on. The platter matches their silver spoons. (*Houston Chronicle*)

Wendy Gramm and her husband, U.S. Senator Phil Gramm, were acquired by Enron in 1993 in a cash and stock deal worth tens of thousands of dollars. Enron's equity interest in the couple is now worthless. (Paul Hosefors/*New York Times*)

Even as Enron's finances faltered in late 2000, construction continued on the company's new $300 million building, which had four floors designed specifically for trading. (Getty Images)

Enron's hard working board of directors, 1998.

Sherron Watkins watches Jeff Skilling as he testifies before Congress on February 25, 2002. Watkins, who is writing a book about her experience, still works at Enron. (Reuters)

One of the Confederate Hellcats that Ken Rice purchased as an office decoration for Enron Broadband Services. Cost: about $30,000.

Linda Lay, wife of Ken Lay, cries that she and her disgraced husband have "nothing left" while appearing on the *Today* show on January 28 and 29, 2002. (Reuters)

The Lays' version of "nothing" includes their homestead, which occupies the entire 33rd floor of this swank River Oaks high-rise. Their 12,827 square-foot abode was recently appraised at $7.8 million.

Located near the intersection of Avarice Avenue and Gluttony Drive, Linda Lay's new boutique in Houston, Jus' Stuff, is *the* place to shop for antiques and other gewgaws once owned by the rich and infamous.

Jeff Skilling's $4.2 million Mediterranean-style mansion in River Oaks, Houston's most prestigious neighborhood. The fence and gate in front of the house were built a few weeks after Enron declared bankruptcy.

Bill and Sherri Saunders. She was fired on December 3, 2001 after working at Enron for twenty-four years. Her retirement fund, once worth nearly $1 million, is now worth less than $100,000.

Belfer, Ken Lay, and Jeff Skilling. Despite her wealth of assets, Enron began treating Mark like a favored Third World country. In 1998, Enron forgave all of the principal and interest on a $955,343 loan the company had granted her in 1997. In early 1999, the company allowed even more debt forgiveness, pardoning an additional $700,000 loan the company made to her in 1998.

She also spent plenty of the company's money. While traveling, she insisted on limousines and the finest hotels. And she was apparently allergic to commercial airlines. According to Enron's proxies, her personal use of the company's jets cost over $141,000 for 1997 and 1998 alone. One estimate put her air travel at 300,000 miles per year, meaning the cost of keeping Mark aloft in Enron's jets for business travel likely cost millions of dollars per year. Personnel at Enron International dreaded Mark's visits, not because she would see anything they didn't want her to see but because, as one executive said, "whenever her jet touched down, we knew it was going to cost our project $60,000."

In addition to the salary, loans, and perks, Mark earned big cash bonuses on many of Enron's international projects. Her 1998 employment agreement with the company shows she was paid more than $3 million for two relatively small overseas projects. And she apparently made an enormous amount of money on the Dabhol project. Lead project developers in Enron's international business were paid between 3 and 4 percent of the net present value of a project when they closed the deal. When Mark pushed through Phase Two of the Dabhol project, the energy facility was given a net present value of $1 billion, according to one source close to the project. That means Mark likely split a bonus of $30 to $40 million with one or two other people.

Of course, with all her newfound wealth, Mark couldn't live in just any Houston neighborhood. She was a Big Shot and she belonged in River Oaks. So in September 1998, she bought a beautiful $2-million property complete with 2.3 acres of land and a big red brick home, in an area of River Oaks known as Tall Timbers. It wasn't quite up to style, though, so Mark had the house completely remodeled in 1999.

The remodeling left her with a 10,286-square-foot home with five bedrooms, six bathrooms, two half bathrooms, and a swimming pool. Not bad for a girl who started on a rural farm.

Later in 1999, to celebrate the financing for Phase Two of Dabhol, Enron held the party to end all parties for Mark and her team. Numerous politicians from India were flown to Houston. There was a sit-down dinner. The entertainment was provided by Cirque de Soleil. Every attendee was given a small piece of fancy crystal. It was an impressive event. And true to Rebecca Mark's style, no expense was spared. That same attitude would prevail at Azurix.

25

Enron's Waterworld

NOVEMBER 1999 Rebecca Mark's glorious fantasy was coming to an end. And Jeff Skilling was enjoying every minute of it.

Most of Azurix's board members, including Mark, Skilling, and Ken Lay, were sitting around the large wooden conference room table in the Azurix office on the tenth floor of 3 Allen Center in downtown Houston. It was November 1999. Scarcely six months had passed since Azurix's initial public offering (IPO)—in which it raised $695 million—and yet the newly born water company was essentially broke. The cash shortage was so bad, there were questions about whether the company would even have enough money to make payroll. Just a few days earlier, on November 4, 1999, Azurix's stock had dropped by 40 percent after the company warned that it would miss its fourth-quarter profit targets. The company blamed the shortfall on high start-up costs.

"How could this have happened?" demanded Skilling, who sat at the opposite end of the long conference table—as far away as possible—from Mark.

"Look. You know how this happened. We've been buying up businesses all over the world. Argentina has been a disaster. We are trying to build Azurix by getting a presence in lots of markets," responded Mark.

"Alright, alright, enough," snapped Lay, who had been quieting the sniping between Skilling and Mark throughout the day.

The meeting was taking far too long and too little progress was being made to satisfy Lay, who liked his meetings orderly and efficient. Lay had hoped that by spinning off Azurix, he'd be done with the enmity between Skilling and Mark, but the corporate structure of the new company had only exacerbated the old tensions. Skilling was on Azurix's board, a position from which he could continue to hector his old nemesis. But the friction between Mark and Skilling wasn't the biggest problem. Money was. Through poor planning and extravagant spending, Mark had gone through nearly all of the money Azurix had raised in its IPO.

Much has been written about the various dot-com and Internet companies and their "burn rates," the term used to describe how much cash a company uses as it tries to prove its business model, get customers, and begin producing revenues, and, everyone hopes, profits. One of the most talked about companies of that period was Amazon.com, the giant on-line book retailer. In early 2000, the company had garnered 20 million customers but had also accumulated losses of $1.2 billion and had a burn rate estimated at $115.7 million per month. But even the mighty Amazon was no match for a company with Rebecca Mark at the helm.

Azurix didn't burn cash, it incinerated it. Between June and the end of 1999, Azurix—despite having just a fraction of the customers that Amazon had—consumed cash at a rate of $115.8 million per month. Much of that was being spent by the company's development teams, which were scouring the globe for water companies they could buy. According to one executive at Azurix, those teams were spending more than $60 million a month on hotels, consultants, and airfare. But by late 1999, the teams were finding that there weren't nearly enough good projects for sale. That meant that by the time Lay, Skilling, and Mark met around the conference table that day in downtown Houston, the company's business model was doomed. The privatizations that it had believed would happen in numerous countries around the world were not occurring. To stay alive, Azurix needed more cash, and the only place it could go, at least in the short term, was back to Enron. That gave Skilling all the advantages he savored: He was smelling fear, he was ready for confrontation, and better still, he was in a position to humiliate Rebecca Mark. As one Azurix insider noted, "Skilling's whole push seemed to be about 'How can I embarrass Rebecca?'"

It was the worst possible turn of events for Mark, who had dreamed that Azurix would be her escape vehicle, the way to once and for all get away from that bastard, Skilling. Azurix was going to be *hers*. She would be in control. Meetings would happen when *she* decided they'd happen, not when Lay or Skilling wanted them to happen. Azurix was part of her divorce settlement with Skilling. There had been an unspoken agreement: Skilling could have the CEO job at Enron. In return, he would support her bid to create Azurix. Mark would have her own company, and along with it, she'd get the chance to prove, once and for all, that she belonged at the top, in control. Azurix would allow her to show that her skills and her brainpower were equal to any of those jerks at Enron, especially Skilling.

It wasn't turning out that way. The water business was far more difficult than she'd ever imagined. Azurix had become just another money-losing headache for Enron. Just like the Dabhol project in India, problems kept popping up everywhere Mark looked. The French water companies Compagnie Générale des Eaux (now part of conglomerate Vivendi Universal) and Suez-Lyonnaise des Eaux were slowly drowning Azurix in almost every country that had concessions open for bids. The two French companies had been active in the global water business for about a century. They were providing water to nearly 160 million people around the world, and they were none too pleased that a bunch of yahoos from Texas were swimming in their pool.

And the Divine Ms. Mark hadn't exactly helped Azurix's cause. Instead, she went out of her way to piss off the French. "We waste enormous quantities of water because no market exists," she told the *Economist*. By trying to create commercial water markets, Mark claimed Azurix was creating "something completely different, unlike the French who have piddled around with this industry for the past 150 years."[1]

The water-soaked Gauls were none to happy with Mark and thereafter pledged that the next time they "piddled," it would be on Azurix's grave. They wouldn't have to wait long.

Rebecca Mark needed to prove that she meant business. She needed a big acquisition. and she needed it in a hurry. And by mid-1998, she became convinced that Wessex Water was the perfect choice. Wessex was among the most profitable water utilities in the United Kingdom. It provided water or wastewater service to about 2.5 million people in southwestern England, principally in the counties of Avon, Dorset, and Somerset, as well as in parts of Devon, Gloucestershire, Hampshire, and Wiltshire.

Colin Skellett, Wessex's CEO, vividly remembered the first meeting he had with Rebecca Mark and the late Cliff Baxter (a high-ranking Enron executive who specialized in mergers and acquisitions and who committed suicide in January 2002). The June 1998 meeting was held in Bath, a former Edwardian-era spa town and present-day dormitory for London's business elite in southwestern England, where Wessex has its headquarters. Mark, who was fond of expensive hotels, liked the Royal Crescent Hotel, known for its expensive lodging and Georgian architecture. Mark and Baxter told Skellett, the Wessex CEO, that they wanted to keep their negotiations quiet. But Mark apparently couldn't quite manage to restrain her love of the high life. "This large black stretch limousine turned up outside the Royal Crescent," recalled Skellett. "It was Rebecca with her short skirt and long legs. If you want to arrive discreetly in Bath, having a blond in a short skirt in a long limousine is not the way to do it. She made quite a splash when she arrived."

Mark and Baxter told Skellett and Wessex chairman Nicholas Hood that Enron was in a hurry to get into the water business and wanted to buy Wessex as quickly as possible. As Skellett remembered, Mark offered to buy Wessex for about $10.30 per share, a 30-percent premium over the $8 the company's shares were fetching at the time. Skellett was convinced that a deal was possible. But he and Hood needed a few days to sort out the proposal and discuss it with Wessex's board. They arranged to meet a few days later, again at the Royal Crescent. Skellett and Hood were a bit late for the meeting. And according to Skellett, Baxter went out in front of the hotel to smoke a cigarette. While there, the hotel's doorman reportedly asked Baxter, "So are you the guy who's here to buy Wessex?" Baxter, said Skellett, was stunned. "After that they became paranoid about security," Skellett recalled with a chuckle.

Despite the breach of security, the two sides sealed the deal, and on July 24, 1998, they announced that Enron would buy Wessex in a deal worth $2.88 billion. Not only would Enron's new water business (which was christened Azurix shortly after the Wessex purchase) get a big utility, it would get a group of well-trained personnel with technical expertise in the water business whom Azurix could deploy elsewhere. The water business is "a logical extension of Enron's expertise developed in the worldwide energy business," crowed Ken Lay in a press release sent out the day the deal was announced. Wessex's operations combined with Enron's "expertise in energy infrastructure project development, asset management, regulatory, finance and risk management services, will enable the new company to become a strong competitor in the global water industry," he predicted.

On the surface, it wasn't a bad idea. Enron had been a pioneer in both the gas trading business and the electricity trading business. And it figured it could do the same with Azurix in the water business. "I don't know how many times I heard that water was going to be 'just like gas and power,'" recalled a young MBA who was among the first people hired at Azurix. "But it was a lot."

Rebecca Mark desperately wanted to apply her deal-making skills to other sectors and believed water was the next logical step. And she had several reasons to believe it. First and foremost, the water treatment business is energy intensive. Water engineers point out that about one-third of the cost of moving and treating water is energy related. Enron viewed itself as the king of the energy business, and therefore, it could get a twofer in the water business. Enron could not only provide the power and the energy risk management tools a given water utility might need, it could also run that utility itself, thereby increasing its potential profits.

Furthermore, Enron saw the global water business as a regulated business that was going to be deregulated and operated by private companies (again, a parallel to gas and power). When that deregulation occurred in countries around the world, Enron wanted to be there, with assets on the ground. Once it owned a big asset such as Wessex or a water utility in another country, it could use its risk management and trading skills to make money by selling water to water-short regions and buying it from water-rich areas. It might also be able to profit by selling lower-cost power from an Enron power plant to the water utility. To do that, it would buy water utilities in target countries. The business plan, known as a "roll-up" strategy, had worked in such other sectors as trash and funeral homes. It would surely work in water. The idea was simple: The buyer would acquire a lot of small mom-and-pop companies and then use their cash flow to pay off the debt needed to buy them in the first place. In the process, the buyer would gain economies of scale.

Enron estimated the value of the worldwide water market at over $300 billion. Although Suez and Vivendi were the dominant players, Mark convinced Ken Lay that Enron could capture water contracts in Europe, Latin America, and Asia that would complement their existing energy businesses in those regions. And because they were Enron, there was no way they could be wrong. Or was there?

The world's water utilities have few interconnection points, a fact that makes moving and trading water very difficult. In the gas business, pipelines intersect in numerous locations. In the electricity business, large utilities may not share generating plants but their power lines often have overlapping service territories. That means that utilities can ship or "wheel" power from one location to another over existing power lines, and they can do it almost instantly, at very little cost (other than the small loss of power that occurs in the power lines themselves).

Water is a different story. Unlike gas and power, it's heavy, 8.33 pounds per gallon. That means it's very expensive to move long distances. In addition, water is a highly variable commodity. Gas and power have very little variation. A BTU of gas and a kilowatt of electricity are virtually identical, no matter where they are delivered. Not so with water, which can have wildly divergent characteristics, like taste, salinity, and turbidity.

Those characteristics matter. They matter a lot. Water comes freighted with an entirely different political and social sensibility than gas or electricity ever will. Water has religious, nationalist, and political overtones in virtually every region of the world. And unlike gas and power, people are not willing to pay high prices for it. Water is viewed as a birthright, not a luxury. And towns, cities, and countries are willing to dispatch activists, lawyers, and even armies to protect what they view as "their" water. As Mark Twain famously wrote, "Whiskey's for drinking, water's for fighting."

Heckmann said that in early 1998, he warned the Enronistas that water is so fraught with logistical, practical, and political problems that they had better go slowly, if at all. "Water has been the basic premise of life since the beginning of man," Heckmann remarked. "That's not true for power. So you have ageless beliefs and developments on how water should be used, treated, and cared for. So communities jealously guard their water rights and water developments. They tend to be built around water and sewer businesses that are typically manned by union people. There's nepotism galore because the most important thing in these businesses is stability, not cost."

Alas, the history of water and its political significance mattered little to Rebecca Mark. At Enron International, she'd made her reputation by moving at warp speed and then accelerating from there. Her focus was on doing deals and more deals, not on thinking about strategic moves or big-picture analysis of water's geopolitical significance. So in the months after the Wessex acquisition, she negotiated what was, in essence, her divorce settlement with Skilling: She'd get her own publicly traded company. And she'd get it as soon as was humanly possible.

The early 1999 decision to accelerate the initial public offering astounded some of the early hires at Azurix. They couldn't understand why the company, which was still developing its business plan, would go public so quickly. "By the time you distilled it down, it was clear that the business we were in was the IPO business, not the water business. They'd picked the water business. But the business, really, was to have an IPO so they could take advantage of the equity market," explained one executive who was hired in late 1998.

The equity markets were booming. In 1998 alone, American companies raised $36.8 billion from initial public offerings. Of that amount, more than $2.7 billion was raised in IPOs conducted for nearly four dozen Internet companies. Azurix's idea to take on the world water business was certainly as good as dogfood.com or any of the myriad other digital Ponzi schemes that were attracting millions of dollars of new funding. So they decided to set their IPO for June 9, 1999.

Despite the fertile ground for IPOs, the folks at Azurix probably should have paid attention to the problems plaguing another Houston company that had launched massive roll-ups of smaller companies. In January 1999, Service Corporation International, the world's largest funeral home company, announced it wouldn't meet Wall Street's profit projections. Although the company blamed falling death rates, it appeared that the funeral giant, headed by its rapacious founder, Robert Waltrip, had grown too fast and had acquired far too much debt to remain profitable. The company's stock got crushed by the news, falling by more than 40 percent in one day.

Mark wasn't watching other companies. She and her acolytes were in a hurry. And within a few days of going public, Mark's stock options in Azurix were worth about $50 million.

But as any good cook knows, haste makes waste. In the case of Azurix, it led to a decision that arguably sealed the company's fate almost before it was born. The Wessex acquisition had been costly. Enron had bought the company at the absolute top of the market.

However, there was plenty of cash flow, so Wessex could pay for itself. That wouldn't be true for the Buenos Aires deal.

Alberto Gude's first instructions to his new charges were simple: "Don't tell anyone you are British."

Gude, who was vice president of information technology at Enron, wasn't being silly. He was being prudent. It was summer 1999 and he already had plenty of other problems. Gude had recently flown from Houston to Buenos Aires so he could help Azurix set up its computer systems and sort through the mess of electronic records Azurix had inherited from the previous operator of the city's utility.

It didn't matter to him that the chaps from Britain were just regular engineers from Wessex Water. It didn't matter that they were going to help Azurix run the water utility. Local history mattered. And by luck or by fate, when the British lads arrived, it was nearly seventeen years to the day since British warships and infantry had routed Argentine forces in a series of land and sea battles over a small set of islands called the Falklands, or Las Malvinas, to the Argentinians. Gude, a practical man who was born in Cuba, knew that the Argentinians were still mad about the Falklands War and, furthermore, having a British passport was not going to win friends and influence pretty girls in the pubs of Buenos Aires.

Sending British water wonks to Argentina isn't the same as sending coal to Newcastle, but it was just about as sensible. However, Azurix's management had no other options. Wessex was their cornerstone, their multibillion-dollar red carpet into the water business. And all of Wessex's employees were, therefore, needed. So as soon as Azurix won the bid for the entity known as AGOSBA, short for Administración General de Obras Sanitarias Buenos Aires, calls were made to Wessex's headquarters in Bath, looking for people able to go to Argentina in short order. It was, by all accounts, a disaster from the get-go.

"They sent the guys from Wessex—none of whom spoke Spanish—all the way from England. Plus, there was the whole lack of cultural sensitivity regarding the Falklands," one senior member of Azurix's management team recalled. Although this second British invasion of Argentina is amusing, Azurix had other problems in Buenos Aires. First and foremost was the cost.

Within a few days of submitting the final bids, it became obvious that Azurix had blown it. Mark's company had agreed to pay $438.6 million for the right to provide some 2 million people in and around Buenos Aires with drinking water. The next-highest bid was about $150 million. Adding insult to injury was the fact that Azurix was not only going to have to come up with new headquarters and new personnel, it was also going to have to invest heavily in infrastructure just to get the plants up and running.

The stupendously high bid was the result of poor planning, poor communication, and poor judgment. For instance, shortly after Azurix won the bid for AGOSBA, the company's lead managers found out that the headquarters building, where the utility had been run for many years, was not included in the deal. The majority of the staff needed to run the utility wasn't included, either. Nor were the billing and collection systems. As an Azurix engineer later said, Azurix "didn't buy a water company in Buenos Aires. We bought the right to create a water company."

Within days of his arrival, Gude discovered that AGOSBA's billing records were a disaster. "Suddenly, 16,000 records were missing. Every week more records would be lost," said Gude. That meant that customers who were supposed to be getting water from Azurix would likely be able to get it for nothing because the company wouldn't know how to find them. Gude and others suspected that former employees of the water utility had obliged their friends by deleting their names and billing records from the company's files before the facilities got turned over to Azurix. That meant that right off the bat, Azurix's revenues would be far lower than it had expected.

There was another problem: Many of the existing utility customers paid their water bills in person. Every month, they traveled to the utility's offices and paid for their service in cash. Again, the AGOSBA deal didn't give Azurix the utility's offices. Instead, their new storefront was several blocks away from the old office. That meant that all of Azurix's new customers who were accustomed to paying their water bill in cash wouldn't know where to go. Azurix officials had to be creative. And after some thinking, they came up with the only feasible solution: Hire some pretty young women.

There was no way the company's clerks could handle all of the customers that would be coming by the old office to pay their bills. They needed a group of people to redirect the old customers—with their payments in hand—to the new office. So the company hired a bevy of young women. On that first billing day, the young women stood outside the old utility building and directed customers to the new Azurix office, where cashiers took the money (as well as the names and addresses) of all the people who came in to pay their bills.

It was an unconventional solution to a sticky business problem. But it worked pretty well. And the newly imported water engineers from Wessex Water were more than a little impressed. "They came from a very staid, regulated British utility business and now they're in South America, they've got good-looking girls in tight shirts and tight skirts with the Azurix logo on their shirts, and they're snuggling up to the customers," one Azurix veteran said, laughing. "It was hilarious."

If the Buenos Aires debacle wasn't going to kill Azurix, Rebecca Mark's free-spending ways were.

"Azurix operated as if it were a Fortune 500 company from the beginning," said Skellett, the CEO of Wessex. "The water business is pretty much a nickel-and-dime business. Your whole focus is on driving out every bit of cost. To them expenses didn't seem to matter. In the first year, we were bemused. We thought they knew what they were doing."

Ah, but that's just it. All graduates of the Harvard Business School *act* like they know what they're doing. They went to Harvard, didn't they? But when it came to managing cash and cash flow, Rebecca Mark was just as clueless as her fellow Harvard Business School graduate—

Jeff Skilling. Like Skilling, Mark spent cash as though she owned a currency printer. Several sources at Azurix said she spent tens of thousands of dollars decorating her office with expensive rugs, imported drapes, and artwork. And though some executives argued that her posh office was justifiable, no one agreed with her decision to build the "stairway to heaven."

By mid-1999, Azurix was growing at a rapid clip. New people were being hired to perform various tasks—no one was exactly sure what, but they were important, weren't they?—and they had to have desks and offices. Before long, the tenth floor at 3 Allen Center where Azurix was headquartered was too small for the young company. The building manager agreed to let Azurix take over the ninth floor, and people were already moving down there. But darn it, what if people working on the tenth floor needed to see some of the people who were working on nine? They couldn't be sending people down the stairwells or on the elevator, could they?

Something had to be done. So Mark decided that the company should have its own stairway connecting the ninth and tenth floors. Architects were consulted. Engineers engineered. And soon, the stairway, a beautiful, curved stairway with glass panels under the banisters, was under construction. Never mind that it took months to build or that insiders say it cost a reported $1 million. Many workers at Azurix were stunned. "I could have used that $1 million to buy another company," said one high-ranking executive.

There were other big hits to Azurix's cash flow. The company spent $5.5 million building a swank new office in London, a few blocks from Big Ben. Azurix signed a fifteen-year lease on the 23,000-square-foot office that was going to cost the firm £83,000 a month. "It was meant to be the European headquarters for Azurix, so it was definitely top-of-the-line space," commented a source who managed the company's facilities. Azurix never moved in.

Azurix also planned to spend tens of millions of dollars buying Synagro Technologies, a Houston company that processes sewage sludge. Synagro was going to be an integral part of Azurix's growth plan. But in late October 1999, Azurix suddenly called the deal off, apparently after company officials realized they couldn't afford to buy Synagro. That story played out with Enron later paying Synagro $6 million to settle lawsuits related to Azurix's actions.

The company took another big hit in November 1999, when Britain's director general of water services announced a 12-percent rate cut for all of Azurix's customers in southern England. The rate cut had been rumored for a long time. And several water industry officials said Azurix should have known the move was coming. Prepared or not, it was another major blow. The company's cornerstone, the utility that was supposed to throw off lots of cash to fund expansions into other areas, was hamstrung. Azurix insiders were stunned. "It couldn't have been predicted," said one Azurix veteran. "The stars lined up against us."

Despite the constant drain on Azurix's cash reserves, Mark didn't spare expenses when it came to her salary. Azurix paid Mark $710,000 a year to head a company that was losing money hand over fist. In addition to her salary, the company made sure that Mark didn't have to fly with commoners during her free time. In 1999 alone, the company gave Mark an additional $101,146 to cover her personal use of the company's aircraft.

Amanda Martin—Ken Rice's girlfriend—was also well paid. Rumor had it that Ken Lay moved Martin to Azurix, in part to get her away from her married boyfriend, Rice. Whatever the reason, Martin became Azurix's executive director and president of North America. Her salary for 1999: $400,000. But her future was not compromised when Azurix folded. She went back to a cushy job at Enron Corp., where she made still more money. In 2001, Martin's cash compensation from Enron totaled $8.4 million, which included a salary of $349,487, a long-term incentive bonus of $5.1 million and $2.8 million in "other" payments. Martin also received another $2 million by exercising her stock options.[2]

Azurix even spent huge amounts of money to get rid of executives. Shortly after her shouting match with Skilling in the tenth-floor conference room at Azurix's office, the Azurix Board of Directors gave Mark an ultimatum: Either get rid of several of your top executives, or resign. Naturally, Mark chose the former. She fired three of her top executives—Rod Gray, Alex Kulpecz, and Ed Robinson—a move that cost her about $7.6 million. Gray, Azurix's former chief financial officer and vice chairman, got more than $3.5 million in severance pay from Azurix. Kulpecz, a mergers and acquisitions specialist who spent a grand total of fourteen months at Azurix, got about $2 million in severance, including $181,817 in housing expenses and up to $83,787 to cover "schooling and bus expenses" for his children. Robinson, another mergers specialist, got a bit more than $2 million, in addition to a computer and a Palm Pilot.

The Azurix board had seven members. They included Lord John Wakeham, the distinguished member of the British House of Lords, Lay, Skilling, Pug Winokur, Joe Sutton, John Duncan, and Rebecca Mark. They were not paid for their service on the Azurix board. They did, however, get stock options in Azurix.

In early 2000, the board authorized Mark's plan to save Azurix by getting another capital infusion from Wall Street. The company floated $599.8 million in junk bonds, one-third of which paid 10.75-percent interest in an effort to stabilize the business and continue buying new utilities around the world.

It didn't work. By the summer of 2000, Azurix's losses, once a torrent, were a geyser. A few months earlier, an algae bloom in an AGOSBA water treatment plant had fouled the city of Buenos Aires's drinking water. The entire city was in an uproar over the taste and smell of the tap water. Revenues from Argentina, once a sporadic stream, were now a bare trickle.

The handwriting was on the wall. And on August 25, 2000, Mark resigned as chairman and CEO of Azurix and gave up her seat on Enron's Board of Directors. Her string of business failures has likely assured that she will never get another job in corporate America. The woman who prefers clothes from Armani and Escada is all dressed up with nowhere to go. Not that she needs to go anywhere, mind you.

Three months before she quit Azurix, she sold 104,240 Enron

shares, a move that brought her total stock-sale proceeds to $82.5 million. Counting all the salary, stock options, and no-payback loans that she got from Enron, Mark probably banked somewhere in the neighborhood of $100 million. That's a truly staggering sum when you consider that her misguided deals in India, Argentina, and elsewhere cost investors at least $2 billion.

But those failures were in the past. None of them mattered. She was rich, gorgeous, and married again. Her new husband was Michael Jusbasche, a rich Bolivian-born businessman. The two were moving into her house in River Oaks and would continue supporting a few local causes. The failure of Azurix was no longer a concern. In early 2002, Mark told *Vanity Fair* that the company "wasn't a disaster. We couldn't survive as a public company because we didn't have earnings sufficient to support the growth of the stock."[3]

Oh.

So Azurix wasn't a disaster. It just didn't have "earnings sufficient to support the growth of the stock." That's a beautifully crafted phrase to describe a dog of a company that should never have gone public in the first place. In the end, Mark's vision—the commoditization of water, water trading, yet more fawning profiles of her in the business press—landed with a stinging belly flop. And Azurix, the company that was to "become a major global water company" lasted as a publicly traded entity for just twenty-one months.[4]

The bath Enron took on Azurix would prove very costly. Mark's debacle had been financed with—*what else?*—off-the-balance-sheet entities, so that Enron didn't have to reflect Azurix's debts on its balance sheet. And those interlinked entities, called Marlin and Osprey, would play a pivotal role in drowning Enron. There's no doubt the Azurix mess was poorly thought out, but Rebecca Mark and her team weren't really corrupt. Misguided maybe. They made some bad judgments and didn't pay attention to expenses. Perhaps their idea was just ahead of its time. But they never purposely misled investors or committed fraud. That would not be the case at another overhyped Enron venture, Enron Broadband Services.

26
Hyping the Bandwidth Bubble

JANUARY 20, 2000
Enron closing price: $67.25

Stock analysts and professional money managers have an unspoken etiquette: During meetings with companies, you should always leave the meeting room when using your cell phone to give buy or sell orders. It's a simple rule, born out of a desire to show respect for the company and for fellow analysts. No one wants to listen to someone else's transactions while trying to follow the points of a speaker on the podium.

But at Enron's January 20, 2000, meeting with Wall Street analysts at the Four Seasons Hotel in downtown Houston, that etiquette was routinely ignored. About 150 analysts had crammed into the ornate Oriental-theme ballroom at the swank hotel to hear Jeff Skilling's prognostications. Skilling talked about Enron's growing trading business, its success in energy services, and, of course, a little bit about pipelines. By midmorning the price of Enron stock was ramping steadily upward, climbing $2 or more per hour. The analysts in the room began suspecting that something was afoot. A year earlier, in the same room, Skilling had announced the formation of Azurix, Enron's water business. And there had been lots of rumors. A month earlier, Skilling and other Enron officials had made the rounds in Manhattan, talking with stock analysts at Goldman Sachs and elsewhere about the company's planned entry into the telecom business. A few analysts had mentioned the potential telecom play in their notes to investors, but none of them had all the details.

By 2:30 P.M. or so, tens of portfolio managers and analysts were on their phones. "They weren't even leaving their chairs, they were calling their traders and saying, 'Buy it, I don't care what the price is, buy it,'" recalled one attendee. Everyone knew something was up. Finally, as the clock approached 3:00 P.M. and the close of trading on the New York Stock Exchange, Skilling told the analysts what several had suspected: Enron was getting into the Internet business. "The broadband explosion is real, it is here *now* and it will fundamentally change the existing Internet delivery platform," Skilling told the increasingly excited managers and analysts. Enron was going to apply the expertise it had learned in gas and power to the Internet infrastructure. It would trade capacity in new-tech pipelines, the hair-thin glass strands that carry light waves. And it would steal market share—and billions of dollars—from those slow-moving dinosaurs of yesteryear, the phone companies. Skilling said Enron's bandwidth trading and "intermediation" (one of Skilling's favorite words) would "bring fundamental changes to the Internet."

Then Scott McNealy walked in the room.

McNealy, the toothy billionaire and CEO of equipment maker Sun Microsystems, was on hand to partner with Skilling on an announcement: Enron was going to buy 18,000 of Sun's top-of-the-line servers and use them in its fiber optic network. "Enron is a natural partner for us because together we have the technology and expertise to transform the way that next-generation applications are developed and delivered on the Internet," McNealy told the excited crowd.

Fortune magazine later wrote that McNealy's appearance "was like Jesus showing up at a tent revival. Analysts swooned; they cheered."[1] Swoon they did. Within days of the Enron meeting, Edward Tirello Jr., an analyst with the investment firm Deutsche Bank Alex. Brown, wrote, "All we can say is WOW! Just when we began to ponder the potential with a very healthy skepticism, Enron brilliantly anticipated the reaction and thrust Sun Microsystems' billionaire CEO Scott McNealy into the mix."[2]

The meeting occurred at the height of the Internet craze. Enron wanted a way to capitalize on it and succeeded magnificently. The day before the meeting, Enron's stock was selling for $53.50. By the time the New York Stock Exchange closed on January 20 and the money managers at the meeting had phoned in their buy orders, Enron's shares had soared more than 25 percent, closing at $67.25. Enron was suddenly a "New Economy" stock.

For Enron and Skilling, the timing of the broadband announcement could scarcely have worked out better. In January 2000, telephony and the Internet were the New New Things. If Global Crossing, with its mountain of debt and world of fiber optic promise, was worth $53 per share, then Enron, with its huge energy business, should be worth more, right? Plenty of other technology stocks were carrying huge valuations when Skilling made his sales pitch. On the same day that Enron closed above $67, shares of Internet portal Yahoo! were selling for $351. Shares in equipment maker Cisco Systems were selling for $112, and a single share of tiny software maker Vignette cost $196.

Skilling and other leaders at Enron "saw the Internet stock bubble and they were pissed off that they didn't get to ride that wave," said Stan Hanks, an engineer who helped design Enron's fiber optic network. "This was payback. This was Skilling and the others saying to Wall Street that 'this boring old company, this natural gas company is smarter than all you fucks put together.'"

Payback or not, Skilling was able to count on the cooperation of a complicit group of Wall Street cheerleaders—oops, I mean analysts—none of whom knew much, if anything, about the challenges that Enron faced in the telecom business.

At about the same time that Enron announced its broadband play, John Sidgmore, the vice chairman of phone giant MCI WorldCom, dismissed Enron's ploy out of hand. "Honestly, what possible expertise could Enron have to help in the communications industry?" he asked a reporter from *Fortune*. "They have zero experience that I know of."[3] Sidgmore is now MCI WorldCom's CEO.

Despite the gas giant's lack of experience, Enron's acolytes were singing hosannas to Skilling and his crew. The response from Merrill Lynch analyst Donato Eassey was almost embarrassing. Eassey didn't just suspend his skepticism, he put it through the nearest shredder, then burned what was left over. Eassey—apparently relying on numbers provided by Enron, which pegged its broadband trading revenues at $13.6 billion per year by 2004—estimated that Enron's operating profits from broadband would total $2.1 billion within four years. "They said the natural gas market would not open up in the 1980s, and it has in a big way," said Eassey. "It was the same with electricity. All the naysayers out there for broadband will be wrong, too."[4]

Raymond Niles, director of integrated gas and power research at Salomon Smith Barney Inc. in New York, jumped on the bandwagon, too. "Trading bandwidth is a home run for the companies that traded energy commodities," he said. Niles told reporters that Enron would succeed in the bandwidth provisioning and trading business because it would be able to transfer the skills it learned in trading energy to the new business.[5]

It wouldn't be the first time the analysts were wrong about Enron. And if only they'd bothered to check out the qualifications of Enron Broadband Services' new boss, they might have been a wee bit more skeptical.

When Rebecca Mark started Azurix, she bought expensive antiques and rugs. When Ken Rice took charge of Enron Broadband Services in early 2000, he bought motorcycles.

Both executives wanted to impress potential customers. Mark was going to do it by showing them how tasteful and classy she was. Rice was going to show that he was mucho macho. And for a man who routinely cheated on his wife and took dangerous vacations with Skilling (hiking on glaciers in South America, racing off-road vehicles in Australia, riding motorcycles in Mexico) that meant that any old motorcycle just wouldn't do. Hondas and Harleys were too pedestrian. Rice wanted more flash, more horsepower, and since money was never a concern, he ordered three of the rarest motorcycles in the world. According to sources at Enron Broadband, he bought two bikes for Enron and one for himself. The source says Rice paid for the bikes with his credit card so he could get the frequent-flyer miles that came with the big purchase. By the way, the source says Rice paid Enron for the Hellcat that he ordered.

Most people have never heard of Confederate Motorcycles. But don't worry. Even hard-core motorcycle enthusiasts look puzzled when asked if they know who makes the Hellcat. That's because Confederate, based in Abita Springs, Louisiana, has only built a few hundred motorcycles since it went into production in 1997. The company's hand-built machines have become a favorite of the motorcycle cognoscenti and what Confederate founder Matt Chambers calls "super net-worth individuals." And since Rice was both racing cognoscenti and "super net-worth," he ordered the Hellcats. Never mind that each motorcycle cost about $30,000 or that they were hardly the type of machinery that Enron Broadband Services needed to succeed.

Although Rice shared the title of co-CEO of Enron Broadband Services with an old Portland General guy, Joe Hirko, it was clear to almost everyone at the company that Rice was the one in charge. Rice was close to Skilling, and no one believed that Hirko was going to stay very long. Hirko left Enron a few months after the analysts' meeting, but not before cashing out Enron stock worth $35.1 million.

Rice figured his new company needed an image. The badder that image, the better. And the Hellcat is one baaaaad machine. Lower slung than a Harley, the Hellcat has a bigger engine, lighter frame, and sleeker design than a run-of-the-mill road hog.[6] It's a bike designed to turn heads, not corners. If you want to ride it, fine. But as Chambers explained, his company builds the "Bentley or Duesenberg of motorcycles. It's not an everyday rider." In other words, the Confederate Hellcat is just flat impractical for transportation. However, as office furniture for a telecom start-up with billions to spend, it's perfect. And though a stock Hellcat is certainly a fine-looking machine, Rice wanted a little bit extra. So he spent another $3,000 or so having one of the bikes customized at a small motorcycle shop in West Houston. The tank was painted maroon and black with "Enron Broadband" emblazoned on each side. The transmission case was adorned with Enron's multicolored tilted-E logo. In addition, Rice had the words "Enron Broadband" etched in a circular fashion into the metal of the transmission case. In the middle of that, in cursive script, was etched "Bandwidth hog."

The coup de grace was on the speedometer, a little custom number that undoubtedly cost several hundred bucks. Rather than have the readout on the dial denoted in mph (for miles per hour) Rice had the dial read Gb/s, for gigabits per second. It was an expensive little fillip, but money was no object. Enron Broadband Services and Ken Rice were on a mission. That mission, it appears, was to spend lots of money very quickly. And Rice certainly succeeded at that task.

Ken Rice wasn't always so flashy. Rice began working at InterNorth in 1980, after graduating from the University of Nebraska with an electrical engineering degree. He was viewed as a smart and capable worker. "He was a good Cornhusker," recalled one former InterNorth executive, using the term for Nebraska's mascot. "He had good Midwestern values." Rice used his engineering skills in a group that managed InterNorth's pipelines. It wasn't a glamorous job, but InterNorth was in constant need of personnel who could handle the mundane task of making sure the company's pipes were in good repair and able to handle increasing volumes of gas. While working in the pipeline group, Rice went on to get his MBA from Creighton University. Then, about the time Houston Natural Gas merged with InterNorth, the company began needing salesmen to find new markets for deregulated natural gas. The company chose Rice to be part of the sales team.

Gregarious and charming, Rice was well liked by virtually everyone at Enron. Men were attracted by his sense of humor. Women found him to be "an attractive man in a boyish sort of way," recalled a woman who had worked at Enron. Within a few years of his promotion, Rice was one of Enron's best salesmen. He was also gaining a reputation as an inveterate philanderer. Despite being married since 1981 to his wife, Teresa, Rice was, according to several sources within Enron, seducing a number of young analysts and associates at the company throughout the early 1990s. His well-known affair with Amanda Martin started sometime in the mid-1990s.

Rice's extracurricular activities did not diminish his value to Enron, particularly when the company was trying to prove the concept of the Gas Bank. To make the concept work, Enron needed to sell some big, long-term gas supply deals. And it wasn't having much success. That changed in 1991 when Rice helped close the New York Power Authority gas supply contract. That deal, along with another one the following year, with Sithe Energy, made Rice's reputation. They helped prove Skilling's Gas Bank could work, and Skilling was extremely loyal to people like Rice and Lou Pai, who'd been selling and trading gas with him since the earliest days of the Gas Bank. Skilling had approved huge bonuses for Rice on those early gas deals and later, from his stint trading electricity. So for the rest of the decade, Ken Rice coasted, cheated on his wife, and raced expensive automobiles. By the time he got to Enron Broadband Services, he'd made so much money he didn't have to work.

And he didn't. Although Rice was the CEO and chairman of Enron Broadband Services, he didn't go to work every day. Instead, he'd show up at the office three, sometimes four times a week. Often dressed in jeans, cowboy boots, and a polo shirt, he'd check the *Bloomberg* terminal for the latest quotes on his stock portfolio and attend a few meetings. But even then, he was hardly the most diligent employee. "He'd watch cartoons during meetings," said one former Enron Broadband Services employee. "We had a wireless high-speed network in the building so he'd turn on his laptop and watch cartoons while we tried to do meetings. And he'd tell everybody to watch it with him." Another employee, who confirmed the cartoon episode, said Rice was simply a "six-year-old in a forty-year-old's body."

Always interested in cars and racing, the newly rich Rice became enamored with Ferraris. And since he had so much time on his hands, and EBS had so much money, Rice had the neophyte telecom company sponsor a Ferrari race car that he and other EBS employees then followed during the racing season. The cost of the sponsorship to Enron: $120,000. Rice personally owned two of the super-swank Italian sports cars, a 360 (cost: about $160,000) he used for racing and a 550 Marinello (about $200,000) that he drove to work and around town. Although Rice quickly figured out ways to spend Enron's money at EBS, he didn't give much thought—and apparently didn't care—how his company was going to make money. And several insiders warned Rice that the company's bandwidth trading business model was fundamentally flawed.

But Rice and his second in command, Kevin Hannon, didn't listen. That wasn't overly surprising. Rice was watching cartoons. Hannon already knew it all. Hannon, the president and chief operating officer of Enron Broadband, was a longtime trader. He'd risen through the ranks to become one of Enron's top executives. He was also one of Skilling's key cronies, which was the only qualification needed to run a billion-dollar telecom business.

Hannon was an Easterner, an MBA, and a real creep. A former risk manager in the natural gas trading unit at Banker's Trust, Hannon was hired by Enron in the early 1990s to help set up the company's gas trading operations. He went on to manage all of the company's trading operations in North America before moving to the broadband unit. It's safe to say that almost no one at Enron liked him. Known for his hair-trigger temper and surfeit of self-importance, Hannon would loudly berate his employees for little or no reason. One female assistant who worked at Enron Broadband and dealt with Hannon on numerous occasions, summed up her feelings toward him by saying, "He's just slimy."

Gelatinous or genteel, Hannon was out of his league when it came to telecom. One executive in the broadband unit recalls going into Hannon's office a few months after the former gas trader had begun working there. The executive was describing the details of provisioning a DS-3 circuit—which can carry about 45 megabits of information per second and is a basic building block of the telecom industry—on the company's fiber optic network. "I went into a meeting and he asked me what a DS-3 is," said the source. "He didn't know the most rudimentary information about the business."

Hannon's confidence, Rice's incompetence, and Enron's overriding belief that it could dominate any market it chose were a lethal combination that allowed them to ignore early warning signs that their business plan was fatally flawed.

In spring 2000, about four months after Skilling announced Enron's broadband play, one of the company's best gas and power traders, who had been hired specifically to manage Enron Broadband Services' trading business, presented a report to Rice, Hannon, and several other top executives. The report showed conclusively that future pricing for bandwidth looked terrible. The trader, an MBA from a prestigious Eastern school, showed them pricing models that predicted a train wreck: Bandwidth prices would get destroyed by a looming capacity glut.

That meant bad things for any trading business because traders can only make profits if prices go up *and* down. "The problem is that models only show the prices going down," the trader warned them. "We can't trade it if prices fall. And there's nothing to show that that won't happen."

The trader recommended that Rice and his crew immediately try to sell the company's fiber optic network and find another business. They didn't listen. Within weeks of delivering the report, the trader was back trading natural gas. "They figured that they were so smart they could figure out a way to make it work," said the trader.

So began Enron Broadband Services' sprint toward its date with insolvency.

27

Andy Fastow Arrives . . . in River Oaks

FEBRUARY 28, 2000
Enron closing price: $64.81

By late February 2000, Andy Fastow had succeeded in enough financial foolishness at Enron to be both Big Rich and Big Important. So he bought a house in River Oaks.

It was only fitting. Fastow's wife, the former Lea Weingarten, was an heiress with deep roots in River Oaks. Lea's aunt, Joan Schnitzer, a principal beneficiary of the Weingarten real estate fortune, had a house in River Oaks. So did her father, Jack Weingarten. A woman like Lea, the daughter of a former Miss Israel, a stylish woman with a lofty Houston pedigree, belonged there.

Other Enron Big Shots already lived in the 77019 zip code. Ken Lay had been in River Oaks for years. Jeff Skilling and Rebecca Mark lived there, too. So it made sense that when Andy Fastow started pulling down the big money, he bought a house on Del Monte Drive in the heart of River Oaks. The property deal, closed on February 28, 2000, cost a reported $1.5 million. The house on the property was perfectly serviceable. The Harris County Appraisal District had appraised the value of the home alone at $388,000. But it was completely unsuitable for a Big Shot. Lea and Andy were going to tear it down and build another, bigger, grander house. Their house—at 3005 Del Monte

Drive—was going to be newer and bigger than practically any other on the street.

His across-the-street neighbor would be Denton Cooley, the renowned surgeon who performed the first successful heart transplant in America. His down-the-street neighbors on Del Monte would include Gordon Bethune, the chief of Continental Airlines, and Rich Kinder, the former president of Enron who had gone on to start another energy company, Kinder Morgan Inc.

Never mind that Fastow and his wife already had an enormous, nearly new house in the prestigious Southampton Place neighborhood near Rice University, close to the center of Houston. In fact, Southampton provided the name for one of Fastow's most egregious special-purpose entities, an off-the-balance-sheet shell company that allowed Fastow and several cronies to make enormous profits. As for the no-longer-adequate Southampton Place property, it's a beautiful red brick home with gas-burning lamps on both sides of the entry door. There are two floors, five bedrooms, four and a half bathrooms, two fireplaces, and two recreation rooms. With 4,710 square feet of living space, it's nearly twice the size of other homes in the neighborhood and covers nearly every square inch of the property. But alas, it just wasn't quite ritzy enough. Just a few years earlier, Skilling had lived in Southampton Place, too, just around the corner from Fastow.

"Andy wanted to keep up with the things that Skilling was doing. Skilling had a house in River Oaks. For Andy to be at that level, he needed the big house, too," said one finance executive who worked closely with Fastow.

In addition to the money, Fastow was getting a bit of notoriety. A few months earlier, *CFO* magazine had named him one of their CFOs of the year, giving him its "CFO Excellence Award for Capital Structure," an award given him for helping make Enron into "a master of creative financing."[1] The magazine praised Fastow's work in the financing structure created so that Enron could buy Azurix as well as several power plants while keeping the debts off its balance sheet. When the award was announced, Skilling praised Fastow to *CFO* magazine, saying Enron needed "someone to rethink the entire financing structure at

Enron from soup to nuts. . . . Andy has the intelligence and the youthful exuberance to think in new ways. [He] deserves every accolade tossed his way."

Along with being recognized as important, Fastow wanted to live near the people he'd already helped make rich. In September 1999, Jim Flores bought Oscar Wyatt's mansion near the entrance to the River Oaks Country Club. But Flores would likely never have been able to buy the Wyatt place if not for a pair of deals he and his partner, Billy Rucks, had done with Enron Finance Corp. in the early 1990s. Their company, Flores & Rucks, had borrowed money from Enron to produce oil from a pair of offshore oil wells. The deal had made both men into zillionaires. And Fastow, who had been hired at Enron Finance by Skilling a short time before, had helped get the Flores & Rucks deal done.

Fastow didn't have as much money as Flores, but he certainly had enough to afford River Oaks. Two years earlier, he and Lea had bought sixty-eight acres in Vermont. And they were considering a vacation home closer to Houston—a nice $250,000 house in Galveston. But the Del Monte house brought real prestige. It would show the Weingarten family—long one of the most prominent Jewish families in Houston, the founders of a grocery and real estate empire[2]—that Andy Fastow *belonged*. He was no longer an interloper from the East Coast. He was a finance whiz who had shown these Houston energy folks how to do really complex deals.

River Oaks would be the landing pad for Andy Fastow, the Jekyll and Hyde of the Enron disaster.

Andrew Fastow was born December 22, 1961, in Washington, D.C. His father, a buyer for a drugstore chain, moved the family to New Providence, New Jersey, when Fastow was a young boy. Throughout his youth, Fastow, the middle of three boys, showed an interest in finance and the stock market. He also showed leadership abilities. He was on the tennis and wrestling teams, played in the school band, and was elected president of his high school's student council.

After high school, he attended Tufts University in Boston, where he studied both economics and Chinese. While at Tufts, he met Lea Weingarten. The two began dating and later married. Fastow graduated magna cum laude from Tufts in 1983. About that time, he and Lea moved to Chicago, where both of them earned their MBAs at Northwestern University. They also both got jobs at Continental Bank, where Andy worked on troubled loans, leveraged buyouts, and other deals. And though Andy was fairly well regarded there, his wife, Lea, was put on Continental's fast track. One source, who claims to be a "good friend of Andy's," said that Lea "was the brains in the family. Andy was always very cocky, just never very bright."

In late 1989 or early 1990, the source says that Lea's father, Jack Weingarten, introduced Andy to Jeffrey Skilling. A few months later, the Fastows were on their way to Houston. Both of them got jobs at Enron. Lea worked in the treasurer's office in the Corporate Finance Department. Andy went to work for Jeffrey Skilling at Enron Finance. Working with Skilling, Fastow learned how to structure complicated deals like the one with Flores & Rucks. He also absorbed Skilling's methods of managing people and his view of the world.

"Fastow very much admired Skilling," commented one source who had worked with both men. "He and Skilling were very close. He wanted to be big and powerful like Skilling."

"If you ever crossed him, he never forgot and would do everything possible to make life miserable for you," said the source. "I'd get calls from bankers complaining because Andy was a pain to deal with. They'd be in meetings and Andy would start yelling obscenities. He'd just fly off the handle. If you were a banker and didn't give him what he wanted, he remembered. He had a short temper and was a vengeful person."

Fastow stayed at Enron Gas Services until about 1996, when Skilling promoted him to lead the company's new retail power business. The idea was to sell power to residential customers in newly deregulated markets like California. But the concept was flawed. Profit margins in the residential electricity market are razor thin. Also, Enron was going to be facing powerful, well-funded, well-entrenched incumbent utilities that weren't eager to share their sandbox. And Fastow, who always believed he could hedge any risk that came down the pike, couldn't figure out how to keep Enron's customers if electric prices fell. Nor could Fastow figure out a business plan that would work if energy deregulation happened more slowly than Enron had hoped.

In early 1997, shortly after Skilling became Enron's president and COO, he yanked Fastow out of retail energy and made him a vice president in the company's finance group. He stayed there until March 1998, when Skilling named Fastow the company's CFO.

It was a job Fastow was not suited for. Although Fastow knew how to set up dozens of off-the-balance-sheet entities, he didn't understand how to manage the company's overall finances, said one longtime Enron employee who was also an MBA. "He was very good at maintaining relationships with financial institutions and lining up people who were willing to contribute cash, but that was all he knew. Any time he spoke about finance was met with derision. He once argued in front of a credit rating agency that Enron should get a higher credit rating because it would allow Enron to borrow more. He didn't understand the basic functions of a CFO. There were no systems in place to set up the structure of the balance sheet, to balance short- and long-term debt, and whether the debt should be at floating or fixed interest rates."

Although Fastow was a table pounder and a screamer at work, he wasn't predisposed to that behavior, according to another former Enroner. "Fastow is such a quiet guy," he said. "Socially, he's very reserved. He doesn't talk a lot. I think he was taking cues on how to become a big dog and that included ranting and raving. He innately wasn't that way. But he saw [Kevin] Hannon, and [Lou] Pai, and [Cliff] Baxter act like that so he evolved into being able to do that."

While with his family, Fastow seemed to be a milquetoast soccer dad. His rabbi, Shaul Osadchey, of Congregation Or Ami, described him as "very unassuming and quiet—not at all pushy. You'd never even know what he did for a living." Several sources said Fastow spent a lot of time with his two young sons, helping coach their sports teams. He played tennis and the trombone. He did fund-raising for Houston's Holocaust Museum and other charities. And he also became an art snob.

Even though Andy and Lea Fastow finally had the house in River Oaks, they were never going to belong in Houston society unless they got plugged in with the arts. The oil and gas nouveau riche have always bought legitimacy and respect through the arts, and Houston was no exception. Hugh Roy Cullen had helped bankroll the launching of the Museum of Fine Arts in Houston. Dominique de Menil, heiress to the Schlumberger megafortune, funded the creation of a museum, the Menil Collection. So in the late 1990s, he and Lea, particularly Lea, began reading up on modern art and contemporary artists. She started buying art and attending lectures. They even began thinking about ways to start giving away their vast new wealth.

Yes, by early 2000, things could not have been better. Enron's stock was sky-high.

Lea and Andy had a berth in River Oaks. They were going to build an 11,500-square-foot home that would be one of the finest in the entire neighborhood. It would cost them $1.5 million or more, but that wasn't a problem. Lea and Andy Fastow were rolling in dough. They had so much money they'd have their own foundation—the Fastow Family Foundation—and all before Andy hit forty.

Andy and Lea had already figured out the return on the Southampton deal he'd done with Enron. For an investment of $25,000, he was going to clear about $4.5 million. They would put all of that money into the foundation. His bonuses and salary would cover all the decorating expenses for the new house. As the managing partner of the myriad partnerships he'd set up, there were plenty of other opportunities to make big money from Enron. And he was going to take advantage of as many as he could.

28

Strippers and Stock Options

MAY 31, 2000

Enron closing price: $72.875

Lou Pai had two passions in life: money and watching young women take their clothes off—but not necessarily in that order. And at Enron, he was able to gorge on both. By spring 2000, though, it appears that Pai's predilection for strippers had him on a one-way trip to divorce court.

His wife of twenty-four years, Lanna Pai, had tolerated his infidelities long enough. She and their two children (and lots of Enron employees) had been hearing the rumors about Lou and the strippers for years, and now she wanted out—for good. Pai, the small (about 5'-5" tall), spookily quiet math brain, was not worth the trouble. They'd been quarreling for months. Court records show their marriage was troubled. On June 15, 1999, Lanna Pai filed a document in Harris County District Court in her divorce action against her husband. The court granted Lanna Pai a temporary restraining order that prohibited Lou Pai from "causing bodily injury" to her or to their children, "threatening" her or their children, and "destroying, removing, concealing, encumbering, transferring or otherwise harming or reducing the value of the property of one or both of the parties."

It appeared that if they were going to split the sheets for good,

Lanna wanted her share of the fortune that Lou had been accumulating at Enron. So Lou Pai began doing what lots of other Enron insiders were doing. He began selling his Enron stock.

Pai didn't mind. He already had more money, stock, and real estate than he'd ever dreamed possible. He was going to stay quiet and out of sight, just like he always had, but now he could do it in style with his babe-a-licious girlfriend, a former topless dancer named Melanie Fewell.[1] Pai had been sleeping with Fewell since the early 1990s even though both of them were married. And in 1996, according to the *New York Times,* Fewell's then-husband named Lou Pai as a problem in their marriage, describing Pai in court documents as her "paramour" and employer.[2] But soon, both Pai and Fewell would be free, and they were going to have plenty of space to keep their privacy. For instance, they could go to Pai's own 14,000-foot-tall mountain.

Reportedly the only person in Colorado to own his own "fourteener," Pai has title to a huge ranch that contains Culebra Peak, which at 14,047 feet is the fifty-first-highest point in the lower forty-eight states. The 77,500-acre parcel formerly known as the Taylor Ranch has long been controversial with the largely Hispanic locals in San Luis. Several generations of local people had been cutting wood, hunting, fishing, pasturing their livestock, and recreating on the property, thanks to an 1844 Mexican land grant. María Mondragón-Valdéz, a historian and community activist who is doing her doctoral dissertation at the University of New Mexico on land rights in Colorado and has researched the long history of the Culebra Peak land grant, said that the people in San Luis (the oldest town in Colorado) have grown used to absentee landowners like Pai. But there was something different about the way Pai went about his business. The previous owner, Jack Taylor, who had controlled the land since the 1960s, at least lived on the land and occasionally talked to the locals. Lou Pai did everything, said Valdéz, "clothed in secrecy and insulated from public contact."

Pai began buying the Taylor Ranch in 1997, and by 1999, through a series of interconnected corporations, Pai controlled the entire ranch. And he immediately began excluding everyone from the property.

Where the Taylors had let mountaineers access the peak for a fee, Pai kept everybody out. His crews erected stout fences and bulldozed a security path immediately behind the fencing. He put up lots of big signs that bore "No Trespassing" in bold letters. The signs carried an additional message just below, which read "For Any Reason Whatsoever."[3]

Pai was going to do whatever he damn well pleased on his ranch. Screw the locals and their ancestral rights to the land and the water of Culebra. For decades, the farmers in the valley below Culebra had used earthen *acequias* to guide water from the mountain into their fields. *Acequias,* long ditch systems that transport water, are found throughout Texas, New Mexico, and Colorado. They were introduced into the New World by Spanish missionaries who learned the technique from the Moors. According to Valdéz, the *acequias* below Culebra Peak are the oldest in Colorado and hold the state's oldest recognized water rights. When Pai took over, Valdéz continued, he began damming the mountain streams to create a Chinese garden effect on his ranch, thereby depriving his downstream amigos of much of the water that had previously flowed their way. Pai's fences, locked gates, and impatient security men also hindered the locals' efforts to open and close the water gates—which sit on Pai's land—that divert water into the *acequias.*

Either by design or by happenstance, Lou Pai had made himself into a villain worthy of *The Milagro Beanfield War*, but he didn't give a damn. Many of the people who lived around San Luis in the heart of the Sangre de Cristo mountain range had hated the previous owner of the ranch, Jack Taylor, but they quickly grew to have a particular loathing for Lou Pai, America's most unlikely land baron.

Lou Lung Pai was born in Nanjing, China, on June 23, 1947. His father, Shih-i Pai, who died in 1996, was a highly regarded aeronautical engineer who did pioneering research into the drag and lift characteristics of airplanes and missiles. The elder Pai moved permanently to the United States in the year of Lou Pai's birth to take a teaching job at Cornell University. In 1953, he left Cornell for a job at the University of Maryland, where he stayed until he retired in 1983. Lou Pai, one of four children, got his undergraduate degree from the University of Maryland. He served two years in the U.S. Army before returning to Maryland to get his master's degree in economics. He worked in Washington, D.C., for a few years, then moved to Houston in the 1980s to take a job with Conoco. In 1987, he was hired at Enron by Bruce Stram, a friend from graduate school, to work in the company's strategic planning department. Pai's work in planning went well, but he had a gift for trading, a gift that was discovered shortly after Jeff Skilling began setting up the company's Gas Bank. Pai proved himself so quickly that Skilling feared Pai would defect and go to another Houston company, Natural Gas Clearinghouse (the company that later became Dynegy).

Pai was quickly promoted to vice president. But Pai's supervisor at the time regretted the move almost immediately. By promoting Pai, said the executive, "I violated two principles of mine. First, the person should take a leadership role. Second, the person going into the job needs to take on more responsibility and carry the corporate flag. Turns out I violated both of them. Pai didn't have leadership capability and he didn't have management capabilities."

But management capability was never a prerequisite for advancement at Enron under Jeff Skilling. Pai was proof of that. He was the most asocial of those in Skilling's inner circle. Pai was happiest when he was left alone, and by being one of Skilling's chosen few, he was able to achieve that goal throughout his Enron tenure. "I'd get on the elevator with him and he wouldn't make eye contact. He was so strange," one woman who worked with Pai remembered.

Stories of Pai's fascination with strippers were legion at Enron. One executive recalled getting an expense report from Pai in 1990, shortly after Pai began working for him. "It was $757 for one lunch. He and two or three coworkers had gone to Rick's [a Houston strip club]. I said, 'I'm not approving this. You are going to have to take care of this yourself.' I couldn't understand why he would do that kind of thing. You just don't do that in business." But that executive didn't stay at Enron long. And Pai reverted to his old ways, ways that Skilling tolerated.

Without Pai, some Enron insiders thought Skilling would have never been able to establish Enron's burgeoning trading business. Pai had the intellectual firepower and focus needed to create the computer programs and systems that allowed Skilling to fulfill his vision of changing Enron into a quasi-investment bank. Pai was "the one person smart enough" to handle the job, as one banker who worked closely with him put it.

Skilling liked Pai because "Pai was willing to go to any length" to get a deal done, recalled one Enron veteran. And by 1997, after a stint as president and chief operating officer of the Enron trading arm, Pai was made chairman and CEO of Enron Energy Services, another business unit that Jeff Skilling hyped, and then hyped some more.

The idea behind the business was simple: Sell long-term energy supply contracts to big industrial users. Enron succeeded quite well in signing up customers who were attracted to Enron's promise of fixed-price contracts for electricity and natural gas. But Enron Energy Services apparently failed to make any money.

By 2000, Pai and his second in command at Enron Energy Services, Thomas White, (whom the senator from Enron, Phil Gramm, would later introduce to a Senate committee as "one of the most outstanding managers in corporate America") were overseeing a division with more than a thousand employees. And like the rest of Enron, the focus was on mark-to-market revenue, not cash. In fact, Enron Energy Services appeared to be nothing more than a gigantic cash drain on Enron. That was true despite financial reports that showed huge growth. In 1999, the division reported losing $68 million on sales of $1.8 billion. In 2000, it reported a $165-million operating profit on revenues of $4.6 billion. But like everything else associated with Pai's company, those numbers appeared to be a mirage.

To entice new industrial customers to sign long-term contracts, Enron Energy Services often paid them huge amounts of money to sign the contract. In one case—a fifteen-year energy supply deal with pharmaceutical giant Eli Lilly—Enron Energy Services paid the firm $50 million up front.

In other cases, the company used mark-to-market accounting to create the illusion of profits. In one deal, signed in February 2001 with Quaker Oats, Enron Energy Services agreed to supply fifteen different Quaker plants with natural gas, electricity, and trained personnel to maintain the company's boilers. Under the terms of the deal, which was later reported by the *Financial Times*, the company guaranteed Quaker would save about $4.4 million per year in energy costs. Then, before turning on a single light, Enron projected it would make $36.8 million profits over the life of the ten-year deal and immediately booked $23.4 million of that amount.[4]

"Everybody I talked to always thought the mark-to-market thing would come back and bite us," said one veteran of Enron Energy Services. "You always had to find new deals to cover the previous deals."

And just as the traders on Enron's trading floor got paid to do big trades, the deal makers at Enron Energy Services got paid to book big deals, regardless of whether they were profitable or not. "The deal makers got paid all their bonuses up-front" when their deals closed, said one of Pai's coworkers. "We didn't know if a deal would be good or bad or ugly. I kept arguing that we need to stretch out these bonuses and pay them out based on their success. But Lou always wanted to have them paid right away."

According to his coworkers at Enron Energy Services, Pai never appeared overly concerned about his company's profitability. Those same coworkers admired his intellect, if not his work ethic.

"Pai had a brilliant mind. He could think of several complicated things at one time," one source remarked. "While everyone was struggling to understand one part of the problem, he had everything figured out. Everyone who met him was impressed with him." However, few people thought he applied himself once he got to the energy services business. He rarely took phone calls. He often sat in his office alone, reading the paper. Another source said Pai would often come in at 9 A.M. and leave by midafternoon. "And he never took any work home."

What Pai lacked in Protestant work ethic, he made up for in his compensation negotiation skills. In the early days of the trading business, "Pai would be in here every few weeks trying to renegotiate his contract," said one Enron veteran. "I'd throw him out of my office. But Skilling would always agree to sweeten his deal." Another longtime Enron employee who worked with Pai in the trading business said, "Everything Lou wanted was stock options. It was stock, stock, stock. Then when he went to Enron Energy Services, he got a whole other bunch of stock in that deal."

Stock and stock options were the cocaine that drove the Internet Bubble. And Enron was the biggest junkie on Wall Street. Enron was more aggressive in awarding options than almost any other company in the Fortune 500. By the end of 2000, over 13 percent of all of Enron's outstanding stock was held in options, and a big hunk of them were held by executives like Pai.

Skilling and Enron chairman Ken Lay could dump Enron stock options on Pai and the rest of the favored few because the accounting treatment for stock options was so favorable. For companies, giving stock options was better than a free lunch: It was a lunch the company got paid to eat.

If Enron paid Pai a bonus of, say, $1 million in cash, the company would have had to report that expense on its profit-and-loss statement. But with options, even though Enron incurred real costs in granting them to Pai, the company didn't have to record the expense on its profit-and-loss statement. Furthermore, Enron (and every other company that used options) could deduct the cost of the options as an expense from its tax liability. All of that means that corporate honchos can reward themselves with a boatload (or two) of stock options without hurting the company's profit reports. Then, when the options are exercised, the company could treat the appreciation in the value of the shares—the option holder's profit—as an expense for tax purposes.

By the end of 2000, Enron's incredibly generous stock option ploy turned what would have been a federal income tax bill of $112 million in 2000 into a $278-million refund. That's better than any free lunch. Of course, Enron wasn't the only company using options to its advantage. Between 1994 and 1998, the number of options granted by companies in the Standard & Poor's 500 jumped from 1.6 billion options to over 4.4 billion. And all of those options had a big effect on those companies' profits. Between 1995 and 2000, the average earnings growth rate of America's biggest companies would have been reduced by nearly 25 percent if those companies had been required to report their stock option grants as expenses on their financial statements.

Stock options may be better than free for corporate fat cats, but they can cost shareholders real American money. The most commonly recognized problem is shareholder dilution. When an executive exercises an option on, say, 1 million shares of stock, the company must add those shares to the existing number of outstanding shares. Thus, a company that had 100 million shares outstanding before the executive exercised the option would have 101 million shares available on the open market after the transaction. That hurts the existing shareholders because their shares have been diluted (albeit fractionally) by the addition of the new shares.

To combat the problem of dilution, many companies buy back their shares on the open market after executives exercise their options. The buyback reduces dilution, but it reduces the amount of cash available to the company for other expenses like equipment and inventory. If the option grants are really large, the company may even borrow money to buy back its shares, a move that weakens its balance sheet.

About the same time Lou Pai began selling huge blocks of his Enron stock, Warren Buffett, the chairman and CEO of Berkshire Hathaway Inc.—and the unofficial conscience of corporate America—protested the widespread use of stock options by American companies. In his company's annual report, Buffett wrote, "Whatever the merits of options may be, their accounting treatment is outrageous." In August 1999, Federal Reserve chairman Alan Greenspan estimated that excessive use of options had caused American companies to overstate their profits by 1 to 2 percentage points over the previous five years.

But those factors paled in comparison to the real danger of the massive stock option grants that had been passed out by Enron: They created a huge incentive for the company's top management to cut corners, to keep important information hidden.

Enron's annual reports show just how effectively Skilling was using those options. During the Kinder era, the number of stock options available to be granted to employees stayed relatively constant, and by the time of his departure, Enron had about 25.4 million shares of its stock tied up in outstanding options. However, at the end of 1997, Skilling's first year as president and COO, the number of outstanding options that Enron employees could exercise had ballooned to 39.4 million shares. By 1999, Skilling was handing out Enron stock options like they were nothing more than cheap candy. By the end of that year, Enron had granted more than 93.5 million shares of stock to its employees in the form of options—incredible, and nearly quadruple the number that existed under the more fiscally conservative Kinder.

Skilling had turned Enron into a stock option colossus. And with their future potential wealth closely tied to the appreciation of the company's stock, Enron's top executives like Fastow, Pai, and Skilling had millions of reasons to keep bad deals and bad debts from surfacing in the company's financial reports.

By late spring 2000, Lou Pai was in his early fifties—older than any of the other members of Skilling's mafia. And he had more responsibility than almost any of the other members of the Enron Executive Committee. He was the chairman of The New Power Company, a company that Enron was betting would be able to gain market share in retail energy markets by offering homeowners and others electricity and gas at prices lower than what they were paying their local utilities. Enron had placed a huge wager on New Power, which was nearly ready for its initial public offering.

In addition, Pai had already been the chairman and CEO of the energy services business for three years. He was ready to slow down. He'd prowled Houston's titty bars for more than a decade, and he'd found the one woman who really lit his fire. And besides, he was already Big Rich. He'd spent about $23 million buying Culebra Peak and the ranch in Colorado. And he still owned about a zillion Enron stock options. It was time to sell and move on with his life. So he did just that. On May 31, 2000, Lou Pai became one of the first Enron Big Shots to take a huge payout under the company's supergenerous stock option scheme. When the markets closed that day, Pai had sold $79.9 million worth of his Enron stock.

Lou Pai was cashing out. And there was more insider selling to come. Lots more.

29

Casino Enron: Cash Flow Problems, Part 2

SUMMER 2000

By mid-2000, Jeff Skilling had achieved his goal: Almost all vestiges of the old Enron, the stodgy, slow-growing pipeline-based entity that transported gas and generated a bit of electricity were gone. In its place, Enron had become a trading company. And with that change came a rock-'em, sock-'em, fast-paced trading culture in which deals and "deal flow" became the driving forces behind everything Enron did.

Traders ran the place. All of the company's top executives—particularly those close to Skilling—were either traders or had helped run trading operations. And all of them believed in Skilling's vision of Enron as a trading company. Enron Broadband was run by Ken Rice and Kevin Hannon, both of whom had overseen groups of traders. Chief Financial Officer Andy Fastow had learned the trading business while in Skilling's group in the early 1990s. Greg Whalley, the president of Enron Wholesale Services, the entity that ran the company's trading operations, had worked in Europe as one of Enron's chief power marketers and had done risk management work for the company. Mark Frevert, the chairman and CEO of Enron Europe, had overseen the company's European trading operations. Other top execs like Lou Pai had been involved in trading for years.

Enron's massive new edifice to itself, a forty-story, 1.2-million-square-foot building was going to be a monument to trading. The building, designed by acclaimed architect Cesar Pelli, would have four trading floors—each big enough for 500 "transaction desks"—with state-of-the-art communications systems. Ken Lay and Jeff Skilling would move their offices from the fiftieth floor of the old building down to the seventh floor of the new one. Instead of overlooking all of Houston, their new offices would be on a balcony overlooking one of the new trading floors. And they wouldn't have to take elevators to get to the traders: Two snazzy curved stairways were going to connect their floor with the trading area.[1]

The new tower had been under construction for nearly a year and was costing Enron a fortune. Pelli's design, which would mimic the glass-sheathed oval tower Enron already occupied, was going to give Enron the most expensive building in downtown Houston. The highest price ever paid for a downtown office building was about $170 per square foot. The new Enron tower was going to cost about $250 per square foot, a figure that would make the final bill about $300 million.[2]

Enron was wasting even more money in Europe. The company's European trading operations were located in an impressive new building dubbed Enron House, located at 40 Grosvenor Place, in the heart of London, on land owned by the Duke of Westminster. Although the building cost $74 million to construct, Enron spent another $30 million in bringing it up to the company's lofty standards. When the company moved into Enron House in November 1999, the top executives, including Enron Europe CEO Mark Frevert, could sit in their top-floor offices and look down on rear gardens at Buckingham Palace. Rent for the new digs? A bargain at a mere £8 million a year.

But cost control in Houston or London was never a consideration for Skilling and Lay. After all, EnronOnline, the company's new web site, was the toast of cyberspace. In the few months since it had been launched in November 1999, the web site had quickly become the biggest e-commerce site the Internet had ever seen. The trading site had been the brainchild of a trader, of course, named Louise Kitchen, a brash young Brit who had been Enron's head natural gas trader in Europe. Cocky and impatient, Kitchen was emblematic of Skilling's new version of Enron. At just thirty-one years old, she was young, she was rich (in 2001, her total pay from Enron was $3.47 million), and she believed there was no end to what she—and Enron—might do.

While she and her team were developing the site, Kitchen said, "I didn't need a pat on the back from Ken Lay or Jeff Skilling. It was obvious that we should have been doing this ages ago."

Kitchen's attitude was typical among the traders. They were the über-Enroners, the ultimate Masters of the Universe. "The traders didn't kowtow to anybody," recalled John Allario, who spent five years at Enron. The traders made the biggest salaries and the biggest bonuses, and they were the ones Jeff Skilling courted. When the traders "decided to do a trade, they weren't hindered by anything else Enron was doing."

Kitchen, along with another thirty-something trader, a Canadian named John Lavorato, were rapidly consolidating their power within Enron. And within a few months of EnronOnline's debut, the pair was heading all of Enron's North American trading operations. There were hundreds of traders, lined up in banks of computer screens, keyboards, telephones, and adrenaline. In the first five months of 2000 alone, the web site did 110,000 transactions with a total value exceeding $45 billion. Deals could be done in seconds, rather than minutes or hours.

Electricity, natural gas, coal, oil, refined products, bandwidth, paper, plastics, petrochemicals, and even clean air credits were for sale on Enron's web site. Within a few weeks of its launch in November 1999, EnronOnline was the biggest e-commerce entity in the world. In all, the company was selling over 800 different products.

EnronOnline was the logical outgrowth of Enron's gas trading business, which was launched shortly after Skilling conceived the Gas Bank concept. What had been done by phone and fax was now being done on the World Wide Web. And the gas business was a primary reason for Enron's trading prowess. The company's trading business surged, in large part, because of tremendous increases in gas consumption in the United States. Between 1983 and 2000, demand for natural gas in America rose by nearly 30 percent, to 22.5 trillion cubic feet per year.

Enron transferred what it learned in gas to the electricity business. Once confined to trading among utilities, Enron elbowed its way into electricity trading in the mid-1990s. The company even bought Portland General Electric to assure itself of a place at the utility table. But the Portland General purchase was, by any measure, a failure for Enron. The company was in nearly constant battles with state regulators in Oregon and by 1999, just three years after it announced the purchase of the utility, Enron announced it would sell the power company to Sierra Pacific Resources. With or without Portland General, Enron had become a monster in megawatts.

Enron was selling gas and power, but all the while it was collecting still more information that provided a constant feedback loop. Enron owned pipelines and power plants, and with EnronOnline, it could instantly tell which direction the market was going. It could also tell who was buying, who was selling, and where it should be placing its own bets in the marketplace.

"We'd get a lot of information because our pipelines were coast to coast and border to border," said one trader who spent many years trading gas for Enron. "We had the models, the computer systems . . . Enron gave you every tool that was ever needed for you to be successful. You just had to pick the right side of the market and have the balls to put on big positions."

In a very short time, Enron had remade itself from pipeline company to the largest energy marketer in the country. But Skilling wasn't satisfied. He wanted more. So in May 2000, Enron announced it would buy London-based MG plc, one of the biggest metals traders in the world, for $446 million. Ken Lay said the deal would allow Enron to claim a major role in the $120-billion-per-year metals market. "Our business model, which we have proven in the natural gas and electricity markets, will give us a tremendous advantage in an industry that is undergoing fundamental change."

There it was again: Enron knew how to trade gas. It knew how to trade electricity, and now it would apply those lessons to the metals business.

Surely, Enron would succeed. The company owned pipelines and power plants, valuable assets that gave it visibility in the gas and electricity markets in North America, South America, Europe, and Asia. It had a big trading operation in Europe. EnronOnline was becoming the de facto standard for traders all over the world. Commodity traders on Wall Street relied on EnronOnline for pricing on dozens of different products and invariably had one of their computer screens tuned to the web site. And Enron had a battalion of talented traders backed by one of the most sophisticated trading platforms ever developed. The company's traders could assess the risk on any deal almost instantaneously. Any deal they made was instantly processed and accounted for in the company's massive data center. Almost any position Enron took in the commodities market was quickly hedged with a countervailing position. Furthermore, its had a battalion of traders who were among the sharpest in the business. They made more money, had bigger egos, and drove faster cars than just about anybody.

Enron's size in the market was demonstrated in other ways. As one of the biggest players in the trading business, Enron was able to help make the rules by which the game was played. But one of those rules would play a major role in its downfall.

During the early days of the Gas Bank, Enron began inserting a provision—called the material adverse change clause—into its derivatives contracts. The clause became a binding part of the contract that allowed Enron to demand that its counterparty put up collateral on their contract if the counterparty experienced a material adverse change to its business. For example, say Company Z entered into a five-year contract to sell 1 million gallons of gasoline per month to Enron. But six months after the contract was signed, Company Z's refinery blew up. Enron could invoke the material adverse change clause and demand that Company Z come up with the cash value of the contract so that Enron would not be left holding the bag. But the material adverse change clause works both ways. Company Z could also invoke the clause if a catastrophe befell Enron. But no one would ever demand that Enron would have to provide cash under the material adverse change. Enron was too strong to fail. Right?

The institution of the material adverse change clause was just one way that Enron dominated the trading business. And Skilling became convinced that Enron simply couldn't lose. In the lingo of Rich Kinder, Skilling began "smoking his own dope."

Skilling had made Enron into *the* trading company that everyone was talking about. Enron had become the 900-pound gorilla in the marketplace. It didn't just own the casino. On any given deal, Enron could be the house, the dealer, the oddsmaker, and the guy across the table you're trying to beat in diesel fuel futures, gas futures, or the California electricity market. With all of those advantages, Enron's trading business must have been a cash machine. Right?

Wrong.

Like every business Jeff Skilling created while he was piloting Enron, the trading business was a loser. Sure, trading was glamorous and sexy, but it generated virtually no cash for Enron. And that was a problem. Instead, Enron's trading operation had an insatiable appetite for cash. Unlike other on-line energy marketplaces like Altra or the consumer goods auction site, eBay—which matches buyers and sellers for a fee—EnronOnline was the principal in every transaction. That's a very expensive place to be.

If a seller agreed on Enron's posted price for, say, natural gas to be delivered on a certain date, that seller could sell it immediately to Enron. The company would then take title to the gas and try to sell it to another party. That may not sound like a big deal, but by mid-2000, Enron was doing several billion dollars worth of trades every day. And because it was in the middle of every transaction, Enron would have to hold some of those commodities for days or even weeks before it could get the price that it wanted on its trades. That meant Enron had to have billions of dollars in cash at the ready. That sort of ready cash needed to clear and fund each sale and purchase—often called a company's "float"—can be enormously expensive. And the bigger the float, the bigger the expense.

Every day that Enron held onto a big position in a commodity, it had to pay interest on the money it borrowed to take that position. For instance, one of Enron's gas traders might be betting that gas prices would rise and therefore go "long" on gas contracts in the amount of 500 million cubic feet of gas. At $3 per 1,000 cubic feet, the gas could be worth $1.5 million. That might not sound like much. But Enron had hundreds of traders. Some going long, others going short in gas and dozens of other commodities. Supporting all of those positions required huge amounts of capital. And as the number of transactions handled by EnronOnline grew, so did its appetite for capital. The new operation had to have enough cash to keep a liquid market in 800 different products, each of which was seeing a big surge in volume.

In the first six months of 2000, Enron borrowed over $3.4 billion to finance its operations. The company's cash flow from operations was a *negative* $547 million. Enron was losing money—real money, *cash money*—hand over fist by just being in business. Interest expenses were surging.

By the end June 2000, the Enron company was paying about $2 million *per day* in interest to banks and other lenders. The $376 million in interest charges for the first half of 2000 was more than Enron paid in all of 1996 (the last year of Rich Kinder's tenure), during which the company's total interest costs were $290 million. Of course, Skilling was able to make Enron's revenue look great. But once again, the surging revenue was due to the illusion of mark-to-market accounting. If Enron signed a five-year electricity supply contract for a department store, all of the revenue was booked immediately. With tricks like that in near-constant supply, it's not surprising that during the first six months of the year, Enron's revenues totaled $30 billion, nearly double the $17.3 billion recorded for the period a year earlier.

Beyond that, personnel costs, particularly in Europe, were out of control. At its peak, Enron Europe had about 5,000 employees, the vast majority of whom were trying to profit from the continent's electricity market, a sector that was only about two-thirds the size of the North American power market. At one point, salaries alone for Enron Europe totaled about $150 million per year. But Skilling was unconcerned, said one Enron Europe veteran. "Skilling never worried about costs. He only worried about revenues. If at the end of the year you had started with a $10 million target and you came back with $12 million, you were a hero. And it didn't matter if you'd spent $15 million to make that $12 million."

Despite EnronOnline's voracious appetite for capital, Skilling was able to convince a nearly constant parade of reporters that Enron's trading business was invincible. Other companies were going to explode as Enron figured out how to buy and sell every part of an individual company's traditional business. Enron was going to intermediate everything, commoditize everything. Just as Ford Motor Company didn't have to own the steel mill to build cars, Enron was going to speed the breakup of every business in the world into its individual parts.

"We believe that markets are the best way to order or organize an industrial enterprise," Skilling told the *Financial Times* in June 2000. "You are going to see the deintegration of the business systems we have all grown up with."[3]

If Enron was going to help that "deintegration," its trading business was going to have to keep growing. And that meant Enron would need more capital, lots more capital. But there was a problem: Enron could not raise capital by adding more debt. More debt on its balance sheet might lower the company's credit rating, which would further increase the company's already high interest costs.

Skilling needed more cash but no more debt. Andy Fastow was going to have to do more financial engineering. And Fastow, of course, was more than willing to help.

30
LJM2

SUMMER 2000

No one at Enron—or anyone else, for that matter—ever accused Andy Fastow of excessive humility. And throughout 2000 and early 2001, the company's chief financial officer was at the apogee of his self-diagnosed genius. Fastow was fully convinced that his skein of partnerships and off-the-balance-sheet entities, with its mind-numbingly complicated spiderweb of interconnections and interdependent relationships, was the ultimate advance in financial engineering. "I can strip out any risk," Fastow once bragged to a coworker. From a distance, it certainly looked that way.

Fastow was both the chief financial officer of Enron and in effective control of a series of partnerships that were charged with investing in Enron assets. That fact gave him a huge amount of leverage when he began raising money for LJM2. Fastow controlled which banks got lucrative investment banking business from Enron. Enron was *the* hot stock on Wall Street. And Fastow, with his inside knowledge of the company, should have been able to provide investors with a good return on their capital.

Nevertheless, the first investment banking firm he approached about investing in LJM2, Donaldson, Lufkin & Jenrette Securities Corporation, turned him down, saying it was uncomfortable with Fastow's dual role as general partner of LJM2 and Enron CFO.[1] The high-minded fellows at Wall Street giant Merrill Lynch had no such qualms. Shown the lure of an Enron-related partnership that promised returns of 30 percent or more a year, Merrill expected to raise $200 million or so. Instead, the firm raised $394 million. And a good chunk of that came from Merrill's own people. Nearly 100 Merrill execs invested a total of $16.6 million of their own money in LJM2. Merrill itself put in an additional $5 million.[2]

The other big Wall Street firms pitched in, too. LJM2 got multimillion-dollar investments from Dresdner Kleinwort Wasserstein, Credit Suisse First Boston Corporation, J.P. Morgan Chase, Lehman Brothers, and Citicorp. Insurance giant American International Group kicked in $30 million.[3]

The banks weren't necessarily investing because they liked Fastow. In fact, a lot of investment bankers despised him. But they feared losing Enron's investment banking business. In some cases, it appears that Fastow even said there would be a quid pro quo: If the banks didn't invest in LJM2, they'd lose Enron's business. Many of the bankers, including people from Chase Manhattan, Barclays, and Deutsche Bank were so flabbergasted by Fastow's strong-arming that they called to complain to Enron's former treasurer, Jeff McMahon.

The complaints didn't matter to Fastow. Once he corralled the cash he needed for LJM2, he began using a panoply of off-the-balance-sheet special-purpose entities in an effort to help Enron book ever more revenue while it simultaneously avoided adding any losing projects to its financial statements. On December 21, 1999, Fastow used LJM2 to buy part of Enron's stake in a power plant the company was building in Poland called Nowa Sarzyna.[4] LJM2 paid $30 million for the stake in the plant, and Enron got to record a profit of approximately $16 million on the sale, a move that helped Fastow's boss, Jeff Skilling look better. But Enron was just using LJM2 as a parking place for the asset. On March 29, 2000, due to a restriction in Enron's original loan on

Nowa Sarzyna, Enron and Whitewing were forced to buy back LJM's share interest in the plant for $31.9 million. Fastow's company made nearly $2 million by holding the asset for less than ninety days.

Fastow's special-purpose entities became a fast-and-dirty way for Enron to manufacture additional revenues in a big hurry. In the last eleven days of 1999, Fastow's companies did seven separate deals with Enron. In addition to the power plant in Poland, Fastow's LJM2 entities borrowed $38.5 million from Whitewing, bought a stake in some of Enron's loans, bought part of Enron's stake in a natural gas gathering system in the Gulf of Mexico, bought a stake in a trust Enron had invested in called Yosemite, and bought part of Enron's stake in a company that provided financing for natural gas producers.

The advantage Fastow brought to Enron with the off-the-balance-sheet entities was the ability to do deals quickly. Enron was "looking for a quick way to sell assets to generate income," said one longtime Enron finance person. "If you control both sides of the deal, you can do it very quickly at any price you want. That's an advantage versus a situation where you're trying to sell it to a third party, it might take a year or more. It was a way for them to control the entire process."

Fastow helped Enron control the process through a flock of entities with names like Osprey, Osprey Trust, Timberwolf, Bobcat, Egret, Condor, Rawhide, Sundance, Ponderosa, Harrier, Porcupine, and Mojave. He also created a quartet of misbegotten entities known as the Raptors.

The sham deals quickly became one of Enron's main business units. In 1999 alone, Fastow's deals inflated Enron's profits by $248 million—that's more than one-fourth of the $893 million in profits Enron reported that year. Fastow's key lieutenant in tending this financial house of cards was Michael Kopper, the Enron employee who bought Enron's interest in the JEDI project in 1997. Kopper and his domestic partner, William Dodson, owned the entity known as Chewco, which had borrowed heavily in order to do the JEDI deal.

By 2000, Kopper and Fastow were working hand in hand. And Fastow was rewarding him. In 1999, it appears that Fastow helped Kopper get a bonus that was double the amount normally given to employees at his level. Kopper, a graduate of Duke University and the London School of Economics, was well liked by his coworkers at Enron. He was smart and capable. But Kopper's coworkers said he also quickly became enamored of the wealth that Fastow's partnerships were showering upon him. After that, "Kopper became Fastow's puppet," said one senior Enron finance person who worked closely with both men.

The huge amounts of money coming from the partnerships undoubtedly helped Kopper and the other Enron employees become inured to Fastow's frequent screaming fits and temper tantrums. One of Fastow's key aides was Ben Glisan, who became the company's treasurer in May 2000. Glisan succeeded Jeff McMahon, a former Arthur Andersen employee who had complained to Enron president Jeff Skilling about Fastow's dual-role position at Enron. Rather than address McMahon's concerns, Skilling moved McMahon from his spot as treasurer to another division at Enron.

Fastow's two-headed role at Enron allowed him to exact very good deals when negotiating on behalf of LJM1 and LJM2. If an Enron employee was pushing too hard for Enron's interests, Fastow would retaliate. In one case, Fastow told an Enron lawyer, Jordan Mintz, to fire one of his subordinates because he was "representing Enron too aggressively" in some negotiations.

Another Enron finance executive felt Fastow couldn't be trusted in negotiations or anything else. "Fastow would tell you anything you wanted to hear to your face. He'd lie to your face. Then go somewhere else and say something totally different."

Truth and trust apparently began to matter less and less to Glisan and Kopper as they began seeing just how many spiffy baubles Fastow's newfound wealth could buy. Fastow was partial to fancy watches. He often wore a Franck Muller model known as a "Master Banker" (no snickering, please), a spiffy analog watch that showed the time in three different time zones. Its cost: about $9,000. Soon, Kopper and Glisan were wearing Master Bankers, too.

Fastow made sure to share the wealth. The most lucrative deal came on March 20, 2000, when Fastow and his cronies set up Southampton Place, L.P. The general partner of Southampton was yet another shell company called Big Doe LLC. (Get it? Big Dough?) The bulk of the money for Southampton came from Big Doe, which was controlled by Kopper, and the Fastow Family Foundation, controlled by Andy Fastow. Those two entities each put $25,000 into Southampton. The other investors in Southampton included Glisan; Kristina Mordaunt, an Enron Broadband Services lawyer who had worked closely with Fastow on LJM-related projects; and three other Enron employees.

Southampton was needed to clean up the derivatives mess Fastow had created in June 1999 with the Rhythms NetConnections deal. Remember Swap Sub and the put option on Rhythms stock that Enron bought—a put that was based on the value of Enron's own stock?

Sometime in March 2000, Enron's president, Jeff Skilling (who was apparently informed and involved in many—if not all—of the company's off-the-balance-sheet deals) decided that the company's option deal with Swap Sub was flawed. Skilling decided Enron should simply sell its Rhythms stock and liquidate the put option it had with Swap Sub.

Fastow, wearing his LJM1 hat, convinced Enron that it should pay a total of $16.7 million to Swap Sub to unwind the deal. (No one at Enron knew that Swap Sub had just been purchased by Southampton.) In exchange for the $16.7 million, Enron would get back the stock it had originally given to Swap Sub and the put option Enron owned on the Rhythms stock would be terminated. Enron's negotiator on the deal, chief accounting officer Rick Causey, agreed to the price and the deal was done.

Why Causey agreed to pay Southampton $16.7 isn't clear at all. In fact, it was just plain boneheaded. Swap Sub owed Enron a ton of money. The Rhythms put options, at the time the deal was canceled, were worth $207 million to Enron because Rhythms stock had fallen dramatically in value. Nevertheless, Fastow somehow persuaded Causey, the eagle-eyed accountant, to pay Southampton big bucks to get out of the Swap Sub deal. Causey's tough negotiating provided an incredible windfall to Fastow and his partners in Southampton.

On May 1, 2000, less than two months after putting $25,000 investment in Southampton, the Fastow Family Foundation got $4.5 million. Glisan and Mordaunt, who put in $5,800 each, received a cool $1 million. It's not clear how much Kopper made from Southampton, but he was making out like a bandit on fees from his other Enron-related deals. Between the end of 1997 and late 2000, Kopper collected about $1.6 million in management fees for the work he did on Chewco.

It didn't take long for Kopper, the owner of Big Doe, to begin spending his big dough. Now that he was getting Big Rich, the Southampton neighborhood wasn't good enough for him any more. He needed something ritzier. So in September 2000, Kopper and his partner, Dodson, bought a smallish house in the ritzy Avalon Place neighborhood just across Kirby Drive from River Oaks. (Kopper and Dodson would sell their old house in Southampton a few months later. But in keeping with Andy Fastow's tradition of selling valuable assets to friends, the two men sold their house to—who else?—Andy Fastow's parents.)[5]

Kopper was only doing what Fastow had done. Just as Fastow was planning to tear down the house he bought in River Oaks, Kopper and Dodson were going to tear down the little house they bought on Ella Lee Lane. And like Lea and Andy Fastow, Kopper and Dodson were going to build something grander.

And where was the Enron board while company insiders were making gazillions of dollars? They were, as usual, asleep at the wheel.

On May 1, 2000, about the same time Fastow, Kopper, and the others were making enormous returns on the Southampton deal, Glisan and Causey presented yet another Fastow-led deal to the company's Finance Committee. The new deal, called Raptor, was described as a "risk management program to enable the Company to hedge the profit and loss volatility of the Company's investments." The presentation said Fastow's company, LJM2, would be one of the main investors in the new entity. It also identified some of the risks that came with the Raptor deal. They were "accounting scrutiny" and "a substantial decline in Enron stock price."

The Finance Committee apparently didn't have any serious objections to the Raptor deal and voted to present it to the full Board of Directors the next day. On May 2, 2000, the full board approved the deal. But Fastow quickly decided his first Raptor needed a friend. So in June, he went to the board's Executive Committee, which quickly approved Raptor II. In August, the full Board of Directors approved the creation of Raptor IV. Fastow apparently created Raptor III without getting the board's approval.

Each of the Raptors was capitalized with $30 million in cash from LJM2. But Fastow was able to get LJM2's money out of the Raptors almost immediately. And if the board members had bothered to ask any hard questions about them or about how much money Fastow and LJM2 were making on the deals, they probably wouldn't have been so agreeable. Although the board was told the investors in the Raptors would only make a return of about 30 percent per year, the truth was far different. Fastow and his investors were making a killing. In October 2000, Fastow, while wearing his LJM2 hat, told his LJM2 investors that the internal rates of return on Raptor I, II, III and IV, were 193 percent, 278 percent, 2500 percent, and a projected 125 percent, respectively.

Those are amazing returns. But Fastow wasn't just making money on the Raptor deals. In between September 1999 and July 2001, Fastow's LJM1 and LJM2 did about twenty different deals with Enron. And Fastow's flimflam partnerships made a profit *on every transaction* they did with Enron. It looked like Fastow couldn't lose. Using Enron's stock instead of cash to prop up his financial house of cards seemed like a great idea. Enron's stock had begun 2000 stuck at about $43. However, thanks to the hype surrounding Enron Broadband Services, it quickly began to climb into the ionosphere. By the middle of the year, it was trading in the $70s. On August 23, 2000, it hit its all-time high, $90 a share. Enron's stock—it seemed—was better than cash.

Given that rising stock price, Fastow apparently convinced Enron to pledge a total of $1 billion worth of its stock to the Raptors. Like Swap Sub, the Enron stock would provide the "capital" that the Raptors needed to do transactions. In return, the Raptors would help Enron lock in tens of millions of dollars in gains on stock it held in newly public companies like hardware maker Avici Systems and The New Power Company, the energy company headed by Lou Pai that planned to sell electric power to individual homeowners.

The solution to preserve the gains in Avici and New Power was the same one that Fastow had come up with for the Rhythms deal: derivatives and more derivatives.

The Rhythms–Swap Sub transaction had used a put option. The Raptor deals were based on a more complicated derivative, a contract called a "total return swap." The total return swap that Enron got from the Raptors allowed the company—in theory—to preserve its investments in Avici and New Power. If the price of the stock in Avici and New Power increased above a certain price, the Raptors would benefit. The Raptors would get to keep any increase in the value of the stock above that set price. If the stocks fell below the set price, the Raptors would be required to pay Enron the difference between the set price and the current price.

But just as with Swap Sub, the Raptors were predicated on flawed logic. The ability of the Raptors to pay Enron for any decline in the value of Avici and the other stocks was based on the value of Enron stock. If Avici and the other stocks declined in value *at the same time* that Enron's stock declined in value, the Raptors wouldn't have enough money to pay Enron back. Fastow may not have known it, but he'd made a multibillion-dollar bet that Enron's stock wouldn't go down. Given Enron's lofty stock price, it must have seemed like a good idea at the time. And as one Enron managing director said, "It worked for a few months. It worked like a charm."

Indeed it did. By November 2000, the notional value of the derivatives deals Enron had done with the Raptors totaled an astounding $1.5 billion.

There was another bit of faulty thinking in the Raptor deals. In exchange for the loan of Enron stock, the Raptors gave Enron promissory notes pledging to repay the $1 billion. So far, so good. However, Fastow and Enron's bean counters made a fatal error in accounting for the promissory note. It was a mistake that would come back to haunt the company.

While the accountants slept, Enron's attorneys were starting to worry about the Raptor deals. On September 1, 2000, Stuart Zisman, an attorney who'd been looking at the Raptors, sent an e-mail to his superiors in Enron's legal department that said, "We have discovered that a majority of the investments being introduced into the Raptor Structure are bad ones. This is disconcerting . . . it might lead one to believe that the financial books at Enron are being 'cooked' in order to eliminate a drag on earnings."

Enron *was* cooking the books and Andy Fastow was the chef de cuisine. So where was Andersen this whole time? It was, as usual, cashing Enron's checks. In exchange for its work on the Raptor deals, Andersen charged Enron a total of $1.3 million.

Enron's bet on the Raptors, combined with Andersen's tacit approval and Fastow's dual role as Enron CFO and off-the-balance-sheet profiteer, was the kind of conflict of interest that federal investigators and regulators were always interested in. Those regulators included people like Arthur Levitt.

31

The Big Five Versus the SEC

Accounting is being perverted.
—SEC Chairman Arthur Levitt, fall 1998[1]

JUNE 27, 2000
Enron closing price: $68.75

About $270 million in tax credits was at stake. But to make the deal work, a group of Enron managers needed an opinion letter from an auditor at Arthur Andersen. So they scheduled a meeting in a conference room in the Enron building and invited the auditor over for a chat. As soon as he got in the room, they held him hostage.

"One of the guys slid a chair in front of the door and announced, 'Nobody leaves until I get that opinion letter,'" recalled one of the people at the meeting. For the next thirty minutes or so, said one of the managers who had been present, the Enron employees threatened, cajoled, and badgered the Andersen employee. They explained the accounting, the reasons Enron needed the opinion letter, and the reasons Andersen should give it to them. After a bit more wrangling, the Andersen auditor, thoroughly upset by the heavy-handed tactics, agreed to produce the letter. The Enron hotshots got up from the table, removed the chair from the door, and everyone had a lovely day.

It was just one of many meetings Enron managers had with their counterparts from Andersen. But for one of the Enron execs in the meeting, it was a turning point in his understanding of the relationship between the two firms. The event, the exec explained, "showed me that those guys from Andersen were whores."

That kind of meeting would have been unimaginable a few decades ago, when certified public accountants, and the firms they worked for, were viewed as impartial arbiters of business. They were CPAs, certified *public* accountants. Their duties were to their clients, sure, but they had a larger duty to the public. And they took that duty seriously. But by the late 1990s, when Enron began barricading doorways that standard had been irreparably eroded—and it worried Arthur Levitt, the chairman of the Securities and Exchange Commission.

Throughout the mid- and late 1990s, Levitt had observed the changes infecting the once-honorable accounting profession. And to Levitt, a former broker and former chairman of the American Stock Exchange, nearly all of the things he was seeing were bad. In 1998, the Tampa, Florida, office of Big Five accounting firm PricewaterhouseCoopers found that its employees were routinely buying stock in companies they audited. The news from Tampa forced the firm to do a companywide audit of its partners' and managers' stock portfolios. In January 2000, the firm said it had found 8,000 violations of its internal policies prohibiting auditors from owning stock in companies the firm audited. About half of PricewaterhouseCoopers's partners had conflicts of interest.[2]

The blurring of the line between the accounting firms' auditing business and their consulting practices was even more worrisome. Figures collected by the SEC, an agency created in 1934 to protect American investors, found a dramatic rise in the amount of consulting work being done by the accounting firms. In 1981, the average accounting firm derived just 15 percent of its income from consulting services. By 1999, firms were collecting half of their annual revenues from management consulting and other nonaudit services. That consulting income was particularly important for the "Big Five" accounting firms: KPMG, Ernst & Young, Deloitte & Touche, PricewaterhouseCoopers, and Arthur Andersen.

The surge in consulting coincided with some terrible auditing work by the accountants. In the seven previous years, investors had lost some $88 billion in market value because of auditing failures.[3] Companies were restating their annual financials with alarming regularity (a restatement occurs after a company realizes its prior financial reports were incorrect). Since 1997, 362 companies monitored by the SEC had been forced to restate their results, a figure that amounted to nearly 1 percent of all filings to the agency. Those restatements had cost investors dearly. The market capitalizations of nine of those companies had declined by a total of $41 billion in the week following the restatement. And one of the poster children for bad behavior was Arthur Andersen.

Andersen, auditor for trash giant Waste Management Inc. for thirty years, had been caught fudging the numbers. The SEC found that Andersen had helped the trash company inflate its earnings by more than $1 billion. In 1998, the company was forced to restate its earnings from 1992 to 1997. Andersen had to pay the trash company an undisclosed amount of money to settle the dispute. During its investigation of Andersen, the SEC allegedly found that the accounting firm's consulting fees were five times what it was being paid to audit the trash company. Furthermore, the SEC alleged that Andersen's audit team at Waste Management was "cross-selling" consulting services and that the auditors were sharing in bonuses derived from the consulting business. The relationship between Andersen and the trash company was far too close. Almost every chief financial officer and chief accounting officer at Waste Management had come to the company from Andersen. The link between the two companies wasn't a revolving door, it was a gravy train.

Although those problems were bad enough, the accounting firm's problems with Waste Management weren't over. In September 1999, Andersen and the trash company agreed to settle a spate of shareholder lawsuits for a total of $220 million. In addition to the Waste Management problems, Andersen's lax approach had caused a series of other debacles, including a growing controversy over its handling of the audits of consumer products maker Sunbeam.

While the company was controlled by Al ("Chainsaw Al") Dunlap, audits failed to raise questions over Dunlap's aggressive "sales" of goods that were still in Sunbeam's own warehouses. Sunbeam's auditor: Arthur Andersen.

Despite Andersen's shoddy record in the business, the firm was able to convince some Big Shots to brag about what a great business partner Andersen could be. One promotional video produced by Andersen featured a testimonial from then Halliburton CEO Dick Cheney, who told viewers, "I get good advice, if you will, from their people based upon how we're doing business and how we're operating." That advice, he added, was "over and above just the sort of normal by-the-books auditing arrangement."[4]

While current vice president Cheney was praising Andersen's willingness to go beyond mere auditing, that very same "over and above" stuff was driving Levitt crazy.

Appointed to head the SEC in 1993 by President Bill Clinton, Levitt was widely viewed as a moderate. And he believed that with proper coercion, he could get the accounting industry to reform itself. Beginning in about 1996, he started delivering speeches, meeting with business and accounting executives, and talking with SEC officials about the rules needed to protect investors from the kind of slipshod accounting that had caused so many problems at Waste Management, Sunbeam, and other companies.

In one 1998 speech, Levitt criticized business leaders who handled "accounting hocus-pocus" with little more than "nods and winks." Accounting irregularities were nothing more than fraud, Levitt insisted. The solution, he told *Fortune*, was wholesale change, regardless of how it affected corporate management. "It's a basic cultural change we're asking for, nothing short of that."[5] The Big Five weren't eager for any kind of cultural shift. They'd grown fat and happy with business just the way it was. During the 1990s, their combined revenues had doubled, to $26.1 billion.[6] During the same time period, their consulting businesses had grown even faster, so that consulting was bringing in three times as much revenue as auditing.[7]

The strength and size of the Big Five was a growing concern to Levitt for another reason: The SEC's budget was far too small for its growing workload. Between 1991 and 2000, the number of complaints and inquiries received by the agency had jumped by 100 percent, but the SEC's enforcement staff had increased by just 16 percent. During that same time period, corporate filings increased by nearly 60 percent, but staff needed to review those filings had increased by just 29 percent.[8] Furthermore, the SEC couldn't keep its employees. Between 1998 and 2000, one-third of the agency's staffers quit.

The SEC was being overwhelmed, and that meant the agency had to have more confidence that corporate filings were honest and reliable. And the only way to get that was to make sure the Big Five and other accounting firms were playing fair. Levitt fervently believed in the motto of one of his predecessors at the SEC, William O. Douglas, who

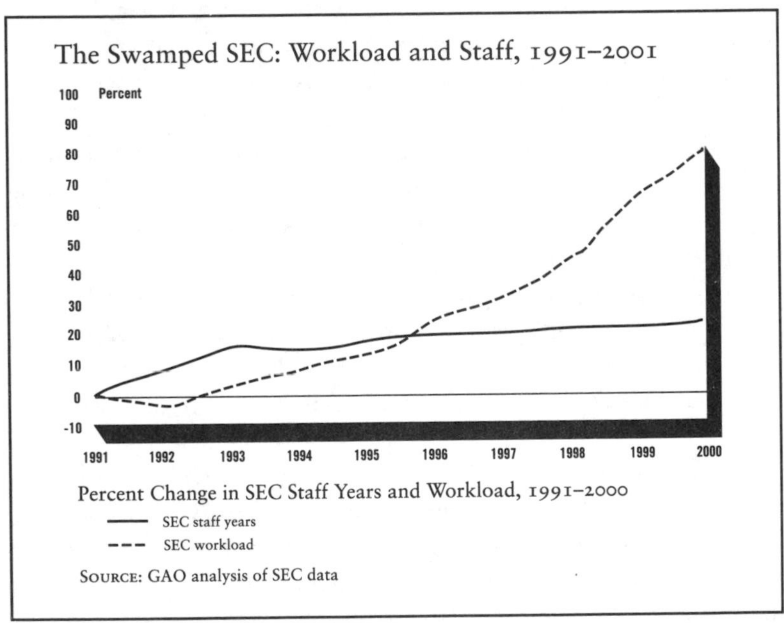

Percent Change in SEC Staff Years and Workload, 1991–2000

SOURCE: GAO analysis of SEC data

said, "We are the investors' advocates." Douglas also said that the SEC's enforcement powers were "the shotgun behind the door."

By the time of the SEC commissioners' June 27, 2000, meeting, Levitt was convinced that the SEC needed more firepower. The other commissioners readily agreed. And by the end of the meeting at SEC headquarters, directly across the street from the Supreme Court building in Washington, D.C., Levitt had what he wanted: a unanimous vote by the commissioners on a rule that Levitt figured would help assure that the public accounting profession retained its duties to *the public*, and not be wholly beholden to the companies that employed them. The rule—even though, with footnotes, it stretched for nearly 60,000 words—was really quite simple: It said accountants must be independent. And it set out four instances that would impair an auditor's independence. That independence would be impaired whenever, during the audit and professional engagement period, the accountant: "(i) has a mutual or conflicting interest with the audit client, (ii) audits the accountant's own work, (iii) functions as management or an employee of the audit client, or (iv) acts as an advocate for the audit client."[9]

Levitt didn't know it at the time, but Andersen's relationship with Enron—the firm's biggest client—violated every one of those standards.

By the late 1990s Andersen had become so reliant on Enron that it simply could not afford to lose the company as a client. Enron understood that and used that fact to its advantage. Andersen's revenues from Enron were enormous. In 1999, the firm billed Enron $46.8 million for its auditing, consulting, and tax work. In 2000, that figure rose to $52 million.

In addition to the big money, Enron's finance department—just like Waste Management's—was packed with Andersen alumni. The company's ex-treasurer, Jeff McMahon, had worked at Andersen. So had his replacement, Ben Glisan. So had Enron's chief accounting officer, Rick Causey. A number of other, lower-level Enron employees, including a vice president named Sherron Watkins—who would soon play a major role in Enron—had also worked at Andersen. And the accounting firm's lead partner on the Enron account, David Duncan, even worked out of Enron's building! Duncan also maintained a close personal friendship with Causey. The two men played golf together, went to lunch together, and took vacations together, including at least one trip to one of golf's most prestigious events, The Masters.

With all those close ties, Enron knew that it could control Andersen. And it did.

In 2000, Carl Bass, a partner at Andersen, raised questions about the partnerships Enron was creating. In particular, Bass questioned the Raptors, the bastard entities that were controlled by Andy Fastow. In an e-mail to a superior in Andersen's Chicago office, Bass said, "I will honestly admit that I have a jaded view of these transactions." Enron didn't like Bass's complaints. And in a client-satisfaction survey, Enron labeled Bass "too rule-oriented." Bass's bosses later told him that Enron believed he was "caustic and cynical toward their transactions" and that they wanted Bass taken off the Enron account. Andersen quickly complied.

Andersen did as Enron desired because the accounting firm had grown dependent on Enron's fees. And since half or more of Andersen's billings to Enron were related to consulting, the firm had to kill Arthur Levitt's proposal. So Andersen, along with the other members of the Big Five, began a jihad. The firms began lobbying and giving huge political contributions to members of Congress. By the end of 2000, according to the nonpartisan Center on Responsive Politics, the accounting industry had given $14.7 million in campaign contributions and had spent $12.3 million on lobbying. Much of that money was aimed at one effort: snuffing out Levitt's reforms. Who was the biggest recipient of the cash? Well, when it came to contributions from Andersen, the member of Congress—House and Senate—who benefited the most is a familiar one: Phil Gramm. According to Federal Election Commission records, Gramm has received $76,850 from Andersen since 1989.[10]

In addition to their contributions to public servants, the Big Five hired one of the sharpest securities lawyers in the country to refute Levitt's efforts. He was a former general counsel of the SEC named Harvey Pitt.

Pitt wrote a paper attacking Levitt's approach and gave the Big Five ammunition in their assault on the SEC proposal. Tactics included big donations to members of Congress and even threats from congressional members to cut the SEC's already thin budget. The push by Pitt and the Big Five left Levitt with little hope. His effort to break up the marriage of auditing and consulting was doomed. And before the end of 2000, Levitt was forced to acknowledge that Congress had folded in the face of campaign cash and a bit of pressure.

That was good news for Enron. It meant that the SEC wouldn't get to look too closely at what Andersen was doing at Enron. It also meant that Enron could continue hyping—and profiting from—one of its biggest and most volatile businesses: derivatives.

32

Derivatives Hocus-Pocus

DECEMBER 13, 2000
Enron closing price: $74.50

Phil Gramm really has no shame. His wife, Wendy Gramm, has a little. But just a little.

In late 1998, Mrs. Gramm's attorney told her that her husband's position in the U.S. Senate allowed him to vote on matters that could directly benefit Enron. And by sitting on the Enron Board of Directors, she might have a conflict of interest.

So, rather than resign her board position, Gramm asked Enron to quit granting her stock options and to henceforth give her cash instead. Her actions were hardly heroic. After all, she was still getting her fat annual director's fees from Enron. But at least Mrs. Gramm took a baby step toward avoiding the appearance of crony capitalism.

The esteemed Democrat-turned-Republican senator from Texas bothered with no such concerns.

When a commodities regulation bill came up in the Senate that had a direct effect on Enron's massive derivatives trading business, *Phil Gramm sponsored it.* The Commodity Futures Modernization Act of 2000, a wide-ranging bill, bounced through both halls of Congress throughout 2000. And with the help of Gramm, who happened to chair the Senate Banking Committee, it was passed unanimously by the Senate on December 13, 2000. President Bill Clinton signed it into law eight days later. Gramm hailed the measure, saying it "protects financial institutions from over-regulation" and that it "guarantees that the United States will maintain its global dominance of financial markets."

Global dominance is always a worthy goal. But Gramm's bill also contained a provision that congressional aides referred to as the "Enron exemption." This bit of legislative legerdemain made into law a regulatory exemption on derivatives contracts that was first rushed into place by the Commodity Futures Trading Commission in 1993. The chair of that body when the exemption first appeared? Yep, Wendy Gramm.

Why didn't the senator abstain from voting on the matter when it came before the Senate? In early 2002, a Gramm spokesman told one reporter that the senator had a policy of "noninterference" when it came to his wife's affairs. He told another reporter that Phil Gramm had not written the section of the bill affecting Enron. "We were not involved with that part of it," croaked a Gramm spokesman.

Therefore, how could it possibly be a conflict? Never mind that in 2001, Enron paid Wendy Gramm a total of $119,292.

Conflict of interest or just the way business is done, Gramm's bill kept the feds out of Enron's business and allowed Enron to continue stoking its ballooning financial statements with an ever-larger diet of derivatives.

In 2000, 7 *percent* of Enron's total revenues—$7.23 billion (identified as "other" revenue on Enron's income statement)—came from its derivatives business. Derivatives had an even bigger impact on the company's balance sheet. Of the $65.5 billion in assets Enron claimed on its balance sheet at the end of 2000, *nearly one-third of the assets*—$21 billion—were financial derivatives (derivatives on Enron's balance sheet are identified as "price risk management activities"). As recently as 1996, the last year of Rich Kinder's tenure at Enron, the company had just $2.47 billion in assets from derivatives, and those assets represented just about one-eighth of Enron's $16.1 billion in total assets.

How was it possible for Enron to grow its assets-from-derivatives position so quickly?

Easy. They made it up.

"There are no government-set rules for reporting derivatives. So Enron could do whatever what they wanted in calculating the value of those derivatives," said economist Randall Dodd, the director of the Derivatives Study Center, a Washington, D.C.–based think tank. By the end of 2000, according to Dodd, the notional value (face value) of Enron's derivatives book was a staggering $758 billion.[1] Enron could create billions of dollars in revenue by simply changing a few assumptions about the value of its derivatives contracts. Remember the price curves discussed earlier? If Enron needed more revenues to prop up its financial statements, it simply adjusted the prices on some of its contracts.

For instance, suppose Enron were to sign a fifteen-year contract that allowed it to buy 1 billion cubic feet of natural gas per year from a producer at a price of $3 per thousand cubic feet. When it completed the deal, Enron might assume that in fifteen years, gas would be selling for $4 per thousand cubic feet. The company would then calculate the value of the entire fifteen years of the contract and immediately—using mark-to-market accounting—record all the projected income from the deal on its books. But if Enron suddenly needed additional revenue, the company could go back into that same contract and assume that gas prices were going to be higher than $4 in fifteen years. The company could raise its price assumption to $6 or even $8 per thousand cubic feet. And because there are no benchmark prices that extend out that far and no regulators to prevent Enron from making that assumption, the company could instantly inflate its revenue figures.

If Enron was selling products like gas or paper or metals to a customer over a long term at a fixed price, the company could simply assume that prices for the commodity would fall even further than their original projections. Again, instant revenue.

There was one check on the system: Enron's auditor, Arthur Andersen, had to validate Enron's price curves. But as one top Enron finance person put it, "Andersen was a rubber stamp."

At the end of 1999, Enron had just $5.1 billion in derivatives assets. Twelve months later, it had $21 billion in assets from derivatives.

The growth of Enron's derivatives business was no more phenomenal than the overall growth of the global derivatives boom. In 1987, the total value of outstanding derivatives was less than $1 trillion. By the first half of 2000, the value of all the outstanding financial derivatives in the United States was over $60 trillion, according to the International Swaps and Derivatives Association.

One of its most innovative products was weather derivatives, an area that Enron pioneered. The company began selling them in 1997 and found a receptive market. Electric and gas utilities were particularly interested in the offering because it allowed them to hedge the risks they faced from extreme weather patterns, which are the biggest variable in the power business. The contracts worked like an insurance policy that utilities purchased from Enron. If temperatures deviated from normal temperature ranges during an agreed-upon time period, Enron would pay the customers to offset their losses. Enron could package the weather derivatives in a panoply of different ways that allowed the utilities to protect themselves against weather that was too cold, too warm, or even too snowy.

Although Enron's derivatives business grew throughout the Skilling era, EnronOnline and the California electricity crisis caused its derivatives exposure to explode. They also, it appears, helped send the company into bankruptcy.

By trying to manipulate the California energy market, Enron unwittingly made it a whole lot more expensive for the company to keep its trading business afloat. Enron's moves sent gas prices through the roof. Electricity prices surged by a factor of eight or more. EnronOnline, which was already struggling to find enough cash to provide liquidity in 800 different products, was, with the surging prices in California, forced to find yet more capital to keep trading. By late 2000 and early 2001, natural gas that was formerly trading for about $3 per thousand cubic feet in California was selling for as much as $60. Electricity that was selling for $30 in late 1999 was going for $1,500 a year later. And

EnronOnline, which was standing in the middle of every deal, had to cover the capital costs of both sides of each transaction. The "float" Enron needed to keep EnronOnline going was soaring.

By the end of the first quarter of 2001, Enron was having to borrow heavily to just stay in business. That quarter, the company borrowed another $1.2 billion, a move that brought its long-term debt load to $9.7 billion. Cash flow from operations was a negative $464 million.

In addition, its exposure to California utilities was enormous. By early 2001, Enron was owed tens of millions of dollars—perhaps even hundreds of millions, the company wouldn't say exactly how much—by California electric companies that could not pay their bills. Enron's derivatives positions, particularly the ones that appear to be related to California, also soared. In 1999, Enron had less than $800 million worth of liabilities related to energy marketing firms, the firms that were selling electricity into the California market. By the end of 2000, that total had grown to $6.1 billion.

By playing the California market, Enron made itself a political target and accelerated the ruin of its finances. As one Wall Street analyst told me, Enron's push to profit from California's energy crisis proved the old adage that "pigs get fat, hogs get slaughtered."

33

Ken Rice: Missing In Action

JANUARY 25, 2001

Enron closing price: $82.00

Ken Rice was missing in action, and the executives on the forty-fourth floor of the Enron building were starting to get worried. Enron's annual conference with Wall Street analysts at the Four Seasons Hotel was supposed to begin in less than forty-eight hours. All of Enron's other business segments were ready with their conference materials. The lead executives had been briefed, their scripts had been approved, and each executive had gone over the script.

But Rice, the chairman and CEO of Enron Broadband Services, was nowhere to be found. He hadn't been in the office for days. That wasn't unusual. Rice was rarely in the office. Although he was the head of the broadband division, Rice didn't feel compelled to work overly hard at establishing Enron's new business. That was fine for him, but his underlings *did* have a business to run and they didn't have his millions. And with the analysts' meeting coming up, they simply had to have Rice's full attention. Billions of dollars of Enron's market capitalization were on the line. The broadband executives knew that broadband was going to be a central part of Jeff Skilling's presentation and that sheets explaining the broadband division's strategy were going to make up the bulk of the packets the analysts were going to receive.

Moreover, Skilling was going to tell the analysts that Enron's stock was worth $126 per share and that the broadband division alone was worth $40 of that per-share figure. What would happen if Rice didn't show for the analysts' meeting? What would happen if Rice did appear but couldn't handle the presentation? What if he botched the answer to a question?

The dangers were great, increasing with every passing hour. The lead executives at Enron Broadband had spent the past several days looking for Rice. They called his cell phone. They left him voice mail. But there was no response. Nothing. "We were trying not to tell anybody that we couldn't find Ken," recalled one executive who was at Enron Broadband during that time. "We started to wonder if he was all right. Finally, I had to threaten his assistant. I told her, if you don't get Ken on the line in two hours, I'm going to Skilling."

Twenty minutes later, Rice was on the phone. "Hey, what's going on?" asked Rice.

"Well, we need you here in the office, the analysts' conference is in two days," said the executive, who was having difficulty hearing because of all the background noise on Rice's end of the line. "What's all that noise? What are you doing?" he asked.

"Oh, I'm out racing my cars," Rice replied.

The executive was floored. He and his coworkers had been putting in ten-hour days getting ready for the analysts' conference. They had been fretting over what to say to the analysts. They knew that Enron Broadband Services wasn't meeting expectations and that the company's broadband strategy was failing. They'd known that for months. But they had to keep the lid on it. Too much was riding on the analysts' conference. And now here was Rice, the Accidental CEO, out on a lark, racing his expensive cars, without a care in the world.

"Well, we need you to come in to the office so we can brief you on your presentation at the analysts' conference," the executive told Rice.

"Oh, okay."

The next day, Rice appeared at Enron's headquarters and went over the script for the meeting. After going over the particulars of the script, the broadband executives were satisfied that Rice was competent enough to deliver the information. But when it came time for Rice to ascend the stairs at the Four Seasons to deliver his spiel, his handlers in broadband were still worried. So they pulled him aside. "Whatever you do, don't answer any questions," a broadband executive told Rice. "You don't know enough to answer any questions. Let us handle them."

So Ken Rice—the leader of Enron's Next Big Thing—delivered his speech and sixty-four pages of Power Point slides to the analysts. He told them that during 2000, despite the fact that his company had lost $60 million on revenue of $408 million,[1] Enron was proving that its business model "can be directly extended to the communications industry" and that the "depth of opportunity for Enron in broadband is significantly greater than previously anticipated." Rice told the analysts that his company's prospects had never been better. Opportunities in data storage, bandwidth trading, and other areas looked great. They looked so good in fact, that Enron Broadband Services alone was worth $36 billion.

But if Enron Broadband was so great, why was Ken Rice dumping his own Enron shares?

In the three weeks before he climbed the podium at the Four Seasons, Rice had sold more than 45,000 shares of Enron stock in about forty different transactions. Rice's profits: just over $2.6 million. Indeed, Rice was selling stock on the very same day he was hyping it. According to Securities and Exchange Commission filings, Rice sold 3,000 shares the day of the meeting, for a total profit of $169,445.

Yes, Ken Rice was doing just fine. He told the analysts exactly what Enron had wanted him to. And better still, he didn't answer any questions.

Jeff Skilling wrapped up the meeting. Just as he had during the January 2000 analysts' conference, he told the Wall Street analysts and the money managers that Enron was a dynamo. "Enron has built uniquely strong franchises with sustainable high earnings power," Skilling told them. "These franchises can be significantly expanded within existing markets and extended to new markets with enormous growth potential." Enron's pipelines, its trading business, its broadband business—all of them were incredibly valuable. The punch line, he told them, was that Enron was worth far more than the $79 or so it was trading at. In fact, Enron was doing so well that Wall Street should price the stock at $126 per share.

With that, the meeting ended.

Rice and Skilling thought it had gone well. But several of the analysts hadn't liked what they had heard. And it wouldn't take long before a few of them started shooting holes in Enron's story.

34

Analysts Who Think

FEBRUARY 21, 2001

Enron closing price: $73.09

Lou Gagliardi and John Parry didn't expect to be praised. They knew someone from Enron would be calling, and calling soon. They didn't have to wait long. On February 21, 2001, just a few hours after his report on Enron was made public, Parry's phone was ringing. It was an Enron official, who immediately began berating him for daring to question Enron's profitability and business model.

Gagliardi and Parry were analysts at John S. Herold, Inc., a Connecticut-based investment research firm, and they'd been following Enron for several years. They'd followed Azurix, Enron's expensive abortion in the water business. They'd been briefed on the broadband business. In the preceding few years, they'd gone to almost every analysts' conference that Enron had held. They knew—and had spoken with—many of Enron's leaders. But Gagliardi, Parry, and their fellow analysts at Herold, including the company president, Art Smith, were wary. The Enron story was getting old and the company's numbers just weren't adding up. If business was so great, why were Enron's profit margins shrinking? Enron "is a force to be reckoned with in international power and trading," wrote Gagliardi, Smith, and Parry, in the report issued that day. But they pointed out that Enron's profits from its trading business were falling dramatically. In 1995, the analysts estimated that Enron's profits from its trading business—as measured by earnings before interest, taxes, depreciation, and amortization—were 6.5 percent. By 2000, that percentage had fallen to 2.7 percent.[1]

The Herold analysts blamed Enron's falling profitability on energy companies like Houston-based El Paso Corporation, Dynegy, and Duke Energy, all of which had jumped into energy trading to capture some of the trading business that was being gobbled up by Enron. More important, those companies' trading businesses appeared to be growing faster and adding more profits to their respective bottom lines than Enron's. Gagliardi and his peers were "particularly concerned about the sustainability of ENE's [ENE was Enron's trading symbol on the New York Stock Exchange] above average revenue growth with competitors nipping at their heels."

Enron was not worth the $126 per share that Jeff Skilling had touted just a few weeks earlier at the analysts' meeting in Houston. Nor was it worth the $73 per share that it was commanding at that time, said the Herold analysts. Instead, Enron should be valued at multiples like those given such New York investment banking houses as Merrill Lynch and Goldman Sachs. Those firms were trading at fourteen times their projected 2001 earnings. Enron was trading at forty-four times its projected earnings. The bottom line: Enron was way overvalued.

Given its falling profitability and the fact that other trading firms were garnering lower valuations, Enron's stock was actually worth no more than $53.20 per share, they said.

"We admit that Herold remains an 'old economy' valuation fan: we make no apologies, we like hard assets," wrote Gagliardi and the others. Enron was a "premier energy trader" but, they said, "we suspect its shares have been levitated by a touch of 'irrational exuberance' in a perhaps frothy market."

The Herold report was the first time any major Wall Street research or investment banking firm had dared question Enron's valuation. It was the first time a major research firm had dared to doubt Enron's story. And it did so at a time when almost every other Wall Street analyst was cheering and Enron was near the peak of its popularity. A *Fortune* magazine article on Enron would come out nearly two weeks later raising similar questions, but Gagliardi, Smith, and Parry were the first analysts willing to stand up and say that Enron deserved more scrutiny than it was getting.

That meant they were going to hear from Enron. When the phone call came, it didn't come from the company's senior management or executive committee. It didn't come from Chief Financial Officer Andy Fastow or from Chief Executive Officer Jeff Skilling; it came from Enron's investor relations flack, Mark Koenig.

"He wouldn't talk on the merits of the paper," recalled Gagliardi, who later tried to engage Koenig in a conversation during a meeting in New York. "I asked him what was wrong with our report, And he'd say something like, 'Oh it's just terrible.' They weren't going to engage us in the facts."

The experience of the John S. Herold analysts was a classic example of Enron's attitude toward Wall Street: If you can't control them, try to intimidate them.

The analysts at John S. Herold were able—and more important, *were willing*—to take on Enron because they are truly independent. Herold doesn't do any investment banking. It's a research-only firm that sells its reports to fund managers, investment houses, and others. It doesn't put out buy or sell ratings. Instead, it estimates earnings for various companies and then writes reports that explain those estimates. In short, Herold has nothing to gain or lose by hyping or panning a specific stock. And for Enron, that meant trouble.

Up until the Herold report was issued, Enron had been able to keep the Wall Street analysts in line. Virtually every analyst who covered the company had a buy rating on Enron. That was hardly coincidental.[2]

"If you ever wanted to do investment banking with Enron, your analyst had to have a strong buy rating on the stock," said John Olson, an analyst at Sanders Morris Harris, a boutique investment banking firm in Houston. "It was borderline extortion." And that extortion was based on the huge investment banking fees that Enron generated. If firms like Goldman Sachs, Merrill Lynch, or Salomon Smith Barney wanted part of an investment banking deal at Enron, their analyst had to be touting Enron's stock. Olson recalled that Ken Lay often reminded analysts, "We are for our friends." To Olson, the translation was easy: No strong buy recommendation, no investment banking fees.

Olson knows this terrain well. An analyst with decades of experience in the energy business, he spent several years at Merrill Lynch in the early 1990s. But Olson was never a fan of Enron. And throughout his tenure at Merrill Lynch, he never put a buy rating on Enron, a fact that infuriated Ken Lay and Rich Kinder. It also infuriated Olson's superiors at Merrill, who were certain that they were missing out on some of Enron's lucrative investment banking business. As one Houston analyst put it, "Olson was calling bullshit on Enron at Merrill Lynch and they finally ran his ass off."

Olson, whose career includes stints at Drexel Burnham Lambert and Goldman Sachs, said that at Merrill Lynch, the firm's leaders were "trying to turn the research department into a deal machine." That meant the analysts had to "either be very encouraging, or provide strong buy recommendations for current or prospective banking clients, so the firmwide bonus would be unusually generous. And if you didn't do that, you'd get whacked."[3]

Enron could make sure the Wall Street firms kept their analysts in line because the company was a deal machine. Between 1986 and 2001, the biggest Wall Street firms made about $323 million for underwriting stocks and bonds issued by Enron. According to data from First Call/Thomson Financial, Goldman Sachs led the list with $69 million. Credit Suisse First Boston took in $64 million, and Salomon Smith Barney, a division of Citigroup, got $61 million. But the $323-million figure is likely only a part of the total amount of money Enron paid to the Wall Street firms. In addition to the underwriting business, Enron was constantly involved in mergers, acquisitions, and divestitures that generated enormous fees for the investment banking houses.

Between January 1999 and December 2001, Enron was involved in forty-one separate merger and acquisition transactions, according to data from *Bloomberg*. Each of those deals could mean tens of millions of dollars in revenue for each Wall Street firm. And Enron's activity dwarfed that of its competitors in the energy business. During that same time period, Dynegy was involved in fifteen merger or acquisition deals, while another Houston pipeline company, Kinder Morgan Inc., did just a dozen deals.

To illustrate how much money was at stake, CSFB Corporation, an investment banking firm, advised Enron on its then pending $2.9-billion sale of Portland General Electric Corporation. If CSFB was able to collect just 3 percent of the sale proceeds, a not unreasonable amount in the investment banking business, the firm would have been paid $87 million.

All those investment banking deals allowed Enron to control Wall Street's analysts better than any other company in modern American history. By carefully controlling which firms got access to Enron executives and which firms were selected to do investment banking deals, as well as through selective browbeating of analysts, Enron was able to prevent analysts from asking too many questions. And Skilling was artful in his personal manipulations. Skilling would sometimes meet with analysts one-on-one, and he "would give little truths," said Carol Coale, an analyst with Prudential Securities in Houston. "He'd get your confidence." But Coale added, Skilling only told the analysts enough to string them along, to keep them believing in Enron's story.

The result of all these techniques was an almost lockstep endorsement of Enron by Wall Street's biggest securities firms. The herd mentality was led by David Fleischer of Goldman Sachs, who, despite a 90-percent drop in Enron's stock price, accounting problems, restatements of earnings, and other calamities, kept Enron on Goldman's "recommended list" until the stock was nearly worthless. Fleischer, Ray Niles of Salomon Smith Barney, Ron Barone of UBS PaineWebber Incorporated, and the other leading Wall Street analysts who covered Enron make sheep look like independent thinkers. Although Fleischer and his compatriots were sheeplike in their devotion to Enron, their greed was pure wolf.

Throughout its hypergrowth period, Enron refused to become too closely tied to any specific Wall Street firm. Instead, it played all of the Wall Street firms against each other. "Enron did business with everybody," said Kurt Q. Holmes, an energy hedge-fund analyst and manager who has worked on Wall Street for eleven years, including five years at Morgan Stanley. "Nobody could count on their business. You had to please them to get their business. And there was a lot of business. Enron would spread it around very effectively and it managed the relationships ruthlessly."

The June 1999 initial public offering of Enron's water company, Azurix, offers a good example of Enron's desire to spread the fees around. Although it wasn't a large IPO, the deal had six companies involved, including Merrill Lynch, Credit Suisse First Boston Corporation, Donaldson, Lufkin & Jenrette Securities Corporation, PaineWebber Incorporated, BT Alex. Brown Incorporated, and NationsBanc Montgomery Securities LLC. In a typical securities offering like the Azurix deal, the investment banking firms would collect 6 percent of the proceeds. That means the firms involved in the Azurix IPO probably split a jackpot of nearly $42 million from the IPO, which raised about $695 million for the new water company.

In May 2001, according to *Bloomberg*, Enron used six banks—A. G. Edwards & Sons Inc., Banc of America Securities, Dain Rauscher Wessels, First Union Securities Inc., Salomon Smith Barney Inc., and UBS Warburg—to manage a $151-million unit offering for Northern Border Partners LP, one of scores of Enron-controlled partnerships.[4] According to Wall Street analysts, for a deal of that relatively small size, no more than four underwriters are ordinarily involved.

Although it's impossible to determine exactly how much Enron was paying the Wall Street firms for their investment banking, several former Enron officials have said that company insiders often reminded Wall Street that they were paying more investment banking fees than any other Fortune 500 company.

"Enron bragged to everybody," said Chris Wasden, who worked on mergers and acquisitions for Azurix. "The guys at Enron wanted to make sure that everybody in the Enron family was getting full benefits from all the big banks. So we would coordinate activities with investment banks." Wasden recalled a specific meeting in 1999, where Enron officials said that in 1998, Enron paid more in fees than any other company in the United States. The numbers from Enron's bankruptcy appear to bear that out. According to the December 2, 2001, bankruptcy filing, Enron owed $185 million to two offices of Chase Manhattan Bank, a subsidiary of J.P. Morgan Chase; $74 million to UBS Warburg; and $71 million to Credit Suisse First Boston. Bear Stearns & Co. has said it will lose $69 million from the collapse of Enron, and Commerzbank AG has said it will lose a bit less than $45 million.

The massive fees the banks were being paid by Enron, coupled with Enron's pressure-packed spin on its story, led to remarkably favorable coverage from the Wall Street firms that were getting fees from the company. And that coverage continued right up to the time of Enron's bankruptcy. Consider the situation on November 12, 2001. In the previous four weeks, Enron had announced that it was being investigated by the SEC. It had fired its CFO, Andy Fastow. It had written off $1.2 billion in equity stemming from Fastow's creative financing deals, a write-down that Ken Lay couldn't explain to analysts. It had written off $1.01 billion in bad investments like Azurix and broadband. Every day, the *Wall Street Journal* and the *New York Times* were reporting new, ever more salacious developments about the Enron saga. Yet the tally sheet among Wall Street firms included eight analysts with a strong buy, three with a buy, one with a hold, and one with a strong sell.[5]

Although Enron's financial statements were difficult to understand, one part of the company's reports was crystal clear: the cash flow statements. And had the analysts bothered to glance at them, they would have seen a dreadful record. Sure, Enron was burning through cash, but a quick review of the cash flow statements during the Skilling era showed a systemic sickness at Enron: Out of the nineteen quarters that Skilling was either president or CEO of Enron, the company was cash flow positive from operations in just six of those quarters. And four of those six instances occurred in the fourth quarter of the year.

Something was fishy with Enron's cash flow, and it didn't take a genius to see it.

But it appears the herd mentality mattered more than hard financial acumen. "Enron is uniquely positioned to be the GE of the new economy," Donato Eassey, Merrill Lynch's energy stock analyst, told *Bloomberg* in February 2001. "This isn't a management team to bet against." Eassey resigned from Merrill in December 2001, shortly after Enron went bankrupt.[6]

Enron was the hot stock of 1999 and 2000. To be against the Enron juggernaut was undoubtedly difficult. And Enron's hard-edged tactics toward analysts who asked impertinent questions made it easier for the company to keep the analysts safely corralled. If an analyst asked a question that Enron's management didn't like, "they'd insult you," said Holmes. "Basically, they'd say if you are too dumb to understand it, then why are you here? They could mesmerize the analysts into accepting everything that was said. Some analysts even said they stopped trying to model Enron and they didn't feel bad about it."

The analysts, said Holmes, started to believe that as long as Enron's earnings per share were increasing, then everything was going to be fine. But things inside Enron weren't fine. Spending was out of control.

35

Air Enron

MARCH 27, 2001

Enron closing price: $60.46

Robin Lay wanted to come home.

The sand and the sun and the beautiful people were fun, but Robin, Linda Lay's daughter from her previous marriage, had been in the South of France long enough. It was time to go back to Houston and be with her mom and dad. So sometime in mid-1999, Ken or Linda Lay made a few phone calls, and a few hours after that, an Enron jet was dispatched—empty, except for the pilots, to fetch her.

Never mind the cost. Never mind the squadrons of commercial airliners that fly from France to Houston every day of the week. Never mind that Robin was an adult in her early thirties who should have been able to fend for herself. At Enron, what mattered to the Lays was what mattered. So a crew of pilots clambered aboard one Enron's Falcon 900s and launched the plane on its twelve-hour flight from Houston's Intercontinental Airport to Nice, France.

The Falcon 900 is a lovely airplane. Capable of cruising at 560 miles per hour, its three engines can propel the twenty-three-ton plane from San Jose to New York in under five hours. Its wide leather chairs and suave couch make first-class seats on a commercial jetliner look shabby. For creature comforts, the thirteen passengers and three crew members can relax—it comes equipped with a lavatory, a full kitchen, and of course, a small bar. In the universe of private jets, it's hard to beat the Falcon. But all that luxury comes with a hefty price tag. Enron's internal billing system estimated the cost of flying the Falcon 900 (a new one costs about $30 million), at $5,200 per hour.[1]

That means Robin Lay's excursion from the Côte d'Azur to the Côte de Smog cost Enron a cool $125,000.

No other part of Enron's business better reflected the company's out-of-control egos and out-of-control spending than the aviation department. While other parts of the company were burning through cash at record rates, Enron executives were cruising five miles high in ultra-luxe style. By spring 2001, Enron had six jets in its fleet. There were two Falcon 900s, three Hawker 800s, and a Falcon 50.

At first blush, that number of airplanes seems excessive. But given all of Enron's international business, perhaps it was not. Most large corporations have a fleet of corporate jets. Aviation industry sources say that when retailing giant K-Mart went bankrupt in early 2002, it had six aircraft. Big companies, particularly companies that have far-flung operations, need planes that can transport people quickly and efficiently to their destination at a moment's notice. Enron's operations were certainly far-flung. Its international operations included power plants in China, pipelines in Argentina, oil wells in the Indian Ocean, and offices on five continents. During the development of the Dabhol project in India, some Enron executives were flying to Bombay on a monthly basis.

Enron did need access to private jets, but it was also obvious that during the Skilling era, the company's hangars and planes became a high-altitude playground for the company's Big Shots.

Car races in Canada, shopping in New York, vacations in Cabo San Lucas (an upscale Mexican resort town on the tip of Baja California), a "business" trip to London—all were taken on Enron jets, at Enron expense by Enron's most senior executives, and not a thought was ever given to how much all of it was really costing.

"The biggest abuser of the planes was Ken Lay and his family," said one longtime Enron pilot, who lost over $2 million in retirement and deferred compensation after the company's bankruptcy. Whether the destination was the Lays' chalet in Aspen or a quick trip to Cabo San Lucas, Ken and Linda Lay always flew in the newest Falcon 900 in the Enron fleet. It didn't matter whether a smaller, cheaper plane was available. Nor did it matter whether the Lays were using the plane for personal use. Aviation department officials understood that a Falcon 900 should be available for the Lays at a moment's notice. Sometimes, the Lays needed two jets: a His and a Hers.

"Several times, Mr. Lay was going to New York, but Mrs. Lay could not leave at the same time. She'd have something to do, so she'd have to leave an hour or two later. So we'd fly him to New York and then follow that plane with another one. Then, the airplanes would have to deadhead [return empty] back to Houston. It was extravagant. It was a waste of money. It'd happen eight or more times a year," says one member of the aviation team. "Here it was Mrs. Lay. We always had to make something available for her. We had to do everything possible to accommodate her."

Making the plane available wasn't enough. There were also snacks. Linda Lay had Ken on a very specific diet. That meant the pilots always had to make sure that the planes were stocked with specific types of low-fat cheese imported, of course from France. In addition, the plane had to be stocked with skim milk and chicken salad for the exclusive use of the Enron chairman. Linda Lay demanded tuna salad.

The Lay family was constantly finding new and inventive ways of using the planes as their personal pickup truck. When Robin Lay moved to France, Ken and Linda wanted to go visit. And since there seemed to be plenty of room in the Falcon 900, they decided to take Robin's bed with them. "We were supposed to take a king-size bed, but we couldn't get the box spring through the door. I said, 'Unless you want me to cut it in half, it's not going.' So we left it in the hangar. We ended up taking the mattress and the headboard and the side rails," said one pilot who made the trip. A few months later, when Robin moved back to the United States, the Enron planes were used to carry her furniture, including the bed, back to Houston. According to Enron's proxies, the Lays' use of company planes grew steadily between 1998 and 2000. In 2000 alone, Ken Lay's personal plane use was estimated at $334,179.

However, what Lay's plane use actually cost Enron was far higher than that modest amount. The $334,000 figure is what Enron reported to the Internal Revenue Service as a perquisite provided to Lay. And Lay was required to pay the income tax only on that amount. The total cost of the plane use was absorbed by Enron, and that cost was likely several multiples of the $334,000 figure. Here's why: If Ken and Linda Lay used the Falcon 900 to fly from Houston to London for personal use, Enron's aviation department used IRS mileage guidelines, called the standard industry fare level, to calculate the taxable value of the trip.[2] Thus, even though the Lays' trip, one-way, cost Enron about $52,000 (London is about ten hours from Houston), the IRS required Lay to pay taxes only on about $5,800—the federally approved value of the perquisite Lay was receiving.

Ken Lay is likely in the highest tax bracket, which means when all is said and done, the real cost to Ken and Linda Lay for a quick hop to London to see the hottest show in the West End was a tax bill that was higher by about $2,320. No wonder they never flew commercial.

The extravagance wasn't limited to the Lays. Whenever Enron had a board meeting, the company always dispatched a company jet to pick up the board members, no matter where they were. That usually meant Enron's jets would fly empty for several thousand miles to make life easier for board members who were already being paid an average of $86,829 per year for the grueling work of sitting on Enron's board. Although flying an airplane like a Falcon 900 with no passengers on board is incredibly expensive, "nobody cared if we had to deadhead an airplane," said one aviation department employee. "Wherever the board members were, we'd deadhead to that city and pick them up and bring them to Houston. They didn't want to fly commercial, even though it would have been a whole lot cheaper."

On many occasions, Enron ran into emergency situations where it didn't have enough jets, so it chartered extra planes. There was certainly an emergency in 1999, when company executives—golfing fans—decided that they had to attend The Masters in Augusta, Georgia. "We had three or four chartered jets, plus three or four company jets doing constant shuttles back and forth," recalled one retired aviation employee. "We were doing as many as four round trips per day. One jet would go to Augusta and another would come back. We had four planes going back and forth for that whole week." The employee said that numerous Enron executives went on that junket, including Chief Financial Officer Andy Fastow, Chief Accounting Officer Rick Causey, Chief Risk Officer Rick Buy, and Enron Broadband Services' CEO, Ken Rice.

On another occasion, Kevin Hannon, the president of Enron Broadband Services, used an Enron jet to take his wife on a shopping trip to New York. Before he left, he asked his secretary to call the aviation department to find out how long it would take to get from the airport in Teterboro, New Jersey, to their shopping destination. The aviation department then called the limousine service in New York, which provided the travel time: thirty minutes. However, that's not what Hannon was told when he finally got into the limo at Teterboro. The driver, according to two sources within Enron's aviation department, told Hannon the drive to the shopping mall would be about seventy-five minutes, not thirty minutes. So Hannon immediately grabbed the cell phone that was in the back of the limousine, called his secretary in Houston, and had her call the Enron aviation department to find out—and he wanted the exact name of the person—who at the limo company had given the wrong drive-time information. "He was ready to hang somebody," said one source in Enron's aviation department. "He was very, very demanding. He wanted to know who made the mistake. He was very arrogant, very hard to deal with."

Mary Wyatt, the former vice president of administration at Enron, recalled that some executives viewed having a private jet available for them almost as a birthright. Wyatt, who worked at Enron from 1984 to late 1998 and was in charge of managing the aviation department, said, "One year, Rebecca Mark [at that time an Enron International] came in with a $6-million airplane budget. Another time, they were working on a deal in South America and Rebecca Mark called and wanted a plane to take her somewhere, I don't remember where, down there. We didn't have a plane available. So she went ahead and chartered a jet. Here I was, faced with laying off people who were making $30,000 per year, and she charters a plane to go somewhere and it cost $100,000 for that one trip. It made me so mad I could just spit."

Several people in the aviation department have similar recollections of Mark, who often used Enron's jets to fly her to her *très chic* vacation home in Taos. One pilot insisted that Mark, not Ken Lay, was the worst frequent flyer. Mark was "the biggest abuser of corporate planes at Enron," according to this longtime pilot. "We would fly her to India, just her, one person. We'd fly her to Malaysia. One person. We'd fly her to Indonesia. She was always chasing a pipe dream. My guess is that two-thirds of her trips weren't worth going on. She just liked flying around the world. She was impressed with Rebecca. That's the bottom line."

The travel costs associated with the aviation department weren't limited to airplanes. Nearly every executive who flew on the planes expected to be picked up by a limousine at the airport. That limo would then be on standby during the executive's visit to that city.

A few—very few—Enron employees worried about costs when it came to using the airplanes, sources within Enron's aviation department said. The thrifty ones were the old-school people from Enron Oil and Gas (the profitable exploration and production outfit that Enron sold in 1999) and the pipeline folks. The oil and gas people seldom used the corporate fleet because they felt it was too expensive. Instead, they flew commercial. When pipeline people used the company jets, they seldom used limousines. "The one who was conservative in that area was [pipeline executive] Stan Horton," said the source. "He'd take a cab. Or he might have a limo pick him up, but nine out of ten times, he'd take a cab back to the airport. He didn't have a limo driver waiting around for him while he was in his meetings. Instead of a limo, the pipeline guys would take a couple of cabs back to the airport. They were also careful on how much catering was ordered for them. They didn't want to waste anything. The other executives didn't care. They wanted the best of everything."

The comments about the pipeline guys are revealing. Throughout the Skilling era, the pipeline business, while always profitable, was ignored. But pipeline executives are, as a general rule, cheap. They know that the only way to make money on a long-lived asset like a pipeline is to cut costs. Rich Kinder was a pipeline guy. And he didn't like the corporate airplanes. "Every airplane bought during Kinder's era was bought over his objection," said one high-ranking executive who worked closely with Kinder. "But the fleet kept growing and growing. Ken Lay wanted to have the best toys."

During the Kinder era, Enron flew five planes, which included two Cessna Citations. The Citation is a small, but economical, jet. It can carry about six passengers at about 400 miles per hour and is a relative bargain at about $1,500 per flight hour. It's a perfectly functional jet for trips from Houston to either coast or almost any location within the United States. Whenever Kinder flew, he always took the smallest airplane available, which usually meant the Citation. And the Citations were perfect for managing the company's pipelines, which are often located in remote areas that don't have long, well-maintained airstrips, places like West Texas and New Mexico, where Enron had significant businesses. In short, Kinder was cheap, and everyone at Enron appreciated that about him. One source, a female executive who worked at Enron for nearly two decades, said, "The joke within the company was 'When Rich leaves, let's see how many planes Ken buys.'"

It didn't take long. Within a few weeks of Kinder's departure from Enron, the company sold the Citations. In their place, Enron bought two Hawker 800s, at a cost of about $10 million each. The Hawkers are nice airplanes. They are big enough to stand up in. They're equipped with microwave ovens, coffee makers, a toilet, and big comfortable leather chairs. And to be fair, they are faster than the Citations and can seat eight passengers instead of six. They also cost—at $4,200 per hour—nearly three times as much to operate.

With Kinder gone and the lowly Citations tossed overboard, personal plane use by Enron's executives taxied for takeoff. "Kinder was a control person, he kept a lid on everything," said one pilot. "When Skilling took over and the executives found out they could use the planes for personal use, they went nuts." That meant trips to Cabo San Lucas for Skilling and his buddies. It also meant frequent trips to southern Colorado so that Enron executive Lou Pai could visit his gigantic ranch.

Pai was such a Big Shot that he couldn't be expected to drive to the airport. You see, Pai lived in Sugar Land, an upscale suburb located about twenty miles southwest of downtown Houston. Enron's jets were kept in a hangar at Intercontinental Airport, about twenty miles north of downtown. So when Pai wanted to visit his Colorado ranch, he called the Enron aviation department and had one of the Falcon 900s dispatched to pick him up at the Sugar Land airport. The jet would fly the forty miles or so from Intercontinental to Sugar Land, a trip that takes about twenty minutes. "That happened probably ten or twelve times," said a pilot who worked for Enron for twenty-four years and flew Pai on many occasions. "And we'd have to do that on both parts of the round-trip." That means the jet would deadhead for twenty minutes (cost: about $1,700) to Sugar Land, pick up Pai, fly the two hours to the airport at Alamosa, Colorado (cost: about $10,400), drop Pai off, and then deadhead back to Houston (cost: another $10,400). When Pai wanted to return to Houston, the process would be reversed. Thus, each time Pai visited his ranch on the Enron jet, the company would incur costs of about $45,000.

But there was a final bit of aerial nuttiness that occurred in Enron's aviation department. And to fully understand the nuttiness requires a bit of knowledge of the world of superexpensive aircraft. Among the world's ultrarich, owning a big expensive airplane is the closest thing there is to an actual penis-measuring contest. Sure, you can a own mansion or a yacht. But compared to owning and operating a big airplane, houses and boats are relatively cheap. Jets are *maximo macho*. They represent freedom. They are the super-first-class ticket that ferries the extremely well-heeled to their mansions and yachts. And the bigger and more expensive the jet, the bigger—and allegedly, more potent—your manhood.

That means, of course, that dinky little Citations just don't cut it. The Big Rich own Falcon 900s. The Really Big Rich prefer the G-V (pronounced G5). That's short for the Gulfstream V (not to be confused with the earlier model, the Gulfstream IV), one of the newest designs in corporate aircraft. Capable of flying nonstop from New York to Tokyo, a G-V is the ultimate status symbol. Nathan Myhrvold, the whiz kid of Microsoft, owns a G-V. So do New Economy whizzes Larry Ellison of Oracle and Steve Jobs of Apple. If those guys had G-Vs, Ken Lay surely needed one, too.

Sure, the Falcon 900s were nice. But when Lay was flying to Europe, the Falcon had to stop in Gander, Newfoundland, or somewhere else on the East Coast, for refueling before crossing the Atlantic. The G-V didn't. So on March 27, 2001, near the end of a quarter in which Enron's cash flow from operations would be negative to the tune of $464 million, at a time when the company's debt load was soaring and analysts were raising doubts about the company's ability to sustain its phenomenal growth, Enron bought a brand new G-V. And the spiffy new toy—with its list price of $41.6 million—was promptly reserved for Ken and Linda Lay. Sources close to the matter said Linda even picked out the fabric and finishes for the plane's interior.

"Everybody knew that Mr. Lay wanted the G-V. He was the one who took it before the board," said one aviation employee familiar with the issue. "A lot of us felt we didn't need the G-V. So what if you have to stop in Gander?" But Ken Lay believed Newfoundland was for losers. Real men flew nonstop to Europe. And the company's new G-V (serial number 609, now for sale by TAG Aviation)[3] allowed him to really stretch his legs. The new plane seated sixteen passengers, had two toilets, a DVD player, a ten-disc CD player, and three eighteen-inch LCD monitors.

In 2001, Lay justified Enron's fancy fleet by telling a reporter that "all these planes give my CEOs something to aspire to." The G-V was Lay's aspiration, the sleek symbol of his success. With the G-V, the son of a poor Baptist minister was arriving in the highest possible style.

Alas, his ego trips aboard the G-V were few. He took the G-V to Europe fewer than a dozen times, and most of those were pleasure trips, including visits to London, Amsterdam, and Venice. Of course, he took several friends and family members with him when he went on those trips, including former Enron president Mick Seidl and Harry Reasoner, a senior partner at Enron's law firm, Vinson & Elkins. And each time, when Lay and his pals flew back to Houston from their European adventures, they flew nonstop.

36

Skilling Says a Bad Word

APRIL 17, 2001

Enron closing price: $60.00

Fayez Sarofim was the king of Houston's moneymen. He advised more of the city's "high net worth" crowd (it's gauche to call them rich) than just about anybody. A billionaire himself, Sarofim hadn't become Houston's top money manager by embracing fads or the stock market flavor-of-the-week. Instead, he'd always sought—and invested in—companies that he felt comfortable with, companies he could understand. The strategy had served him well. In the previous decade, he'd beaten the annual performance of the S&P 500 eight times. He wanted smart clients, patient clients who understood his approach. And he limited his clientele to a select group. Unless you had $5 million or more to invest, Fayez Sarofim & Co. wasn't for you. And even though Sarofim knew Ken Lay from Houston's social scene and knew the Enron story as well as anyone, he didn't like the company. Sure, his clients had asked him—and the small group of money managers he employed—why they weren't investing in Enron's stock. Surely, with about $40 billion under management, Sarofim could put a bit of his money to work in Enron, a hometown company, right?

The questions got particularly thick when Enron's stock was soaring during the late 1990s and early 2000. But Sarofim and his representatives always had the same answer: "We don't understand how they make money. And we don't buy anything we don't understand."

Ken Lay and Jeff Skilling may have been the princes of Houston's business community, but they hadn't passed Sarofim's smell test. And on April 17, 2001, Sarofim's hunch was proven right.

During a conference call with analysts, Jeff Skilling, who'd been Enron's CEO for just two months, discussed the company's first-quarter results. They appeared impressive. The company's revenues—through the mirage of mark-to-market accounting—had nearly tripled from the same quarter the previous year, escalating to $50.1 billion. Trading volumes of gas, electricity, and other commodities had soared. "First-quarter results were great," Skilling told the analysts. "We are very optimistic about our new businesses and are confident that our record of growth is sustainable for many years to come." Skilling then opened the call to questions and began patiently responding to analysts who consistently congratulated him on the company's latest numbers. Then, Richard Grubman got on the line.

The managing director of a $2.8 billion Boston-based hedge fund called Highfields Capital Management, Grubman wasn't a typical analyst. He didn't preface his questions with any congratulatory lines, he didn't work for an investment bank, and he wasn't buying Skilling's story. Grubman and Highfields were shorting Enron's stock in the belief that it was going to fall in price.

The Highfields–Harvard University connection is worth mentioning here. The Highfields hedge fund was founded in 1999 with $500 million of Harvard's endowment money. By mid-2001, it was managing some $2 billion of Harvard's endowment and was the school's main private-investment fund. Enron board member Herbert Winokur is a member of the Harvard Corporation, the university's seven-member governing body. If Enron's stock price fell as Grubman suspected it would, then Harvard—alma mater to Skilling and Winokur—was going to make a lot of money.[1]

Why, Grubman asked, didn't Enron provide the analysts with more information prior to the conference call? Where, for instance, was the cash flow statement and balance sheet? Skilling responded that Enron had never provided those reports before analyst calls. Grubman wasn't satisfied. "You're the only financial institution that can't produce a balance sheet or a cash flow statement with their earnings" prior to conference calls, he said.

"Well, thank you very much," replied Skilling. "We appreciate that. Asshole."

Skilling's lackeys in the Enron conference room chuckled at their boss's brazenness. The analysts listening to the call were stunned. Corporate bosses never liked difficult questions, and they didn't like analysts who pushed them too hard. But calling an analyst an asshole? That just wasn't done. Call him whatever you want in private. Chew him out when he's in your office. But *on the conference call*? In front of all the analyst's peers?

"It was an indication we should have been paying attention and we should have been pushing hard questions all the way along," said one Houston-based analyst who was on the call. "It was a form of intimidation, and it was Skilling's message to his long-term shareholders that he wasn't going to acknowledge those types of pressures, he was going to keep saying the story was strong and people like that [the short sellers] didn't belong on the call and didn't deserve an answer."

A lot of Houston's old-money crowd, the ones who'd been steered away from Enron by Fayez Sarofim, were shocked when they heard about Skilling's comment. They were also relieved that Sarofim hadn't invested their money in Enron. "It showed that Skilling wasn't ready for prime time," a member of one of Houston's oldest and wealthiest families told me. "That marked the beginning of the end."

It *was* the beginning of the end for Skilling. Although Skilling's obscenity was deleted from the audio replay of the conference call, the damage had been done. Several of the major energy publications ran stories about it. Several members of Enron's Board of Directors were outraged. Some even called for Skilling to resign. They wouldn't have to wait long.

37

George W. to the Rescue, Part 1

MAY 29, 2001

Enron closing price: $53.05

It's a good thing George W. Bush has a laissez-faire approach to business. Otherwise, it might look like he was just trying to help his pals at Enron.

Although the California energy crisis was raging throughout Bush's first few months in the White House in 2001, the president refused—for nearly six months—to consider the possibility that the Golden State's power markets were being manipulated. In some parts of the state, electricity rates had gone from $30 per megawatt hour to an alarming $1,500 per megawatt hour. Rolling blackouts—and threats of blackouts—had the state in a near-constant uproar. One of the state's biggest utilities, Pacific Gas & Electric, went bankrupt, and another, Southern California Edison, almost did. By the time Bush had spent about 180 days in the White House, the state of California had spent nearly $8 billion buying power on the open market just to keep the lights on.

Despite the crisis, Dianne Feinstein, a U.S. senator from California—the largest state in the union—couldn't get an appointment with Bush. Maybe it was because she was a Democrat. Maybe it was because Bush lost California to Al Gore during the election. Whatever the reason, the

White House rejected her request for a meeting and even did her the favor of sending back a form letter that misspelled her name.[1]

The White House had plenty of time for Enron, though. On April 17, 2001, Vice President Cheney had a private meeting with Enron chairman Ken Lay. During the meeting, Lay offered suggestions for Cheney's energy task force and lobbied Cheney against price caps in California. Lay even handed Cheney a memo that said, "The administration should reject any attempt to re-regulate wholesale power markets by adopting price caps." Even temporary price restrictions, the Lay memo said, "will be detrimental to power markets and will discourage private investment."

Cheney quickly adopted Lay's argument. The day after his meeting with Lay, Cheney mocked the idea of price caps. He told the *Los Angeles Times* that caps would only provide "short-term political relief for the politicians." He also said price restrictions would discourage investment, a matter Cheney called "the basic fundamental problem."[2]

In late May, Bush visited California and, like Cheney, attacked the idea that price caps—something California governor Gray Davis and Feinstein had been begging for—might help the state restore order to its electricity system. "Price caps do nothing to reduce demand, and they do nothing to increase supply," Bush said flatly.

Bush and Cheney were wrong. Enron and several other power companies had been manipulating the California energy market for months and collecting huge revenues for their efforts. Using strategies with colorful names like Death Star, Get Shorty, Fat Boy, and Ricochet, Enron had apparently figured out ways to play the state's power system and drive up prices. Finally, on June 18, 2001, after weeks of rising intrigue, the Federal Energy Regulatory Commission approved limited price caps for California. The move quickly settled the state's power markets.

Of course, Bush didn't just help Enron in California. Bush and Cheney allowed Enron to write part of the administration's energy task force plan for America's national energy policy.

Ken Lay had helped George W. Bush every step of the way during his journey to the White House. Lay had been one of Bush's first "Pioneers," each of whom pledged to raise $100,000 for Bush. Lay had made Enron's fleet of airplanes available to the Bush campaign. The Bush campaign used Enron's jets to fly to different events on eight different occasions—that's more than any other corporation. During the 2000 election cycle, Lay contributed more than $275,000 to the Republican National Committee. Enron's total donations to the party exceeded $1.1 million. Enron gave $250,000 to help fund the Republican Party National Convention in Philadelphia. When the outcome of the election was in doubt after the polls closed in November 2000, Lay and his wife, Linda, gave $10,000 to help finance the Bush campaign's Florida operation during the recount after the election.

After Bush prevailed in the election (thanks to an assist by the U.S. Supreme Court), Ken and Linda Lay gave another $100,000 to help finance Bush's inaugural gala. In all, Enron and its top execs kicked in $300,000 for the inauguration festivities. Naturally enough, the day after the inauguration, Lay went to a private lunch party at the White House, where he got to schmooze with the new president one-on-one. A few weeks later, Lay had dinner with the president. Beyond all that, Enron's connections in the White House went much further than George W. Bush. The new president's chief economic adviser, Larry Lindsey, was on Enron's payroll before going to the White House, earning $100,000 in consulting fees from the Houston company. Marc Racicot, the former governor of Montana, lobbied for Enron before Bush named him to lead the Republican National Committee. Robert Zoellick, Bush's choice for U.S. trade representative, served on an Enron advisory council. Thomas White, Bush's secretary of the army, was the vice chairman at Enron Energy Services, a money-losing charade of a company. Nevertheless, when White left Enron, he owned more than $25 million in the company's stock. Bush's chief strategist and political guru, Karl Rove, owned more than $100,000 of Enron stock when Bush took office.

With Bush in office and his pals in the White House, Lay was only too happy to provide them with guidance.

Lay recommended a total of twenty-one people for various federal posts. Three got the spots Lay asked for. But they were critically important jobs to Enron. Lay was particularly interested in the Federal Energy Regulatory Commission, or FERC, because that agency regulates the transmission and sale of natural gas in interstate pipelines and the transmission and wholesaling of electricity on interstate wires—both of which are key parts of Enron's business. Lay recommended that Bush appoint Pat Wood, the chairman of the Texas Public Utility Commission and a strong proponent of deregulation, to the FERC. Bush did. Lay also recommended Nora Brownell for the FERC. In fact, Lay placed a number of phone calls to urge the appointment of Brownell. Again, Bush did as Lay asked. Lay asked Bush to appoint Glenn L. McCullough to the chairmanship of the Tennessee Valley Authority, a powerful agency in the Southeast that operates more than two dozen hydroelectric dams and other power plants that had a terrible relationship with Enron due to a dispute over huge electricity contracts Enron did not want to fulfill. Again, Bush did as Lay requested.

Bush's White House provided Lay and Enron with unprecedented access. In addition to the meeting with Lay, Enron officials met with Cheney's task force (the National Energy Policy Development Group) five times and talked with that task force by phone on at least six other occasions about the measure. Their effort shows.

The National Energy Policy Development Group's final report, "Reliable, Affordable and Environmentally Sound Energy for America's Future," released in mid-May of 2001, contains a number of provisions very favorable to Enron. For instance, the report recommends the creation of a national electricity grid, a move that could allow Enron to trade electric power more readily in all regions of the country. The report says permitting for gas pipelines should be expedited,[3] a factor that would help Enron, already one of the largest pipeline companies in the world, build more capacity more quickly. The report says America needs legislation that would create a market-based program for trading of pollution credits. That would allow electric utilities to create a market in which they could trade the amount of pollutants such as sulfur dioxide, nitrogen oxide, and mercury coming out of their power plants. (Trading of pollution credits is touted as a way for market forces to reduce overall pollution levels emitted by industrial plants and energy facilities.) Surely it's just a coincidence that Enron was one of the biggest traders of pollution credits in America. In early 2001, Enron paid the Environmental Protection Agency more than $21 million for a batch of pollution credits in sulfur dioxide. Enron bought forty-five times more credits than any other company participating in the auction.

The report talks about the California crisis, the need for energy efficiency, increased domestic natural gas production, and, of course, India. Didn't you know that the cost of butane in Bombay is critical to soccer moms in Seattle? Cheney's group recommended that "the President direct the Secretaries of State and Energy to work with India's Ministry of Petroleum and Natural Gas to help India maximize its domestic oil and gas production."

Not only could Lay get Bush's ear on appointments, he could get federal reports to mention countries like India, where Enron, with the Dabhol electricity and liquefied natural gas project (which is also mentioned in Cheney's report), was a major investor.

To be fair, the energy report discusses world energy prices and the growing importance of America's access to energy-rich areas like the Caspian Sea. It also discusses America's growing reliance on energy from Mexico and Canada. But the State Department, which participated in the writing of the energy report, didn't add the India section, the White House did. Personnel in the State Department who worked on the report said the language about India was inserted into the task force's energy plan after it came under the control of the White House in late March 2001.[4]

Ken Lay's money on George W. Bush had been well spent.

38

Broadband Blues

JULY 13, 2001

Enron closing price: $48.78

Paul Racicot shouldn't have been so cocky.

The day before, July 12, 2001, Enron's broadband unit had reported terrible numbers. It lost $102 million on revenues of just $16 million, one-tenth of the sales reported in the year-earlier quarter. Those results followed a first quarter in which the business lost $35 million on revenue of $83 million.

Enron's much-ballyhooed broadband strategy was getting a royal spanking. Even Jeff Skilling had been chastened (a little). "This quarter was the absolute evidence that there is a serious problem in the telecom industry," Skilling said, while discussing the company's second-quarter numbers. "Revenue opportunities just dried up. People are not contracting." Yet despite the numbers and Skilling's microdose of humility, Racicot, a thirty-three-year-old Master of the Universe with a lofty title (vice president of global bandwidth risk management for Enron Broadband Services) sat across from me in his office on the forty-fourth floor of Enron's headquarters—an office that sat just a few feet away from row upon row of desks where bandwidth traders were supposed to be (but weren't) exchanging valuable fiber optic capacity—and boldly proclaimed that Enron was still going to rule the world of broadband.

Enron's business, he said, was "growing faster than we expected it to grow." And then, parroting Skilling's line, Racicot said, "Anything we want to intermediate, we can."

Racicot was offering the company line, just as Skilling and his cronies had done repeatedly in the previous year. Enron was going to kill all those old, slow, good-for-nothing telephone companies. It was smarter, faster, and meaner than everybody else. Eight months earlier, Skilling told a reporter, "People think of telecommunications as being a high-tech business. They use high-tech equipment, but they use archaic business models. The business model is straight out of John D. Rockefeller's Standard Oil Co."

For a few months after the January 20, 2000, meeting, few people bet against Skilling and his crew. In July 2000, Enron announced it was teaming with video rental giant Blockbuster Inc., to sell movies on demand over the Internet. At first glance, the deal looked hot. Enron's chairman, Ken Lay, called it a "killer app for the entertainment industry." Blockbuster boss John Antioco said Enron and his company had created the "ultimate bricks-clicks-and-flicks strategy."

It sounded too good to be true. It was. And by July 13, 2001, it was becoming clear that the Blockbuster deal—along with almost everything else Enron Broadband did—was too good to be true. Enron's broadband play was turning out to be little more than an elaborate pump-and-dump fraud.

The first energy company to plunge into the fiber optic business was the Tulsa-based pipeline and energy giant, Williams Companies. In 1985, Williams recognized the value of its pipeline routes. The company had some old pipelines that no longer carried oil. Why couldn't they carry information instead? So the company began stringing fiber optic cable in some of its old pipelines. The idea was a smash. In 1995, the company sold its WilTel subsidiary, which had an 11,000-mile fiber network, to LDDS WorldCom—now WorldCom—for $2.5 billion in cash. By 1998, Williams, through its new subsidiary, Williams Communication, was at it again, building another fiber network.[1]

Like Williams, Enron got into the fiber optic business almost by accident. When Enron bought Portland General Electric in 1997, a small group of people at the utility were building a fiber optic ring around the city, and they were considering some long-haul fiber projects. Enron executives quickly saw the similarities between telecom and electricity: Both were commodities that couldn't be stored and had to be delivered immediately, and both had historically been controlled by monopolies that were now dealing with a deregulated market. So Enron began investing tens of millions of dollars in its fiber optic network.

But there were loads of obstacles in Enron's way. Chief among them was the surfeit of fiber optic capacity. Companies like Level 3, Extant, Qwest, Broadwing, Global Crossing, and Williams were laying scads of fiber optic cable, too. Between 1996 and the end of 2000, the amount of installed fiber cable in the United States more than quadrupled, increasing from 4 million to about 18 million miles. And each of those companies was eager to carry the same traffic that Enron was targeting. They, like Enron, believed the Internet revolution would quickly spawn new demand for high-speed communications. Video-on-demand, Napster, and video conferencing would fill the new glass pipes as soon as they were installed.

At the same time, as miles and miles of new fiber were being laid in sewers and along railroads and highways, new technology was allowing each fiber to carry ever-increasing amounts of information. The process, known as dense wave division multiplexing, uses tunable lasers that split light into multiple colors, each of which is capable of carrying an individual signal. Thus, a fiber that was previously capable of carrying eight high-capacity signals could, with a set of new lasers, be expanded to carry sixteen—or more—signals and do it at relatively low cost.

In their hubris, Lay, Skilling, and other executives at Enron's broadband unit believed they didn't need to know how the telecom industry really worked. "Everybody in electricity said it wouldn't work, that we couldn't do in electricity what we did in [natural] gas," Lay told *Fortune* in early 2000. "But it took four years for us to become the largest supplier of electricity in the U.S. They were wrong."[2]

Had Lay and Skilling taken the time to understand the differences between the natural gas business and the telecom business, they might have saved Enron billions.

Lay, Skilling, and their cronies thought that selling a bit in a fiber optic cable was going to be just like sending a BTU of gas through a pipeline. And there are some similar characteristics: Both pipelines and fiber networks stretch over thousands of miles and require complicated switching systems, highly trained personnel, and marketing people with strong ties in the industry who can sell capacity on the network to various customers. But sending a few dollars' worth of gas through a fat steel pipe is far different from shooting photons through hair-thin glass pipe. In a gas pipeline, the value of the commodity is just the price of the natural gas, and that value is posted on numerous exchanges throughout the country. Furthermore, natural gas is a fungible commodity that can be replaced by any other natural gas from any other company. When it comes to gas, a BTU is a BTU.

With photons traveling through glass pipes, the value of each photon is highly variable and may be far more valuable than the cost of the pipe itself. For instance, a light beam carrying the TV telecast of the Super Bowl or the World Cup championship to billions of people is far more valuable than a parallel light beam carrying *Debbie Does Dallas* to Room 207 of a Motel 6 in Las Vegas.

Simply put, when it comes to fiber optics, a bit is not a bit.

Companies that use fiber optic capacity on transcontinental glass cables (pipelines) aren't buying a commodity, like natural gas, they are buying a service. And because those glass circuits are hauling highly valuable information, like the Super Bowl telecast, they are willing to pay a premium price for security and reliability. But Enron didn't own the fiber curb-to-curb, and that meant it could not provide all the security and reliability that buyers required. Why? Enron Broadband Services didn't have access to all of the existing fiber networks. Which leads to the next flaw in Enron's hype machine.

America's natural gas pipelines are interconnected in several locations around the country. So when companies trade gas, they specify price based on specific delivery points like the Henry Hub on a certain date. Everyone in the business accepts those places and several others as standard delivery points. The telecom business has a bare handful of accepted hubs. Fiber optic networks are idiosyncratic. Each cable of fiber might have 120 strands of glass in it, each one of which may be carrying multiple signals of varying capacity. Also, the different fiber networks don't have common termination points. For instance, in New York City, the biggest telecom interconnection hub is located at 60 Hudson Street. But there are half a dozen other data centers in the New York region that are also used by the phone and fiber companies to terminate their networks. In addition, the telecom industry is still grappling with the problem of who will own and operate the switches and other electronics at the hubs where the carriers' fiber actually intersects.

That lack of easy interconnection means that provisioning a new circuit between two fiber networks can take weeks, or even months. Enron tried to surmount this problem by creating "pooling points" that would act as a Henry Hub in each of two dozen major cities. But the phone companies like AT&T, Sprint, and WorldCom had little incentive to spend the money required to string fiber cable to those pooling points for the sole purpose of interconnecting with Enron. Nor could Enron—which was already spending hundreds of millions of dollars to lay fiber across the continent—afford to build interconnections with every major fiber carrier.

Furthermore, the phone companies—those backward followers of John D. Rockefeller—didn't see any prospective gain in doing business with Enron or in allowing Enron to trade their fiber capacity. Doing business with Enron would let Enron, and everyone else, know how they were pricing their fiber optic capacity. A transparent pricing market would further erode their already shrinking profit margins.

So what did all of those factors mean for Enron Broadband Services? In short, Lay, Skilling, and their cronies were hyping their ability to trade fiber capacity service that was:

- enormously overabundant,
- falling in price by 50 percent or more every twelve months,
- largely controlled by incumbent phone companies that had no desire to trade with Enron,
- nearly impossible to trade because of security concerns,
- not an essential commodity like electricity and gas.

Other than that, Enron's business model was perfect.

Despite the flaws in their business plan, the executives at Enron Broadband Services could rely on a tool the other telecom companies didn't have: financial tricks. By spring 2000, the fledgling company was under great pressure to show revenue growth—and fast. So it turned to an entity owned by Enron's financial-magician-in-residence, Andy Fastow.

In June 2000, Enron sold some of its unused in-the-ground fiber optic cable (called "dark fiber" because it hasn't been connected to lasers and switching equipment) to LJM2, the partnership run by Andy Fastow, Enron's chief financial officer. The deal meant $100 million in revenue to the telecom unit, $30 million in cash, and a $70 million promissory note from LJM2. Enron's profit on the deal was $67 million, even though prices for dark fiber—as well as lit fiber—were plunging at the time LJM2 did the deal. In June 2000, for an investment of $100 million, an adventurous telecom investor could have purchased about 33,000 miles of dark fiber, nearly twice the 18,000 miles of fiber that Enron controlled.[3] Enron Broadband and Fastow apparently agreed that LJM2 would pay an inflated price for the company's dark fiber and LJM2 would be made whole later. It appears that's exactly what happened. Fastow's partnership sold part of the dark fiber to an unknown third party for $40 million. In December 2000, LJM2 sold the remaining dark fiber—despite a market in which fiber optic capacity was falling by half or more every six months—to yet another (unnamed) Enron-related partnership for $113 million. The deals allowed LJM2 to make a $2.4 million profit from Enron's fiber.[4] The attitude seemed to be: We don't care how much money Fastow makes as long as Enron Broadband Services can show some revenue.

Although the LJM2 fiber deal was shady, it would pale in comparison to the buzz Enron generated on the Blockbuster transaction. On the surface, the Blockbuster deal certainly looked like it could be big. The twenty-year deal would bring huge amounts of paying data traffic onto Enron's fiber optic network. It would also allow Blockbuster to have a new avenue into American homes that didn't include expensive storefronts and retail personnel. But there were huge logistical and copyright problems with the arrangement, and none of them had been fully considered. First and foremost was Enron's network. Sending movies over a network requires huge amounts of bandwidth. Transmitting one movie to a customer usually requires a copper or glass pipe that can carry at least one megabit of information per second. That's a fairly easy task when the signal is carried via a coaxial cable, like the one used most often by American cable providers.

It's a much harder problem when trying to cram that much information through a pair of tiny copper telephone wires. To supply movies over digital subscriber lines (DSL) over a large area, Enron was going to have to pay for an expensive network of machines all along the information highway. To deliver a single movie from Los Angeles to a home in Salt Lake City, Enron would have to install tens of thousands of dollars' worth of expensive routers, switches, and servers all along the way, including new equipment at the central office closest to the customer's home (a central office is usually the first interconnection point from the customer's home to the telephone or data network). Finally, the system proposed by Enron and Blockbuster was going to require a set-top box to sit atop the customer's TV set.

That much hardware costs a lot of money. So much in fact, that the entire proposition was destined to be a massive money loser.

Shortly after the Blockbuster deal was done, an analyst at Enron Broadband figured that in 2001, Enron would lose $347 million on

$52 million in revenue if it could garner 2 million paying subscribers to the new venture. By 2002, if the firm was able to garner 5 million customers, each of whom was renting three movies a week, losses would rise to $476 million. Even under the absolute best projections, extending out to 2005, if Enron could gain 50 million subscribers (that would mean the company would have to have about *one-half* of all the households in America as subscribers), each of whom was renting six movies per week, the Blockbuster-Enron outfit would still be losing a whopping $3.38 billion per year. The analyst found that *one-fourth* of all of the Blockbuster-Enron subscribers would have to rent ten to fourteen movies per week just for the deal to break even!

Nevertheless, Enron continued hyping the deal all through 2000 and early 2001. By March 2001, at its absolute peak of service, Enron was beaming Blockbuster-supplied movies to only about 1,000 test customers in four cities (selected for their ease of installation), and many of those customers didn't even pay. The analyst who'd done the economic projections on the Blockbuster deal said he showed his models to Enron Broadband president Kevin Hannon and other top-level officials in the company. "I was told, basically, we have no intention of developing and delivering this service. We just want to prove the concept. We'll sell the contract to someone else and then book the revenue."

That's exactly what Enron did. In the fourth quarter of 2000 and first quarter of 2001, Enron Broadband, using the wonders of mark-to-market accounting, claimed $110.9 million in profits from the deal, even though the company had never collected a dime in real cash. The company did it by creating a partnership called Braveheart (apparently a reference to Mel Gibson's 1995 movie). Then, Enron's negotiators somehow snookered the smart investment bankers at CIBC World Markets, an arm of Canadian Imperial Bank of Commerce in Toronto, to pump $115.2 million into the partnership. In return, CIBC got a promise from Enron that it would get nearly all of Enron's profits for the first ten years of the movie-delivery project.[5]

Despite the hype, within eight months of its launch, the "ultimate bricks-clicks-and-flicks strategy" was on the fritz. Enron pointed the finger at Blockbuster, which was pointing right back at Enron.

Racicot told me the reason the deal failed was because Blockbuster "couldn't deliver the movies." That may be the case. The movie studios certainly had no reason to do licensing deals on their hottest movies. Their distribution channels were just fine, thank you very much. For its part, Blockbuster expected the deal would last twenty years and that the business would be built up slowly, over time. And even though the Blockbuster deal fell apart, the deal was still a success for several Enron Broadband salesmen, who got huge bonuses for doing the deal. According to one internal auditor, several of them even went on a weekend ski trip to Colorado—at Enron's expense, of course—to celebrate their big deal.

Despite the downturn in telecom and the loss of the Blockbuster transaction, July 13, 2001 was still a good day for Ken Rice, the good-for-nothing CEO of Enron Broadband. He sold nearly 772,000 shares of Enron stock that day and pocketed more than $28 million in proceeds.

It isn't clear exactly how much stock Kevin Hannon sold. Several Enron insiders speculated that Hannon refused to be named an officer of Enron Corp. so that he wouldn't have to report his stock sales. And as Enron began to slide toward bankruptcy, speculation about Hannon's stock sales was a common topic of discussion among Enron employees. In June 2002, Enron filed a document in bankruptcy court that showed Hannon sold stock in 2001 valued at $5.5 million.[6]

Rice wasn't the only one bailing out. That same day, Jeff Skilling went to visit Ken Lay.

39

Sleepless in Houston: Cash Flow Problems, Part 3

JULY 13, 2001
Enron closing price: $48.78

Ken Lay's trip to India had been nearly useless. He'd spent three days meeting with Indian officials and hadn't made any progress. The Indians had stopped paying Enron for the electricity from Dabhol months earlier. Enron, faced with mounting losses, had been forced to shut the plant down. Despite Lay's best efforts, the Indians insisted throughout the negotiations that Enron's price on the Dabhol power project was simply too high and that the government could not afford the power from the plant. Despite the bad negotiations, he and Jeff Skilling were making happy noises to the press about the state of the Dabhol project. Skilling said Enron's contracts on the mega-power plant "are very clear. They have very strong provisions, so they will be enforced." Enron has "zero intention of taking any economic loss on the project. Zero."

The Indians, however, were resolute. After meeting with Lay, Vilasrao Deshmukh, chief minister of the Indian state of Maharashtra, told reporters that India "cannot afford the cost of Phase Two power and we do not need all the power from Phase One.... We have asked Enron to slash their tariff." The Indians' refusal to honor the contract was costing Enron dearly. The last payment the company got for the electricity generated by the plant was in December 2000. The plant hadn't generated any electricity since May 29, when the company decided to shut it down rather than generate more power at a loss.

Of course, just because Dabhol was failing didn't mean that Enron officials couldn't make piles of money from the deal. In 2001, Sanjay Bhatnagar, the CEO of Enron India—and a Harvard MBA who served as Enron's ramrod on the Dabhol project in India—exercised stock options worth $15.4 million.[1]

As Lay and Skilling sat in Lay's fiftieth-floor office on Friday, July 13, they discussed Dabhol and a long list of other things. As the last issue wrapped up, Lay assumed they were finished. But Skilling had one more thing: He was going to resign as CEO.[2]

Lay was shocked. He thought that Skilling was doing fine. He'd screwed up badly with the asshole comment in April, but most other things had gone fairly well. Why quit now? he asked. It was about his children, Skilling explained. He'd been away a lot and hadn't spent enough time with them. Pretty soon the teenagers were going to be going to college and Skilling would have missed his chance. Lay agreed that family time was important, but that wasn't the only reason, was it? Skilling hemmed and hawed for a while, then admitted that he wasn't sleeping. He was worried about Enron's stock price.

The significance of the falling stock price was apparently lost on the imperial chairman of Enron. But Skilling surely understood it. It had fallen below $48 in mid-June before staging a small rally. But it was once again flirting with the $48 level, and Skilling knew that spelled disaster. Given the fragile nature of the financing behind Andy Fastow's special-purpose entities, Skilling had good reason to worry about Enron's sagging stock price. And there were plenty of other reasons for Skilling's desire to jump ship. First and foremost was the worst cash crisis Enron had ever seen.

By the end of June, the company's cash flow from operations was a negative $1.3 billion, and the company had been forced to borrow $1.97 billion just to keep the doors open. Interest costs were soaring, largely, it appears, due to the cash Enron needed to keep EnronOnline in business. In the first six months of the year, the company paid $426 million in interest, or more than $2.3 million per day. Short-term and long-term debt were soaring, too. Between the last day of 2000 and the end of June 2001, Enron's short-term debt load more than doubled, rising from $1.67 billion to over $3.45 billion. Long-term debt went from $8.55 billion to $9.35 billion.

Cash was flying out the door in unprecedented quantities. In the previous few months, the company had spent $325.9 million to buy back the shares of its failed water company, Azurix. It had spent hundreds of millions more buying paper mills that were turning out to be almost useless in Enron's trading business. The metals business was killing the company. In mid-2000, Enron paid $446 million for MG, the huge metals trader. But Enron's losses in the metals business had already reportedly exceeded $500 million, and the news just kept getting worse. The London Metal Exchange was concluding a long investigation into Enron's trading activities, and it wasn't pleased. About the same time Skilling and Lay met, the exchange hit Enron with the second-largest fine ever levied against a company for what it called "seriously inadequate" compliance with its trading rules. The exchange's $264,000 fine against Enron was second only to the multimillion-dollar penalty levied against a group of banks in the wake of the Sumitomo Corporation copper trading scandal, in which a rogue trader lost some $2.6 billion for the Japanese firm. In Enron's case, the exchange said the company's shoddy work "jeopardized confidence" in the exchange's delivery mechanism.

The $264,000 fine wasn't a lot of money in Enron's world. But it was indicative of a bigger problem: Enron's core businesses were in deep trouble. Aside from the pipelines, which, of course, always made money, danger signs were everywhere.

Enron Broadband Services, the company that just seven months earlier Skilling said was worth $36 billion, was stinking it up. The day before, during a conference call with analysts, Skilling told them, "It's like someone turned off the light switch" in the telecom sector. Enron had no choice but to cut spending in broadband and hope for better

Enron by the Numbers

All figures are from Enron Corp. SEC filings (All figures are in $ millions)

	2000	1999	1998	1997
Revenues	$100,789	$40,112	$31,260	$20,273
Net Cash from Operating Activities	$4,779	$1,228	$1,640	$501
Net Income as Originally Reported	$979	$893	$703	$105
Net Income Restated 11/08/01	$847	$643	$590	$9
Long-Term Debt	$8,550	$7,151	$7,357	$6,254
Employees (per *Fortune* magazine)	20,600	17,900	17,800	15,555
Rank on *Fortune* 500	7	18	27	57

*From 1997 to Feb. 2001, J. Skilling was Pres. and COO of Enron**

	1996	1995	1994	1993	1992	1991	1990
Revenues	$13,289	$9,189	$8,984	$7,986	$6,415	$5,698	$5,336
Net Cash from Operating Activities	$1,040	$(15)	$460	$468	$330	$814	$1,081
Net Income as Originally Reported	$584	$520	$438	$333	$306	$232	$202
Net Income Restated 11/08/01	N/A	N/A	N/A	N/A	N/A	N/A	N/A
Long-Term Debt	$3,300	$3,000	$2,805	$2,600	$2,458	$3,108	$2,982
Employees (per *Fortune* magazine)	7,456	6,692	6,955	7,100	7,776	7,731	6,962
Rank on *Fortune* 500	94	141	129 svc 500				

From 1990 to 1996, Rich Kinder was Pres. and COO of Enron

	3q 2001	2q 2001	1q 2001
Revenues	$138,718	$100,189	$50,129
Net Cash from Operating Activities	$(753)	$(1,337)	$(464)
Net Income as originally reported	$(644)	$404	$425
Net Income Restated 11/08/01	$(635)	$409	$442
Long-Term Debt	$6,544**	$9,355	$9,763

*From January 10, 1997 to January 1, 2001 Skilling was Pres. and COO of Enron. He's CEO from February 1, 2001 to August 14, 2001.

**Although Enron's long-term debt in the third quarter of 2001 declined, the company's short-term debt soared. At the end of 2000, Enron's short-term debt was $1.6 billion. By November of 2001, it was $6.4 billion.

days. The metals trading business wasn't working. Enron was still saddled with the remnants of Azurix, including the British utility, Wessex Water. Another one of Rebecca Mark's stellar achievements, the international power business, was in similarly poor condition. Enron had invested about $900 million in Dabhol, and its return was a big fat zero. And Lay didn't have a clue about how to deal with the Indians. Despite her faults, Mark had developed personal relationships with the key players in India. She might have been able to make some headway on the impasse just as she had after the project was scrapped by the Indian government in 1996. Or maybe Joe Sutton could have made a difference. The former army man had worked side by side with Mark in India and knew everyone, too. But Mark and Sutton were gone. After repeated clashes with Skilling, they'd cashed out tens of millions of dollars in stock options and hit the door.

Cash was getting harder to come by. Skilling had already sold everything that wasn't nailed down. In 1999, after months of tense negotiations, Skilling agreed to sell Enron's 53-percent ownership stake in its exploration and production subsidiary, Enron Oil and Gas. And though that deal gave Skilling about $600 million in cash to play with, it also stripped Enron of one of its best-run and most reliable businesses. By getting rid of Enron Oil and Gas, Skilling and Lay had also lost one of Enron's most experienced and professional executives, Forrest Hoglund.

Skilling had done all he could by using overseas subsidiaries and tax tricks. When Skilling took over from Kinder, Enron had just a handful of subsidiaries, the list of which covered about ten typed pages. By the end of 2000, Enron had hundreds of subsidiary companies in countries all over the world. And the list of subsidiaries—many of them in tax havens like the Cayman Islands—now stretched for fifty-five typed pages. Skilling had also done plenty of aggressive tax work. In 2000 alone, some $296 million—about 30 percent—of Enron's profits reportedly came from aggressive use of tax reduction strategies.[3] But it was likely becoming clear to Skilling that his bag of subsidiary and tax tricks was nearly empty.

The international business was a mess. The company owned between $7 billion and $9 billion worth of overseas assets. A few of them were profitable. But most weren't producing enough revenue to cover the amount of money Enron had invested in them. Skilling and Lay had hoped that Project Summer, the summer of 2000 initiative to sell all of the company's best international assets, would bail them out and give them a big dose of cash. Sutton, the leader of Project Summer, had packaged about $7 billion worth of assets, including Dabhol, and had tried to sell them to a group led by the president of the United Arab Emirates, Sheik Zayed bin Sultan al-Nahayan. The sheik and other investors in Europe and the Middle East were going to buy almost everything Enron owned overseas, including projects in Turkey, Japan, Brazil, Argentina, Qatar, and the Caribbean. But the sheik was having health problems and the supercomplicated deal fell apart. Sutton left Enron on November 1, right after the deal collapsed.

Enron was also running out of ability to manufacture cash from deals known internally as "prepaids." The prepaids were a complicated way of hiding debt. Enron would sell long-term commodity contracts it had signed with its customers to investment banks, that, in turn, would immediately give Enron cash for the contracts. In one deal, made on December 28, 2000, Enron sold a contract to a Channel Islands–based entity called Mahonia that was actually owned by J.P. Morgan Chase & Co. Enron's contract with its customer called on Enron to deliver natural gas worth $394 million to the customer from 2001 to 2005.[4] Mahonia agreed to buy the contract from Enron for $330 million, a discount of about 7 percent. Enron then agreed to buy gas from another J.P. Morgan entity, called Stoneville Aegean, for the full value of the contract—$394 million.[5] Enron agreed to pay for the Stoneville gas in monthly installments.

Although the Mahonia deal sounds complex, its purpose was simple: It allowed Enron to raise cash without adding debt to its balance sheet. The accounting rules allowed the company to disguise what was really a loan—Mahonia's cash advance to Enron for the value of the contract, which Enron then repaid in monthly installments—as a sale.

And Enron got another valuable accounting benefit: It was able to count the cash it got from Mahonia as cash flow from operations.

Enron had been doing prepaid deals with various banks since the mid-1990s. But these deals became bigger and far more frequent under Skilling. By doing them, Enron was trading a reliable future revenue stream for cash that could be used to fund the company's immediate needs. They were, said one finance expert at Enron, "the financial equivalent of crack cocaine. If you want to destroy incentives to generate cash, this is what you do. It was like a credit card."

By the time of Skilling's meeting with Lay, Enron was addicted to the crack cocaine of prepaids. In 2001, the company raised about $5 billion in cash from prepaid deals with banks that included J.P. Morgan, Citigroup, and others. Enron was slowly being suffocated under the weight of its multibillion-dollar addiction. And the pushers on Wall Street were expecting Enron to pay its debts. The prepaids were only delaying the inevitable.

Skilling undoubtedly knew every detail of the company's finances. And though the prepaids were worrisome, Enron's falling stock price was the biggest problem. The Raptors that Fastow had created were all either insolvent or nearly so. Enron had been able to prop them up temporarily, but it was becoming clear that Enron was going to have to write off the Raptors. And the write-off would be huge, hundreds of millions of dollars.

Skilling almost surely knew about the problems with two other off-the-balance-sheet entities, Whitewing and Osprey. Whitewing had borrowed billions from investors in the United States and overseas in order to buy a variety of Enron's international assets. In return for loaning the money to Whitewing, the investors got interest-bearing promissory notes from Osprey, a trust controlled by Whitewing, that were to be paid back in 2003. But Enron was on the hook if the assets Whitewing bought from Enron fell in value. And by July 2001, that was clearly the case. Furthermore, the investors were assured that if Enron's shares fell below $48.55, Enron would distribute extra Enron stock to Whitewing's investors in order to cover any losses. In addition, the deal with the Osprey notes required Enron to issue more stock if Enron's stock fell below $47. (Enron's make-whole obligations in the Whitewing and Osprey deals are actually derivatives, similiar to the total return swaps that Enron employed with the Raptors.)

If Enron had to issue stock to prop up the two entities, the additional stock would dilute the holdings of Enron's existing stockholders, and that would lead to further decreases in the stock price. Wall Street's love affair with Enron would evaporate. Analysts would downgrade the stock, and the price would fall further. The downgrades and selling would feed on each other, meaning Enron's stock would get hammered. All of the stock options that Skilling had awarded to hundreds of Enron employees—the options he'd used to attract them and buy their loyalty—were going to be worthless.

The financial house of cards that Skilling and Fastow had built in order to hide debt and pump up Enron's profits was starting to crumble, and Skilling could see it. He wanted out before the shit hit the fan.

In addition to the financial problems, Skilling knew that many of his buddies were either getting ready to leave or had already left Enron. He almost certainly knew that his pal Ken Rice was getting ready to leave Enron Broadband. Rice's heavy stock sales were a clear indicator he wasn't going to stay. Lou Pai, Skilling's trading genius since his earliest days at Enron, had already left the company. In fact, Pai's stock sales had been so heavy prior to his departure—on May 18, 2001, he sold 300,000 shares in one day—that both Lay and Skilling had asked him to be more moderate. Pai had refused, of course, and ended up selling $270.2 million in stock before leaving.

Cliff Baxter, another Skilling crony, was gone, too. And like Pai, he left with his pockets stuffed full of cash. Baxter, who served a brief stint as Enron's vice chairman, sold $34.7 million in stock before leaving Enron.

Although Skilling's resignation wouldn't be made official until August 14, it appeared Lay was already hedging his bets, too. Lay had been selling his Enron stock on a regular basis throughout 2001. In the two weeks prior to his meeting with Skilling, Lay sold 31,500 shares of

Enron stock. On July 13, he sold another 3,500 shares of Enron stock and pocketed $104,750 for his trouble. Lay continued selling 3,500 shares a day for the next few days. On July 20, he sold a total of 78,500 shares for a one-day gain of over $2.1 million.

Like Ken Rice and Jeff Skilling, Ken Lay was also bailing out. And even though he'd never heard of a woman named Sherron Watkins, she was about to become a major player in his life.

40

Sherron Watkins Saves Her Own Ass

AUGUST 15, 2001

Enron closing price: $40.25

It didn't make any sense at all. Jeff Skilling, after just six months as CEO of Enron, had quit, saying he wanted to spend more time with his family.

"I am resigning for personal reasons. I want to thank Ken Lay for his understanding of this purely personal decision, and I want to thank the board and all of my colleagues at Enron," Skilling said in a press release.

There were problems with Skilling's story. To begin with, Skilling was never considered much of a family man. He was divorced. He and his ex-wife had three children. Skilling loved his kids, but few saw him as a fanatical family man. Second, by quitting, Skilling had left lots of money on the table. In 2000, Skilling's pay package had totaled some $10.1 million, more than double the amount he'd been paid in 1999. By leaving early, he was forgoing millions of dollars—perhaps tens of millions. Finally, it just didn't fit. Skilling had always been in it for the power, for the glory, for the thrill of having people think he was important. And *now*, now that he was finally in charge of the whole enchilada, he was throwing in the towel? No way.

Stock analysts were puzzled. "Investors generally don't like uncertainty, and this has added a level of uncertainty," stock analyst Andre Meade told *Bloomberg*.[1] The surprise announcement punished Enron's stock. When news of Skilling's departure hit the stock market, the company's stock fell by more than 6 percent. Since the time Skilling became CEO in February 2001, Enron's stock had fallen by nearly half.

Rumors were flying. One prominent rumor said Shell Oil had been planning to buy Enron. The two sides had talked for weeks, but Shell was scared off by Enron's impenetrable accounting. The rumors, combined with Skilling's announcement, just added more selling pressure to Enron's stock, which was already being hammered with questions about Dabhol and the company's apparent involvement in price gouging in California's electricity markets.

Sherron Watkins didn't believe any of Skilling's explanations. And she was going to do something about it. An eight-year veteran of Enron, Watkins was typical Enron: smart, aggressive, and not timid about speaking her mind. That characteristic hadn't won her a lot of friends. At the same time, there was no doubting her guts. If she had questions about the weird accounting that she was seeing as a member of Andy Fastow's financial group, she was going to bring them up to whomever she pleased. And Watkins knew the only person who could address her questions was Ken Lay. She also knew that as soon as she spoke out about Enron's accounting mess, she was going to catch hell.

Watkins's boss, Andy Fastow, was going to be livid. Fastow controlled people like Watkins through fear. His volcanic temper and intimidating tactics had allowed him to quell any dissent at Enron. But Watkins was running out of choices. She'd been given the opportunity to peer behind the curtain at Enron's finances, and she didn't like what she saw. The off-the-balance-sheet shenanigans that Fastow had been up to were eventually going to kill Enron if something wasn't done about it. So the day after Skilling quit, Watkins sent Lay an anonymous one-page letter.

In her memo, she told Lay that Skilling might be "resigning for 'personal reasons,' but I think he wasn't having fun, looked down the road and knew this stuff was unfixable and would rather abandon ship now than resign in shame in two years." She also discussed Fastow's most aggressive accounting flimflams, the Raptors. She concluded by saying, "I am incredibly nervous that we will implode in a wave of accounting scandals."

The next day, Watkins went to Cindy Olson, Enron's chief of human resources, and told Olson that she had authored the letter to Lay. Olson advised Watkins to meet with Lay. Watkins agreed. And she set up a meeting with Lay for August 22. Before the meeting, she wrote another memo. This one was longer, 2,370 words. The memo was both prescient and concise, laying out the problems with the off-the-balance-sheet entities and even giving Lay a game plan for dealing with the accounting problems created by Skilling and Fastow.

In her memo, Watkins addressed Fastow's bastard financing head on. "Is there a way our accounting guru's [*sic*] can unwind these deals now?" she wrote. "I have thought and thought about a way to do this, but I keep bumping into one big problem—we booked the Condor and Raptor deals in 1999 and 2000, we enjoyed wonderfully high stock price, many executives sold stock, we then try and reverse or fix the deals in 2001, and it's a bit like robbing the bank in one year and trying to pay it back two years later. Nice try, but investors were hurt, they bought at $70 and $80 a share looking for $120 a share and now they're at $38 or worse. We are under too much scrutiny and there are probably one or two disgruntled 'redeployed' employees who know enough about the 'funny' accounting to get us in trouble."

Watkins's letter to Lay would prove to be a pivotal event in the collapse of Enron. She was exposing Andy Fastow and his partnerships, the ones that were designed to make Fastow rich while hiding Enron's debts and bad deals. And though Watkins deserves kudos for her courage, there is another fact that cannot be denied: In writing the letter, Sherron Watkins had little to lose and much to gain.

Half a dozen former Enron employees tell almost identical stories about Watkins: She was a calculating, vindictive woman who was facing almost certain firing by Fastow, who didn't like her and was likely to fire her at his earliest opportunity.

Watkins had already been fired once by Enron. Her position at

Enron Broadband Services was terminated in spring 2001, apparently because of the company's faltering business prospects. But in June 2001, she was able to get a job inside Fastow's finance group as a "noncommercial" person. Commercial people at Enron were the stars. They developed and wrote deals and made big bonuses. Noncommercial personnel evaluated the deals and did the grunt work. And it was while working in that capacity that Watkins was able to look at Fastow's myriad off-the-balance-sheet deals.

Watkins's family has a long history in Tomball, Texas, a tiny burg about thirty miles northwest of downtown Houston. Descendants of German Lutherans who came to America in the 1830s, her mother's family, the Kleins, held key merchant jobs in the town. Her uncle ran the local supermarket. A cousin ran the funeral home. Her mom was married to the mayor. One of her ancestors had served as the town's mayor during the nineteenth century. Watkins left Tomball to study at the University of Texas, where she earned a master's degree in accounting. She started her career in 1982 at Arthur Andersen as an auditor. She stayed with the firm for eight years before joining New York–based MG Trade Finance, the trading arm of German giant Metallgesellschaft, which was once Germany's fourteenth-largest company.

Watkins's experiences at that company undoubtedly prodded her to speak up at Enron. When she joined MG in 1990 to help manage the company's trading business, Metallgesellschaft was slowly becoming more aggressive in the commodities futures business. MG began specializing in derivatives and was signing long-term contracts with energy distribution and marketing companies to supply them with gasoline and other refined oil products. The company was selling fixed-price contracts on future deliveries of fuel. Those contracts appealed to MG's customers who were concerned about sudden increases in oil prices. But the company's strategy was blown apart in late 1993, when world oil prices plummeted, leaving it with enormous losses in energy derivatives. The losses were so big, Metallgesellschaft had to be rescued by a consortium of German banks.

One of Watkins's peers at Metallgesellschaft, Jeff McMahon, had also worked with her at Andersen. In 1993, McMahon, who was one of MG's internal auditors, warned his superiors that poor internal controls could cause problems for the company. McMahon's warnings went unheeded. Like Watkins, McMahon left MG after it fell apart and went to work at Enron. And the two became good friends.

At Enron, Watkins worked on some of the original off-the-balance-sheet partnerships, including the Joint Energy Development Investment Limited Partnership, or JEDI. She then went to work in Enron's international business for several years before landing at Enron Broadband Services in early 2000.

It was at the broadband division where Watkins made a number of enemies. One former coworker in that enterprise called Watkins a "conniving, manipulative self-promoter to a dangerous extreme. She was poison in the well. She brought down people and deals to try to make herself look the hero," said the source. Several others from the same unit question why, given Watkins's knowledge of all the fraud and mismanagement at Enron Broadband Services, she didn't mention any of those things in her letters to Lay.

When Watkins's letter was made public, many people at Enron began speculating that her memo was an effort to ally herself closely with Jeff McMahon, who'd spent about two years as Enron's treasurer. Like Watkins, McMahon didn't like Fastow or his off-the-balance-sheet deals. In March 2000, McMahon had gone to Skilling to complain about the many conflicts of interest inherent in the LJM partnerships being run by Fastow. Rather than address the problem head on, Skilling offered McMahon a job as the chief executive officer of another Enron company, Enron Industrial Markets. McMahon took the job, and the LJM matter disappeared. As one source explained it, "McMahon's future was over at Enron. By going to Skilling, he'd laid out his cards saying 'This place stinks.'"

Watkins may have been hoping that her letter would force Lay to deal with the off-the-balance-sheet problems and perhaps even get rid of Fastow. That would leave the position of chief financial officer open. And that meant either McMahon, or perhaps even Watkins herself, could move up into Fastow's old spot. Either way, Watkins would be protected.

Whatever her motives for writing the letter, they were effective. Watkins was able to mark herself as a whistle-blower without really going public. By writing the letter, she protected herself from getting fired. That move was certainly good insurance for her position at Enron, but it was also clear that her letter was having repercussions inside the company.

Predictably, Andy Fastow was enraged when he heard that Watkins had talked to Lay. One source close to the matter said that shortly after Fastow heard about Watkins's memo and her subsequent meeting with Ken Lay in his office, Fastow stormed into Watkins's work area and told her immediate supervisor, "I want that bitch [Watkins] out of here tonight." Fastow then went into Watkins's office and ripped her company-issued laptop off her desk. "Fastow took the laptop and threw it in his closet in his office," recalled the source. "He thought that would take care of the memo problem. But Fastow's such a dope he doesn't know that everything is backed up on the network."

The other almost immediate reaction caused by Watkins's memo was a half-hearted effort by Ken Lay to investigate the matters she had raised. Although Watkins's memo advised Lay to hire a law firm other than Vinson & Elkins to examine the partnerships, Lay ignored her advice. He promptly contacted Enron's longtime law firm and asked it to look into the issues Watkins was raising. A few weeks later, the law firm assured Lay that the off-the-balance-sheet matters were not a problem. That wasn't a surprise; Vinson & Elkins had helped Enron set up many of the partnerships.

Like Arthur Andersen, Vinson & Elkins—one of the biggest and most prestigious law firms in Texas—was a captive of Enron. In 2001, Enron paid the firm $30 million for its services, a figure that amounted to about 7 percent of the firm's total billings. Many of its alumni, including Enron's general counsel, James Derrick, went on to work at Enron. Clearly, Vinson & Elkins was the wrong firm to investigate Fastow's partnerships.

But Ken Lay apparently didn't consider the law firm's conflicts of interest. It would prove to be one of the many poor management moves he would make as his firm sprinted toward bankruptcy.

Meanwhile, Watkins was looking out for her financial interests. She sold $31,000 worth of Enron stock in late August. She went on to sell another $17,000 block of stock options in early October—probably a good move on Watkins's part. And whatever she took out of Enron was a pittance compared to Ken Lay's plunder.

On August 21, the day before he met with Watkins and got her memo about the accounting problems, Lay wrote an e-mail to all of the company's employees. "As I mentioned at the [August 16] employee meeting, one of my highest priorities is to restore investor confidence in Enron. . . . This should result in a significantly higher stock price." Perhaps it's just coincidence, but that same day, August 21, Lay sold 68,620 shares of Enron stock, netting himself just over $1 million. The day before that, Lay had sold 25,000 shares, taking home nearly $387,000.

Lay was cashing out while he could. And although Enron was getting shaky, Lay still had a few cards to play. The Dabhol project in India was a major problem. But he had some friends in Washington, friends who owed him a favor or two.

41

George W. to the Rescue, Part 2

SEPTEMBER 28, 2001
Enron closing price: $27.23

George W. Bush was Enron's defender in California. In India, he was the company's bill collector.

Since the Indian government wasn't going to pay Enron the money it owed the company for the Dabhol power plant, the Bush administration was going to have to do some arm-twisting. If it didn't, American taxpayers were going to be on the hook for hundreds of millions of dollars. Two federally backed agencies, the Overseas Private Investment Corporation, which provided a total of $391.8 million in insurance on the project, and the Export-Import Bank, which provided $302 million in loans,[1] had backed Enron's Dabhol project, and by summer 2001, it was looking like their entire investment was going to be lost.

So the Bush administration made Dabhol one of its highest priorities. Beginning in June 2001, officials within the National Security Council began directing an effort to coerce the Indian government to make good on its deal with Enron. Governments are always looking out for the business interests of their corporations, particularly well-connected companies that provide big campaign contributions. But the Bush administration's interventions on behalf of Enron are remarkable because they occurred at such a high level. The National Security Council was created during the Truman administration to help the president wage war and manage diplomacy, not collect bad debts. Nevertheless, a trove of e-mails and memos obtained by the *Washington Post* shows that the Security Council coordinated an effort involving the State Department, Dick Cheney's office, the Overseas Private Investment Corporation, the Treasury Department, and others to help Enron. For months, the security agency continually monitored Enron's efforts to force the Indian government to buy its stake in Dabhol. For his part, Lay hoped that at the very least, the administration might be able to prevail on the Indian government to pay Enron for the electricity it had already produced—about $64 million worth—but had not been paid for.

On June 27, Lay got some high-level help. During a meeting with Sonia Gandhi, the president of India's opposition Congress Party, vice president Cheney brought up the Dabhol dispute. Although Cheney's exact message to Gandhi isn't known, an e-mail the following day from an unnamed official at the National Security Council proclaimed, "Good news is that the Veep [Cheney] mentioned ENRON in his meeting with Sonia Gandhi yesterday."[2]

Cheney was actually the second person in the Bush administration to pressure the Indians on Dabhol. During an April 6 lunch meeting in Washington with Indian foreign minister Jaswant Singh, Secretary of State Colin Powell told his Indian counterpart that "failure to resolve the matter could have a serious deterrent effect on other investors." Powell later defended his intervention on Enron's behalf, saying that he raises "commercial issues with governments all the time."

On July 5, the National Security Council sent an e-mail to the vice president's office, the office of the U.S. trade representative (headed by former Enron employee Robert Zoellick), and the Overseas Private Investment Corporation, saying, "We would like to host a second interagency meeting on Enron, Wed. July 11 at 10:30." Later that month, the U.S. assistant secretary of state for South Asia, Christina Rocca, brought up the Enron debacle while meeting in New Delhi with Indian officials. A few weeks after that, America's ambassador to India, Robert Blackwill, told businessmen in Bombay that the Enron dispute was causing American companies to rethink investments in India. "I know this personally from speaking with some of the premier American business executives with major investments in Asia," Blackwill said. Blackwill's comments came just a few weeks after Ken Lay's fruitless trip to meet with Indian leaders on Dabhol.

In August, Lay, feeling the Bushes were firmly behind him, even began sounding like he had a position in the administration. He told the *Financial Times,* "There are U.S. laws that could prevent the U.S. government from providing any aid or assistance to India going forward if, in fact, they expropriate property of U.S. companies."[3]

It was a dumb thing to say. The American government was already walking a tightrope with India. It had imposed economic sanctions on both India and Pakistan in 1998 after the two countries tested nuclear weapons. And now, as the United States was trying to normalize relations with India, Lay, the president's buddy and main benefactor, was acting like he had a say in American foreign aid. The reaction from India was predictable. Madhav Godbole, who headed a special committee formed by the Indian government to address the Dabhol problem, said the dispute is "a commercial one and has nothing to do" with potential economic sanctions on India.

Despite Lay's blunder, the Bush administration kept pushing Enron's position. In September, the administration asked the Treasury Department's representative to the World Bank to "get the World Bank to express concern" to the Indian government about the Dabhol project.[4] This effort was apparently made in spite of the fact that the World Bank had consistently refused to endorse or fund the project when Dabhol was proposed in 1992.

Furthermore, the Bush administration needed to get the Dabhol matter out of the way so it could concentrate on more important issues like the ongoing tensions between India and Pakistan. Those long-running tensions were a particular problem for the United States in the wake of the September 11 terrorist attacks because the U.S. government needed the cooperation of both countries.

The Dabhol problem "was a nightmare situation for the Bush administration that had to be taken off the table," said one Enron executive who worked closely with OPIC and administration officials. The Indians refusal to deal with the problem "was like an open sore. It was like a splinter that festers. If it wasn't taken care of it would only get worse and worse and create a greater impediment to the administration's ability to do other things."

In late September, Cheney went to bat for Enron again. On September 28, the Overseas Private Investment Corporation provided Cheney's office with a list of talking points on Dabhol prior to the vice president's meeting with Indian foreign minister Singh.[5] Given his own history in the private sector at Halliburton, Cheney was certainly aware of the need to preserve the investments made by the Overseas Private Investment Corporation and the Export-Import Bank. If foreign governments didn't honor investments made by Enron, then investments made by Halliburton and other companies could also be at risk.

In October, Undersecretary of State Alan P. Larson raised the Dabhol debacle with both Singh and National Security Adviser Brajesh Mishra and "got a commitment to 'try' to get the government energized on this issue prior to" a November 9 visit to Washington by Indian Prime Minister Atal Bihari Vajpayee."[6] At that meeting, President Bush was scheduled to discuss the Dabhol matter with Vajpayee. However, that discussion was apparently later called off just before Bush's meeting, likely because of Enron's accelerating financial meltdown.

The Bush administration's flurry of efforts to rescue Enron's bad investment in Dabhol apparently did little to sway the Indian government. If anything, it may have hardened India's resolve when it came to Enron. By late September or so, Ken Lay must have begun realizing that his efforts to resolve the dispute were not going to work. Enron insiders say the company's total investment in Dabhol was about $900 million, and yet its return on the project had been almost zero.

Enron was drowning in a sea of bad deals. The trading business, Azurix, Enron Broadband, metals trading, and now, once again, Dabhol. Everything Lay and Skilling had touched had begun to hemorrhage. And Ken Lay couldn't stop the bleeding. The money was flying out the door. Enron was spending insane amounts of cash. Indeed, at about the same time that Lay's pal Dick Cheney was talking to the Indians about Dabhol, Enron's Big Shots were spending millions of dollars—*on art.*

42

You Gotta Have Art

SEPTEMBER 4, 2001

Enron closing price: $35.00

The scaffolding was still up in the lobby. Workmen were still adding windows and finishing a hundred different tasks. But several floors of the building were finished, and a few Enron employees were moving into their new workspaces. And though the new building was lovely, it wasn't quite right. If the new $300 million Cesar Pelli–designed building, dubbed Enron Center South, with its spiffy trading floors, was going to make a statement, it had to be decorated. It needed art. Expensive, trendy art. And Lea and Andy Fastow—the modern-day de Medicis—were just the ones to make sure Enron made the right decisions.

Beginning in summer 2000 and continuing right through autumn 2001, as Enron began to spiral downward, the Fastows were the driving force behind an amazing art-buying binge. Even though Lea hadn't been an Enron employee since 1997, she became the de facto head of a team of Enron employees that included Jeff Shankman and Mike McConnell, as well as two local museum curators, that began scouting the art world for new pieces to add to the company's growing collection. They spent $575,000 on a soft sculpture by Claes Oldenburg. They paid $690,000 for a wooden sculpture by Martin Puryear, a record amount for his work sold at auction.[1] The committee also bought works by sculptor Donald Judd, painter-printmaker Vic Muniz, video artist Nam June Paik, photographer Julie Moos, and painter Bridget Riley.

In July and August 2001, Lea Fastow oversaw the installation of several of the newly purchased art pieces in the new building, including several by Muniz. "[One of them] was nine or ten feet high," said a source. "It cost about $110,000, and there were half a dozen of those." But the piece ended up in a hallway, said the source, where viewers couldn't get far enough away to get an overall impression.

There was a giant green glass globe that was designed specifically for the lobby of the new building that reportedly cost the company some $2 million. Lea Fastow was also heading projects involving a lighting installation that would link the two buildings that was to be created by Danish modernist Olafur Eliasson. There was going to be an installation on one of the trading floors by video artist Bill Viola. Company insiders say that while Lea Fastow was acting out her role as art princess in Houston, Andy Fastow was reportedly buying art for Enron offices in other parts of the country, including an office in Denver.

Conserving money was not a concern. And Lea Fastow relied on Enron to cover her art-related expenses. Those expenses were usually fairly small. But according to a source close to the art-buying committee, Mrs. Fastow also billed Enron for her limousine use. On December 8, 2000, her limousine costs totaled $832.46. She used a limousine again the following night that cost Enron $456.30. But the real fun was had during a trip Lea Fastow took to New York City aboard one of the company's planes. On March 13, 2001, according to the source, she and one or two other members of the art committee went on an art-buying trip. Their total bill for food and lodging during their stay in the Big Apple: $14,168.41.

The art-buying binge on Enron's behalf paralleled the Fastows' own efforts to become movers and shakers in the Houston art scene. They bought a number of modern art pieces for themselves, including a painting by minimalist Agnes Martin and another by Ed Ruscha, both of which were lent for display to the Menil Collection, one of Houston's most prestigious museums. The Fastows' art contributions quickly became controversial when Walter Hopps, the founding director of the museum, insisted that they be removed. Hopps claimed the Fastows were using the Menil to increase their social standing and to increase the value of their personal collection.

While the Fastows were buffing their social image, they were simultaneously working toward a vision for Enron. The company would amass a world-class art collection that would bring even greater glory to the energy colossus. Enron would build a collection with hundreds of works. Enron's getting into the art business wasn't a new idea. Other corporations had big art collections. For instance, *Forbes* magazine has a significant collection that includes rare toys, art, and Fabergé Easter eggs. Enron would have its own significant collection. It would commission new artworks and create educational programs. And Lea and Andy Fastow, would, of course, be at the epicenter of all of it.

By August and September 2001, the art buying at Enron was accelerating, said one source involved in the process. The company had spent about $4 million on twenty different pieces. But as the summer ended, for reasons that aren't clear, the Fastows began to hurry the process. "There was a big rush," said a source in the Houston art business. "They paid rush charges to get things framed and out of the New York galleries. I don't know if it was some time frame that floors [in the new building] were opening and they wanted them hung, or something else. But they paid lots and lots of money" to expedite the shipping of art from New York and San Francisco to Houston.

The Fastows were busy watching what was happening in the art world and tracking their growing riches courtesy of LJM1 and LJM2, but no one at Enron was watching what the Fastows were doing or spending on their artsy endeavors. Enron was paying for multiple paintings for each floor of the new building, some of which cost $30,000 to $40,000 each. "No one was tracking any of the purchases or the existing assets," said one internal auditor. "Enron didn't even know what was ordered because it was all done by Lea Fastow. She was buying art all over the place. The purchase orders were done by her. The shipping was handled by her. And everyone in the building deferred to her."

Although few people knew it at the time, there was plenty of reason for the Fastows to be in a hurry. Andy Fastow's lucrative run on the Enron teat was about to run out.

43

Revenge of the Raptors

OCTOBER 19, 2001

Enron closing price: $26.05

Ken Lay read the *Wall Street Journal* story, of course. He had to. The story, by reporters Rebecca Smith and John R. Emshwiller, shook him to his socks. The third paragraph contained everything he needed to know. Andy Fastow, the story said, "and possibly a handful of partnership associates, realized more than $7 million last year in management fees and about $4 million in capital increases on an investment of nearly $3 million in the partnership, which was set up in December 1999 principally to do business with Enron."[1]

The LJM deals that Fastow had promised would be so good for Enron were being very good indeed for Andy Fastow. Ken Lay needed to take action, and he needed to take it right damn quick. But he didn't. He didn't immediately march down to Fastow's office and demand an explanation. Nor did he summon the company's Executive Committee to discuss how the news about Fastow's compensation might affect the company. Instead, he called a meeting of the Enron Board of Directors. And for some reason, the board couldn't summon the gumption to call Fastow immediately, either.

Maybe Lay and the board were just being loyal. Perhaps they figured Wall Street would go bonkers if Enron fired Andy Fastow right away. Maybe they just didn't know what to do.

There had been inklings of Fastow's partnerships in the previous few days and Enron had acknowledged taking losses on them, but no one from the company was saying anything. Enron's PR flacks refused to talk to the *Journal*. So did Fastow. So did Michael Kopper, Fastow's pal, who quit Enron in order to buy out Fastow's interest in LJM2 in July 2001.[2] The company's inaction, coupled with its silence were—once again—driving the stock price down. On October 19, Enron's stock closed at $26.05, a decline of 10 percent from the price a day earlier.

Everybody wanted to know more about Fastow's payouts. The October 19 story followed an earlier *Journal* story, on October 17, which reported that Fastow had made $4.6 million from his stock options at Enron. The short sellers were coming out in force, and if Enron had been cooking the books, then the stock was going to fall further and that meant an opportunity to make money.

Also, the Wall Street guys were still asking questions about the events of October 16. That day, Ken Lay had stunned Wall Street by announcing that Enron was losing money, lots of money. For the third quarter of 2001, Enron announced it had lost $618 million. It was the company's first quarterly loss since 1997. The loss was primarily caused by the company's decision to write off $1.01 billion in bad investments. That total included a $544-million loss on investments in New Power, various broadband businesses, and several technology companies. There was a $287-million charge for lousy assets associated with Rebecca Mark's misadventures at Azurix and a $180-million charge to restructure Enron Broadband Services. Finally, there was a $35-million charge that piqued everyone's interest: It was for bad deals Enron had done with Fastow's LJM2.

There was more. Lay stunned the Wall Street analysts when he causally dropped another bombshell: Enron was taking a $1.2-billion reduction in shareholder equity.

The Raptors had come home to roost.

*

Beginning in August 2001 and continuing into October, the accountants at Andersen and Enron were realizing that the Raptors were totally insolvent. It appears that several Andersen auditors were reaching that conclusion at about the same time they got an e-mail from Enron's head of research, Vince Kaminski.

An average-size man of seemingly boundless energy, Kaminski could as easily discuss French literature (in French) as complex mathematical models for future commodity prices. A polymath and polyglot, Kaminski started working at Enron in 1992. A native of Poland, he had three degrees, a Master of Science in international economics and a Ph.D. in mathematical economics from the Main School of Planning and Statistics in Warsaw and an MBA from Fordham University. In addition to being smart, Kaminski had the added virtue of being honest, a factor that quickly put him at odds with Andy Fastow.

In 1999, Kaminski, the company's head of research, had objected to the very first deal that Fastow had done with LJM1. Two years later, his opinion of Fastow hadn't changed. On October 2, Kaminski sent an e-mail to an accountant at Arthur Andersen to alert the firm about the problems Enron faced with the Raptors. About the same time, Kaminski also notified Enron's chief risk officer, Rick Buy, that he and the people in his research group would no longer do any work on any of the LJM or Raptor transactions, even if it meant he would be fired.

Kaminski's stand, coupled with the ongoing decline in Enron's share price and the drop in the stock prices of Avici and New Power, left Enron with virtually no choice: It had to "unwind" the Raptor deals. And in doing so, the company would have to correct the blunder Enron's accountants had made in their initial accounting for the Raptors.

In mid-2000, when Fastow's LJM2 set up the Raptors, Enron pledged 55 million shares of its own stock, worth about $1 billion, to off-the-balance-sheet entities. The Raptors used the stock as capital to hedge against the possible decline in value of the Avici and New Power stocks. In exchange for the loan of Enron stock, the Raptors gave Enron a promissory note pledging to repay the $1 billion. But in accounting for the promissory note, Enron's finance team made the mistake of accounting for the note as an asset, and therefore made it an *addition* to Enron's shareholders' equity. (Shareholder equity is the net worth of a company. It represents all the assets stockholders might claim after all creditors and debts—liabilities—have been paid.) But the lending of the stock to the Raptors wasn't an asset for Enron. It was a liability. Therefore, the promissory note should have been regarded as a *reduction* to Enron's shareholder equity.

It was going to be embarrassing, but Enron had to write down the entire Raptor transaction. To do so, Enron decided to repurchase all of the 55 million shares it had lent to the Raptors. That meant it had to cut shareholder equity by $1 billion. In addition, Enron had to write off an additional $200 million in shareholder equity because of losses on the stock investments the Raptors had made.

Enron's own spokespeople didn't realize the importance of the gigantic reduction in shareholder equity. The day after the write-down was mentioned, one of the company's flacks, Mark Palmer, downplayed the importance of the vanishing $1.2 billion when he told the *Wall Street Journal* that the lost equity was "just a balance-sheet issue" and therefore wasn't really "material."[3]

Not so fast, hoss. Stock analysts and credit-rating agencies carefully watch shareholder equity numbers. In particular, credit rating agencies like Moody's Investors Service use the shareholder equity number to assess the creditworthiness of a given company by comparing the equity to the company's total debt load. By writing down $1.2 billion, Enron's debt-to-equity ratio—the figure that credit rating agencies use to determine a company's ability to pay its debts—surged from 46 percent to 50 percent. In fact, right after Enron's shareholder equity write-down, Moody's said it was considering downgrading Enron's long-term debt because of "significant write-downs and changes reflecting substantially reduced valuations" on several Enron businesses.[4]

Enron's death spiral had begun.

44

"An Outstanding Job as CFO"

OCTOBER 23, 2001

Enron closing price: $19.79

After Milberg Weiss sued, Ken Lay should have kept his mouth firmly shut.

Enron's credibility had been decimated. The October 16 write-down, followed by the October 19 *Journal* story, had made Wall Street wary. Those events, combined with Dabhol, the all-too-sudden departure of Jeff Skilling in August, and ongoing questions about Enron's profitability, had left Ken Lay with scant credibility. He could not afford to waste what little he had left.

He had other reasons to keep quiet. First, the board of directors still hadn't heard Andy Fastow's side of the LJM story. Although the board discussed the Fastow matter on October 19, the board waited until the following Monday, October 22, before it authorized two of its members, Charles LeMaistre and John Duncan, to call Fastow and ask him whether the *Wall Street Journal*'s story—the one that said he'd made millions from LJM—was accurate. But the two men didn't ask Fastow the question when they talked to him on that Monday. They scheduled another phone meeting, on October 23, at which they'd query Fastow.[1]

Before answering any questions from anybody inside or outside of

Enron, Lay wanted to have LeMaistre and Duncan's report. Then he'd know how best to handle the Fastow matter.

Second, the Securities and Exchange Commission was snooping around. On October 22, Enron announced the SEC had begun looking into Enron's dealings with Fastow. The news killed Enron's stock again. By the end of trading on October 22, Enron's stock had fallen 21 percent, closing at $20.65.

Finally, the class-action lawyers were closing in. That same day, October 22, Milberg Weiss Bershad Hynes & Lerach—the mega-law firm that corporate Big Shots love to hate—had filed suit against Enron, alleging that Lay, Fastow, and other Enron insiders had failed to disclose material information to the company's shareholders.

Of all the issues Lay was facing, the lawsuit had to be among the most worrisome. Milberg Weiss was one of the most aggressive law firms in the business. Its lawyers had made tens of millions of dollars suing companies like Enron for alleged breaches of securities laws. There was even a term for getting sued by the firm, it was called "getting Lerached" a phrase that referred to the no-holds-barred tactics of Milberg's lead attack-dog litigator, Bill Lerach. One CEO who decried Lerach and his tactics called him "lower than pond scum." Now that he was a defendant in a lawsuit, Ken Lay must have known that everything he would say or do would be parsed and scrutinized by Mr. Pond Scum and his pack of lawyers. And with Milberg leading the way, a school of other feeder sharks was certain to follow, eager to snack on Enron's faltering business.

The same day that Milberg Weiss sued Enron, Lay held a meeting with sixty of Enron's highest-ranking employees, the managing directors. In a meeting at a conference room at the Hyatt Regency, just across the street from Enron's headquarters, Lay tried to reassure the directors that everything was going to be fine and that he had confidence in Fastow. "Ken said, 'We support Andy. We don't think he's done anything wrong,'" recalled one Enron official who attended the meeting. Lay also insisted there was nothing wrong with the deals that Enron had done with Fastow.

Lay's sales pitch didn't work. Many of the managing directors were "saying Andy needs to go," according to one official who attended the meeting. The most vocal member of that group was Kaminski. During the open-floor segment of the meeting, Kaminski told Lay and the other directors that Enron needed to reveal all of its deals with Fastow, deals that he called "terminally stupid" and "improper." Kaminski was so inflamed about Fastow's flimflams and complained about them for so long, that Enron's new president, Greg Whalley, finally had to ask him to stop. Many of the managing directors agreed with Kaminski. Although they didn't know very much about the off-the-balance-sheet deals with Fastow, the general feeling was that Enron needed to make a bold move, expose the problems, and move on.

Lay was adrift and wasn't sure what he should do. He "didn't have anybody who he could trust," said one source close to the situation. After Skilling's departure, he had appointed Whalley and a new vice chairman, Mark Frevert. Both men were fairly capable, but they had virtually no high-level management experience. Beyond that, Enron insiders said Frevert had planned to leave Enron shortly after Jeff Skilling resigned, but Lay imposed on him to stay. Frevert didn't need to stay. In 2001, Frevert got cash payments from Enron that totaled $17.2 million. According to Enron bankruptcy documents, that sum includes an amazing $7.4 million in income from what Enron calls "Other." The filing defines "Other" as relocation costs, severance costs, consulting, and income imputed due to use of corporate aircraft.[2] That amount was in addition to his stock sales, a mere $54.8 million.

Only Ken Lay surpassed Frevert in the final playoff of the Enron Greed Bowl. In 2001, Lay's cash payments from Enron totaled $103.5 million.[3]

Worse yet, Whalley and Frevert had only been in their positions since late August. Lay didn't really know them that well. "Whalley and Frevert were new. There was nobody Ken could call for the unvarnished truth or even an unvarnished perspective," said one Enron managing director. "Ken was on his own."

Whether it was bad advice or his own vanity, Ken Lay just couldn't keep quiet. And Enron scheduled another conference call with Wall Street analysts for the morning of October 23.

When the call began, Lay—who, according to a source close to the situation, insisted on handling the script for the call himself—once again defended Fastow. He insisted that Fastow's partnerships had been fully disclosed to investors and that the board had taken measures to insure that no conflicts existed with Fastow's dual roles inside the company. He said that Enron had constructed a "Chinese wall" between the company and Fastow's partnerships and that deals were only done when they were "in Enron's best interest." Lay acknowledged the interest in the Fastow matter, saying, "We know there are a lot of rumors getting out, a lot of speculation. It's done a lot of damage to us over the last few days. We want to get the facts out."

The analysts weren't convinced. David Fleischer, an analyst at Goldman Sachs and one of Enron's biggest cheerleaders, told Lay, "What you are hearing from many is that the company's credibility is being questioned and there is a need for disclosure. . . . There is an appearance that you are hiding something."

Lay was still in defend-Andy-Fastow mode. He responded, "Obviously, the board and even the lawyers and auditors realized that there would be an apparent conflict of interest there and the board prescribed certain methods for it to be dealt with, so Enron would never be compromised. We are very concerned the way Andy's character has been loosely thrown about in certain articles, as well as the company's reputation."

Lay should have stopped there. He didn't. "I and Enron's Board of Directors continue to have the highest faith and confidence in Andy and think he's doing an outstanding job as CFO," Lay said.

The defense of Fastow should have been enough fireworks for one conference call. But the analysts wanted more details about other financial land mines that Enron was facing: Whitewing, Osprey, and Marlin.

Enron had used the off-the-balance-sheet entities to buy some of its overseas assets at inflated prices in an effort to make Enron's financial statements look better. Whitewing, Osprey, and Marlin—like the Raptors—were backed by Enron stock and contained financial backstops for Enron's partners in the deal. Each entity had different price trigger points. One trigger required Enron to issue more stock to cover any losses incurred by the other partners in Whitewing if Enron's stock fell below $48.55. Osprey had two different trigger prices, $59.78 and $47. The Marlin deal required Enron to issue more stock if the price fell below $34.13 per share.

So who was asking questions about the off-the-balance-sheet entities? None other than Jeff Skilling's buddy, Richard "Asshole" Grubman from Highfields Capital Management, the firm that had been shorting Enron's stock for months. Grubman knew from the company's financial statements that Enron had borrowed billions of dollars from Whitewing and another entity, Marlin, which owned a number of water assets obtained during the Azurix disaster.

Grubman questioned Lay repeatedly about the value of the assets in Marlin, an off-the-balance-sheet entity that was used to hide debt Enron used to fund Azurix. His questioning implied the assets in Marlin were only worth about $100 million. If that were true, it likely meant that Enron would have to find about $1 billion to pay off debts related to Marlin. The Whitewing exposure could cost Enron billions more.

Lay, the man who "wanted to get the facts out" refused to address Grubman's questions head on. Instead, he and Rick Causey, Enron's chief accounting officer, disputed Grubman's figures and said that Enron could sell assets to deal with the Whitewing problem. When Grubman persisted, Lay jumped on him, saying he was trying to monopolize the conversation. "You've done your best to drive down the price of the stock," Lay said testily. He then told the conference-call operator to go to the next question, saying, "Let's move on."[4]

Lay wanted to move on, but Grubman was pointing to a problem that Lay would have to acknowledge—and soon.

45

Fastow Goes Bye-Bye

OCTOBER 24, 2001

Enron closing price: $16.41

Ken Lay *was* hiding something from the analysts. The same day as the analysts' conference call, Lay apparently heard back from his fellow Enron board members, LeMaistre and Duncan. The two men had finally talked to Andy Fastow. They'd asked the CFO how much money he'd made from LJM1 and LJM2. When they heard the answer, they could barely believe it.

Fastow told the two men he'd made an astounding total of *$45 million* from LJM1 and LJM2. Fastow, the man who had a fiduciary duty to Enron's shareholders, told the board members he'd invested $1 million in LJM1 and $3.9 million in LJM2. For that investment, in less than two years, he'd made $23 million from LJM1 and another $22 million from LJM2.[1]

That was hardly Fastow's only source of income. Over the previous three years or so, Fastow had sold 687,445 shares of Enron stock, with total proceeds of $33.67 million. And Fastow didn't stop: On August 16, 2001, he had actually bought another 10,000 shares of Enron stock—perhaps he thought it was a good investment. There was more. Back in January and February 2001, Fastow, along with other top Enron executives, had received huge bonus payments that were based in large part, on the amount of Enron's profits. Fastow's total take from the bonuses: more than $3 million. All that cash was, of course, in addition to Fastow's annual salary of $440,698.[2] So, in other words, Fastow was dunning Enron four different ways. He was: (1) on the Enron payroll, (2) making money from the LJM1 and LJM2 deals, which *never* lost money on their dealings with Enron, (3) cashing in stock options that were more valuable because his LJM1 and LJM2 shenanigans helped artificially inflate the price, and (4) getting a cash bonus from Enron because the stock was doing so well.

Nice work if you can get it. The other side of the story is that while Fastow was getting rich, Enron's employees were getting poor. On October 17, Enron froze all of the assets in the Enron Corp. Savings Plan. The company said it was freezing the assets because it was changing the administrators of the retirement plan. That may have been the case, but by freezing the assets, the company also prevented Enron employees from selling their Enron holdings as the shares plummeted. At the end of 2000, the Enron Corp. Savings Plan contained $2.1 billion in assets, and 62 percent of that total was invested in Enron stock. By the time the asset freeze ended on November 19, the value of Enron's stock had fallen from $32.20 to $9.06, and thousands of the company's employees had lost the bulk of their life savings.

Lay didn't deign to tell anybody on Wall Street that Fastow had made such an incredible fortune at Enron. In fact, Lay and his cronies on the Enron board kept Fastow's $45-million windfall from LJM1 and LJM2 as their own dirty little secret until May 2002, when LeMaistre finally revealed the figure during his testimony before the U.S. Senate.

Lay didn't have a conference call to announce his next move. Instead, on the afternoon of October 24, Enron issued a terse, six-paragraph press release saying that Fastow's rival, Jeff McMahon, would be the company's new chief financial officer. "Andrew Fastow, previously Enron's CFO, will be on a leave of absence from the company," said the release. "In my continued discussions with the financial community," Lay said, "it became clear to me that restoring investor confidence would require us to replace Andy as CFO."

That day, Enron's stock closed at $16.41, down more than $3 from the day before. Lay was clueless about what to do next. His company was falling apart. The problems with Whitewing, Marlin, and other plunging-in-value assets like Dabhol and broadband were leading a handful of Wall Street watchers to compare Enron's collapsing fortunes to the 1998 failure of the giant hedge fund Long-Term Capital Management. Like Long-Term Capital Management, which was led by a group of cocky, self-absorbed traders and Nobel Prize–winners, Enron's arrogance was now costing it dearly.

On October 24, the same day Fastow was put on "leave of absence," Peter Eavis, a sharp-eyed columnist at TheStreet.com, who'd been crying bullshit on Enron's story for months, wrote, "Lay has shown himself to be woefully out of touch with the market's views. Arguably, that's downright reckless for a trading company that is dependent on potentially skittish short-term financing." Eavis added that Lay was showing "an unhealthy reluctance to address key problems until they're unavoidable... is it any wonder people compare this lot to Long-Term Capital Management?"[4]

Five days after Eavis's column appeared, Moody's cut Enron's credit rating to two notches above junk status. Enron's stock fell again, to $13.81. If Moody's and the other credit agencies were to cut Enron's debt to junk status, it could force the company to pay off billions of dollars in debt early, compelling it to issue tens of millions of new shares to cover the debt. The new shares would dilute the existing ones, reducing their value even further.

The destruction of Long-Term Capital Management had taken just five weeks. Enron's fall, it appeared, might happen even more quickly.

Ken Lay was going to have to take drastic action. It was either merge or go bankrupt. He had to try a merger, and by early November, Dynegy, Enron's longtime rival, was the only company interested enough—or able to—pull off a merger.

So where was Jeff Skilling during the crisis? Enjoying his cash.

46

Posh PJ's

NOVEMBER 2, 2001

Enron closing price: $11.30

Enron may have been falling apart, but that didn't mean Skilling and his fiancée, Rebecca Carter, couldn't go to a pajama party. Skilling and his future bride were young and good-looking, and they knew many Houston socialites. So there they were, among the hippest of the hip at the opening-night party at Hotel Derek, a place that calls itself "wickedly stylish."

The hotel, decorated by Hollywood designer Dayna Lee, was going to be the place in Houston where the fabulously fashionable go for a good night's sleep. The dress code for the soiree was announced as "posh PJ."

In the first sighting of Skilling in Houston since he left Enron, according to an account from the *Houston Chronicle*, he arrived in a "long flannel robe over slacks and sandals." The future Mrs. Skilling chose to forgo pajamas "in favor [of] a fetching black halter dress." The dinner for the guests, ninety or so of Houston's finest, was held at the hotel's new restaurant, Ling and Javier, a high-dollar joint featuring fusion cuisine that mixed Chinese and Cuban foods. Then there was disco dancing and more eating. "It was after 1 A.M. Saturday before all the guests headed upstairs to tuck into the new rooms that evolved from the $14.5 million makeover of the former Red Lion Hotel," reported the *Chronicle*'s Shelby Hodge.[1]

The paper didn't report a cost for the event or whether party goers had to pay to attend. Whatever the charges, Jeff Skilling could afford it. On August 15, the day after he announced that he was resigning from Enron, Skilling sold 140,000 shares of Enron stock. The sale was reported to the Securities and Exchange Commission as a "planned sale." Skilling's proceeds from the sale: $7.9 million. The sale brought Skilling's total stock sales to $70.6 million. Of course, that wasn't the only money Skilling made from Enron in 2001. He also got a salary of $1.1 million, a bonus of $5.6 million, and incentive pay of $1.9, for a total of $8.6 million.[2]

Jeff Skilling was living a wickedly stylish life. Ken Lay was sweating bullets.

47

Greenspan Gets the Enron Prize

NOVEMBER 13, 2001

Enron closing price: $9.98

Dynegy closing price: $46.94

It would be his last act as a Big Shot.

During his career, Ken Lay had been to countless $1,000-a-plate dinners where he'd eaten a henhouse-full of lukewarm chicken breasts and a bushel of cold asparagus while listening to political candidates tell the well-heeled crowd how they were going to help the little people. The Enron Prize, though, was different. It was Lay's chance to hobnob with rulers, the people who really run the world.

By giving Rice University a few million bucks, Lay and Enron had been able to elbow their way to the front of the line when it came to discussions of international politics. Instead of giving the prize on a regular schedule, for instance, every two years, Enron decreed the prize would be awarded "periodically." So when South African president Nelson Mandela came to the United States in October 1999, the company decided he would get the prize, even though the same honor had been bestowed upon Georgian president (and former Soviet Union foreign minister) Eduard Shevardnadze just seven months earlier. Furthermore, the prize gave Lay another way to ingratiate himself even further with the friends of the Bushes.

The prize—officially called The James A. Baker III Institute for Public Policy Enron Prize for Distinguished Public Service—allowed Lay to cement his ties to the Bush family's consigliere and Enron's former lobbyist, James A. Baker III.

Better still, the Enron Prize allowed Lay to become something of a statesman. It gave him a way to take the stage next to Baker, the former secretary of state, and pontificate on world politics while rewarding such Bush family allies as Colin Powell (who got the Enron Prize in 1995) and such global leaders as former Soviet Union president Mikhail Gorbachev (1997). The dinners and cocktail parties that came with the prize provided Lay with an additional opportunity to chat with people who could advance Enron's international projects. When Lay and Baker gave the Enron Prize to Mandela, Lay got some face-time with Prince Bandar bin Sultan, the Saudi Arabian ambassador to the United States. With the Gorbachev award, Lay got to chat up über-execucrat Henry Kissinger.

The November 13, 2001, event at the Rice University campus in central Houston was not much different from previous Enron Prize award ceremonies. Federal Reserve chairman Alan Greenspan certainly fit the Friend-of-the-Bushes profile, and he was clearly high-profile. And like the other awards, Lay almost surely had an ulterior motive.

Indeed he did. In late October, Lay had called the president of the Federal Reserve Bank of Dallas, Robert McTeer, to discuss Enron's worsening condition. (Incidentally, Jeff Skilling was a member of the Houston branch of the Dallas Fed from February 2000 to January 2002. In December 2000, Skilling had given a presentation on Enron to Fed chairman Alan Greenspan and members of the Fed's Dallas branch.[1]) On October 26, Lay called Greenspan himself. Although the call was reportedly brief, it must have been obvious to Greenspan that Lay was hoping that he might help engineer the same type of bailout for Enron that the Federal Reserve had for Long-Term Capital Management, in 1998. As it teetered on the edge of collapse, Long-Term had only about $1 billion in cash to cover its losses. Yet through very heavy borrowing, it had amassed $100 billion in assets and a derivatives position with a notional value of $1 trillion.[2] If the Federal Reserve System hadn't helped rescue Long-Term Capital Management, the deepening Asian financial crisis would have been made even worse. Greenspan later told reporters that there was great risk of "serious distortions to market prices had Long-Term been pushed suddenly into bankruptcy."[3] So the Fed stepped in and engineered a rescue plan that was paid for by American and European banks and brokerage houses.

Enron was big, but it was no Long-Term Capital Management. Sure, several Wall Street investment banks had several billion dollars' worth of exposure to Enron, but that was fairly small compared to Long-Term. Also, the fourteen banks that participated in the bailout of Long-Term had reason to provide capital to the failing firm: All of them had lent huge sums of money to the hedge fund. If Long-Term went bankrupt, the banks would have had to spend years in court fighting over the firm's assets. By keeping the giant hedge fund afloat for a while longer, the banks had a chance to recover more of their original loans to the firm. Beyond that, the bankers understood and trusted the founders of Long-Term, particularly John Meriwether, the brilliant former Salomon Brothers trader. Meriwether, despite his faltering hedge fund, was *one of them*. They liked and respected him.

Ken Lay and Enron were from Texas, too far from Wall Street to really matter. The button-down types at the New York Federal Reserve—the arm of the bank that orchestrated Long-Term's rescue—didn't care about them. Nor did it trust them. The departure of Skilling, the idiocy of the Andy Fastow partnerships, along with Lay's lame defense of his former CFO, had shredded Enron's credibility.

Furthermore, Enron might have claimed more revenues from its derivatives business than Long-Term did, but by the end of the third quarter of 2001, Enron's total assets from its derivatives business amounted to less than $19 billion, an amount that made it less than one-fifth the size of Long-Term at its zenith. Enron claimed more than $40 billion in other assets on its balance sheet that it could use to pay off its derivatives position. Greenspan apparently figured a collapse of Enron, if it happened, wasn't going to be catastrophic.

Nevertheless, Lay was clearly hoping Greenspan or someone else—

anyone else—at the federal level, would help his company. In fact, on October 28, two days after he called Greenspan, Lay called Treasury Secretary Paul O'Neill and compared Enron's problems directly to those of Long-Term Capital Management. O'Neill, according to the White House's version of the events, then instructed Peter Fisher, the deputy treasury secretary, to talk to Enron officials about their predicament. Fisher was also to assess how the possible failure of Enron would affect the overall American financial market.

By the time Greenspan got to Houston, it was clear that both Lay and his company were in desperate straits. Dynegy was going to buy Enron for about $9 billion in stock, and John Henry Kirby's company would disappear forever. The company would be called Dynegy. There was no job for Ken Lay. Dynegy's CEO and chairman, Chuck Watson, would be the boss, and his people—Steve Bergstrom, who was Dynegy's president, and Rob Doty, its chief financial officer—would keep their spots in the new company. Dynegy would have eleven of the fourteen seats on the new board. Enron could have three.

Whatever was going to happen to Enron, it was likely that Greenspan—a committed free-marketeer—realized that he couldn't help the company even if he wanted to. So the bespectacled chairman of the Federal Reserve did what he was invited to do: In his plodding, drier-than-sand style, he delivered a speech that was desperately unremarkable. The speech, which featured a recitation of world energy supplies and prices, lasted about ten minutes and contained such hilarious lines as "The long-term marginal cost of extraction presumably anchors the long-term equilibrium price and, thus, is critical to an evaluation of the magnitude and persistence of any current price disturbance."[4]

Greenspan's only remarkable comments came during a question-and-answer session afterward. When asked about his advice for people now entering the job market, he said, "I do not deny that there are innumerable people who succeed in business by being less than wholly ethical. But I will say to you that those are the rare examples; the best chance you have of making a big success in this world is to decide from square one that you're going to do it ethically."[5]

In all of his remarks, Greenspan didn't mention Enron once. But his prescription for business success—along with his refusal, apparently for reasons of propriety, to accept any Enron lucre—likely made Ken Lay wince. When Greenspan flew out of Houston, the only thing he took back to Washington was the nice certificate that came with the Enron Prize. Greenspan left behind both the lovely crystal trophy that came with the Enron Prize and the check—the amount of which Rice has kept a closely guarded secret—that went with it.[6] Enron had purchased senators, governors, lobbyists, secretaries of state, and a few presidents. It could not buy Andrea Mitchell's circumspect husband.

By the time Greenspan left Houston, Ken Lay was probably wishing he could take the cash that came with the Enron Prize back to 1400 Smith. He needed it. Enron was—once again—in a cash crisis. This one would be fatal.

48

One Restatement Too Many

NOVEMBER 19, 2001

Enron closing price: $9.06

Dynegy closing price: $43.60

The November 19 restatement was one restatement too many.

Enron had already restated its earnings once. On November 8, the company announced that it had overstated its profits—thanks to Michael Kopper and Andy Fastow's off-the-balance-sheet deals—by a total of nearly $600 million since 1997. Enron's portrayal of growth under Jeff Skilling had been a mirage. Chewco, LJM1, LJM2, and the rest had allowed Skilling and Fastow to manufacture profits that didn't exist, and Enron had been forced to come clean.

The $105 million in profits that surprised analysts at the end of 1997, Skilling's first year, had been almost entirely fabricated. That year, the company made $9 million, not $105 million. The off-the-balance-sheet deals had allowed Enron to overstate its 1998 profits by $113 million; the 1999 profits were too high by $250 million; and the 2000 profits, by $132 million.

In its November 8 filing, Enron admitted that between June 1999 and September 2001, it did two dozen deals with LJM1 or LJM2 that should have been consolidated onto Enron's books. The company also said that Fastow made "in excess of $30 million" for his hard work on the deals—it was actually *in excess of $45 million*, but what's $15 million among friends? In the effort to clean up the mess and regain a modicum of credibility, the company also announced it had fired Enron treasurer Ben Glisan and Broadband Services lawyer Kristina Mordaunt, both of whom had made an ever-so-easy $1 million by investing in Fastow's Southampton partnership deal.

Although the November 8 restatement was bad, it wasn't fatal. In fact, Wall Street kind of liked it. That's because it was accompanied by news that Dynegy, Enron's rival, was going to buy the company. In the week after the restatement, Enron's stock actually rose in price, breaking a long downward trend. By November 14, Enron closed at $10 a share, its highest level since November 5. Enron's suddenly stable stock price gave some analysts and more than a few people at Enron and Dynegy hope that the merger might actually work.

Then came the November 19 restatement.

Enron was coming apart far faster than anyone had imagined. The November 19 filing with the Securities and Exchange Commission showed that Enron was restating its third-quarter financial results for the second time in eleven days. When the company filed its original 10-Q (the quarterly financial statement that public companies must file with the SEC) on October 16, it said it lost $618 million in the third quarter of 2001. On November 8, it said the third-quarter loss was $635 million. On November 19, it said the loss was actually $664 million.

As disturbing as that information was, it was a fairly minor matter compared to the grenades Enron buried in a section called "Recent Events." Enron said that the November 12 downgrade of its debt by Standard & Poor's, to a notch above junk status, had "caused a ratings event related to a $690 million note payable that, absent Enron posting collateral, will become a demand obligation on November 27, 2001."

In nonfinance jargon, it meant Enron was toast. Unless the company could come up with $690 million, in cash, by November 27, the owner of the promissory note (Enron never said who it was) could come in and start seizing and selling Enron's assets.

Just below that note was another bit of information that surely had

Richard Grubman smiling. During the October 23 conference call with analysts, Grubman had asked Ken Lay about the health of Marlin, the off-the-balance-sheet entity Enron used to hide debts it incurred while setting up its misbegotten water venture, Azurix, and Lay had insisted that everything involving Marlin was just dandy. But in its November 19 filing, Enron acknowledged that if the company's debt was downgraded to junk and its stock price was below an unspecified price, Enron would have to "repay, refinance or cash collateralize additional facilities totaling $3.9 billion." Of that amount, nearly one-fourth was due to debt from Marlin.

Rebecca Mark's ghosts of bad water deals past were coming back at the absolute worst time for Enron.

The November 19 filing stunned Chuck Watson and his team at Dynegy. They'd been working night and day for two weeks to put the merger together, and now Enron was saying that it had billions of dollars in additional debts that would have to be covered—in cash—if it was to stay solvent. Watson phoned Lay to complain about the lack of disclosure, and already anticipating legal action, he followed it up with a letter. "We have not been consulted in a timely manner regarding developments since November 9," wrote Watson. "We were not briefed in advance on the issues in your 10-Q. Our team had to make repeated phone calls to your finance and accounting officials in an attempt to obtain information. Some of the most significant information in the Q was never shown to us at all."[1]

A source close to the Dynegy team said the merger was hampered from the beginning because Lay's team was continually changing its story. "It was clear that the Enron negotiators didn't have a clue. They didn't know how the business was going to run. They also didn't know what would happen if the deal didn't go through." Furthermore, said the source, "Lay didn't have a clue. He was like a deer in the headlights."

The Enron team—which consisted mainly of Lay; Enron's new president, Greg Whalley; new vice chairman, Mark Frevert; and new treasurer, Jeff McMahon—didn't have a Plan B. If the Dynegy merger failed, Enron would have to go into bankruptcy. And yet, despite their precarious position, Lay, Frevert, and Whalley hadn't thought through what the November 19 filing would mean to Dynegy. By not telling them in advance, Lay and his team had just alienated the only friends they had left.

There was another bomb in Enron's November 19 filing: The balance sheet showed that Enron's short-term debt had nearly doubled in just twelve weeks. At the end of the second quarter of 2001, Enron's short-term debt was $3.4 billion. By September 30, 2001, it had soared to $6.4 billion.

The disclosures in the November 19 document provided more fuel for what was already a raging meltdown in investor confidence. On November 20, Enron's stock dropped by almost one-fourth, closing at $6.99.

At the same time the company's credit situation was declining—most of its debt was just one notch above junk—the company's cash reserves were disappearing. Those pesky material adverse change clauses—the clauses that Enron had insisted that its counterparties use when doing business with Enron—were coming back to bite the company at the worst imaginable time.

As part of the merger agreement, Dynegy advanced $1.5 billion in cash to Enron to help the company stabilize its shaky finances. In return, Dynegy got preferred stock in one of Enron's most valuable assets, the Northern Natural Gas pipeline. If the deal failed and Enron didn't pay back the $1.5 billion, Dynegy would get the pipeline. The Dynegy team assumed all along that all or part of that $1.5 billion cash would be left over when the merger was finalized. It wasn't. Within a week of the original merger agreement being signed, all of the cash—and more—according to sources at Enron, had been used to collateralize Enron's derivative contracts.

In addition to the money from Dynegy, Enron got a $550-million loan from J.P. Morgan Chase and Citicorp that was backed with the assets of Enron's Transwestern Pipeline Company. It also got another $450-million loan from the two giant Wall Street banks that was backed by assets on the Northern Natural pipeline. And it borrowed another $3 billion from banks that had already given Enron lines of credit. In all, Enron borrowed about $5.5 billion in cash to keep its doors open.

It wasn't nearly enough. The situation was simple: Enron was being held hostage by the cash needs of its trading business. Enron barely discussed the problem in its November 19 filing, saying only that it was using cash to provide "collateral deposits to trading partners."

Enron's counterparties were invoking the material adverse change clause against Enron. The message was simple: Enron's worsening credit situation was a material change in the company's financial situation. Therefore, Enron had to cover its trading positions with cash or the counterparties would tell the world that Enron was no longer creditworthy, and that would create an even bigger run on Enron's treasury. The material adverse clause, instead of saving Enron from a catastrophe, was accelerating the company's cash crisis. The lack of federal regulation of derivatives contracts—the exemptions engineered by Senator and Mrs. Phil Gramm, regulations that might have forced Enron and its trading partners to have proper collateralization in the first place—was being played out. As Randall Dodd of the Derivatives Study Center explained, "Enron had to come up with a whole lot more capital at a time when it was capital short."

According to Enron's November 19 filing, it had $18.7 billion in liabilities from derivatives and commodities futures contracts on its books. Nearly all of those positions were going to have to be collateralized. To do it, Enron needed many billions of dollars in cash it didn't have and couldn't borrow.

It was déjà vu all over again.

Ken Lay had nearly lost Enron to the trading disaster caused by Enron Oil in Valhalla, New York, in 1987. Back then, Lou Borget and his traders had gotten in over their heads. Borget's team had piled losses on top of losses until they were faced with a position in the oil futures market that totaled about $1.5 billion. Enron would have gone bankrupt had its counterparties required the company to collateralize all of its positions with cash. Enron only escaped that mess because Enron executive Mike Muckleroy and his team of traders were able to bluff the market and unwind Borget's positions. Those trading losses forced Enron to take an $85-million charge against earnings in the third quarter of 1987, and a chastened Ken Lay christened the mishap an "expensive embarrassment."

Now, a shade more than fourteen years later, Lay had been snookered again. But instead of a $1.5-billion problem, Enron's vaunted trading business had more than $18 billion in liabilities. And there was no one like Muckleroy to the ride to the rescue.

In 1987, Lay blamed the problems at Enron Oil on Borget and his rogue traders, even though he and the other top executives at Enron had been warned several times in the preceding months that Borget had falsified records. Fourteen years later, Lay and Enron were being stung repeatedly by disclosures about Fastow's self-serving scams, deals that Lay and the Enron Board of Directors had blithely approved.

But none of it was Ken Lay's fault. Of course not. Someone else was to blame. During a November 12 conference call with analysts, Lay pointed the finger at others. Referring to Fastow, Kopper, and their cohorts, Lay said, "I'm sorry those six people seem to have gone somewhat over the edge in their dealings or transactions, but you can't be absolutely protected from that in any business."

The delicate executive wouldn't need to be protected much longer. The end was fast approaching.

As Enron's stock price spiraled downward, nearly every one of Enron's trading parties was demanding that the company collateralize its positions. The finance team was scrambling to find cash everywhere it could, while trying to avoid doing anything that might spook the credit rating agencies. Sure, the cash outflows were hurting the company, but a downgrade meant death.

49
The Downgrade

NOVEMBER 28, 2001

Enron closing price: $1.10

Dynegy closing price: $36.81

The days after Enron's November 19 restatement were chaotic. The top executives from Enron and Dynegy had to convince the credit rating agencies that the merger was going to work. If they could do that, they could prevent the agencies from downgrading Enron again. But with each passing day, all of the agencies—Standard & Poor's, Moody's, and Fitch—were increasingly nervous. Billions of dollars were riding on their decision about the fate of Enron's debt.

Moreover, the two sides had to figure out a new structure for the merger. Enron's still-sliding stock price had changed all of the agencies' assumptions. When the merger was announced on November 13, Enron's stock was trading at $9.98. Ten days later, as the New York Stock Exchange quit trading for the long holiday weekend, Enron's shares were worth just $4.71. As the price kept sliding, Dynegy had to continually recompute the value of Enron and make an appropriate offer. That offer would then have to be approved by Enron's board. It was a time-consuming and frustrating process.

In addition, Dynegy's lead executives and negotiators on the merger deal, CEO Chuck Watson, president Steve Bergstrom, and chief financial officer Rob Doty, were increasingly dismayed by Enron's actions. The November 19 filing had left the three men angry and more than a little wary of what Enron might do next. But Watson was negotiating from a good position. He, Bergstrom, and Doty had been working together for a long time. Bergstrom had been president of Dynegy since 1995. Doty had been the CFO for more than eighteen months. Watson trusted the two men and knew them well.

Ken Lay was far more isolated. Whalley and Frevert were smart, but they weren't enough. Lay really needed some tough negotiators and some top-notch public relations people. He also needed someone who could help him understand Enron's real financial condition.

Despite Lay's handicapped position, the two sides continued their negotiations over the Thanksgiving Day holiday. Rather than stay in Houston, the two sides moved their talks to the Doral Arrowwood Resort and Conference Center in Rye Brook, New York.[1] There, the two sides holed up in a series of conference rooms with their staff members and their bankers. In one set of rooms, Lay huddled with his investment bankers from J.P. Morgan Chase and Citigroup. Watson and his team from Dynegy relied on bankers from Lehman Brothers.

The investment bankers had a lot at stake in the merger, too. In particular, J.P. Morgan Chase and Citigroup had huge credit exposure to Enron. In the previous few weeks, they had helped raise $1 billion in loans—backed by the value of Enron's pipelines—to help keep Enron solvent. Lehman had its own interests and its own conflicts. During the merger talks, Lehman was pressuring Enron to make good on a $179-million derivative transaction it had made with the beleaguered energy trader.[2] The payments on the transaction were about to come due, and Lehman wanted to make sure the merger deal included a provision for its own exposure.

There were other conflicts that hampered the negotiations. The biggest problems came from Enron's own twisted accounting. As members of the Enron team began to understand an issue, they would tell Dynegy what they had learned. Then, said a source close to the negotiations, Enron's team would "go back and find something else that they'd have to tell the folks from Dynegy. Enron was just figuring it out a few hours before they talked to the people at Dynegy. No one at Enron had a full understanding of all the potential implications" of the company's accounting problems.

Dynegy also had questions about the profitability of EnronOnline. The Dynegy team had always assumed that Enron's on-line trading operation was making money. However, as the Dynegy negotiators began inspecting the business more closely, it became increasingly obvious to them that despite the enormous volumes that were being generated on the web site, Enron was actually losing money on its trading business. And the plunge in Enron's stock price and potential credit problems had driven away many, if not most, of the entities that were used to trading on EnronOnline. That meant Enron was being forced to offer higher prices for commodities than competing on-line marketplaces, a fact that was making the exchange lose even more money.

By the end of the holiday weekend—November 26, a Monday—it appeared the two sides had worked out another deal. The original merger agreement had called for Enron shareholders to get 0.2685 shares of Dynegy stock, worth about $10.50, for each share of Enron stock, an amount that valued all of Enron's stock at about $9 billion. That offer was now far too generous. Enron's stock was no longer worth $10. So Watson's team decided to offer no more than $6 per share, or about $5 billion. From Enron's side of the table, that offer looked good. *Hell, any offer looked good.* By the time the New York Stock Exchange closed on the 26th, Enron's stock was trading for just $4.01. If Enron's shareholders could get Dynegy shares worth $6, at least they'd get something. There were a few other provisions, including another cash infusion of $500 million by J.P. Morgan Chase and Citigroup to keep Enron afloat and an agreement by some of Enron's creditors to delay the repayment dates of certain Enron debts until after the merger was completed.

The cash infusion was critical. And Enron had been appealing to deep pockets all over the world in an effort to find the money it needed to stay in business. While it was negotiating with Dynegy, Enron appealed to the billionaire Saudi prince Alwaleed Bin Talal, as well as two buyout firms, the Carlyle Group Inc. (whose employees include George H. W. Bush) and the Blackstone Group. All of them turned Enron down.

Without cash to keep Enron going, the Dynegy deal wasn't going to work. In fact, as the hours passed, the Dynegy team began realizing that the stock price no longer mattered. Enron's cash management was so poor, they couldn't do the merger.

"What drove Dynegy away faster than anything else were questions about Enron's cash position," said one source close to the Dynegy side. "That was the thing that broke the camel's back. It set off big alarms among the Dynegy people. They'd ask Enron 'What's your cash position?' And Enron couldn't provide it. It wasn't that they wouldn't provide it, they *couldn't* provide it. They didn't know how much cash they had or where it had gone. That's when the Dynegy team said, 'We have to get out of this.'"

Although Watson and his team were probably going to pull out of the merger anyway, their decision was made for them. At 10:57 A.M. on November 28, Standard & Poor's slashed Enron's credit rating to junk status. The rating agency said the move was caused by "concerns about the viability of the merger agreement with Dynegy and liquidity implications of the possible failure of that transaction." A few hours later, Moody's and Fitch followed suit. In fact, the agencies slashed Enron's debt so far below investment grade that Enron needed a ladder just to see daylight. Moody's cut Enron's rating five notches. Standard & Poor's slashed it by six. Fitch cut it by ten.[3]

The response from the stock market was almost instantaneous. On November 27, Enron's shares had closed at $4.11. In the hours after the announcement by the credit rating agencies, Enron's stock fell to as little as 60 cents. Trading volume on Enron stock was incredible. About 342 million shares of Enron stock changed hands, an amount that broke the previous trading volume record of 309 million shares set on September 22, 2000, by Intel. Dynegy shares took a beating, too, closing down 12 percent, at $35.97.

In a conference call that afternoon, Watson lamented the implosion of the deal, saying Dynegy wasn't "going to do anything to jeopardize our stakeholders. And sometimes a company's best deals are the very ones they did not do." Bergstrom added that Dynegy was no longer trading with Enron. "Unless," he added, "Enron puts up sufficient credit support." In other words, Dynegy, like every other trader, was going to insist that Enron collateralize any position it took with cash. And Bergstrom knew better than anyone that Enron didn't have any. The two men—already anticipating ligitation—refused to take any questions and ended the call by saying, "We will talk to you later."

Ken Lay didn't have a conference call. Instead, Enron issued a glum release quoting Lay: "We are evaluating and exploring other options to protect our core energy businesses. To do this, we will work to retain the employees necessary to the continuing operations of our trading and other core energy businesses."

Continuing any operations was impossible. With its credit downgraded to junk, Enron was going to have to repay the $3.9 billion in debts associated with Whitewing and Marlin right away. It didn't have it. The till was empty and there was no way to borrow more money. Ken Lay was out of options.

50
The Bankruptcy

DECEMBER 3, 2001
Enron closing price: $0.40
Dynegy closing price: $27.17

The meeting of the board of directors on Saturday, December 1, was perfunctory. Everyone on the board knew what had to be done. After a brief discussion, the group voted unanimously on a motion to declare bankruptcy. A few hours later, during the early morning hours of December 2, a group of lawyers from the firm Weil, Gotshal & Manges submitted Enron's bankruptcy filings to the Federal Bankruptcy Court in New York's Southern District. They did it via the court's web site. Enron, the company that had hyped its ability to trade bandwidth, to use the Internet to access new markets, to transform the world, had filed bankruptcy without using a single sheet of paper.

Ken Lay made sure to keep blaming someone else. Along with the bankruptcy papers, Enron filed a $10-billion lawsuit against Dynegy, claiming breach of contract.

There was more foolishness. Even though Enron's trading business had helped drive Enron into the ground, Ken Lay still believed in it. Sure, Enron's reputation was forever tarnished, his employees' pension funds had been decimated, and thousands of Enron employees were about to be fired. But Lay just *knew* that he had to preserve the company's trading business. So in the days leading up to the bankruptcy, Lay's company quietly provided payments totaling $55.7 million to about 500 employees. In exchange, the employees agreed to stay on at Enron for ninety days.

Of course, the traders got the biggest bonuses. John Lavorato, the head of Enron's trading business, got $5 million—that was in addition to more than $2.3 million Enron had paid him in salary and long-term incentives. Louise Kitchen, the woman who had helped create EnronOnline, got $2 million. Jim Fallon, who had overseen the spectacular failure of broadband trading at Enron Broadband Services, got $1.5 million. Paul Racicot, the trader and Enron Broadband employee who had told me five months earlier that Enron could "intermediate" any business it chose, got $400,000. Jeff McMahon, who had succeeded Andy Fastow as CFO, got $1.5 million. Several dozen others got bonuses ranging from a few hundred thousand dollars to more than $1 million. John Arnold, a gas trader who reportedly helped make $700 million for Enron by trading gas on the West Coast, is said to have gotten total bonuses in 2001 of $8 million. When asked by a reporter about the bonuses, Enron spokesman Mark Palmer (who got a bonus of $200,000) explained they were paid to "protect and maintain the value of the estate."

By the morning of December 3, a Monday, the traders at Enron were happy. Most of them had gotten substantial retention bonuses. Their bosses had told them that they didn't have much to fear from the bankruptcy. Enron was going to fire a substantial number of people, but the personnel cuts wouldn't really affect the trading division. The news of the bankruptcy was stressful, but that was countered by the fact that the traders didn't really have anything to do. Enron's counterparties had quit trading with the company more than a week earlier because of worries about Enron's credit rating. So the traders, the whizzes who traded gas, power, crude oil, propane, and dozens of other commodities, sat at their desks and watched TV or read the paper.

Thousands of other employees weren't so lucky. Throughout the morning, clumps of employees, several dozen at a time, gathered for meetings with their supervisors. Many of the employees, concerned about the bankruptcy, had already cleaned out their desks and taken their personal effects home. The ax fell for some right away. Others were told that their job status was uncertain. "They told us to check our voice mail tomorrow," one employee, Sanjays Pathak, told me after he came out of the building. "That's a hell of a thing: getting fired by voice mail."

By noon, the line of cars making their way to the front of the Enron building stretched for blocks, snaking out of Andrews Street and then north, onto Smith Street. They moved forward slowly, one at a time, hurried on by a gaggle of impatient cops from the Houston Police Department. Two of the cops were on horseback. Each car would stop for a few moments, to pick up dejected former Enron employees. Some of the people carried boxes, which they hurriedly loaded into the waiting car, driven by a friend, relative, or spouse. The cops weren't helping matters. They even gave a few parking tickets to Enron employees who'd just been fired.

Yuri Solomon, a big man, was one of them. He was in no hurry. He slowly crossed Andrews and was gradually heading north on the sidewalk toward Smith Street. Every few steps, he'd stop and look back at the shiny, oval-shaped building, occasionally shaking his head. In his left hand was a blue plastic sack carrying some of the knicknacks from his desk. In his right hand, he carried a tennis-ball-sized conglomeration of rubber bands. He walked a few more steps, then paused again to look at the half dozen TV trucks and the growing group of reporters and media people in the small park directly across the street from the entrance to Enron's main lobby.

After three years at Enron, Solomon was in no hurry to leave. A technician in Enron Networks, the information technology arm of the company, he had hoped to retire with Enron. Instead, he was out of a job. "You know, my father-in-law works for Southwestern Bell," he said. "When I got hired on here in 1998, he was so happy. He told me, 'That company isn't going anywhere.' Man was he ever wrong."

If only Yuri Solomon had been a trader, he wouldn't have been on the street. But he wasn't. He was just another casualty, one of 4,000 employees Enron fired that morning. And for all of his hard work, Solomon was going to get a special payment. He, like the other fired Enron employees, no matter how many years they'd worked at Enron, would be getting a severance check. It would be for $4,500—approximately one-half the cost of one of Andy Fastow's Master Banker watches.

51

"Salvation Armani"

JUNE 27, 2002

Enron closing price: $0.11

Dynegy closing price: $6.08

Jus' Stuff doesn't sell fancy watches. But $4,500 won't get you very far once you step inside.

One of many quaint boutiques that lie within a mile or so of the River Oaks neighborhood, Jus' Stuff doesn't have anything really unusual. It does, however, have plenty of buzz.

When it opened in late May 2002, Jus' Stuff got the kind of attention millions of small business owners can only dream of. There was an article in the *New Yorker*, a write-up by the *Houston Chronicle* and numerous stories in newspapers around the country. Jus' Stuff became a featured player in *Doonesbury*, the nationally syndicated comic strip drawn by Garry Trudeau. The strips even included the address for Jus' Stuff, 1302 West Gray.

The media attention was drawing the curious and the well heeled. It was also ringing the cash register. On one of its first weekends in business, there was a standing-room-only crowd at Jus' Stuff. There were so many customers that the store ran out of its zebra-print tissue wrap and business cards. But the customers weren't really there for the merchandise. They were there to see all the baubles that come with being among the Big Rich. There were also hoping to catch a glimpse of the new store's owner, Linda Lay.

Jus' Stuff was the Lay family's equivalent of K-Mart's Blue Light Special. The store was the family's way of selling off the accrued detritus of decades of conspicuous consumption, which included several homes in Houston, four properties (one vacant lot and three homes, all worth many millions of dollars) in Aspen, and a multimillion-dollar vacation spot in Galveston. And while the store was drawing gawkers, it was also drawing scorn. Wags were continually coming up with new names for Jus' Stuff, the best of which was "Salvation Armani."

Indeed, if Marie Antoinette were having a garage sale, it would probably look just like Jus' Stuff.

Oh sure, there were a few cheap items. A gold picture frame was going for $35. Nearby was an item whose tag—written in neat cursive hand—said "Very Pretty Turned Wood Candlestick." They cost $175 for the pair. But the good stuff required a much bigger checkbook. For instance, the "Very Old Mirror From France" on the wall near the door was priced at $7,200. The "Antique Religious Italian Metal Altar Candlesticks" were $1,400 for the pair. The "Vermont Target Rifle German Silver Inlay & Patch," which was casually poking out of a big wooden box along with another old rifle, was tagged at $2,550. And of course, no self-respecting millionaire could live without a pair of antique fireguards to protect the fireplace. Jus' Stuff had a pair. The old-looking wooden gewgaws had an oval wood-and-glass medallion affixed near the top of a thinner-than-a-broomstick pole. The tag, written in green ink, proclaimed "Pair—Amazing Antique Fire Guards with Original Needle Work. $5,000." Anything that had descriptors like "antique" or "amazing" on the price tag usually cost several thousand dollars.

Linda and Robin Lay were at the store on the afternoon of June 27, working the phones, talking to coworkers, managing their fledgling small business. It was kind of quaint, really. Here was Linda Lay, who just four months earlier had embarrassed herself by going on national television and announcing that the Lays had "nothing left" and were "fighting for liquidity" (read: Poor people go broke, rich people fight for liquidity). During her weepy interview on NBC's *Today* show, she insisted that Ken Lay was a wonderful guy who "wasn't told" much about the company's finances and that all the facts would come out during the investigation.

Her appearance on NBC was an unqualified public relations disaster. Every commentator in the land mocked her for days afterward. But here she was, stoically working at her store. Sure, she and Ken had been humbled, but they weren't going to roll over and play dead, either. But that didn't mean everyone in Houston was going to visit. "Several Enron executives have told their wives not to even think of going into that store," said one well-placed secretary who's still with the company.

Everything about Jus' Stuff horrified Houston's upper-crust social set. One socialite expressed amazement at the fact that Ken Lay hadn't left town, given the humiliation that came with Linda opening a place like Jus' Stuff. In the span of one year, the Lays had gone from the city's power couple to running a resale store. "I don't know how I could even walk around in Houston if I were Ken Lay," said one well-known socialite. "It'd be like carrying an elephant on my back. It's like she's trying to shoot her husband in the foot."

For the first few weeks the shop was open, an off-duty officer from the Houston Police Department secured the front of the building. The Lays were expecting trouble. And they got a little bit. In early June, a group of three or four dozen neighbors, activists, and artists had a bit of fun at the Lay's expense. Led by Mark Larsen, a Houston-based painter and performance artist, the group conducted a bit of performance art/protest/theater in the parking lot in front of the store. They carried signs that read, "Imelda Marcos is Back" and "After This, Visit The O.J. Simpson Flea Market."[1]

Larsen led the crowd in various chants, including one that went, "We just want to say to you, we think your place smells like poo." The group also did short skits. One skit involved a group of protesters/artistes dressed in their finest furs and fashions for the event who began chanting, "Let us shop. Let us shop."

It was all in good sport, and the protesters had a grand time mugging for the TV cameras and making fun of the Lays. Alas, Linda Lay was locked inside Jus' Stuff, well away from the none-too-respectful hoi polloi out front. The store was unexpectedly closed, reported an amused Wendy Grossman, a reporter for the *Houston Press*, "due to a plumbing problem."[2]

Larsen, a native of Flint, Michigan, a Rust Belt city that has been decimated by a corporate evacuation led by General Motors, told me that he was motivated to organize the event because he felt that the very existence of Jus' Stuff was "blasphemous." He said that other Houston residents joined his protest for a simple reason: "They feel like this country has been hijacked."

While Linda Lay works at Jus' Stuff, Ken Lay works at keeping out of sight. He doesn't go out. He doesn't give speeches. He plays golf and reads a bit. He still goes to the office—not at the Enron building, but at a twelfth-floor corner suite of the River Oaks Bank Building. The sign on his door says "Linda and Ken Lay Family." It's a convenient spot. The office sits just a few hundred feet from the front door of the Huntingdon, the posh high-rise condo at 2121 Kirby where the Lays occupy the entire thirty-third floor. The Harris County Appraisal District values the condo, which has 12,827 square feet of living space, at $7.8 million. Their downstairs neighbor, by the way, whose condo is valued at $1.2 million, is Lanna Pai, the ex-wife of Enron executive Lou Pai.

Indeed, the Lays looked to be prospering quite nicely, despite Linda's statement in her January TV appearance that she and Ken had "nothing left."

Linda Lay's idea of "nothing" is pretty hefty. County property records show that she owns five properties in Houston, including two single-family homes, two duplexes, and a triplex. Combined value of those properties: $1.1 million. There's more. In addition to the condo at the Huntingdon that the Lays own jointly, they own two other properties in Houston, a small apartment building and a single-family home. They also own the retail building occupied by Jus' Stuff. All told, the Lays' property holdings in Houston are worth more than $9.3 million.

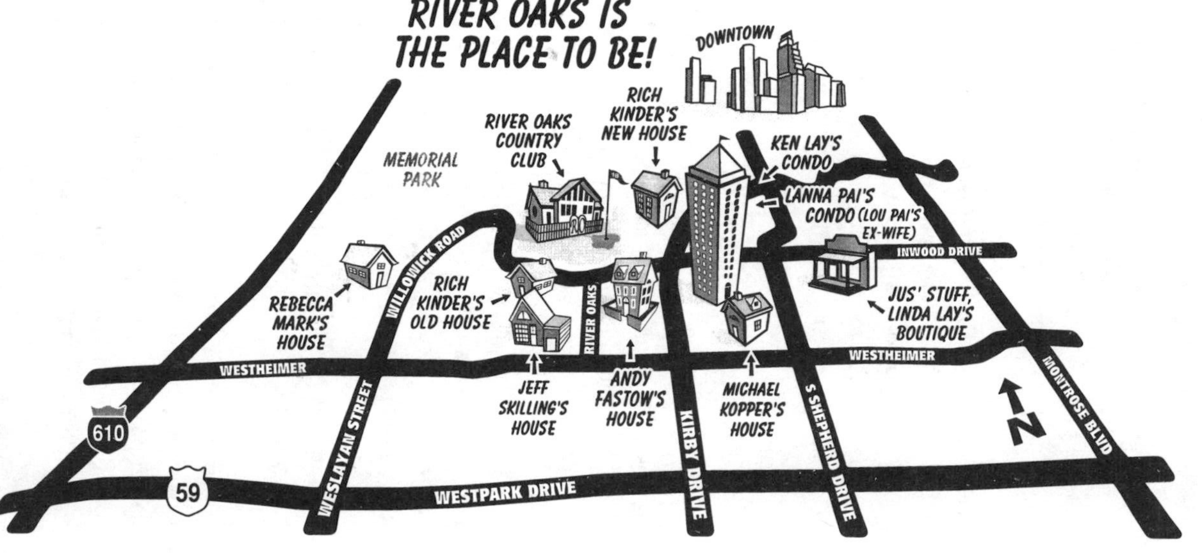

Map by Brian Barry

The Lays are clearly rich. But they won't be pardoned, not by the city they used to dominate.

"Houston has had its share of crooks over the years. I don't know if Lay was a thief or just a huckster," said John Mixon, a law professor at the University of Houston who has observed the changing city since he began teaching there in 1955. "But he violated the code by getting caught and hung out to dry. He's made Houston look bad. And that cannot be forgiven."

Elsewhere in the well-manicured confines of River Oaks, former Enroners are living quite well, and all within two miles or so of each other.

The Lays and the Fastows are the closest neighbors. The Fastows' almost-finished house on Del Monte is just three-tenths of a mile from the Huntingdon. The house is nearly complete. All of the stonework on the exterior has been finished and workmen are busily painting the interior. Andy Fastow, like his former boss, is keeping a low profile. He's still going to his children's baseball games, but that's about the only time he's seen in public. While they wait for the Del Monte house to be finished, Andy, Lea, and their children stay in their huge house in the Southampton neighborhood. A six-foot-wide American flag continues to hang from the second-story porch.

If his legal maneuvers are any indication of his mindset, Andy Fastow is also increasingly worried about his exposure to lawsuits and criminal indictments. In June, Fastow's lawyer asked a federal judge in Houston to rule that Fastow does not have to give depositions or produce documents for plaintiffs who are suing him in civil lawsuits. Fastow's reasoning is that any information he provides to the plaintiffs could be used against him by prosecutors if (or when) he is indicted by federal authorities.

Jeff Skilling lives in a $4.2-million Mediterranean-style mansion with 8,100 square feet of living space and three fireplaces. It sits just seven-tenths of a mile from Fastow's new house on Del Monte. Skilling, too, is keeping an ultra-low profile, and he's fortifying his redoubt. In

March, workmen put the finishing touches on a stout six-foot-high metal fence and electric gate that defends the front side of his property. He and his fiancée, Rebecca Carter, got married the first weekend in March. The two may be in love. They may also be preparing for litigation. As Skilling's wife, Carter (Enron's former corporate secretary) can claim marital privilege and cannot be forced to testify against her husband.

Rebecca Mark, whose house lies just a few blocks west of Skilling's, is—like the others—avoiding reporters and publicity. She helps raise money for causes like the Awty International School, a very chic (the school's web site is in both English and French), very expensive, multilanguage prep school. She's also reportedly doing a bit of work for the Houston Museum of Fine Arts. Her husband, Michael Jusbasche, is occasionally seen at the River Oaks Country Club. Skilling and Lay are also members of the exclusive club, but they haven't been seen there lately. Mark's home in River Oaks is valued at $5.5 million. Her annual tax bill is about $61,000 per year.

Mark Frevert, the former CEO of Enron Europe who spared no expense in setting up Enron's London offices, is living well in River Oaks, too. He and his wife live in a house on Pelham Drive that is appraised at $1.3 million.

Lou Pai doesn't live in River Oaks. But he continues to be as elusive and quiet as possible. In mid-June, he got rebuked by the Colorado Supreme Court. The court ruled that Pai, who had been in constant battles with local landowners over access to his ranch, could no longer exclude local citizens from accessing his ranch. Their traditional land-use rights, the court ruled, were legal and enforceable. The locals could once again access the ranch for grazing, firewood, and timber.[3]

Ken Rice, like the others, is hiding. He reportedly shares an office with Jeff Skilling. He owns a fleet of houses in Houston's Bellaire neighborhood and is reportedly still playing with his fast cars.

By late June 2002, all of these people—Lay, Fastow, Skilling, Mark, Pai, Rice—were named defendants in dozens of lawsuits. The litigation is likely to last for years, maybe decades. They might lose every one of the lawsuits now facing them. But they don't have to worry. They live in Texas. No matter what happens in court, they're still gonna be rich.

The Lone Star State has one of the most lenient bankruptcy laws in America. In Texas, bankruptcy is no cause for shame, it's a tradition. It's also no cause for losing your hard-stolen loot.

If Ken Lay or Jeff Skilling lose a few lawsuits, they could simply declare bankruptcy. By doing so, they'd be allowed to keep a pair of donkeys, 200 acres of ranchland, two firearms, and their homesteads. And in Texas, that homestead can be a mega-mansion. It doesn't matter if the house is worth $10,000 or $7.8 million, it's beyond the reach of any creditors. So are luxury cars, salaries, and any retirement income.[4]

In most states, people who take bankruptcy are allowed to keep an average of about $60,000 in home equity. There is no limit on home equity in Texas. However, several bills now pending in Congress would revamp the federal bankruptcy rules, which would cap homestead equity exemptions at $125,000.[5]

Texas law also prevents creditors from seizing income the Lays are likely to get from their annuities. In 2001, Enron purchased two annuity contracts, with a total value of $10 million, for Ken Lay.[6] One of those annuities, a $4.7-million contract, will pay Ken and Linda Lay $400,000 annually, starting in 2007.

So what about Rich Kinder? Oh, don't worry about him. He's not a defendant in any of the Enron lawsuits. And he won't be taking bankruptcy anytime soon.

After Ken Lay refused to name him as Enron's CEO in 1996, Kinder didn't get mad. He got even. In January 1997, he teamed with another University of Missouri alum, Bill Morgan, and paid $40 million for one of Enron's natural gas liquids pipelines. Enron thought the pipeline wasn't profitable enough to keep. Kinder and Morgan did and built an empire.

The two men did it in what Oil Patch guys call "midstream assets," which means all the pipelines, tanks, and bulk terminals needed to transport and refine oil and natural gas on its journey from the wellhead to consumers. By 2002, the companies they started, Kinder Morgan Inc. and Kinder Morgan Energy Partners L.P., had become monsters of the midstream. The two interconnected companies own and operate 25,000 miles of pipelines and over 70 terminals. Their combined market capitalization is about $10 billion.

Kinder did it by being the anti-Skilling. Kinder Morgan doesn't do *any* trading. Instead, it focuses on old-fashioned Big Iron and cash flow. In interviews for TV and print outlets, Kinder has said several times that he doesn't care about the price of oil or natural gas. "Everything we do, we get paid a fee for service," Kinder told one reporter in 2001 (Kinder refused interview requests for this book). "The strategy is simple: we move as much product as possible and we try to grow the throughput." Also, Kinder knows all of the risks that come with the business. All of the company's assets are right here in the United States. Buy them, then sit back and collect the fees they generate. There's no commodity risk, no currency risk, no political risk, and no price risk. If there's a dispute and a customer doesn't like your price, let them ship it by truck.

The business structure is stupid simple. Kinder Morgan uses a master limited partnership that is Big Oil's equivalent of a real estate investment trust, or REIT. Partnerships like Kinder Morgan have a significant tax advantage over corporations: They are exempt from corporate income taxes as long as they distribute almost all their profits to investors. Those reliable cash distributions allow the company to pay unit holders a hefty dividend—Kinder Morgan Energy Partners was paying over 7 percent in late June— which makes the equity attractive to institutional investors looking for steady returns.

It's been a remarkably successful strategy, one that's been copied by El Paso, Williams, and Dynegy, all of which have created their own publicly traded limited partnerships in recent years. But Kinder Morgan remains the king of the hill. Selected as the *Houston Chronicle*'s company of the year in May 2002, Kinder Morgan is the biggest master limited partnership in America.[7] Much of its growth is likely attributable to Rich Kinder's cheapness. Kinder Morgan owns no corporate jets. It doesn't advertise or buy tickets to sports events. The company's top executives are limited to base salaries of $200,000 per year. Kinder's salary in 2000 (and in 2001) was a whopping $1—yes, that's one dollar. He got no bonuses or stock options, either. In fact, the company's annual report says Kinder is "not eligible for annual bonuses or option grants."

But he's managing to scrape by. Between January 1997 and January 2002, Kinder turned himself from a decamillionaire into one of the truly Big Rich.

In early 2002, *Forbes* magazine named Kinder as the fourteenth-richest man in Texas and the 351st-richest man on earth. His fortune's estimated value: $1.3 billion, nearly all of it in Kinder Morgan stock. In Houston, his riches are surpassed only by those of oilman George Mitchell, who's worth $1.5 billion, and savvy money manager Fayez Sarofim, who has $1.8 billion. By the way, the billionaire's investment company, Fayez Sarofim & Co., which refused to invest in Enron, is a big investor in Kinder Morgan and owns nearly 7 million units of Kinder Morgan Energy Partners (Sarofim personally owns 2 million of those units).[8]

Rich Kinder enjoys another perk Ken Lay will never have again: friends in the White House. Kinder attended the White House Christmas Party and, earlier this year, had snacks in the White House cafeteria with George W. Bush's political Einstein, Karl Rove. In January 2002, Kinder hosted a fund-raiser for Jeb Bush, brother of the president and governor of Florida.

Kinder is also making his mark in River Oaks. For several years, he's lived on Del Monte, a few doors down from Andy Fastow's new house. But by late June 2002, the house he and Nancy are building on Lazy Lane was starting to take shape. The enormous new house—two giant two-story wings joined by a thirty-foot-high rotunda topped by a convex roof—sits on a 3.5-acre lot and will probably have about 20,000 square feet of living space. The land alone is valued at $4.7 million.

Rich and Nancy's new palace is rising on a prairie of immaculate green grass almost directly across the street from the front entrance of one of Houston's most famous homes, Bayou Bend. The fourteen-acre gardens and house located in a sweeping bend in Buffalo Bayou were owned by oil heiress Ima Hogg (yes, Ima Hogg). She was the daughter of Big Jim Hogg, the first Texas-born governor of the Lone Star State. (The governor earned his nickname honestly. One Texas writer, O. Henry, reported that Hogg was "about the size of two butchers.") Miss Ima never married and became a notable collector of rare early American furniture and art. In 1957, she donated Bayou Bend, now a tourist attraction, to the Houston Museum of Fine Arts.

While Kinder and Kinder Morgan sailed through the Wall Street meltdown with nary a complaint, Houston's other energy giants have been afflicted with serious cases of Enronitis. In March 2001, El Paso, a giant natural gas company that, like Enron, jumped into the electricity generation and energy trading markets, had a market capitalization of $34.2 billion. By the end of June 2002, its market capitalization was just $11 billion. Dynegy, another resident of Houston's Energy Alley that copied Enron's moves into trading and broadband, was worth $15.6 billion in early 2001. By June 2002, the company was being investigated by the Securities and Exchange Commission for allegations of financial wrongdoing and was worth just $2.76 billion. Williams Companies, the Tulsa-based company that convinced Enron to get into the broadband game, had been worth $20.4 billion. By the end of June 2002, it was worth $3.68 billion.

The collapse of Enron took a big human toll, too. On June 2, 2002, El Paso's treasurer, Charles Rice, committed suicide. His death followed the suicide of Enron's Cliff Baxter in January. At Dynegy, the company's founder and CEO, Chuck Watson, the man who believed he could take over Enron, was forced out of the company in May. He was followed a few weeks later by the company's CFO, Rob Doty, who quit about the same time that Dynegy announced it was laying off several hundred workers. El Paso, Dynegy, and Williams are all undergoing huge restructuring plans. All are planning to sell assets and drastically cut the amount of resources they allocate to trading.

Of course, these companies aren't alone. The implosions of WorldCom, Tyco, and other companies are symptomatic of the system that allowed Enron to happen. That system is seriously broken and needs immediate reform.

On June 24, 2002, Felix Rohatyn, a former managing director of Lazard Freres, wrote an opinion piece in the *Wall Street Journal* that offered several excellent reforms. The first on Rohatyn's list: *independent* corporate directors. The move would mean that corporate boards would no longer be solely controlled by the company's CEO and his cronies. Rohatyn recommended that pension funds, particularly the big public pension funds like the California Public Employees' Retirement System (which is one of many funds suing Enron), nominate their own candidates to corporate boards. "It's in their interest to do so," wrote Rohatyn. "After all, the collapse of Enron cost public pension funds about $3 billion."[9]

Second, Rohatyn recommended that Wall Street banks must be more closely regulated. For more than six decades, the big banks were regulated by the Glass-Steagall Act, a law created in 1933 that kept banks, insurance companies, and brokerage houses from merging with each other. The law that repealed Glass-Steagall, the Gramm-Leach-Bliley Financial Services Modernization Act—named for the Republicans who sponsored it, Senator Phil Gramm of Texas, Representative Jim Leach of Iowa, and Representative Thomas Bliley of Virginia, and signed into law in 1999—allows big banks to offer an unprecedented array of services. It also allows them to have unprecedented conflicts of interest.

In his op-ed piece, Rohatyn said conflicts of interest among Wall Street banks have become "rampant because we have gone too far in a deregulatory direction. . . . The securities industry and its regulators must police the behavior of investment houses and their analysts."

One place to start those regulations is with J.P. Morgan Chase, the giant bank that advised Enron during its merger talks with Dynegy. In addition to acting as adviser, for which it was to be paid an estimated $45 million, J.P. Morgan Chase had helped the beleaguered company raise $1 billion in loans—backed by the value of Enron's pipelines—to keep the company afloat during the merger. The bank was an investor in Andy Fastow's LJM2 scheme. Morgan Chase was also involved in a series of highly questionable transactions with Enron that were known inside Enron as "prepaids." These deals, the most famous of which was a $394-million transaction called Mahonia, allowed Enron to disguise what was essentially a loan by presenting it as a long-term commodity contract. (Several large insurers who provided surety bonds to cover the bank's exposure on the Mahonia deal are being sued by J.P. Morgan Chase, in the bank's effort to recover the $965 million in bond coverage. The insurers want the suit dismissed and are alleging the bank acted improperly in the transaction.) Throughout all of J.P. Morgan Chase's dealings with Enron, the company's own equities analyst, Anatol Feygin, was covering Enron and guiding investors concerning the value of the company's stock. Not surprisingly, Feygin had a "long-term buy" recommendation on Enron stock, a rating he maintained until the Dynegy merger deal collapsed.

Thus, when it came to Enron, J.P. Morgan Chase was an adviser, a lender, an investor, and a source of completely unbiased, objective stock research.

Finally, Rohatyn said America's corporations must begin dealing honestly with stock options. This suggestion should be a no-brainer. Stock options cost shareholders money, and yet the current financial reporting requirements do not reflect that truth. Rohatyn's recommendation was simple: Make companies charge the cost of any stock grants against the company's revenues in the year they are granted. Rohatyn was following up on Federal Reserve Chairman—and winner of the Enron Prize—Alan Greenspan's recommendation a month earlier that the accounting method used for stock options be reformed. Rohatyn also suggested that outright grants be used, not options. By granting stock, he said the executives' interests would be immediately aligned with those of the individual stockholders.

Although proper accounting for stock options has many prominent backers, President George W. Bush and several powerful Democratic members of Congress, including Senator Joe Lieberman, want to keep the old system just the way it is. Stock options are the holy grail of the technology and general business lobby, and those interests have lobbied Congress heavily to prevent any meaningful reforms from occurring.

Another area needs to be more closely regulated: derivatives. The notional value of the global over-the-counter derivatives market is about $100 trillion. That's ten times the total of America's gross domestic product. To put that in perspective, the total value of the American corporate equities market is about $15 trillion. Derivatives—the complex contracts between corporations—are almost completely unregulated, and that means that investors cannot accurately gauge the value or threats posed by the derivatives. Derivatives, one stock analyst told me, have become "Wall Street's dirty secret." It's time for those secrets to be brought out into the open and to allow federal regulators to examine the financial soundness of the companies that are risking billions of dollars in over-the-counter derivatives like the ones that Enron handled.

The reforms are simple: People who deal in derivatives must be licensed, and they should have to report to an agency like the Securities and Exchange Commission or the Commodity Futures Trading Commission. Derivatives dealers should be required to post agreed-upon amounts of capital to collateralize their trading positions. Finally, the derivatives marketplace must be made more uniform, with policing by regulators who can establish price limits, listing requirements, and other trading parameters.

The bottom line on derivatives is easy to understand: If derivatives dealers want to trade with, and act like, banks and securities dealers, then they should be regulated like banks and securities dealers.

The accounting business has to change, too. There are some simple possible changes that would make corporate accounting more transparent. William W. (Bill) Cooper, a professor emeritus of finance and management at the University of Texas, has offered a good solution: Require firms that use mark-to-market accounting to also report their financial statements using accrual (cost) accounting. That way, investors and analysts will be able to discern how aggressively the firm is pricing various assets and liabilities. "Once you move to mark to market, you don't have the documentation that you have in cost accounting," said Cooper, at an Enron-focused seminar in Austin in late February.

Cooper didn't make his recommendation lightly. Nor can he be easily dismissed. Still spry and cantankerous at age eighty-seven, he's a member of the Accounting Hall of Fame. He has taught at Carnegie Mellon University and Harvard. In the mid-1930s, Cooper worked for a small but growing Chicago-based accounting firm called Arthur Andersen.[9] Simply stated, Cooper knows what he's talking about. And his argument makes sense. If Enron had been required to report its financial results using accrual accounting alongside its mark-to-market results, investors could easily have seen that the company was booking enormous revenues from long-term contracts and that future revenue growth would have been difficult—if not impossible—to maintain.

Another reform that needs to occur right away is the one that Arthur Levitt tried to push through the Securities and Exchange Commission in 2000: Prohibit auditors from providing consulting services to the companies they audit. This may seem like an easy reform to pass in the wake of the Enron scandal, but by summer 2002, the Congress was still divided over the matter. It wasn't getting any help from the White House. President George W. Bush appointed Harvey Pitt to succeed Levitt at the commission. Pitt, the man the Big Five accounting firms hired in 2000 to help them defeat Levitt's reform movement, was taking the same stance now that he was running the agency: that is, there's no reason to prohibit accounting firms from providing consulting to the firms they also audit.

While the Bush administration dawdles, the accounting profession is going through the biggest upheaval in its history. And the June 15, 2002, conviction of Arthur Andersen on federal charges of obstruction of justice assures that upheaval will continue. During the trial, it was revealed that Andersen shredded hundreds of pounds of Enron documents even though it knew the Securities and Exchange Commission had begun looking into Enron. Within weeks of the conviction, Andersen, which had $9 billion in revenue in 2001 as well as 85,000 employees, had nearly disappeared altogether. Meanwhile, the other big accounting firms were busily scrambling to stay in business and out of the courthouse.

The most obvious way to improve the auditing process is to increase the budget of the Securities and Exchange Commission, an agency that has long been undermanned and underfunded. Despite the Enron debacle and numerous other scandals, President Bush seems to believe the agency doesn't need any more resources. In his initial 2003 budget, Bush proposed giving the agency $467 million, a scant increase over the SEC's 2002 budget of $437.9 million. (Bush later advocated a $100 million increase for the SEC.) The U.S. House of Representatives has proposed giving the agency $776 million in 2003. But even that might not be enough. Laura Unger, the former acting chairman of the SEC, has said the agency could use as much as $1 billion per year to handle the hundreds of investigations it currently has underway. In March 2002, the General Accounting Office said the shortage of money and staff at the SEC was forcing the agency to "be selective in its enforcement activities and have lengthened the time required to complete certain enforcement investigations."

Meanwhile, back at Enron, the outrages big and small continue.

In January, the company sold its trading business—you know, the one that was supposed to be the most valuable part of the company—to the investment banking firm, UBS Warburg. The sales price: free. Yes, Enron *gave* its trading business to UBS in exchange for a promise that Enron and its creditors would get one-third of any future profits. But by all accounts, there have been no profits. By late June, most of Enron's best traders, including John Arnold, who got millions in bonuses from the company in 2001, had left the company, and Enron's once-formidable trading floor had almost completely ceased operations.

In February, Ken Lay, Andy Fastow, Rick Causey, Michael Kopper, and Rick Buy all appeared before Congress. All of them took the Fifth Amendment and refused to answer any questions. Jeff Skilling, who's always eager to demonstrate his intellectual superiority, did not take the Fifth. Instead, a combative Skilling testified for hours before lawmakers and insisted throughout that he knew nothing about any financial shenanigans at Enron. "If there was anything inappropriate," in Enron's accounting methods, "I would never have done it."

In March, Enron sold Wessex Water—the jewel in Rebecca Mark's Azurix crown—to a Malaysian company, YTL Power International, for $1.76 billion. Enron paid $2.88 billion for Wessex in 1998.

In mid-April, the company, under the direction of turnaround specialist Stephen Cooper, told a group of Enron employees that Enron's total liabilities in its bankruptcy could be as high as $100 billion. On April 22, Enron notified the Securities and Exchange Commission that its finances were in such disarray it could not come up with a balance sheet and that it would not be filing any financial statements for the foreseeable future.

In early June, the ballpark formerly known as Enron Field, the House That Lay Built, got its third name in two years. In early 2002, Enron Field became Astros Field after the baseball team paid Enron $2.1 million to take its scandal-scarred name off the stadium. It remained Astros Field until Houston-based Minute Maid, a division of Coca-Cola, paid over $100 million for the naming rights. On June 5, the stadium became Minute Maid Park. In announcing the deal, Houston Astros owner Drayton McLane said he chose the juice maker because of its "great financial stability" and because it is "about what we represent—it's a wholesome company."

About the same time the ballpark got renamed, the last four remaining directors who served on the Enron board before its bankruptcy turned in their resignations. Wendy Gramm, Herbert Winokur, Norman Blake, and Robert Belfer all quit.

Their departure marked the end of an epoch at Enron. Of the players who had key roles in the company's dramatic rise and fall, only

Sherron Watkins remained. Her salary, according to people inside the company, is approximately $200,000. In mid-May, a bankruptcy court judge ordered Enron to pay her legal bills, in the amount of $220,000. She is now writing a book about her experience at Enron with Houston writer Mimi Swartz.

As for Enron's big remaining assets, the company continues to take a beating. By mid-June, Enron's finance people were putting the finishing touches on paperwork that will allow the company to write off its entire $900-million investment in the Indian power plant, Dabhol. The Portland General investment has been similarly disastrous, particularly for the utility's employees, who had their retirement funds completely wiped out.

On June 17, Enron filed documents in bankruptcy court that showed total cash payments of $309.8 million to a group of 144 top Enron executives during 2001. In addition, those same executives cashed in stock options worth $311.7 million.[11] There were lots of other perquisites that haven't been made public. According to one Enron insider, since the bankruptcy the company has been canceling club memberships all over Houston. When Enron filed for bankruptcy, the insider said, the company was paying for twenty-nine different country club memberships, each of which were costing the company an average of $28,000 per year.

Sherri Saunders doesn't belong to any country clubs.

By late June 2002—six months after handing out her résumés to the recruiters at the job fair at Enron Field—she had finally found a job that would be good for the long haul. A few months after getting the boot from Enron, she caught on with a small financial firm, but the benefits weren't that good. In early May, she heard about a position at the Houston Medical Center. She interviewed and got a job working as a secretary for the man who runs all the facilities at the complex. So she was undergoing a crash course on the mammoth medical center's transportation and construction projects and its cleaning contractors. It was a bit overwhelming. But Sherri said, "I think it's a great place to get started to learn about the hospital." And her new job has life insurance and top-notch health coverage. "Since I'm the sole support for Bill and [me], I just had to have those benefits."

She'd only been on the job since May 28, so she didn't want me to come visit her at work. She didn't want to create the wrong impression, or at least not appear conspicuous so quickly after being hired. So we talked over the phone several times and traded gossip about Enron.

She and Bill were still living in the same $1,200-a-month, two-bedroom apartment. It's in West Houston in a quiet neighborhood. It has 1,250 square feet of living space. "Probably about the size of Ken Lay's bathroom," Sherri said with a laugh. She and Bill are trying to be upbeat. Their life savings are nearly gone, and Sherri knows she'll probably never have enough money to retire. She'll just have to keep working, probably for the rest of her life. She and Bill still want to do a bit of traveling. But as the newest hire in her department, Sherri knows there won't be any long vacations anytime soon.

Sherri had been reading the papers, of course, following all the latest news. She hadn't been to Jus' Stuff but wanted to know all the details about the shop. When I mentioned I'd driven by Rebecca Mark's house in River Oaks, Sherri lamented that she wished she'd bought stock in Kinder Morgan instead of Azurix. But for some reason, she and Bill had invested $2,000 in Azurix. Why? "Because Rebecca Mark was the golden child. She spent hundreds of thousands of dollars on whatever she wanted. So when she started Azurix, a lot of employees jumped on that bandwagon." Sherri had bought the hype.

She was mad—but not bitter—about her life post-Enron. She'd always worked, and now she was just working somewhere besides Enron. "Opportunities abound," at the medical center, she said. "People are always leaving. Jobs are up for bid and I'll be looking. It's a great place to learn."

As for her pay, Sherri says the new job pays her $36,000. "I was making $46,000 to $48,000 at Enron, and more than that when you count bonus and overtime," she said. "But you know, you can't get greedy."

52

Aftermath

SEPTEMBER 5, 2003
ENRON CLOSING PRICE: $0.05
DYNEGY CLOSING PRICE: $3.57

By the summer of 2003, it was clear that Enron had merely swapped one set of pirates for another set of pirates.

Sure, Jeff Skilling, Andy Fastow, and the others had left the building at 1400 Smith Street with their pockets bulging with cash, but the hot shots who took their places after Enron went bankrupt have managed to stuff their pockets with cash, too.

Consider the case of Neil Batson. By mid-2003, Batson and his law firm, Atlanta-based Alston & Bird, had been unraveling Enron's finances for eleven months. During that period the firm had billed Enron some $60 million in fees and expenses. And yet, despite working as Enron's examiner for all that time, Batson and his minions failed to realize that they might have a conflict of interest in the case. In late May 2003, Batson finally decided to inform the bankruptcy court judge overseeing Enron's case that another auditor should be added to the bankruptcy team because Alston & Bird had some conflicts of interest regarding three banks and two accounting firms that had done business with Enron.[1] Batson's firm told the bankruptcy court that it could not analyze the roles played by Bank of America, Royal Bank of Canada, UBS Warburg, PricewaterhouseCoopers, and KPMG. However, he didn't specify what conflicts of interest Alston & Bird had regarding those firms. Bankruptcy Judge Arthur Gonzalez admonished Batson for not raising the conflict issue sooner, but he approved the appointment of another examiner to look at the five companies and what role they might have had in the Enron disaster.

Batson's belated realization about his conflicts astounded several people who worked at Enron. One longtime Enron employee, a lawyer who'd been working on the reorganization plan, said he knew shortly after Batson was hired that there would be conflicts. "Batson should have seen the conflict immediately. We saw that the banks had entanglements early on," he said.

Batson wasn't the only pirate. Stephen Cooper, the turnaround specialist from New York, also had his hand in Enron's till. Enron was paying Cooper a salary of $1.3 million to help it figure out how to emerge from bankruptcy. But Cooper was making money in other ways. The bankruptcy court allowed him to hire thirty people from his firm, Kroll Zolfo Cooper, at a cost of $864,000 each annually.[2] Those people were charged with directing Enron's turnaround. They might have been qualified for that task, but Cooper's new hires didn't win many friends or influence many longtime Enron staffers. According to Enron insiders, several members of Cooper's team would fly to Houston on Monday morning and then fly home on Friday afternoon. Their lodging and food expenses, were, of course, paid by Enron. And then there was the question of why Cooper wasn't hiring people in Houston to do those jobs. "They could have found lots of people with good credentials right here in Houston," said one longtime Enron employee. "And they could have paid them $150,000 instead of $864,000."

Another law firm, Milbank Tweed Hadley & McCloy, which was representing Enron's creditors, was also doing well. Its fee: $725 an hour. Meanwhile, Weil Gotshal & Manges, Enron's lead bankruptcy counsel, was leading the billings race. By the end of May 2003 it had submitted bills totaling $93 million. In the first seventeen months of Enron's bankruptcy, lawyers and accountants working on the case had done about one million hours of work. Their total billings for that time period: $496 million. That figure makes the Enron bankruptcy the most expensive bankruptcy in American history.[3] Put another way, the amount spent by the lawyers and accountants is nearly twice the amount spent to build the baseball stadium formerly known as Enron Field.

Of course, the lawyers had plenty of critics. Texas Attorney General Greg Abbott denounced the huge fees, saying that the lawyers working the case were "lining their pockets. There is a lot of money sloshing around, and the participants are taking it away from the people who really deserve it."[4]

Finally, on July 11, 2003, Cooper's team revealed their plan for Enron's future. And—surprise!—they found that Enron was really just a pipeline company and that the pipelines were its only significant assets.

Cooper's Chapter 11 reorganization plan offered to pay the company's creditors less than 20 cents on the dollar. Enron Corp. would cease to exist. In its place, creditors would be given control of a new pipeline company—that's right, an old-fashioned, boring pipeline company—called CrossCountry Energy Corp. CrossCountry's main assets would be 9,900 miles of natural gas pipeline with a total capacity of 8.5 billion cubic feet per day.[5] After bankruptcy, Enron would look a lot like it had back in the early 1980s, when pipelines—and the cash they generated—were viewed as good, stable businesses.

Enron's creditors would also get stock in Portland General Electric, the electric utility in Oregon that Enron purchased to solidify its position in the power trading business. The city of Portland wants to buy the utility back from Enron, but the two sides have been unable to agree on a price. Finally, all of Enron's remaining foreign gas and power assets would be consolidated, with creditors controlling a Cayman Islands–based entity called Prisma.[6] The Prisma entity would have assets worth about $1 billion.

The bankruptcy court will have to decide whether Cooper's reorganization plan becomes a reality. For the court to approve the plan, Enron's creditors will have to agree that the reorganization proposal is the best option available. About 29,000 "proofs of claim" have been filed against Enron by its creditors. In the documents released by Enron on July 11, 2003, the company revealed that 22,000 of those claims totaled $310 billion. The filing said there were another 7,000 claims that hadn't yet been given a dollar value. In addition, more claims could be filed against Enron as other subsidiaries go bankrupt.

While the bankruptcy issues continue to slog along, a battalion of lawyers continue pushing a myriad of lawsuits against Enron, its board of directors, its lead executives, banks, accountants, lawyers, and anybody else who came within a mile or so of 1400 Smith. By mid-2003, some 100 Enron-related lawsuits were pending in state and federal courts.

One of the suits came from the U.S. Department of Labor, which sued Enron and twenty company officers on June 26, 2003. The suit, filed under the Employee Retirement Income Security Act, alleges that the Enron board of directors, along with Skilling, Ken Lay, and several others, are responsible for the loss of hundreds of millions of dollars invested in Enron retirement accounts. On the day the suit was filed, Labor Secretary Elaine Chao said the suit, "will strengthen the American work force's confidence in their retirement savings."[7] Perhaps it will, but Chao and her lawyers will have to queue up behind a whole bunch of other attorneys.

The biggest lawsuit is the one being brought by Milberg Weiss Bershad Hynes & Lerach on behalf of the University of California Board of Regents. Everything about the lawsuit is huge. More than 100 lawyers are involved. The volume of paper is mind-boggling. More than seventy-five million pages of documents will be catalogued and put into a document depository for the litigation. Of that number, lawyers expect to get about thirty-six million pages from Enron and another twenty-two million pages from the financial institutions.[8]

The showdown in the courthouse might be averted if the parties are able to reach a settlement. In July 2003, U.S. District Court Judge Melinda Harmon ordered the plaintiffs and the defendants to go into mediation on the lawsuit. But it's doubtful that that route will be effective. Look for a trial in that case to start in the fall of 2005.

Players Update

Everyone at Enron knew Andy Fastow was greedy. But no one knew exactly how greedy he was until his indictment, issued by the Department of Justice, was made public on April 30, 2003. According to the indictment, Andy Fastow and his wife, Lea, made $2.1 million in 1998. The next year, the couple's income was $9.1 million. In 2000, their income reached the astonishing sum of $48.5 million. But somehow, even $48 million wasn't quite enough for the high-living Fastows. The indictment also charges that the couple filed fraudulent income tax returns for each of those three years.

In all, Andy Fastow faces eighty federal counts, including wire fraud, securities fraud, mail fraud, money laundering, and conspiracy to commit wire fraud. If convicted on the charges, he faces over 100 years in prison. His wife, Lea, is in similar trouble. In addition to the fraudulent income tax charge, Lea Fastow was indicted for alleged money laundering and conspiracy to commit wire fraud.

The indictments against the Fastows were part of a highly publicized spate of indictments made public in late April. Other former Enron Big Shots who were indicted include former Enron Broadband Services CEO Ken Rice and another former CEO of the broadband unit, Joseph Hirko. In addition, the unit's former COO, Kevin Hannon, was indicted along with former senior vice presidents Scott Yeager and Rex Shelby and former EBS executives Kevin Howard and Michael Krautz.

While the Enron Broadband guys were doing "perp walks" in front of the TV cameras, other notable Enron refugees have been remarkably quiet. Indeed, Lou Pai and Thomas White, the former bosses of Enron Energy Services, as well as Rebecca Mark, the deal diva at Enron International and Azurix whose bad bets cost Enron at least $2 billion, have been nearly invisible.

There was a bit of news on Pai in February 2003. That's when the Senate Finance Committee released a report on the Enron scandal stating that Pai, the math whiz and stripper aficionado, had—in addition to his salary and stock sales of more than $270 million—been given a one-eighth interest in a jet aircraft by Enron.[9] The jet, a Hawker 800, sells for about $13 million. The jet appears to be just one more example of Pai's absolutely insatiable appetite for money and prestige. You may recall that Pai was the Enron executive who was too darn busy to drive all the way to Houston Intercontinental Airport to board one of Enron's jets, and had the Enron pilots fly the jet to Sugar Land, a distance of about forty miles, to pick him up. Pai's fellow Big Shot at Enron Energy Services, Thomas White, left Enron for a job within the Bush administration as Secretary of the Army. But in April 2003, shortly after American troops got to Baghdad, White was fired by his boss, Defense Secretary Donald Rumsfeld. Meanwhile, Rebecca Mark continues to live very comfortably in her swank house in River Oaks. Her name has been off the society pages.

The former senator from Enron, Phil Gramm, is now working for Swiss banking giant UBS Warburg, which coincidentally is the very company that took over Enron's trading operation in 2002. Gramm's job at the Zurich-based company is to advise clients on corporate finance issues and strategy. Gramm didn't reveal how much he is earning at UBS. But before leaving the Senate, Gramm allowed that his pay at UBS would be "a little better than I'm doing here." Given Gramm's experience in banking regulations, hiring him was clearly a coup for UBS. When asked if he was going to be using his influence in Washington to help UBS, Gramm gave a puzzling answer, saying that UBS was "hiring me for what I know and not who I know. I hope both are valuable."[10]

In other words, Phil Gramm was selling access to the Rolodex he built while in office. And UBS was the firm that offered him the most money. Meanwhile, Gramm's wife, former Enron board member Wendy Gramm, who is a named defendant in several Enron-related lawsuits, has kept a very low profile.

Sherron Watkins continues to do well thanks to her canonization by the media. Watkins, the accountant who took her concerns about Enron to the company's boss, Ken Lay, was repeatedly portrayed as one of the few honest people at Enron. In late 2002, *Time* magazine named

Watkins (along with Cynthia Cooper of WorldCom and Colleen Rowley of the FBI) "Whistleblower of the Year." The three women had their pictures on the cover of *Time* and were feted for what the magazine called their "ordinary demeanor but exceptional guts and sense."[11] The exposure has been lucrative for Watkins. By mid-2003, Watkins was telling reporters that she was being paid $20,000 to $25,000 per speech and that she was doing two speeches per month.[12]

The book that Watkins wrote with journalist Mimi Swartz, *Power Failure*, appeared to be selling well, though it arrived in bookstores on the eve of the U.S. war in Iraq and probably didn't get the attention its publishers had hoped for. In addition to her speaking fees, Watkins was formalizing plans to go into the consulting business, advising corporations on board functions and ethics. And while Watkins has become a media darling, she has some detractors. In an op-ed in the *Washington Times*, Charles Ganske of the conservative American Freedom Center in Austin wrote that Watkins "blew the whistle in a soundproof room. She never aired the concerns she expressed in her memo and conversation with Mr. Lay to regulators, the press, or the company's board, all of whom she could have contacted anonymously." He continued, "a true whistleblower would not have participated in fraudulent transactions, remained silent after Mr. Lay failed to act, and cashed in by selling her own Enron stock while armed with inside information."[13]

Meanwhile, Ken and Linda Lay are still living in the lap of luxury in their posh condo at the Huntingdon. They have, however, quit the Aspen scene. In late 2002 and early 2003, the Lays sold all four of their properties in the Colorado resort town, for a total of $22.6 million. Alas, they took a loss on the properties of about $1 million.[14]

While the Lays have become social lepers in Houston, Nancy and Rich Kinder continue to do very well, thank you very much. On July 19, 2003, Nancy Kinder was one of the lead organizers of a fund-raiser at Houston's Westin Galleria Hotel for George W. Bush's 2004 re-election campaign. About 1,500 members of Houston's smart set paid $2,000 apiece to hear Bush's stump speech. (He didn't mention Enron.)

By the time of the fund-raiser, the Kinders' enormous new house on

Lazy Lane was nearing completion and Kinder Morgan's pipelines continued to be enormously profitable. After George W. Bush's tax cut plan was passed by Congress, Kinder Morgan announced that it would increase the dividend payments to its unitholders. That meant that in 2003, the Kinders would receive about $35.2 million in cash dividends. And yet, thanks to the Bush tax cut, they would pay a mere 15 percent of that income in taxes.[15] By comparison, the wealthiest people in America faced marginal income tax rates in 2003 of 37.6 percent. Even middle class taxpayers earning $90,000 or so per year were paying taxes at rates that were about two times the rate paid by the Kinders. All of which proves that the rich really *are* different from the rest of us: They pay less taxes.

Legislation/Reform Update

One of the most remarkable documents to come out of the post-Enron era was produced on September 18, 2002. On that day, some of the most powerful regulators in the Bush administration sent a letter to U.S. Senators Zell Miller and Michael Crapo to express their opposition to regulation of financial derivatives. In their letter, the regulators—Federal Reserve Chairman Alan Greenspan, Treasury Secretary Paul O'Neill, Securities and Exchange Commission Chairman Harvey Pitt, and Commodity Futures Trading Commission Chairman James Newsome—insisted that derivatives did not need to be regulated because they have "been a major contributor to our economy's ability to respond to the stresses and challenges of the last two years." A then-pending Senate proposal to regulate derivatives, they warned, could increase "the vulnerability of our economy to potential future stresses."

Greenspan and his pals apparently decided to overlook the role that over-the-counter financial derivatives played in the Enron bankruptcy. But some of America's biggest investors think the chairman of the Fed is making a big mistake. In March 2003, the world's smartest capitalist, Warren Buffett, weighed in on the derivatives question. In his annual epistle to Berskhire Hathaway shareholders he warned about the dangers of derivatives and pointed to the failures of Enron and Long-Term

Capital Management as examples of those dangers. Buffett wrote that he and his longtime partner, Charlie Munger, agreed on derivatives: "We view them as time bombs, both for the parties that deal in them and the economic system." He pointed out that many dealers in derivatives are not adequately capitalized and that "large amounts of risk, particularly credit risk, have become concentrated in the hands of relatively few derivatives dealers, who in addition trade extensively with one another. The troubles of one could quickly infect the others. On top of that, these dealers are owed huge amounts by nondealer counterparties." The billionaire from Omaha concluded by calling derivatives "financial weapons of mass destruction, carrying dangers that, while now latent, are potentially lethal."[16]

Buffett and others who are pushing for reform of the derivatives market are not getting much traction in Washington. And the derivatives market continues to grow like kudzu. By the end of 2002, the total notional value of financial derivatives in global markets exceeded $141 trillion, according to figures compiled by the Bank for International Settlements.[17]

Although little progress has been made on policing derivatives, corporate America has finally begun to get religion when it comes to another key area of reform: stock options. Some of the changes may have been spurred by the Senate Finance Committee's February 2003 report. The report found that Enron avoided paying federal taxes in four of the five years before it went bankrupt. Much of that tax evasion was made possible because of Enron's massive use of stock options.

In the wake of the Enron scandal, dozens of companies abandoned the wholesale use of stock options as a form of executive compensation. Perhaps the most important convert to the new reality of stock options is software giant Microsoft. In July 2003 it announced that it would no longer award stock options to its employees. Instead, it would give stock grants. By using stock grants, Microsoft ensures that employees' interests are in line with shareholders'. If the stock goes up, employees and investors both do well. If it goes down, then employees share in the suffering.

The other key reform established since the failure of Enron is the Sarbanes-Oxley Act. Passed by Congress, the measure requires a number of changes in corporate governance. It requires companies to set up a confidential system through which employees can report malfeasance. It requires a company's CEO and chief financial officer to swear to the accuracy of their quarterly and annual financial reports. The law also requires lawyers to notify the Securities and Exchange Commission if they find material violation of financial rules and they cannot resolve the matter with the company for whom they are working.[18]

The requirements of Sarbanes-Oxley, combined with more aggressive prosecutions by the Securities and Exchange Commission, should stem the flood of corporate shenanigans for the next few years. But the new regulations and new policing will not protect investors forever. Crooks will always be able to find a way to cheat the system and steal from investors.

Enron will happen again. It's only a matter of time.

Appendix

The Enron Scorecard

THE BAD, THE WORSE, AND THE UNINDICTED

The Bad

Kenneth Lay, chairman and CEO, Enron Corp. Lay continues to live quietly at the Huntingdon, his high rise River Oaks condo. Lay's lawyers continue to insist that Lay did nothing wrong.

Jeffrey Skilling, president and CEO, Enron Corp. Prosecutors want to indict Skilling in the worst way. But Enron insiders say prosecutors cannot find his signature on any of the key documents. Skilling is still living in his house in River Oaks. A six-foot-high security fence and automatic gate surrounding the property were completed in mid-2002.

The Worse

Andrew Fastow, chief financial officer, Enron Corp. Indicted. Facing about eighty federal counts including securities fraud, conspiracy to commit wire fraud, money laundering, insider trading, and filing false income tax returns. If convicted on all counts, he faces over 100 years in prison. Federal authorities also want to seize over $21 million in accounts owned by Andy and Lea Fastow as well as their family home in the Southampton neighborhood. Trial will begin April 20, 2004.

Lea Fastow, wife of Andy Fastow and assistant treasurer, Enron Corp. Indicted. Faces charges of conspiracy to commit wire fraud and money laundering, as well as four counts of filing false income tax returns. Trial will begin February 10, 2004.

Ben Glisan, treasurer, Enron Corp. In prison. In September 2003, Glisan pled guilty to a single count of conspiracy to commit wire and securities fraud and began serving a five-year prison term. Glisan also agreed to forfeit more than

$900,000 in profits he made from Fastow's Southampton partnership. He also agreed not to seek a refund of $412,000 in income taxes he paid on those profits. Glisan was the first Enron official to go to prison.

Michael Kopper, finance executive, Enron Corp. Kopper was the very first Enron executive to cooperate with the government and plead guilty. In August 2002 he waived indictment and pled guilty to two counts of conspiracy. Settled civil charges with the SEC by agreeing to pay $12 million. Also faces up to fifteen years in prison. Will be sentenced in early 2004.

Lawrence Lawyer, finance executive, Enron Corp. Waived indictment and pled guilty to filing a false income tax return. Feds alleged he didn't report $80,000 in kickbacks. Faces up to three years in prison. Will be sentenced in early 2004.

Dan Boyle, finance executive, Enron Corp. Indicted. Boyle allegedly facilitated a deal between Merrill Lynch and an Enron partnership involving Nigerian power barges. Faces charges of conspiracy to commit wire fraud and falsifying accounting records. Trial will begin August 17, 2004.

Kenneth Rice, CEO, Enron Broadband Services. Indicted. Rice was the star of a 218-count indictment filed in Houston on April 29, 2003. The Securities and Exchange Commission and the Department of Justice allege the let-the-good-times-roll boss of Enron Broadband was a key player in a scheme to inflate the value of Enron's stock. He faces charges of conspiracy to commit wire and securities fraud, wire fraud, securities fraud, insider trading, and money laundering. Feds allege he sold $53 million of Enron stock at inflated prices. Feds have also moved to seize several of Rice's fast cars, including a 1995 Ferrari F355, worth about $80,000, and a 2001 Ferrari 360, worth about $200,000. Trial date: April 2004.

Joseph Hirko, CEO, Enron Broadband Services. Indicted. Hirko was part of the original Portland General gang that dreamed up the idea of using the utility's right-of-way to string fiber optic cable. Faces charges of conspiracy to commit wire and securities fraud, wire fraud, securities fraud, insider trading, and money laundering. Feds allege he sold $35 million of Enron stock at inflated prices. Trial date: April 2004.

Kevin Hannon, COO, Enron Broadband Services. Indicted. Hannon was Ken Rice's right-hand man, and like Rice, he knew next to nothing about fiber optics and telecom. Faces charges of conspiracy to commit wire and securities fraud, insider trading, and money laundering. Feds allege he sold $8 million of Enron stock at inflated prices. Trial date: April 2004.

Rex Shelby, senior vice president, Enron Broadband Services. Indicted. Faces charges of conspiracy to commit wire and securities fraud, wire fraud, securities fraud, insider trading, and money laundering. Feds allege he sold $35 million of Enron stock at inflated prices. Trial date: April 2004.

Scott Yeager, senior vice president for strategic development, Enron Broadband Services. Indicted. Yeager was one of the most technically savvy people at EBS. Faces charges of conspiracy to commit wire and securities fraud, wire fraud, securities fraud, insider trading, and money laundering. Feds allege he sold $55 million of

Enron stock at inflated prices. Trial date: April 2004.

Kevin Howard, vice president of finance, Enron Broadband Services. Indicted. Faces charges of conspiracy to commit wire and securities fraud, securities fraud, wire fraud, and making false statements to federal investigators. Feds allege he was a key player in Project Braveheart, the scam Enron used to improperly book $111 million in revenue associated with a video-on-demand project the company launched in 2000 with Blockbuster Inc. Trial date: April 2004.

Michael Krautz, accountant, Enron Broadband Services. Indicted. Faces charges of conspiracy to commit wire and securities fraud, securities fraud, wire fraud, and making false statements to federal investigators. Feds allege he and Howard worked together on Project Braveheart. Trial date: April 2004

Timothy Belden, managing director, Enron Corp. Belden pled guilty to one count of conspiracy to commit wire fraud in connection with efforts to manipulate energy prices in California. Forfeited $2.1 million and faces up to five years in prison and a $250,000 fine.

Jeffrey Richter, trader, Enron Corp. Pled guilty to conspiracy to commit wire fraud and making false statements to the FBI. Richter faces up to five years in prison and a $250,000 fine for each count.

John Forney, trader, Enron Corp. Arrested in June 2003, and released on bond. He was later indicted on one count of conspiracy to commit wire fraud. The charge was related to Enron's apparent effort to manipulate California's electricity markets.

Hunter Shively, trader, Enron Corp. In March 2003, the Commodity Futures Trading Commission charged that Shively had taken part in manipulating gas prices. The case is still pending.

Kristina Mordaunt, lawyer, Enron Broadband Services. Mordaunt was one of the Enron employees who participated in Fastow's Southampton partnership. She agreed to forfeit $1.6 million in ill-gotten gains to the SEC.

Kathy Lynn, finance executive, Enron Corp. Agreed to forfeit $218,326 to the SEC.

Anne Yeager, finance executive, Enron Corp. Agreed to forfeit $45,000 to the SEC.

Wesley H. Colwell, chief accounting officer, Enron Wholesale Services. In October of 2003, Colwell agreed to pay a $500,000 fine to the federal government to settle charges that he helped manipulate the company's earnings. Colwell, who was a partner at Arthur Andersen before going to Enron, agreed to cooperate with the Securities & Exchange Commission and Justice Department in their investigation into other Enron miscreants. He won't face criminal charges.

The Unindicted

Rebecca Mark, CEO, Azurix, CEO, Enron International. It appears that by leaving Enron in August 2000, the Deal Diva escaped at the right time. She's living comfortably and quietly in River Oaks.

Lou Pai, CEO, Enron Energy Services. Pai continues to live the good life. Although he sold $270 million worth of Enron stock, federal prosecutors appear to be ignoring Pai.

Jeffrey McMahon, treasurer, Enron Corp. McMahon has been a target of prosecutors for months due to his participation in a scheme to sell some power plants owned by Enron in Nigeria.

Richard Causey, chief accounting officer, Enron Corp. Causey's name was in the Houston rumor mill throughout late 2002 and much of 2003, with the presumption that he could be indicted at any time. However, nothing has happened.

Thomas White, vice chairman, Enron Energy Services. Was named Secretary of the Army by George W. Bush. In late April 2003, as the Second Iraq War was ending, Defense Secretary Donald Rumsfeld fired White.

Sources

Various *Houston Chronicle* stories; Department of Justice indictments; Ellen Florian, "Scandal Cheat Sheet," *Fortune*, July 7, 2003, 48–49.

Kenneth N. Gilpin, "Ex-Treasurer of Enron Is Sentenced to 5 Years in Prison," *New York Times*, September 10, 2003.

Notes

1: The Job Fair

1. Gary McWilliams, "The Quiet Man Who's Jolting Utilities," *Business Week*, June 9, 1997.
2. Daniel Yergin, *The Prize: The Epic Quest for Oil, Money, and Power* (New York: Simon & Schuster, 1991), 214.
3. Frank Partnoy, "Testimony of Frank Partnoy," *Hearings before the United States Senate Committee on Governmental Affairs*, 107th Cong., 24 January 2002. Available: http://govt-aff.senate.gov/012402partnoy.htm.
4. All information about Ken Lay's affiliations was taken from various newspaper reports or from the bio of him published on the Enron web site in 2001.

2: John Henry Kirby and the Roots of Enron

1. Bob Burtman, "The Silent Treatment," *OnEarth* (spring 2002): 15, 16.
2. Ibid.
3. David G. McComb, *Houston: The Bayou City* (Austin: University of Texas Press, 1969), 207.
4. Yergin, *The Prize*, 83.
5. Mary Lassell, *John Henry Kirby, Prince of the Pines* (Austin, TX: Encino Press, 1967). This book is the definitive biography of Kirby and was my main source for dates and information on the timber baron.
6. Kenneth Fellows, *Houston Natural Gas Corporation: Its First Fifty Years, 1925–1975* (Houston: Houston Natural Gas Corporation, 1976), 3.
7. See the Kirby Corporation web site. Available: www.kmtc.com/corp/history.cfm.
8. Marks Hinton and Aaron Howard, "Paved in History: The Colorful Stories Behind Houston's Historic Street Names," *Inside Houston Magazine*,

November 2001.

9. Fellows, *Houston Natural Gas Corporation*, 5.
10. Rebecca Busby, *Natural Gas in Nontechnical Language* (Tulsa, OK: PennWell Publishing, 1999), 7.
11. Ibid., 11.
12. Fellows, *Houston Natural Gas Corporation*, 10.
13. Houston Metropolitan Study, *The Houston Metropolitan Study: An Entrepreneurial Community Looks Ahead* (Houston: Houston Metropolitan Study, 1998), 23.
14. Fellows, *Houston Natural Gas Corporation*, 140.
15. Donna K.H. Walters, "Internorth Will Make $2.3-Billion Offer for Houston Natural Gas," *Los Angeles Times*, May 3, 1985.

3: Buy or Be Bought

1. Bettijane Levine, "Feuding Families; Not Just the Sport of the Rich and Famous, Infighting Is an Equal Opportunity Pastime," *Dallas Morning News*, September 28, 1993.
2. Mark Ivey and John Rossant, "The Man Who Strikes Fear in the Heart of the Oil Patch," *Business Week*, November 6, 1989.
3. Ibid.

5: The Lays Move to River Oaks

1. Sally Quinn, "Blond Bombshell from the Texas Boom Town," *Washington Post*, December 17, 1978.
2. Ray Miller, *Ray Miller's Houston* (Austin, TX: Cordovan Press, 1982), 135.
3. Sandy Sheehy, "There Goes the Neighborhood," *Forbes*, October 26, 1992.
4. McComb, *Houston: The Bayou City*, 221.
5. Sheehy, "There Goes the Neighborhood."
6. Ibid.

6: The Valhalla Fiasco

1. Tricia Crisafulli, "Bulk Oil, Nichimen, Among Defendants in Enron Suit Charging Fraudulent Trading," *Platt's Oilgram News*, June 16, 1988.
2. Ibid.
3. Peter H. Frank, "Enron to Close Unit After Costly Trades," *New York Times*, October 23, 1987.

7: "The Smartest Son of a Bitch I've Ever Met"

1. Yergin, *The Prize*, 343.
2. Jeff Nesmith and Ralph K.M. Haurwitz, "Spills and Explosions Reveal Lax Regulation of Powerful Industry," *Austin American-Statesman*, July 22, 2001.
3. Ken Lay, *The Enron Story* (New York: The Newcomen Society of the United States, 1990).
4. Despite such regulation, many argue, rightly, that federal agencies have not been vigilant in policing the pipeline industry on safety issues. Since 1990, fires and explosions from pipelines have killed more than 200 people and

injured more than 1,000 (Nesmith and Haurwitz, "Spills and Explosions Reveal Lax Regulation of Powerful Industry"). However, the steady increase in accidents has not persuaded federal regulators to step up their enforcement and inspection of interstate pipelines. And don't expect that to happen during George W. Bush's administration.

5. Adam Levy, "Inside Enron: CEO Jeffrey Skilling Is Again Propelling the Texas-Based Energy Company into a New Mix of Businesses," *Bloomberg Markets*, May 1, 2001.
6. Tom Skilling continued to pursue meteorology and is now chief meteorologist of WGN-TV in Chicago.
7. John Merwin, "We Don't Learn from Our Clients, We Learn from Each Other," *Forbes*, October 19, 1987.
8. In 1990, Sawhill took over the leadership of The Nature Conservancy. He died in 2000.

8: Banking on the Gas Bank

1. The following web site provides all FERC orders and other useful gas-related information. Available: www.energyservices.net/glossary.htm.
2. Vince Kaminski and John Martin, "Transforming Enron Corporation: The Value of Active Management," *Journal of Applied Corporate Finance* (winter 2001): 43.
3. Mimi Swartz, "How Enron Blew It," *Texas Monthly*, November 2001.
4. Ibid.
5. Lay, *The Enron Story.*
6. By 2002, Rucks and his childhood buddy, Flores, were Big Rich. Flores & Rucks had become Ocean Energy, one of America's biggest independent exploration and production companies.
7. Peter C. Fusaro, *Energy Risk Management: Hedging Strategies and Instruments for the International Energy Markets* (New York: McGraw-Hill, 1998), xiii.
8. Ibid., 73.

9: Mark-to-Market Account-a-Rama

1. There are several biographies of Pacioli. Much of my information on him came from the web site of the Association of Chartered Accountants in the U.S. Available: www.acaus.org/history.

10: Enron Goes International: Teesside

1. In 1947, for reasons that are still unknown, a French ship, the *SS Grandcamp,* holding tons of ammonium nitrate fertilizer, exploded and killed about 600 people, leveling parts of the town of 16,000.
2. These numbers come from John Olson, an energy analyst who worked at Drexel. Lay continued to be an admirer of Milken long after Drexel imploded and Milken went to jail for securities fraud. In 1998, Milken, a convicted felon, gave a speech at an Enron management conference in San Antonio. He delivered his speech while standing in front of a banner that displayed Enron's four values: Respect, Integrity, Communication, and Excellence.

11: The Big Shot Buying Binge

1. Joe R. Feagin, *Free Enterprise City: Houston in Political and Economic Perspective* (New Brunswick, NJ: Rutgers University Press, 1988), 114.
2. Ibid., 121.
3. Ibid., 139.
4. Robert Caro, *Path to Power* (New York: Vintage Books, 1981), 380.
5. Ronnie Dugger, *The Politician: The Life and Times of Lyndon Johnson* (New York: W. W. Norton & Co., 1982), 281.
6. Ibid., 287.
7. Given Brown & Root's strong Houston connections, it is not really surprising that the lead construction company on the contract to build Enron Field was—you guessed it—Brown & Root.
8. Seymour Hersh, "The Spoils of War," *New Yorker*, September 6, 1993, 70.
9. Sandy Grady, "Gulf War Brings Out Hustlers in High Places," *Toronto Star*, September 8, 1993.
10. Hersh, "The Spoils of War," 74.
11. Grady, "Gulf War Brings Out Hustlers in High Places."
12. Ibid.
13. Minority Staff, Committee on Government Reform, U.S. House of Representatives, "How Lax Regulation and Inadequate Oversight Contributed to the Enron Collapse," 107th Cong., February 7, 2002, 3.
14. Ibid.
15. Public Citizen, "Blind Faith: How Deregulation and Enron's Influence over Government Looted Billions from Americans," December 2001, 12.
16. Ibid., 3.
17. Bruce Nichols, "Private Players, Bush League; Ex-Officials Making Run at Corporate Ranks," *Dallas Morning News*, April 15, 1993.
18. Public Citizen, "Blind Faith," 14.

12: "Kenny Boy"

1. Richard A. Oppel Jr., "For a Generous Donor and Bush, the Support Is a Two-Way Street," *New York Times*, June 30, 2000.
2. David Corn, "W.'s First Enron Connection: Update on the Bush-Enron Oil Deal," *Nation*, March 4, 2002.
3. Louis Dubose and Carmen Coiro, "Don't Cry for Bush, Argentina," *Mother Jones*, March/April 2000.
4. Ibid.
5. Ibid.
6. Enron's president at the time, Mick Seidl, hedged Enron's bets. He attended a similar function in Houston for Bush's opponent, Michael Dukakis.
7. Richard A. Oppel Jr. and Wayne Slater, "Bush Plan Mirrors Tax Adviser's; Walker Was Key Architect of Reagan's '80s Proposals," *Dallas Morning News*, February 8, 1997.
8. This information comes from the author's interview with Pinkney Walker.
9. Oppel and Slater, "Bush Plan Mirrors Tax Adviser's."

13: The Dabhol Debacle

1. Patricia Sellers, "Women, Sex, and Power," *Fortune*, August 5, 1996.
2. Toni Mack, "High Finance with a Touch of Theater," *Forbes*, May 18, 1998.
3. Ibid.
4. Sellers, "Women, Sex, and Power."
5. Ibid.
6. Human Rights Watch, *The Enron Corporation: Corporate Complicity in Human Rights Violations* (New York: Human Rights Watch, 1999), 161.
7. Abhay Mehta, *Power Play: A Study of the Enron Project* (Mumbai, India: Orient Longman, 1999), 9.
8. Human Rights Watch, *The Enron Corporation*, 159.
9. Ibid.
10. Ibid., 161.
11. Mehta, *Power Play*, 202.
12. Human Rights Watch, *The Enron Corporation*, 22.

14: OPIC: Sweet Subsidies

1. "Historic Finance and Insurance Projects with Enron—FY 1989 Through FY 2001," fact sheet from OPIC, undated (likely February 1, 2002).
2. Ibid.
3. Ibid.
4. Knut Royce and Nathaniel Heller, "Cheney Led Cheney Led Halliburton to Feast at Federal Trough," Center for Public Integrity, August 2, 2000.

15: A Kinder, Gentler Enron

1. All of the profit figures come from Enron's Securities and Exchange Commission filings. The employee numbers are taken from *Fortune* magazine's annual Fortune 500 rankings.

17: "A Pit of Vipers"

1. Hillary Durgin and Richard Skinner, "Inside Track: The Guru of Decentralisation," *Financial Times,* June 26, 2000.

19: Chewco: The 3-Percent Solution

1. William C. Powers, Raymond S. Troubh, and Herbert S. Winokur, "Report of Investigation by the Special Investigative Committee of the Board of Directors of Enron Corp.," *Enron Corp.*, February 1, 2002 (the Powers report). This report was *the* key document for my research into Chewco as well as all of Enron's other off-the-balance-sheet deals. The report is widely available on the Internet.
2. "Enron Shares Pull Out of Slump as Company Delivers Growth," *Bloomberg News*, February 18, 1998.

20: Sexcapades

1. "Enron Payments to Insiders," published on *Houston Chronicle* web site. Available: www.chron.com/enron, June 17, 2002. The information in this spreadsheet was culled from Enron's bankruptcy filings and lists payments to 144 Enron employees and contractors, including Travel Agency in the Park. To access the file, go to the link on the right titled "Compensation to Enron Executives."

21: The Family Lay

1. "Enron Payments to Insiders," *Houston Chronicle*.
2. Travel Agency in the Park has since changed its name to Alliance Worldwide.
3. David Barboza and Kurt Eichenwald, "Son and Sister of Enron Chief Secured Deals," *New York Times*, February 2, 2002.
4. Ibid.

22: LJM1

1. This chapter relies heavily on the Powers report.
2. This information comes from the Powers Committee interview with Ken Lay. Incredibly, Lay would later say he didn't understand what a special-purpose entity was until October 2001.
3. This information comes from the Powers Committee interview with Vince Kaminski.

23: Buying Off the Board

1. Roger Lowenstein, *When Genius Failed* (New York: Random House, 2000), 38.

24: The Deal Diva, or How to Lose a Couple of Billion Dollars and Still Be a Rock Star

1. Human Rights Watch, *The Enron Corporation,* 3.
2. Ibid., 106.
3. Sellers, "Women, Sex, and Power."
4. Mack, "High Finance with a Touch of Theater."

25: Enron's Waterworld

1. "Nor Any Drop to Drink," *Economist*, March 25, 2000.
2. "Enron Payments to Insiders," *Houston Chronicle*.
3. Marie Brenner, "The Enron Wars," *Vanity Fair*, April 2002, 205.
4. On March 16, 2001, Enron bought back all of Azurix's outstanding stock for $325.9 million. But even after Enron bought back all of the shares, the losses continued. In the third quarter of 2001, Azurix lost $293.7 million.

26: Hyping the Bandwidth Bubble

1. Brian O'Reilly, "The Power Merchant," *Fortune*, April 17, 2000.
2. Karyn McCormack, "And the Latest Fiber Optic Play Is . . . Enron?" SmartMoney.com, February 3, 2000.
3. David Kirkpatrick, "Enron Takes Its Pipeline to the Net," *Fortune*, January 24, 2000.
4. Michael Brush, "Enron Puts Its Energy into Broadband," *MSN Moneycentral*, February 11, 2000.
5. Hillary Durgin, "Sleepless in Louisiana Street," *Financial Times*, December 20, 2000.
6. The displacement of the Hellcat engine is 113 cubic inches. The average Harley engine is a wimpy 88 cubic inches.

27: Andy Fastow Arrives . . . in River Oaks

1. Ronald Fink, "Balancing Act," *CFO Magazine*, June 1, 1999.
2. From the early 1900s through the 1970s, Weingarten's was the major grocery chain in Houston. According to David G. McComb's book *Houston: The Bayou City* (233), the chain was so important that Houston's civil rights activists chose it as the site of their first sit-in. In early 1960, a group of citizens occupied the lunch counter at the Weingarten store at 4100 Alameda. One protester said, "We buy our food here and spend our money here and think we should be able to eat here." Weingarten's quickly closed the lunch counter.

28: Strippers and Stock Options

1. Neela Banerjee, with Shaila K. Dewan, "For Executives Of Enron Unit, the Skill Was in Leaving," *New York Times,* February 15, 2002.
2. Ibid.
3. Alan Prendergast, "The Mystery of Pai," *Westword*, April 18, 2002.
4. Andrew Hill, Joshua Chaffin, and Stephen Fidler, "Enron: Virtual Company, Virtual Profits," *Financial Times*, February 3, 2002.

29: Casino Enron: Cash Flow Problems, Part 2

1. Ralph Bivins, "Firm in a Hurry to Get into New Downtown Tower," *Houston Chronicle*, April 15, 2001.
2. "Will Enron's Failure Pull the Plug on Houston?" *Grid,* January 2002.
3. Durgin and Skinner, "Inside Track: The Guru Of Decentralisation."

30: LJM2

1. Leslie Wayne, "Chagrined Enron Partners Try to Stave Off Both Losses and Scandal's Taint," *New York Times*, March 31, 2002.
2. Ibid.
3. Ibid.

4. This chapter relies heavily on the Powers report.
5. Laurie Cohen and Flynn McRoberts, "As Curtain Lifts, At Least One Man Working Enron Levers Is Exposed," *Chicago Tribune*, February 20, 2002.

31: The Big Five Versus the SEC

1. Jane Mayer, "The Accountants' War," *New Yorker,* April 22, 2002, 69.
2. Mike McNamee, Paula Dwyer, Christopher H. Schmitt, and Louis Lavelle, "Accounting Wars," *Business Week*, September 25, 2000.
3. Ibid.
4. Michael Kinsley, "Blame the Accountant," *Washington Post*, May 31, 2002.
5. Carol J. Loomis, "Lies, Damned Lies, and Managed Earnings," *Fortune*, August 2, 1999.
6. Mayer, "The Accountants' War."
7. Ibid.
8. General Accounting Office, "Major Human Capital Challenges at SEC and Key Trade Agencies," Testimony Before the Senate Subcommittee on Oversight of Government Management, Restructuring and the District of Columbia, Committee on Governmental Affairs, by Richard J. Hillman and Loren Yager, April 23, 2002.
9. The best place to look at the SEC's proposed rule is on their web site. Available: www.sec.gov/rules/proposed/34–42994.htm.
10. For more on Andersen's corporate contributions, go to the *Houston Chronicle* web site. Available: www.chron.com/enron.

32: Derivatives Hocus-Pocus

1. Randall Dodd and Jason Hoody, "Enron: Derivatives and the Damage Done," Derivatives Study Center, March 12, 2002.

33: Ken Rice: Missing In Action

1. Much of the information for this section comes from handouts distributed to financial analysts who attended the January 24 and 25, 2001, meeting. Additional information came from people who attended the meeting.

34: Analysts Who Think

1. Louis B. Gagliardi, Arthur L. Smith, John B. Parry, "The New, New Valuation Metrics: Is Enron Really Worth $126 per Share?" John S. Herold, Inc., February 21, 2001.
2. On May 6, 2001, Off Wall Street, a Cambridge, Massachusetts–based stock analysis firm that doesn't do any investment banking, followed Herold's lead in attacking Enron's story. The report, written by the firm's director of research, Mark Roberts, put a sell rating on Enron and predicted the energy giant's stock would fall to $30. (Enron stock was trading for about $59 per share at the time.) The report was remarkably prescient in its assessment of the accounting tactics being used by Enron's leadership. "Enron management appears to have resorted to a variety of transactions that are of questionable

quality and sustainability to manage and to boost its earnings. These transactions appear to be purposely obscured in Enron's public reporting." It should also be mentioned here that on September 20, 2000, *Wall Street Journal* reporter Jonathan Weil brought to light the dangers of mark-to-market accounting. Weil, writing for the *Texas Journal,* a regional publication of the *Wall Street Journal,* said that although companies like Enron and Dynegy were booking big profits, what "investors may not realize is that much of these companies' recent profits constitute unrealized, non-cash gains. Frequently, these profits depend on assumptions and estimates about future market factors, the details of which the companies do not provide, and which time may prove wrong." Weil's story was the first story by a major business publication to underscore the risks that come with the mark-to-market method.

3. In late July 2002, the U.S. Senate began investigating Merrill Lynch's firing of Olson. A spokesman for the giant brokerage firm insisted "Our research was not compromised."
4. *Bloomberg News*, "Enron Enriched Wall Street Firms, Analysts Ignored Warnings," December 18, 2001.
5. Charles L. Hill, "Statement of Charles L. Hill, Director of Research, Thomson Financial/First Call," U.S. Senate Government Affairs Committee, 107th Cong., February 27, 2002.
6. "Enron Enriched Wall Street Firms, Analysts Ignored Warnings," *Bloomberg News*, December 18, 2001.

35: Air Enron

1. Almost all of the information in this chapter came from extensive interviews with employees of Enron's aviation department. Specifications and cost figures for the airplanes came from published figures.
2. For more information on the standard industry fare level, see the following web site. Available: www.aircraftbuyer.com/news info/taxwatch16.htm.
3. Available: www.tagaviation.com.

36: Skilling Says a Bad Word

1. "Trading Truth: A Report on Harvard's Enron Entanglements," *Harvard-Watch,* January 31, 2002.

37: George W. to the Rescue, Part 1

1. George Skelton, "Price Caps Don't Fit in Cheney's Head for Figures," *Los Angeles Times*, April 19, 2001.
2. Ibid.
3. The entire energy report is on the Web. Available: www.whitehouse.gov/energy.
4. Minority Staff, Committee on Government Reform, U.S. House of Representatives, "Background on Enron's Dabhol Power Project," February 22, 2002, 18.

38: Broadband Blues

1. Robert Bryce, "Fueling Bandwidth Trading," *Interactive Week*, August 13, 2001.
2. David Kirkpatrick, "Enron Takes Its Pipeline to the Net," *Fortune,* January 24, 2000.
3. Daniel Fisher, "Shell Game," *Forbes*, January 7, 2002.
4. Ibid.
5. Rebecca Smith, "Blockbuster Deal Shows Enron's Inclination to All-Show, Little-Substance Partnerships," *Wall Street Journal*, January 17, 2002.
6. "Enron Payments to Insiders," *Houston Chronicle*, June 17, 2002.

39: Sleepless in Houston: Cash Flow Problems, Part 3

1. Fisher, "Shell Game."
2. Powers Committee report interview with Ken Lay.
3. April Witt and Peter Behr, "Enron's Other Strategy: Taxes Internal Papers Reveal How Complex Deals Boosted Profits by $1 Billion," *Washington Post*, May 22, 2002.
4. Christopher Mumma, "Enron-J.P. Morgan Energy Contracts May Be Loans, Expert Says," *Bloomberg News,* February 20, 2002.
5. Ibid.

40: Sherron Watkins Saves Her Own Ass

1. Jim Kennett and Mark Johnson, "Enron Shares Decline After Skilling Resigns as CEO," *Bloomberg News*, August 15, 2001.

41: George W. to the Rescue, Part 2

1. The Sustainable Energy and Economy Network and the Institute for Policy Studies' "Enron's Pawns: How Public Institutions Bankrolled Enron's Globalization Game," March 22, 2002, 31. This is an excellent exposé of the American government's subsidies to Big Business, not just Enron.
2. "Chronology of Administration Dealings with Enron's Dabhol Power Plant in India," *Washington Post*, January 22, 2002.
3. Sheila Mcnulty and Khozem Merchant, "Enron Issues Veiled Sanction Threat to India," *Financial Times*, August 24, 2001.
4. "Chronology of Administration Dealings with Enron's Dabhol Power Plant in India," *Washington Post.*
5. Ibid.
6. Ibid.

42: You Gotta Have Art

1. Stephen Kinzer, "Enron's Fall Reverberates in Houston's Arts World," *New York Times*, December 18, 2001.

43: Revenge of the Raptors

1. Rebecca Smith and John R. Emshwiller, "Enron CFO's Tie to a Partnership Resulted in Big Profits for the Firm," *Wall Street Journal*, October 19, 2001.
2. Ibid.
3. Rebecca Smith and John R. Emshwiller, "Enron Says Its Links to a Partnership Led to $1.2 Billion Equity Reduction," *Wall Street Journal*, October 18, 2001.
4. Ibid.

44: "An Outstanding Job as CFO"

1. Charles LeMaistre, "Response of Enron Board to Warning Signs, Testimony by Dr. Charles A. LeMaistre," Senate Governmental Affairs Committee, Permanent Subcommittee On Investigations, 107th Cong., May 7, 2002.
2. "Enron Payments to Insiders," *Houston Chronicle*.
3. Ibid. Whalley's total stock sales are not known. There were rumors within Enron that he, like Kevin Hannon of Enron Broadband Services, asked not to be named an officer of Enron Corp., so that he wouldn't have to report his sales. However, Whalley was well compensated. His total cash payments from Enron in 2001 totaled $4.6 million. Whalley also exercised stock options valued at $3.28 million in 2001.
4. *HarvardWatch*, 1. Grubman's position on Enron paid off in a big way for Highfields and Harvard. A January 2002 report by *HarvardWatch* estimated that the hedge fund made $50 million by shorting Enron.

45: Fastow Goes Bye-Bye

1. LeMaistre, "Response of Enron Board to Warning Signs."
2. "Enron Payments to Insiders," *Houston Chronicle*.
3. Peter Eavis, "Shell-Shocked Enron Parts with CFO," TheStreet.com, October 24, 2001.

46: Posh PJ's

1. Shelby Hodge, "Hotel Derek Guests Party in Pajamas," *Houston Chronicle*, November 5, 2001.
2. "Enron Payments to Insiders," *Houston Chronicle*.

47: Greenspan Gets the Enron Prize

1. *American Banker*, "Fed Asked to Preserve Enron Documents," March 11, 2002.
2. Lowenstein, *When Genius Failed*, 200.
3. Ibid., 230.
4. Alan Greenspan, "Keynote Address by the Honorable Alan Greenspan," at Baker Institute, November 13, 2001, 5.
5. *Baker Institute Report*, February 2002, 5.
6. Gerard Baker, "A Saint or a Sucker?" *Financial Times*, March 2, 2002.

48: One Restatement Too Many

1. Kurt Eichenwald and Diana B. Henriques, "Web of Details Did Enron In as Warnings Went Unheeded," *New York Times*, February 10, 2002.

49: The Downgrade

1. Eichenwald and Henriques, "Web of Details Did Enron In as Warnings Went Unheeded."
2. Randall Smith, "Lehman Faced Possible Conflict as Enron-Dynegy Merger Failed," *Wall Street Journal*, December 5, 2001.
3. Alex Berenson, "Debt Rankings Finally Fizzle, but the Deal Fizzled First," *New York Times*, November 29, 2001.

51: "Salvation Armani"

1. Wendy Grossman, "Laying Siege: The Tycoon's Gift Shop Sparks a Turf War in Montrose," *Houston Press*, June 13, 2002.
2. Ibid.
3. Steven K. Paulson, "State Supreme Court Rules Locals Have Access to Taylor Ranch," Associated Press, June 24, 2002.
4. Mary Flood, "Executives May Lose Suits, but All Is Not Lost for Them," *Houston Chronicle*, April 8, 2002.
5. Ibid.
6. "Enron Payments to Insiders," *Houston Chronicle*.
7. Bill Hensel Jr., "Company of the Year: Kinder Morgan Energy Partners, Little-Known Pioneer Rising to the Top," *Houston Chronicle,* May 16, 2002.
8. In late July 2002, Fastow, through a spokesman, announced he wouldn't move into the house. The Fastows will sell the house so their children "would have less disruption at a difficult time."
9. Felix Rohatyn, "An Agenda for Corporate Reform," *Wall Street Journal*, June 24, 2002.
10. Patrick Beach, "His Beautiful Mind," *Austin American-Statesman*, March 3, 2002.
11. "Enron Payments to Insiders," *Houston Chronicle.*

52: Aftermath

1. Eric Berger, "Enron Case Growing Longer and Costlier with Second Examiner," *Houston Chronicle*, May 22, 2003.
2. Peter Behr, "Flood of Fees Draining Enron Funds: $496 Million in Charges Rung Up So Far by Lawyers, Others," *Washington Post*, June 28, 2003, A1.
3. Ibid.
4. Ibid.
5. "Enron Forms New Holding Company," *Houston Business Journal*, June 25, 2003.
6. James Norman, "Enron Reorganization Plan Has Key Creditor Backing," *Platts Oilgram News*, July 14, 2003, 1.

7. "Labor Department Sues Enron Over Retirement Plan Losses," *Portland Business Journal*, June 26, 2003.
8. Tom Fowler, "In a Hurry for Enron Trial? October 2005 Looking Good," *Houston Chronicle*, July 10, 2003.
9. Joint Committee on Taxation, "Report of Investigation Of Enron Corporation and Related Entities Regarding Federal Tax and Compensation Issues, and Policy Recommendations," February 13, 2003, 15.
10. William L. Watts, "Phil Gramm to Join UBS Warburg," CBS.MarketWatch.com, October 7, 2002.
11. http://www.time.com/time/personoftheyear/2002/poyintro.html.
12. http://www.corporatecrimereporter.com/watkinsinterview.html.
13. Charles Ganske, "Whistling for Fame and Fortune," *Washington Times*, May 4, 2003, B5.
14. "Ken Lay and Wife Lose $1 Million on Aspen Homes," *Associated Press*, August 4, 2003.
15. Graef Crystal, "Two Secular Saints Are 'Buys' for Shareholders," *Bloomberg*, June 9, 2003.
16. http://www.fortune.com/fortune/subs/print/0,15935,427751,00.html.
17. http://www.bis.org/publ/otc_hy0305.pdf.
18. "Sarbanes-Oxley, One Year Later: Corporate Reform in the Works," *Wall Street Journal*, July 25, 2003.

Bibliography

Books

Busby, Rebecca. *Natural Gas in Nontechnical Language.* Tulsa, OK: PennWell Publishing, 1999.

Dugger, Ronnie. *The Politician: The Life and Times of Lyndon Johnson.* New York: W. W. Norton & Co., 1982.

Feagin, Joe R. *Free Enterprise City: Houston in Political and Economic Perspective.* New Brunswick, NJ: Rutgers University Press, 1988.

Fellows, Kenneth. *Houston Natural Gas Corporation: Its First Fifty Years—1925–1975.* Houston: Houston Natural Gas Corporation, 1976.

Fusaro, Peter. *Energy Risk Management: Hedging Strategies and Instruments for the International Energy Markets.* New York: McGraw-Hill, 1998.

Houston Metropolitan Study. *The Houston Metropolitan Study: An Entrepreneurial Community Looks Ahead.* Houston: Houston Metropolitan Study, 1998.

Human Rights Watch. *The Enron Corporation: Corporate Complicity in Human Rights Violations.* New York: Human Rights Watch, 1999.

Johnston, Marguerite. *Houston: The Unknown City, 1836–1946.* College Station: Texas A&M University Press, 1991.

Lassell, Mary. *John Henry Kirby, Prince of the Pines.* Austin, TX: Encino Press, 1967.

Lay, Kenneth. *The Enron Story.* New York: The Newcomen Society of the United States, 1990.

Lowenstein, Roger. *When Genius Failed.* New York: Random House, 2000.

McComb, David G. *Houston: The Bayou City.* Austin: University of Texas Press, 1969.

Mehta, Abhay. *Power Play: A Study of the Enron Project.* Mumbai, India: Orient Longman, 1999.

Miller, Ray. *Ray Miller's Houston.* Austin, TX: Cordovan Press, 1982.

Newton, Harry. *Newton's Telecom Dictionary: The Official Dictionary of Telecommunications Networking and the Internet*. Gilroy, CA: CMP Books, 2000.

Petroleum Extension Service. *Field Handling of Natural Gas*. Austin: University of Texas, 1972.

Tracy, John A. *Accounting for Dummies*. New York: Hungry Minds, 2001.

Yergin, Daniel. *The Prize: The Epic Quest for Oil, Money and Power*. New York: Simon & Schuster, 1991.

Securities and Exchange Commission Filings

Azurix Corporation, 1999 Form 10-K and proxy statement
Azurix Corporation, 2000 annual report
Azurix Corporation, 1999 Form S-1
Enron 1990 Form 10-K, annual report and proxy statement
Enron 1991 Form 10-K, annual report and proxy statement
Enron 1992 Form 10-K, annual report and proxy statement
Enron 1993 Form 10-K, annual report and proxy statement
Enron 1994 Form 10-K, annual report and proxy statement
Enron 1995 Form 10-K, annual report and proxy statement
Enron 1996 Form 10-K, annual report and proxy statement
Enron 1997 Form 10-K, annual report and proxy statement
Enron 1998 Form 10-K, annual report and proxy statement
Enron 1999 Form 10-K, annual report and proxy statement
Enron 2000 Form 10-K, annual report and proxy statement
Enron Form 10-Q filings, 1997 through third quarter, 2001
Enron Form 144 filings for insider sales
Enron Form 8-K filings
Enron Oil and Gas 1998 Form 10-K
Kinder Morgan Energy Partners, 2001 Form 10-K

Press Releases, Speeches, and Other Sources

City of Houston, Planning and Development Department. Various construction permit records obtained by author under the Texas Open Records Act.

Enron Corp. *Electric Power from Natural Gas*. Houston: Enron Power Corp. and Enron Europe Ltd., undated (approximately 1992).

Enron Corp., Press releases from 1993 through 2001.

Harris County Appraisal District. Real property records for various properties in Harris County, Texas. Available: www.hcad.org.

Lay, Kenneth. *The Measurement of the Timing of the Economic Impact of Defense Procurement Activity: An Analysis of the Vietnam Buildup*. Houston: University of Houston, 1970.

Mark Newby, et al. vs. Enron Corp., et al. Civil Action No. H-01-3624, Consolidated Complaint for Violations of the Securities Laws, filed in the United States District Court, Southern District of Texas, Houston Division, April 8, 2002.

Powers, William C., Raymond S. Troubh, and Herbert S. Winokur Jr. "Report of Investigation by the Special Investigative Committee of the Board of Directors of Enron Corp.," Enron Corp., February 1, 2002 (the Powers report).

Enron Web Sites

The Web contains a wealth of material on Enron. Here are a few good sites.

Available: www.chron.com/enron. The *Houston Chronicle*'s web site. Enron's hometown paper hasn't been great, but it's been dogged in its coverage and the site has most of the important background documents. It also has a complete trove of the paper's stories on Enron, sorted by month, all of which are available at no charge.

Available: www.dailyenron.com. An irreverent, often funny site run by American Family Voices, a new pro-consumer group and advocate for middle- and low-income families.

Available: www.findlaw.com/enron. This site, run by findlaw, an on-line legal news site, has tons of documents about Enron, including employment contracts for key officials, legal documents, and bankruptcy filings.

Available: www.laydoff.com. Run by former Enron employee John Allario, this site has T-shirts, links to former Enron employee info, and other good stuff.

Available: www.nytimes.com/enron. This *New York Times* site has some good stories but doesn't have a comprehensive listing of the paper's coverage of the Enron debacle. If you want all the older, archived stories, you have to pay.

Available: www.viridianrepository.com/Enron/Enron.htm. More irreverent humor at Enron's expense. Bruce Sterling, the sci-fi author and cyber-raconteur, sponsored a contest to come up with the best new Enron logo. This site has all the entrants as well as the winning logo.

Available: www.washingtonpost.com/wp-dyn/business/specials/energy/enron. This site has a complete, free listing of the *Post*'s stories on Enron and other good source materials.

Index

PublicAffairs is a publishing house founded in 1997. It is a tribute to the standards, values, and flair of three persons who have served as mentors to countless reporters, writers, editors, and book people of all kinds, including me.

I.F. STONE, proprietor of *I. F. Stone's Weekly*, combined a commitment to the First Amendment with entrepreneurial zeal and reporting skill and became one of the great independent journalists in American history. At the age of eighty, Izzy published *The Trial of Socrates,* which was a national bestseller. He wrote the book after he taught himself ancient Greek.

BENJAMIN C. BRADLEE was for nearly thirty years the charismatic editorial leader of *The Washington Post*. It was Ben who gave the *Post* the range and courage to pursue such historic issues as Watergate. He supported his reporters with a tenacity that made them fearless and it is no accident that so many became authors of influential, best-selling books.

ROBERT L. BERNSTEIN, the chief executive of Random House for more than a quarter century, guided one of the nation's premier publishing houses. Bob was personally responsible for many books of political dissent and argument that challenged tyranny around the globe. He is also the founder and longtime chair of Human Rights Watch, one of the most respected human rights organizations in the world.

For fifty years, the banner of Public Affairs Press was carried by its owner Morris B. Schnapper, who published Gandhi, Nasser, Toynbee, Truman and about 1,500 other authors. In 1983, Schnapper was described by *The Washington Post* as "a redoubtable gadfly." His legacy will endure in the books to come.

Peter Osnos, *Publisher*